John von Neumann and the Origins of Modern Computing

History of Computing

I. Bernard Cohen and William Aspray, editors

John von Neumann and the Origins of Modern Computing

William Aspray

The MIT Press
Cambridge, Massachusetts
London, England

This book was typeset in New Baskerville.

Library of Congress Cataloging-in-Publication Data

Aspray, William.
    John von Neumann and the origins of modern computing / William Aspray.
       p. cm.—(History of Computing)
    Includes bibliographical references and index.
    ISBN 978-0-262-01121-1 (hc. : alk. paper) — 978-0-262-51885-7 (pb.)
    1. Electronic digital computers—History. 2. Von Neumann, John, 1903–1957.
I. Title. II. Series.
QA76.5.A77446 1990
004'.092—dc20   90-37108
                                                              CIP

The MIT Press is pleased to keep this title available in print by manufacturing single copies, on demand, via digital printing technology.

Contents

Archival Sources and Abbreviations

This book makes extensive use of archival materials. In order to shorten citations, every archival collection has been given a four-letter code, which is used in the notes to the text.

AONA   Record Group 156, Office of the Chief of Ordnance, Research and Development General Records, National Archives, Suitland, Maryland

ATBB   Abraham Taub Papers, Bancroft Library, University of California at Berkeley

CPHO   Center for History of Physics Oral History Collection, New York City

DOEA   Department of Energy Archives, Germantown, Maryland

FASC   Frank Aydelotte Papers, Friends Historical Library, Swarthmore College

HGAP   Herman Goldstine Papers, American Philosophical Society Library, Philadelphia

HGHC   Herman Goldstine Papers, Hampshire College

HSRC   Honeywell-Sperry Rand Litigation Records, Charles Babbage Institute Archives, Minneapolis

HSRH   Honeywell-Sperry Rand Litigation Records, Hagley Library, Wilmington, Delaware

IASD   Director's Records, Historical Studies–Social Sciences Library, Institute for Advanced Study, Princeton, New Jersey

IASE   Electronic Computer Project Records, Historical Studies–Social Sciences Library, Institute for Advanced Study, Princeton, New Jersey

JCMI   Jule Charney Papers, MIT Archives

JCNC   Jule Charney Oral History, Archives, National Center for Atmospheric Research, Boulder, Colorado

LALL   Los Alamos National Laboratory Library
LANA   Los Alamos National Laboratory Archives
LFEM   Laboratory for Electronics Archives, MIT Archives
NMAH   National Museum of American History Computer
            Collection, Smithsonian Institution, Washington,
            D.C.
NWMI   Norbert Wiener Papers, MIT Archives
OHCB   Oral History Collection, Charles Babbage Institute,
            Minneapolis
OHSM   AFIPS-Smithsonian Oral History Collection, National
            Museum of American History Archives, Washington,
            D.C.
OMIK   John von Neumann Papers, National Technical
            Information Center Library, Budapest
OVLC   Oswald Veblen Papers, Library of Congress
PMMP   Princeton Mathematics in the 1930s Oral History
            Collection, Seeley Mudd Library, Princeton
            University
ROLC   Robert Oppenheimer Papers, Library of Congress
SANB   Samuel Alexander Papers, National Bureau of Stan-
            dards Records, National Archives, Suitland,
            Maryland
SCUC   S. Chandrasekhar Papers, Regenstein Library,
            University of Chicago
SRHM   Sperry Corporation Records, Hagley Library,
            Wilmington, Delaware
SUAP   Stanislaw Ulam Papers, American Philosophical
            Society Library, Philadelphia
VNLC   John von Neumann Papers, Library of Congress
WMAP   Warren McCulloch Papers, American Philosophical
            Society Library, Philadelphia

Series Foreword

The MIT Press series in the History of Computing is devoted to the history of computers and information processing in the broadest terms. The series encompasses all aspects of modern computing—systems, hardware, and software—as well as the preliminary development of data processing and the mechanization of calculation. Historically based inquiries into the social, political, philosophic, and economic as well as the technical aspects of the introduction and use of computers and information processing fall within our purview.

The series includes both general works and specialized monographs. Some of the volumes concentrate on a particular development, such as magnetic memory, while others trace in full the technical history of an industrial company of significance in the computer industry. While most of the books in the series deal with the twentieth century, and particularly the most recent part of this century, others trace anterior developments. Thus the series includes a biography of Ada, countess of Lovelace, and another on Georg and Edvard Scheutz, both associated with the work in the nineteenth century of Charles Babbage. The series also includes autobiographical studies of key figures in modern computing.

I. Bernard Cohen
William Aspray

Acknowledgments

An increasingly common phenomenon of the period since World War II is big science, in which tens or hundreds of researchers from many different institutions work together to produce a product. In writing this book, I feel as though I have participated in big history. Literally hundreds of people have participated in the research and writing of this book, and I cannot begin to acknowledge my credit to all of them. However, it would be a serious injustice not to mention a few people who have made special efforts to assist with this book. Garrett Birkhoff, Arthur Burks, Thomas Drucker, Herman Goldstine, and Carol Voelker have read the entire manuscript at least once and have given detailed criticisms. Others who have read and commented on parts of the manuscript close to their own interests include Cuthbert Hurd, Lyle Johnson, Peter Lax, Nicholas Metropolis, Frederik Nebeker, John Palmer, George Platzman, James Pomerene, Emerson Pugh, Joseph Smagorinsky, George Stibitz, Albert Tucker, Nicholas Vonneuman, and Marina Whitman.

The project would have been impossible without the generous assistance with historical source materials given by many archivists and historians, including Bruce Bruemmer at the Charles Babbage Institute, Kathy Marquis and Helen Samuels at the MIT Archives, Elizabeth Carroll-Horrocks and Martin Levitt at the American Philosophical Society, Roger Meade at the Los Alamos Archives, Carol Dreyfus and Peggy Kidwell at the National Museum of American History, Michael Nash at the Hagley Museum, Mark Darby and Gail Malmgreen at the Institute for Advance Study, Clark Elliott at the Harvard University Archives, Spencer Weart at the Center for History of Physics, Roger Anders at the Department of Energy Archives, and Daniel Meyer of the University of Chicago's Regenstein Library. I also thank Robbin Clamons for her extremely able library research assistance on the project and Andrew Goldstein for his proofreading and preparation of the index.

The research for this book was supported by National Science Foundation grants SES-8609543, DIR-8809336, and 90-96106. Generous institutional support was provided for four years by the Charles Babbage Institute and, during the last few months, by the IEEE Center for the History of Electrical Engineering. I reserve my special thanks for Arthur Norberg, who discussed method, strategy, and content with me at great length from the beginning of the project.

Introduction

While on a war assignment in England in 1943, John von Neumann wrote to a mathematical colleague in Princeton that he had recently developed "an obscene interest in computation" and would be returning home "a better and impurer man."[1] Thus began the computing career of that illustrious computer scientist. It was a short career, lasting little more than a decade before being cut off by his death from cancer. But in those few years von Neumann made lasting contributions to the design, application, theory, dissemination, and legitimization of computers. Based on the first careful examination of the abundant archival record left by von Neumann and his associates, this book reveals a full and complete picture of his many different contributions to the field of computing.

Von Neumann entered the computing scene at a critical, transitional point, when the electronic, digital, stored-program computer was being conceived to replace older and less powerful calculating technology. This transition involved two fundamental tasks: to decide what functional units the computing system should comprise and how these units should be interrelated (what von Neumann called the logical design and what we today call the computer's architecture) and to implement the design in electronics so as to achieve a profound increase in calculating speed.

Von Neumann approached these two tasks in somewhat different ways. In the area of logical design, he was a principal technical contributor. The draft report on EDVAC, which he wrote in 1945, gave the first written account of the stored-program computer. Three papers he coauthored with Arthur Burks and Herman Goldstine between 1946 and 1948 presented the first detailed descriptions for the design and programming of such a computer. In engineering implementation, von Neumann made only modest technical contributions. His more important effort was to conceive, raise funds for, and direct the Electronic Computer Project (1945–1957) at the Institute for Advanced Study. This project produced in 1952 one of the first electronic stored-program computers and along the way made many engineering advances in components and systems design.

Although I give von Neumann's work on the design and construction of computer systems detailed coverage, a major purpose of this book is to explain that his contributions to computing were much broader. He was interested in computers primarily for what they could offer to science, and it is likely that he would have regarded his contributions to scientific applications, numerical analysis, and computer theory to be of importance at least equal to those to logical design and system construction.

Von Neumann's interest in the computer as a scientific instrument originated in the need for a more powerful tool to solve differential equations associated with his war work at Los Alamos and his ordnance work for the army and navy. Well before the war had ended he appreciated the value these new computers could have for solving a wide range of scientific problems, especially those relating to nonlinear problems such as occur in fluid dynamics. After the war he built a computer at the Institute for Advanced Study dedicated to scientific applications, and with it he made his crucial test of the scientific value of the computer in a study of numerical weather prediction.

Von Neumann had recognized almost immediately that he could not achieve his scientific goals merely by building high-speed computing equipment. These new computers differed extensively in their "internal economy" from precedent technologies, such as desk calculators and punched-card tabulating systems. For the first time arithmetic was cheap but storage of information was dear. In this new economy, new algorithms were needed to reduce the "cost" of computations and to ensure their reliability. In 1944, within months of becoming involved in the design of computers, he had established a research program in Princeton to study numerical methods for the computer. This interest continued over the next decade and, as much as anyone else, von Neumann was responsible for reviving the moribund mathematical subdiscipline of numerical analysis.

Von Neumann took a wider, more theoretical view of computers than did most of his contemporaries. The EDVAC report in which he introduced the stored-program computer did not use mechanical switches, electromechanical relays, or vacuum tubes for its switching elements, as one might expect, but instead used idealized neurons adapted from a paper on theoretical psychology. One reason for this approach was to distinguish the logical design from the engineering implementation that most concerned his contemporaries; another reason was to highlight the comparison of the computer and the human nervous system as the two principal examples of complicated information processing systems, or automata, to use his term. Over the next ten years, working mostly alone, he developed a theory of automata. It considered such issues as learning, reliability of systems with unreliable components, and self-replication. He regarded this work, which he continued despite his heavy government commitments and his bout with cancer, as one of his most important contributions.

An accurate accounting of von Neumann's contributions to computing must consider all of these topics together. It is equally important to consider his achievements outside computing. At the time he became interested in computing in 1943, he was already an internationally famous scientist who had made fundamental contributions to mathematics, physics, and economics. During and after World War II he was an important consultant and scientific statesman, as an atomic energy commissioner and as the principal scientific adviser to the U.S. Air Force on ballistic missile development. In order to give a sense of his career outside computing, the first and last chapters sketch his career before 1943 and after 1952. These chapters do not do full justice to his many other intellectual accomplishments, however, and I hope that soon someone will accept the ambitious task of writing the full intellectual biography of this brilliant man.

John von Neumann and the Origins of Modern Computing

1

A Mathematical Research Career

The first participants in a new scientific or engineering discipline, as computing was in the 1940s, naturally have been trained in other, more established fields.[1] These pioneers bring with them specialized skills, traditions of how to formulate and approach problems, and values concerning what is important. This intellectual baggage is a strong shaping force on any new discipline.

Some emerging disciplines (perhaps biochemistry is an example) issue from an alliance of only two established fields; in this case the contributions and biases of each are somewhat readily traced. The situation is considerably more complex in computing, which attracted specialists from a number of engineering and scientific fields: computer architecture interested logicians and control engineers, component design and hardware engineering were advanced by electrical engineers and physicists, software became the province of mathematicians, numerical methods were studied by a specialty group within mathematics, and computer theory received attention from mathematicians, psychologists, and various biomedical specialists. Close cooperation among all these groups was required for progress because a computing operation is a complex, interconnected technological system in which performance is limited by the weakest link.

The complexity of computing systems was not recognized clearly in the 1940s. Many of the early participants did not see beyond the myriad details of component design and hardware engineering, and there was little appreciation for the importance of systems

I thank Nicholas A. Vonneuman for having authorized me to use material in this chapter from his book, *John von Neumann as Seen by his Brother*, without the requirement to footnote each citation. I also thank him for checking this chapter for factual errors and suggesting corrections. He is one of the very few surviving witnesses of John's European life and career, and I have greatly appreciated his assistance.

software. One reason for von Neumann's great impact on computing development was his recognition of the complexity of a computing system and his contributions to many (indeed, most) of its different aspects. He was interested in the computer as a tool to solve scientific problems, and to make this tool work effectively he had to pay attention to all its parts. Most of the early participants in the new computer field contributed in a single area, perhaps component design or numerical methods, but von Neumann conducted research in architecture, software, numerical methods, applications, and theory; he also directed a group of engineers working on component design and engineering development. Moreover, his work emphasized areas that were neglected by many of his contemporaries, such as architecture and software.

This chapter traces the intellectual development and early career of von Neumann into the early years of World War II. He did not do any computing of special note during this period. Nevertheless, this period was crucial to his later work, and I include an account of it to lend credence to the position that von Neumann was able to make his many different contributions to computing not only because of his brilliance and hard work but also because of his unusually rich and diverse experience with mathematical analysis, logic and axiomatics, chemical engineering, and physics, which gave him the rounded education needed to work on the many facets of modern computing.

This chapter also lays the groundwork for a sociological argument pursued in the final chapter. Prior to the inception of the electronic, stored-program computer, most mathematicians regarded numerical analysis with disdain and typically relegated computation to their assistants—generally ill-paid women laboring at desk calculators. Only considerable effort would convince the scientific elite of the computer's scientific merits, and an equal effort was called for to convince the military community (the principal funders in the early years) to allocate the substantial resources required to design and construct computing systems. By the late 1930s von Neumann had been publishing important scientific papers for almost twenty years. He had an international reputation and was a senior member of one of the world's leading scientific research centers, the Institute for Advanced Study. His scientific standing was an important factor in winning over the scientific and funding communities, and it was a standing in stark contrast to that of most of the other pioneers of modern computing. Howard Aiken, J. Presper Eckert, Jay Forrester, Alan Turing, Maurice Wilkes, and most others who have won renown for their work in computing in the 1940s and 1950s were young and unestablished. In the United States Vannevar Bush and Samuel Caldwell were almost alone as senior statesmen of science interested in computing, but they were ensconced in MIT's older line of analog computers and never made the transition to the new digital technology.[2] L.J. Comrie, Douglas Hartree, and M. H. A. Newman had some effect on the direction of British computing, but their impact was small in the United States.

Early Life, 1903–1921

John von Neumann, or rather Margittai Neumann Janos Lajos, was born in Budapest on 28 December 1903.[3] His father, Max, was a successful lawyer whose career led him to become the chief counsel and a director of one of Hungary's leading banks, the Magyar Jelzalog Hitelbank.[4] His mother, Margaret, ran the home. Her father, Jakab Kann, had grown up in a poor family but by the 1890s had secured his financial position through a novel system for merchandising agricultural supplies across Hungary. As a wedding present, Kann had given his daughter an apartment in a building he owned, and John grew up there with his parents and his younger brothers, Michael and Nicholas. Other members of the Kann family lived in the same building. The Kann sisters and their families were close, and John grew up in this extended family.

Max and Margaret fostered a rich intellectual environment in their household. The entire family participated in regular discussions of current events, science, music, literature, and theater, as well as school subjects. Governesses were selected who could teach the children French and German. Max entertained at home regularly, and the children met not only his many foreign business associates but also such important Hungarian intellectuals as Rudolf Ortvay, director of the Theoretical Physics Institute at the University of Budapest, Lipot Fejer, a professor of mathematics at the University of Budapest and later von Neumann's thesis adviser, and Sandor Ferenczi, who introduced Freudian psychoanalysis to Hungary. The family had a library that Max had purchased at an estate sale.

John was a precocious child with a remarkably quick mind. He read avidly with almost photographic memory. His special interest was history, and, as a child, he read all the way through a popular forty-four volume set on general history.[5] His talent for languages was strong; he learned French, German, and classical Greek and Latin, as well as his native Hungarian, at an early age. Any topic relating to science or technology, in particular airplanes, interested him, which he credited to his father's influence. Following the example of his grandfather Kann, he also developed an unusual faculty for rapid mental arithmetic that remained with him throughout his life.[6]

John received private tutoring at home until the age of ten, when he was enrolled in the Lutheran Gymnasium (Agostai Hitvallasu Evangelikus Fogimnazium), one of three well-respected high schools in Budapest that attracted students from all over Hungary. Although it was sponsored by the Lutherans, a visiting rabbi provided training in Hebrew writing and literature to Jewish students like John. The strong curriculum offered a humanistic balance of sciences and arts, including eight years of Latin, four years of Greek, three years of Hungarian history, two years of combined study of world history, geography, and world literature, together with physics and mathematics through analytic geometry and calculus. The teachers were knowledgable; many held advanced degrees and pursued independent research programs.[7] There were many gifted students at the school, including John's close friend Eugene Wigner, and peer recognition for intellectual achievement was strong.[8] Not surprisingly, John was admired by his fellow students for his general academic mastery.[9]

Within a few months of John's enrollment at the Lutheran Gymnasium, the senior mathematics teacher, Laszlo Racz, visited Max Neumann to inform him of his son's mathematical talent and encourage him to provide training beyond that offered in the school so that this extraordinary talent would be developed.[10] With the father's approval, Racz contacted a mathematics professor, Jozsef Kurschak, at the University of Budapest and arranged for a young mathematician on the faculty, Michael Fekete, to tutor John regularly in mathematics at home, an arrangement that continued throughout the eight years that John attended the Lutheran Gymnasium.[11] By the time he graduated, the tutoring had evolved into collaboration and resulted in John's first mathematical publication, a paper with Fekete solving a problem on the location of zeroes of certain minimal polynomials, which generalized a result of Fejer.[12]

John's high school years were tumultuous times for Hungary, and the political changes left their mark on the development of his political views and vocational goals. The year that he matriculated at the gymnasium, Hungary entered World War I on the side of the Central Powers. As an outcome of the war, Hungary lost almost two-thirds of its territory and population in the Treaty of Trianon. Budapest fell from its prewar position as the lively and prosperous second capitol of a great empire to being the principal city of a small nation.

The situation was exacerbated by civil strife. In 1919 the liberal Karolyi government was overthrown and replaced by the Hungarian Soviet Republic. The family left Hungary for Italy during the short Soviet rule, returning later in 1919 upon the ascension of the Horthy government. However, that regime instituted restrictive anti-Jewish laws in the 1920s, including quotas on Jews at the University of Budapest. Even so, the Neumann family lived in Budapest with only minor inconvenience, and John's education was not seriously disrupted. These experiences nevertheless hardened John against political extremes and diminished his interest in a career in Hungary.

John entered the University of Budapest in 1921 to study mathematics; however, he adopted the unorthodox practice of attending the university only at the end of each term when examinations were given. Between 1921 and 1923, a good portion of his college years, he spent most of his time in Berlin, where he attended chemistry lectures of Fritz Haber, heard Albert Einstein lecture on statistical mechanics, and came under the influence of the mathematician Erhard Schmidt. In Berlin he also had regular contact with other Hungarian scientists, in particular Denis Gabor, Leo Szilard, and Eugene Wigner.

In 1923 John enrolled at the Eidgenossische Technische Hochschule (ETH) in Zurich to study chemical engineering, because his father wanted him to obtain a practical education.[13] By this time he was already actively involved in mathematical research, as his friend Stan Ulam later recounted: "While Johnny was in Zurich, he spent much of his time ('spare time' as a chemistry student) working on problems of mathematics, writing for publication, corresponding with mathematicians, etc. I remember that he had contacts with Weyl and Polya, both of whom were in Zurich at that time. I also remember that Weyl once left for a short while and that Johnny took over his courses for him during that period."[14] He received the chemical engineering degree from ETH in 1925 and the Ph.D. in mathematics from the University of Budapest in 1926.

A European Research Career, 1921–1930

Hungary could not match the mathematical attractions of Germany, and von Neumann chose to remain in Germany when he completed his formal education.[15] He spent the 1926–1927 academic year as a Rockefeller Fellow at the University of Göttingen.[16] In 1927 he was appointed as a Privatdozent at the University of Berlin, the youngest in the university's history, and for the next several years commuted by train between Berlin and Göttingen. The first half of the academic year 1929–1930 he spent as a Privatdozent in Hamburg.

The decade from 1921, when von Neumann completed his gymnasium studies in Budapest, to 1930, when he left Europe for the United States, constitutes a cohesive phase of his research career. Although some of the research he started was continued at Princeton, his European work differed in emphasis from that in America. The European period included research on measure theory, the theory of integration, and game theory, but it concentrated on two general areas: first, set theory and the logical foundations of mathematics, and second, Hilbert space theory, operator theory, and the mathematical foundations of quantum mechanics.[17] In both of these areas he was influenced by the work of David Hilbert and his associates.

The first great advances in mathematical logic were made between 1870 and 1930.[18] Propositional and quantifier logics were developed and formalized, number theory and set theory axiomatized, the logical paradoxes discovered, and mathematical and philosophical programs for the restoration of the foundations of mathematics advanced. Hilbert was at the center of these developments. In 1899 he had provided a rigorous axiomatization for geometry, and in his famous Paris lecture to the International Congress of Mathematicians in 1900, he had listed as one of the important unsolved problems of mathematics the consistency of the real number system. In 1904 he wrote his first paper attempting to prove the consistency of arithmetic, setting out his formalist approach to the foundations of mathematics.[19] He returned to this problem in 1917, publishing a series of papers in the 1920s. Hilbert enlisted a number of talented young mathematicians, including

Wilhelm Ackermann, Paul Bernays, and von Neumann, to assist with the completion of his formalist program; however, the program eventually foundered over Kurt Gödel's famous proof in 1931 that no formal system (e.g., the one presented in Bertrand Russell and Alfred North Whitehead's *Principia Mathematica*) powerful enough to formulate arithmetic could be both complete and consistent.[20]

Stimulated in part by Hilbert, von Neumann published seven papers during the 1920s on topics of mathematical logic. The first paper (1923) presents in naive (nonformal) set theory a rigorous definition of the ordinal numbers, defining each ordinal as the set of all smaller ordinals. His definition improved on those given by Georg Cantor and Bertrand Russell and was incorporated into subsequent accounts of axiomatic set theory.[21]

Von Neumann's second paper (1925) gives a terse account of a new system of axioms for set theory, which he elaborated in a 1928 paper.[22] His axioms define two types of objects: sets and classes. All sets are classes, but some classes, such as the universal class and the class of all classes, are not sets. Von Neumann used classes to represent formally Ernst Zermelo's imprecisely defined concept of definite properties. The von Neumann account, usually known today as von Neumann–Gödel–Bernays set theory, was the first axiomatization of set theory to be finitely axiomatizable. In this respect it resembles the axiomatizations of geometry given by Hilbert and others—the examplars of mathematical axiomatization—more than Zermelo's system does.[23]

A paper published in 1927 is von Neumann's only direct contribution to Hilbert's formalist program. It gives an expository account of the formalist program and indicates how previous attempts, such as that by Wilhelm Ackermann, had not completely succeeded, especially in providing a formalist foundation for analysis. A technical result is given showing that finite iterations of quantifiers and propositional connectives do not lead to inconsistency when applied to finitary relations, and an incorrect claim is made that this approach could be extended to a proper foundation for analysis.

In a 1928 paper von Neumann returned to his 1923 definition of ordinals in order to give a precise formal definition. The 1928 paper also gives formal definitions of other set-theoretic concepts, including the first definition of transfinite induction. His research program in logic concluded with a 1929 paper discussing restrictions on the formation of sets, necessary and sufficient to avoid the logical paradoxes threatening the foundations of mathematics. Upon learning of Gödel's incompleteness results, which foiled Hilbert's program completely, von Neumann abandoned his research on logic and foundations. He nevertheless maintained a great admiration for Gödel's accomplishments and in the 1930s helped to spread the word about the incompleteness results and played a supporting role in bringing Gödel to the Institute for Advanced Study.

Von Neumann's second major research of the 1920s, on quantum mechanics, was also stimulated in part by Hilbert.[24] The sixth unsolved problem listed in Hilbert's Paris lecture of 1900 is an axiomatic account of modern physics to match the one he had already given for geometry. Toward that end Hilbert had worked in the 1910s and early 1920s with moderate success on axiomatic foundations for the kinetic theory of gases, the theory of radiation, and general relativity theory.[25]

At about the time that von Neumann first visited Göttingen, probably in the summer or fall of 1925, Hilbert gave a seminar on the mathematical foundations of quantum mechanics. Two approaches to quantum mechanics, the wave theory of Erwin Schrödinger in Zurich and the particle mechanics of Werner Heisenberg in Göttingen, had recently revolutionized the subject in different ways. There had been several attempts to reconcile the two approaches, the most notable being the transformation theory of Pascual Jordan and P. A. M. Dirac, but none had succeeded entirely.[26]

In the fall of 1925 Hilbert invited Heisenberg to speak to the Göttingen mathematics colloquium about his new uncertainty principle.[27] The talk inspired von Neumann to begin working with Hilbert and his physics assistant, Lothar Nordheim, on improving the mathematical principles underlying Heisenberg's result. Nordheim provided Hilbert with a simpler mathematical account of the Jordan-Dirac transformation theory. When von Neumann saw it, he immediately went to work on its generalization. Within a few days he had outlined the fundamentals of his own approach to the mathematical foundations of quantum mechanics, based on an extension of the work of the Hilbert School on infinite-dimensional vector spaces (Hilbert spaces), much to Hilbert's satisfaction. This was the subject of a paper Hilbert, Nordheim, and von Neumann published in 1927.[28]

This paper initiated von Neumann's foundational program for quantum mechanics. He published three more papers in 1927 and several in 1929. In 1932 he published his *Mathematische Grundlagen der Quantenmechanik* (*Mathematical Foundations of Quantum Mechanics*), which gave a detailed account of these foundations and developed the related theories of measurement and quantum statistics. The Heisenberg and Schrödinger approaches satisfied his finite set of axioms, and thus his axiomatization represented a kind of abstract unification of the wave and particle theories. His approach had the further advantage of being mathematically rigorous, in contrast to Dirac's account, which used delta functions imprecisely.

Von Neumann's other major breakthrough in this area was his theory of measurement.[29] Physicists had noted that measurements in quantum theory were vague and of a probabilistic character. Many physicists believed this indeterminism was due to hidden parameters, which, once unveiled, would allow the development of a deterministic quantum theory. Von Neumann argued persuasively that this indeterminism was inherent in the quantum theory because of the interaction of the observer and the observed. His account became the standard mathematical foundation for quantum mechanics, and it was shown over time to support most of the new advances in quantum science and technology, though it has had to be revamped for use in quantum field theory. However, the abstract, formalist, mathematically technical character of his account made it much more appealing to the mathematicians than to the physicists, who have not made substantial use of it.

Princeton Mathematics, 1930–1942

Von Neumann was invited to the United States by Oswald Veblen, an internationally famous geometer and a leader in the American mathematical community.[30] Veblen played a leading role in advancing mathematics at Princeton University in the 1910s and 1920s and was partly responsible for the establishment of a research chair in mathematical physics to which Hermann Weyl was appointed in 1928. Weyl, however, relinquished the Jones Chair after only one year in order to succeed Hilbert at Göttingen, thereby creating an opening for a mathematical physicist at Princeton. Veblen first met von Neumann in 1928 at the international mathematics conference in Bologna and was impressed with his virtuosity in mathematics and mathematical physics. Veblen suggested using the income from the Jones Chair endowment to hire von Neumann as a visiting lecturer in mathematical physics. The faculty decided instead to invite the physicist Eugene Wigner, von Neumann's boyhood friend in Budapest and scientific collaborator in Berlin and Göttingen, to share the lectureship with von Neumann.[31]

Von Neumann accepted the offer with alacrity, realizing that mathematical professorships in Germany were scarce.[32] He arrived in Princeton in February 1930, in time to teach during the spring term. For three years he spent half the year teaching at Princeton and the other half teaching at the University of Berlin. Because the political situation was deteriorating in Germany, he was eager to secure a permanent appointment in the United States. Both he and Wigner were regarded by the Princeton faculty as serious contenders for the Jones Chair, but the mathematicians and the physicists, it appears, could not come to an agreement on a candidate.[33]

Veblen then had a second opportunity to help von Neumann. In 1930 the Bamberger and Fuld families, who had made fortunes in the department store business in northern New Jersey, provided an endowment for an advanced research institute, which became known as the Institute for Advanced Study (IAS). The shape of the institute was determined primarily by Abraham Flexner, its first director, and Veblen, who was appointed in 1932 as its first professor, once the decision had been made to devote its first school of study to mathematics. The institute was settled in Princeton and from 1933 until 1939 shared the quarters of the Princeton University mathematics department.

By January 1933 the institute had appointed four mathematicians or mathematically oriented physicists: Veblen and James Alexander from Princeton, Albert Einstein from Berlin, and Weyl from Göttingen. Veblen urged Flexner to make a fifth offer to von Neumann, but Flexner was opposed. He believed that there were sufficient funds for only four appointments and that, having already plucked two mathematicians from the Princeton faculty, the institute should move carefully in its relations with the university. He was probably also concerned about the number of European appointments, since one objective of the institute was to build an indigenous American research program, as he indicated at the 9 January 1933 meeting of the IAS board of trustees.[34]

The circumstances changed quickly, however. In January 1933, only six days after accepting a position, Weyl telegraphed that he had changed his mind. Flexner then reversed his position and supported Veblen's plan, and von Neumann's appointment was secured by the end of the month. Von Neumann remained at the institute for the rest of his career, except for leaves of absence to pursue government duties during and after World War II.

He returned to Europe every summer from 1930 through 1938, but the political situation eventually soured him on life there.[35] He was naturalized as a U.S. citizen in 1937 and became an enthusiastic partisan of the United States. After the war he visited Europe reluctantly and only briefly. For his second year at Princeton he returned from Hungary with his bride, the former Mariette Kovesi, and their marriage produced his only child, Marina, in 1935. The marriage ended in divorce in 1937. Two years later von Neumann returned from summer vacation in Hungary with a new wife, the former Klara Dan, who became one of the first computer programmers.

By the time von Neumann arrived in the United States he had already established an international reputation based on his contributions to operator theory, logic, and the mathematical foundations of quantum mechanics. In the 1930s, he continued his work on operator theory and quantum mechanics while furiously pursuing a number of new research topics. It is beyond my scope here to describe all of his mathematical contributions of the 1930s, but I will account briefly for some of his most important work: the spectral theory of Hilbert space, ergodic theory, rings of operators, and Haar measure.[36]

The search for an adequate foundation for quantum mechanics led von Neumann to extend substantially Hilbert's theory of integral operators between 1928 and 1932. He promulgated a more abstract definition of Hilbert space and reformulated the basic theory of bounded symmetric operators. He also systematically investigated the important case of unbounded operators, which previously had been studied in only a few special cases by Weyl and T. Carleman. This work added greatly to the theory of Hilbert spaces and made it a viable companion to the more familiar theory of finite-dimensional spaces.[37]

An outgrowth of von Neumann's work on quantum mechanics was an interest in the ergodic theorem, which had mainly been known as an important but imprecisely stated hypothesis of statistical mechanics. Following a remark in a 1931 paper by B. O. Koopman that the ergodic theorem could be formulated precisely in the theory of operators on a Hilbert space, von Neumann formulated and proved the mean ergodic theorem for unitary operators. G. D. Birkhoff, who had previously worked in this area, read von Neumann's paper and soon proved a somewhat stronger result, known as the point ergodic theorem.[38] Von Neumann wrote several more papers on ergodic theory, but they were not as influential as his first, which together with that of Birkhoff opened up an active research interest in ergodic theory and influenced research on dynamical systems and statistical mechanics.[39]

Von Neumann's early work on the spectral theory of operators dealt with single operators. As early as 1929 he began to study families of operators—properties of operators characterized by the algebraic structure of the polynomials in the operator or by the action of this algebra on the Hilbert space, for example. Using as an example research on noncommutative algebras carried out in the 1920s by Emmy Noether and Emil Artin, von Neumann deveoped his own theory of rings of operators (known also as W*-algebras and later as von Neumann algebras), which are algebras of bounded operators in a separable Hilbert space. Working alone at first, he analyzed the commutative algebras. Then in a series of landmark papers written in collaboration with F. J. Murray between 1936 and 1940 (the last published only in 1949), he analyzed the noncommutative algebras.[40] This work opened a new field of research and produced a powerful and widely used tool of quantum physics.

Following from an example he and Murray uncovered in their work on rings of operators, von Neumann formulated the axioms of a new subject, which he called continuous geometry. A continuous geometry is a generalization of projective geometry but without points. Instead the emphasis is on the flats (linear subspaces) and their interrelations. This subject was studied in Japan during World War II and by many researchers worldwide since then.[41]

Another of von Neumann's major mathematical contributions of this period was his partial solution of Hilbert's Fifth Problem (another of the twenty-three unsolved problems presented in Hilbert's 1900 Paris lecture).[42] In 1933 A. Haar showed the existence of an appropriate measure (now known as Haar measure) for topological groups. Von Neumann read Haar's paper prior to its publication and in the same issue published his own result, which explained how to use Haar's measure to solve Hilbert's Fifth Problem for the important case of compact groups.[43] Twenty years later Andrew Gleason and Deane Montgomery completed the solution. Von Neumann wrote several more papers on Haar measure, including two proofs of its uniqueness.[44] He also wrote two related papers on almost periodic functions, one in collaboration with Salomon Bochner.[45]

A few years later von Neumann returned to an idea he had suggested in the 1920s and began to publish on the theory of games and mathematical economics.[46] In 1921 Emil Borel had published a note that used examples to describe random strategies in two-person games.[47] Seven years later von Neumann gave a quantitative mathematical model for games of chance, based largely on an analysis he had carried out during the previous two years on variants of poker.[48] His central result was the Minimax Theorem, which has served as a basis for all subsequent work in the theory of games. In this paper he also defined three-person games and suggested how to define a general n-person game.

In economics his first effort was directed toward constructing a mathematical model of economic equilibria for a uniformly expanding closed economy with unlimited resources and constant returns-to-scale in production. The model, first presented at a colloquium at Princeton University in 1932, became more widely known through its presentation at Karl Menger's colloquium in Vienna in 1937, which led to its publication. Although this paper is not as well known as his 1928 paper on the theory of games or his later book with Oskar Morgenstern, one historian of econometrics has credited it with being "the single most important article in mathematical economics" because it gave the first rigorous arguments for the existence of economic equilibria and also developed a set of mathematical tools that became widely used in economics.[49]

Von Neumann did not work on his theory of games after 1928 until the Austrian economist Oskar Morgenstern arrived at Princeton University ten years later, forced by the Nazis from his economics research institute in Vienna. In 1939 Morgenstern and von Neumann started to write a paper on the application of the theory of games to economics. The scope of their research expanded, and they continued to work on the project not only in Princeton but also in Washington, where von Neumann was stationed for war work in 1942. Through a concerted effort they delivered the 600-page manuscript of *Theory of Games and Economic Behavior* to the publisher in January 1943, just days before von Neumann was called away to England on a war assignment.

The book describes the mathematics of the theory of games in great detail and applies it to many different economic problems, including exchange of goods between n parties, monopolies and oligopolies, and free trade. The authors did not expect their book to be embraced or even understood by the economists, and the publisher expected such low sales that he insisted on a subsidy. However, several favorable survey articles and reviews, together with a sympathetic front-page article in the *New York Times* in March 1946, made the book a best-seller by academic standards.[50] It became the starting point for the now-thriving study of the theory of games, as well as for related studies in combinatorics and applications to economics and several other social sciences.[51] The book's great success seems to stem from its axiomatic approach and its reliance on combinatorics as the mathematical basis for economics.

There was little time for the theory of games during the war, but afterward von Neumann resumed his interest.[52] He participated occasionally in the game theory seminars organized by Albert Tucker at Princeton University and was a consultant on this subject to the RAND Corporation. But he never again found time to give game theory the same attention as in the early 1940s. After the war his attention was directed to the new technologies of computing and atomic energy.

By the late 1930s, von Neumann was established as one of the leading international mathematicians and mathematical physicists. He had not yet had any significant contact with computing, though he was knowledgeable about numerical methods from his work in physics and chemical engineering, and he had already gained much experience with the concepts of information processing that was later to help shape his studies of computer theory. By this time he was already well connected in the American scientific power structure and was widely known for his problem-solving ability, legendary quickness of mind, and ability to reduce complex problems to a mathematically tractable form. All of these characteristics made him attractive to the people who were using science to prepare the country for war, and soon he was drawn into the war effort as a scientific consultant. This activity led him directly into computing.

An excursion into the Grand Canyon, Arizona, late 1940s. Klari von Neumann is fourth from the front, and John is at the very rear, in his ever-present business suit, and is facing the wrong direction. (Courtesy of Marina Whitman)

Von Neumann and his daughter Marina on a cross-country auto tour, Santa Fe, New Mexico, 1946. (Courtesy of Marina Whitman)

Klari and John von Neumann in front of their house in Princeton, New Jersey, 1954. (Courtesy of Marina Whitman)

(Top) Von Neumann took great delight in off-color limericks and funny hats. This inflatable hat was given to him as a gift. Princeton, 1950s. (Courtesy of Marina Whitman)

(Bottom) Willy Fellner, Emery Reves, and von Neumann, Zurich, 1926. (Courtesy of Marina Whitman)

Johnny, age 8, looks over the shoulders of (from left) his relative Lusie, brother Nick, cousin Lily, and Lily's friend Lupi Molnar. The governess can be seen in the background. The family home in Budapest, 1912. (Courtesy of Marina Whitman)

Lunch after the wedding of von Neumann's cousin Lily. Seated are (from left) von Neumann, the married couple, von Neumann's wife Mariette, a friend of the newlyweds, Lily's mother-in-law, Lily's father and mother, and Lily's father-in-law. Taken in Lily's dining room, in the same house in which von Neumann grew up. (Courtesy of Marina Whitman)

Johnny as a young boy. (Courtesy of Marina Whitman)

Von Neumann with friends at Princeton in the 1930s. (From left) Angela
Robertson, Mariette von Neumann, Eugene Wigner and his wife, von Neu-
mann, Edward Teller, and H. P. Robertson. Eugene Wigner and H. P.
Robertson were two of von Neumann's closest colleagues at Princeton.
(Courtesy of Marina Whitman)

2

An Education in Computing

World War II was a turning point in the development of computing technology. Change began in the 1930s and early 1940s when several projects were initiated to build faster and program-controlled calculating devices for scientific and engineering applications. Konrad Zuse in Germany, Howard Aiken at Harvard University, and George Stibitz at Bell Telephone Laboratories designed electromechanical calculators, and John Atanasoff at Iowa State University designed an electronic calculator.[1] All of these projects were isolated efforts, however, and had little money or scientific authority behind them.[2] The war provided an incentive to improve computational equipment, since it was useful in the preparation of ballistics tables, aircraft and atomic weapons design, fire control, and logistics, and the U.S. government felt compelled to allocate substantial resources to these problems. Many new computer projects were initiated during and after the war, and a group of highly qualified scientists and engineers were trained in computer design and application. Von Neumann was one of these scientists who became interested in computing as a result of the war, and in many ways his story is representative of that pioneering period in modern computing.

War Work

One casualty of the war was von Neumann's research program in pure mathematics. In 1941 the war occupied about a quarter of his time and the following year almost half. By 1943 he was directing all of his effort to war work and still could hardly keep pace with his heavy schedule as an adviser to several different government organizations.[3] His government consulting career had begun in 1937, soon after he became a naturalized U.S. citizen, at the

Ballistics Research Laboratory (BRL) operated by the Army Ordnance Department in Aberdeen, Maryland. The Aberdeen connection was an important influence on his career, as he explained in a postwar testimonial for Robert Kent, one of the senior BRL officials: "It was through him [Kent] that I was introduced to military science, and it was through military science that I was introduced to applied sciences. Before this I was, apart from some lesser infidelities, essentially a pure mathematician, or at least a very pure theoretician. Whatever else may have happened in the meantime, I have certainly succeeded in losing my purity."[4]

It seems almost certain that von Neumann became involved with the BRL through Veblen, his closest colleague at the institute. G. A. Bliss, F. R. Moulton, and Veblen had mounted a modest mathematical research program at Aberdeen during World War I. The program was largely dismantled after the war, but it was revitalized in 1937 in response to the deteriorating political situation in Europe. Veblen advocated using civilian scientists as military advisers. He proposed a new scientific advisory program for Aberdeen, and it was probably through his intervention that von Neumann consulted at Aberdeen occasionally in the late 1930s. In 1940 the War Department organized a formal Scientific Advisory Committee to review the BRL, and von Neumann was among its initial appointments.[5]

He became involved in other defense research, especially after the Pearl Harbor attack in December 1941. From September 1941 to September 1942 he was a consultant and later a member of Division 8 of the National Defense Research Council (NDRC). In this capacity, he worked with George Kistiakowsky, E. Bright Wilson, and G. J. Kirkwood on detonation waves.[6] His contribution principally concerned the theory of detonation and the arrangement of high explosives in shaped charges as a means to concentrate and direct the physical effect of a detonation.[7] From September 1942 until July 1943 he worked for the Mine Warfare Section of the Navy Bureau of Ordnance on what he called operational research on the physical and statistical aspects of mine warfare and countermeasures to it. The work took him to Washington for the last few months of 1942 and to England for the first half of 1943.

His activities for the government increased when he returned from England, and until the end of the war he led a peripatetic life, moving almost constantly from one project to the next. In late 1943 and early 1944 he spent about a quarter of his time at Aberdeen, working closely on problems in aerodynamics with Theodore von Karman, whom he had known since his youth. He also continued his consulting for the Navy Bureau of Ordnance, as well as his work on high explosives. In September 1943 he became a consultant to Los Alamos on the atomic bomb. Because of the value of his other consulting work to the war effort, he was one of the few scientists excused from full-time residency in Los Alamos.

In early 1944 a project of the Applied Mathematics Panel was organized under his direction at the IAS. With assistance from Valentine Bargmann and Deane Montgomery, he studied numerical methods for the calculations associated with his work for army and navy ordnance. The project was taken over by the Navy Bureau of Ordnance in August 1945 and expanded to include the development of computing methods for the high-speed calculating devices just beginning to be built.

In late 1944 he became an official member of Division 2 of NDRC, following a period as an adviser on the interaction and reflection of blast waves. He consolidated in Division 2 his work in Division 8 on aerodynamics and high explosives, and he began new investigations of the effects of explosive blasts and projectile impact on various structures. In the last months of the war he advised the BRL and the Naval Ordnance Laboratory on their programs to develop electronic and other high-speed calculating machines.

Learning About Computing

During a visit to England in the first half of 1943 von Neumann became seriously interested in computational mathematics.[8] He wrote back to Veblen of his experience:

I think that I see clearly that the best course for me at present is to concentrate on Ordnance work, and the Gas Dynamical matters connected therewith. I think that I have learned here a good deal of experimental physics, particularly of the Gas Dynamical variety, and that I shall return a better and impurer man. I have also developed an obscene interest in computational techniques. I am looking forward to discussing these matters with you. I really feel like proselytizing—even if I am going to tell you only things which you have known much longer than I did.[9]

This letter followed by only a month what may have been von Neumann's first experience in writing a program for a calculating machine.[10] The opportunity to learn about a means to automate gas-dynamical calculations arose through his contact with the mathematician John Todd, the organizer of the Admiralty Computing Service. In April 1943 von Neumann joined Todd on a visit to the Nautical Almanac Office (NAO) in Bath, where calculations were being carried out under the supervision of D. H. Sadler. L. J. Comrie, the previous superintendent of the NAO and a leader in numerical mathematics, had used the NAO's National Cash Register model 3000 accounting machine to calculate tabular functions of integer arguments using sixth differences. Sadler proposed to Todd and von Neumann that the machine be used to interpolate intermediate values, and they wrote the program he desired on the return train trip to London.[11] Later von Neumann wrote to Todd that he "received in that period a decisive impulse which determined my interest in computing machines."[12]

Von Neumann's next important involvement with computing came at Los Alamos.[13] The director of the laboratory, Robert Oppenheimer, enlisted von Neumann as a scientific consultant because of his knowledge of hydrodynamics.[14] He first visited Los Alamos in the autumn of 1943 and almost immediately began to make contributions. In particular he was an important catalyst in convincing the laboratory to use an implosion technique for detonating the bomb.[15] One of the staff physicists, Seth Neddermeyer, had begun implosion detonation experiments at Los Alamos earlier in the year, but the idea was largely ignored by the senior scientists Bethe, Oppenheimer, and Teller. Von Neumann heard about Neddermeyer's work during a visit to Los Alamos in the fall of 1943 and gave a talk describing his own experiences with shaped charges, which convinced the staff of the possibilities of implosion. He explained how conventional explosives could be shaped—that is, placed around fissionable material in such a configuration that a detonation would generate a uniform shock wave that compressed the fissionable material to a critical state.[16]

It was well known from the laboratory's beginning that the equations governing the hydrodynamics of implosions and explosions could not be solved analytically but must be treated either experimentally or numerically. The computing load increased rapidly. The laboratory was fortunate in having the services of Stanley Frankel and Eldred Nelson, who had organized a computing service for the electromagnetic isotope separator at the University of California at Berkeley the year before. The Theoretical Division began operations at Los Alamos with Marchant and Friden desk calculators, which were used by the scientists and the (primarily female) employees known as "computers," who carried out the extensive numerical calculations for them. In the late summer of 1943 Donald Flanders, a mathematician from New York University, was hired to head this hand-computing group, known as T-5. He increased the staff size to around twenty and provided an effective computing service.[17]

The computing demands of the laboratory quickly outstripped T-5's capacity. In late 1943 one of the staff scientists, Dana P. Mitchell, suggested augmenting the operation with IBM punched-card equipment. Mitchell was on leave from the Columbia University physics faculty and knew about the sophisticated astronomical computations made by Wallace Eckert with punched-card equipment in the Columbia computing laboratory established by IBM. Frankel and Nelson soon received permission to acquire the most up-to-date electromechanical IBM accounting equipment for use on the design of the gun-type bomb, in which a gun would be used to shoot one subcritical mass of fissionable material into another to attain critical state.[18] By the time the equipment arrived shortly after, priorities had changed, and the equipment was used instead to study detonation by the implosion method that interested von Neumann.

The implosion simulation required the integration of a hyperbolic partial differential equation in one space and one time variable. The integration was carried out by sending batches of punched cards through a sequence of IBM machines. On each run the machines collaboratively calculated a single integration step; then a set of values was printed, and a new batch of cards was punched with the data to be used as input to calculate the next integration step. Each card required between 1 and 5 seconds of processing by each machine, and a human operator had to intervene at many points. Hand calculations were also being done as a check on the IBM equipment being installed and made ready. Richard Feynman decided it would be instructive to organize a contest to determine whether the desk calculators or the punched-card equipment would be more effective at the implosion simulation. For several days the race was even, but eventually the human computers working the desk calculators tired, and the IBM equipment pulled ahead. Thereafter the IBM equipment was used for all large calculations.

Von Neumann took a great interest in the practice, as well as the results, of computing and insisted on learning how to program the IBM machines.[19] Metropolis and Nelson remember:

In March or April 1944, he spent two weeks working in the punched-card machine operation, pushing cards through the various machines, learning how to wire plugboards and design card layouts, and becoming thoroughly familiar with the machine operations. He found wiring the tabulator plugboards particularly frustrating; the tabulator could perform parallel operations on separate counters, and wiring the tabulator plugboard to carry out parallel computation involved taking into account the relative timing of the parallel operations. He later told us this experience led him to reject parallel computations in electronic computers and in his design of the single-address instruction code where parallel handling of operands was guaranteed not to occur.[20]

Even the best standard IBM equipment was not sufficient to the task at hand, so the laboratory convinced IBM to build more powerful punched-card equipment with the capability to do triple-product multiplications and divisions. This equipment, delivered in late 1944, improved the situation but did not fully meet the computing needs of the Los Alamos scientists.

Through his extensive travels and wide government and scientific contacts, von Neumann was in a position to bring to Los Alamos news of calculating technologies as they became available. The earliest evidence of his actively soliciting information about computing technologies is from January 1944, when he wrote to Warren Weaver, head of the Applied Mathematics Panel of the Office of Scientific Research and Development.[21] Weaver suggested contacting Howard Aiken of Harvard University, George Stibitz of Bell Telephone Laboratories, and Jan Schilt of Columbia University.[22]

Aiken had conceived in some detail, and IBM had engineered and constructed at its own expense, one of the first program-controlled computing devices. It used relays to control the process and electrically powered movements of mechanical counters to perform the arithmetical operations.[23] This machine, known first as the Automatic Sequence Controlled Calculator and later as the Harvard Mark I, was first operated at the IBM plant in Endicott, New York, in January 1943. IBM donated the machine to Harvard, where it was relocated in February 1944 and later operated by the Navy Bureau of Ships. Von Neumann informed the Los Alamos scientists of its existence in the spring of 1944 and arranged to run a problem on it for them that spring or summer.[24] The problem involved the numerical integration of a second-order partial differential equation governing spherical shock implosions. Metropolis recalls the event from the Los Alamos perspective:

Von Neumann suggested that one of the problems scheduled to be run on the punched-card machines be cast in unclassified form and given to Aiken, who was seeking problems to be run on his about-to-be-completed machine. We agreed to do that, and von Neumann took the unclassified form of the problem to Harvard. The running of the problems on the two complexes began at almost the same time, so it developed into a "race" between the punched-card machines and the Mark I, although the Harvard personnel did not know the problem was being run in parallel elsewhere. The problem took three weeks to run at Los Alamos. About two weeks later, von Neumann reported that the Mark I was halfway through the problem. The comparison of the two machines was not fair, however, for the punched-card machine operation computed values to six decimal digits, whereas the Mark I computed values to eighteen decimal digits and integrated the partial differential equation at a much smaller interval size, thereby achieving greater precision.[25]

The Harvard Mark I did not have all the power and flexibility that the Los Alamos physicists desired, and it was already fully booked with projects for the navy. From late 1944 until the time of the Japanese surrender in August 1945, the pressure for computing at Los Alamos remained intense. Richard Feynman and Nicholas Metropolis became more involved in the use of punched-card machinery, and Richard Hamming was recruited from the University of Illinois to join them.

Von Neumann continued to look into the availability of high-speed computing equipment. By July 1944 he had met with Leland E. Cunningham, the head of the machine-computing section at Aberdeen, about a promised improvement in IBM multipliers and talked with Cunningham, Robert Kent, Major A. A. Bennett, and Captain Herman Goldstine about the possibility of the Army Ordnance Department's buying a Bell Telephone relay calculator.

These discussions about computing facilities for Los Alamos dovetailed with von Neumann's work on the reflection and refraction of shocks for NDRC Divisions 2 and 8 and the Navy Bureau of Ordnance. While aerodynamical experiments were being carried out in 1943 at two British laboratories and in 1944 at the BRL in Aberdeen and the Princeton Station of NDRC, von Neumann and others were at work on computational methods for these problems, mainly for use with punched-card machines.[26]

Weaver discussed von Neumann's computing problems with George Stibitz in March and gave von Neumann an introduction to Stibitz.[27] Von Neumann visited Stibitz during the first week of April and reported to Weaver that Stibitz had taught him some of the principles of high-speed computation and even offered to try to make Bell computing facilities available:

I spent the better part of a day with Stibitz, who explained to me in detail the principles and the working of his relay counting mechanisms, and showed me the interpolator as well as the almost-finished anti-aircraft fire-control calculator. We had a very extensive discussion of the possibilities of these machines compared with the I.B.M. type, and their adaptability to the problems in which I am interested. Dr. Stibitz even suggested, what went far beyond my expectations, that he may seek permission for an experimental computation of the kind I suggested on the big machine in the process of its breaking in. . . .

At any rate I am staying in contact with Stibitz, and I am extremely glad that you made this possible.[28]

Weaver also had his deputy, Thornton Fry, locate IBM equipment to use on von Neumann's NDRC calculations. The IBM equipment nearest to Princeton was identified as being at the Thomas J. Watson Astronomical Computing Bureau of Columbia University and Consolidated Edison Company, both in New York City. Weaver put von Neumann in contact with Professor Jan Schilt of the Columbia University Astronomy Department, acting head of the Computing Bureau at Columbia, who was carrying out extensive bombing calculations for the Applied Mathematics Panel using IBM punched-card equipment.[29] Von Neumann visited Schilt that same week in April in which he visited Stibitz. With assistance from Fry and Schilt, arrangements were made to use the IBM machine at Consolidated Edison and to receive programming assistance from Schilt's group at Columbia.[30] By the beginning of July the instructions had been written out for Schilt's group, but no calculations had yet been done.[31] These calculations were apparently carried out in due course, though no documentation of their outcome has been found.[32]

Von Neumann reported what he had learned about the availability of high-speed calculating machinery to Robert Oppenheimer, director of the Los Alamos Laboratory, in a letter of 1 August 1944.[33] Following a discussion of the technical details of the Bell calculator and the IBM multiplier, he concluded about the former:

The answer to our technical questions follow below; they are very favorable. My overall impression is that the machine would be well worth having if a future of, say, 1 1/2 years or more is being envisaged for the project. I think that it would not be necessary to make a very great effort to get a branch of the N.D.R.C. interested, particularly if the Ordnance Dept. has already gone ahead in this matter, which seems likely. . . .

In Cunningham's opinion the simplicity in planning, the reliability of the elements, the self-checking features, and the ability to run overnight without a crew, should alone make the machine 5 times or more faster than any I.B.M. aggregate, quite apart from the other advantages.[34]

The improved IBM multiplier employed a new timing principle in which each of ninety-six timing units emitted a characteristic impulse to which controls could be wired.[35] Von Neumann wrote of this improvement:

[This new timing principle] gives the machine an enormous flexibility. It is clearly more "intelligent" than any tabulator.

However: The machine does not function yet! The relays were steel-and-brass, which seems to be an unusual and, as it turned out, unsatisfactory arrangement. They had to be taken out and will be replaced by better ones. The functioning is now promised for a month from now. Cunningham thinks that the machine will ultimately work at the specified [greatly improved] speeds, but he has little faith in the deadline.[36]

Apparently the timetable for the Bell calculator was too long, for there is no indication that further steps were taken to acquire one for Los Alamos. Improved IBM equipment was used at Los Alamos, but it does not seem to have been of this design.

What is more interesting about von Neumann's letter is the indication it gives of his growing knowledge of calculating systems. The analysis of the Bell calculator is organized around twenty-one questions he had prepared before his visit to Williams and Stibitz. These questions concerned the literature on the calculator, sites and terms of agreement, details of arithmetic operation, input-output (reading, printing, punching, and tables), control, fixed tables (to hold interpolation coefficients), checks and errors, and personnel requirements.[37] From these questions and their answers it is apparent that von Neumann already had a deep and practical understanding of many of the important concepts of high-speed digital computation:[38] (1) separate arithmetic units organized into a system by a controlling device;[39] (2) separate registers to carry out the four basic arithmetic operations and square roots;[40] (3) scaling requirements so that numbers would not overflow a machine's fixed range; (4) three-variable addressing;[41] (5) the general relationship between the times taken to carry out basic operations and the overall operation time of the system; (6) storing tabulated functions in fixed tables; (7) subroutines;[42] (8) entry of data and instructions on a single tape;[43] (9) conditional branching;[44] (10) coding of data and instructions; (11) difficulties associated with problem setup time; (12) cost and speed relationships among hard wiring of instructions, hand setting of switches, and programming by tape; (13) the need for automatic error checking; and (14) the personnel requirements associated with operation and maintenance of a computer system. Von Neumann had come a long way in his understanding of computing systems in a short time. This knowledge served him well when, later in 1944, he came into contact with the ENIAC project at the University of Pennsylvania.[45]

ENIAC and EDVAC

When von Neumann wrote to Weaver in January 1944 to inquire about computing facilities, Weaver's reply mentioned those at Bell Telephone Laboratories, the Columbia-Watson Laboratory, and Harvard University but not those at the University of Pennsylvania's Moore School of Electrical Engineering.[46] Since June 1943 the Moore School engineers had been working on a giant electronic calculator known as the ENIAC (Electronic Numerical Integrator and Computer).[47] It was sponsored by Army Ordnance, which wanted faster computing equipment at the BRL to augment its differential analyzer and desk calculators in the computation of firing tables for its new guns, shells, and fuses.

The ENIAC was of unprecedented size and complexity among computational devices. Its forty panels filled a large room and contained some 1500 electromechanical relays and 17,000 vacuum tubes. Twenty accumulators carried out the addition and subtraction, while other units handled multiplication, division, and square roots. An IBM card reader worked in tandem with a unit known as a constant transmitter to enter data, an IBM card punch worked together with a print unit to provide output, and an IBM tabulator printed tables. Function table units developed by RCA were used to store tabular data, and intermediate results were stored in the accumulators or on punched cards. A problem was set up through a labor-intensive process of setting switches and plugging cables.

The ENIAC used many existing components and units but was differentiated from other calculating devices by its ability to process at electronic speeds, hundreds of times faster than the fastest electromechanical devices. The multiplication of two ten-digit decimal numbers took less than 1/300 of a second.

That Weaver did not inform von Neumann of the ENIAC may seem surprising, since many people now regard it as the first modern computer. Weaver was certainly aware of the ENIAC project through the NDRC and would have had little difficulty in obtaining permission to tell von Neumann about this classified project. One author has suggested that Weaver was silent because the NDRC held the Moore School project in low esteem.[48] Several facts support this interpretation: electronics were untested in calculating equipment, and many people regarded as infeasible a machine with so many vacuum tubes; also the ENIAC's chief engineer, J. Presper Eckert, was young and untested, and the primary mathematical adviser, John W. Mauchly, had no particular standing in the mathematical research community. At least two other explanations for Weaver's silence are plausible. One is that he did not consider the ENIAC because von Neumann had an immediate need for a computer. The Bell and Columbia machines were already in operation and Harvard was receiving a tested machine from IBM—in contrast, the ENIAC did not reach a tested, operable state for two more years. Another explanation may be that Weaver did not then know of any progress on the ENIAC project. The first progress report written by the Moore School staff was dated 31 December 1943 and was probably initially delivered only to the sponsor, Army Ordnance, so it is unlikely that Weaver had seen the report in mid-January when von Neumann approached him.

Von Neumann heard about the ENIAC inadvertently from Herman Goldstine in the late summer, probably August, of 1944. Goldstine, a captain in Army Ordnance who held a Ph.D. in mathematics from the University of Chicago, was the army's liaison to the Moore School and had been instrumental in helping the school to obtain a contract to build the ENIAC. Von Neumann was returning home from a Scientific Advisory Committee meeting at the BRL when he happened to meet Goldstine on the railroad platform in Aberdeen. Goldstine knew von Neumann only by reputation but approached him. As Goldstine recounts: "The conversation soon turned to my work. When it became clear that I was concerned with the development of an electronic computer capable of 333 multiplications per second, the whole atmosphere of our conversation changed from one of relaxed good humor to one more like the oral examination for the doctor's degree in mathematics."[49]

Goldstine quickly arranged for von Neumann to visit the Moore School and see the ENIAC. There is no written evidence for the date of von Neumann's first visit to the Moore School, though Goldstine recalls it as being 7 August.[50] What von Neumann discovered upon his first visit is not open to question. The general design principles for the ENIAC had been decided on, and tests were being run on a two-accumulator prototype.[51] Von Neumann arrived too late to participate in the design of the ENIAC; however, he did participate in discussions on the design of a second computing machine, later named the EDVAC (Electronic Discrete Variable Arithmetic Computer). He and the Moore School team were interested in his continued participation, and Herman Goldstine arranged to have his official duties as a consultant to BRL extended to include this project.[52] Thereafter von Neumann visited the Moore School every few weeks until early 1946, except when he was in Los Alamos or elsewhere on government business.

These discussions about a new computing machine, which began before the ENIAC reached completion, were stimulated by several perceived deficiencies in the ENIAC's design. The exigencies of the war had led Eckert and Mauchly to make some compromises in the ENIAC's design—one was the inefficient method of problem setup, as an ENIAC Progress Report of 31 December 1943 explained: "No attempt has been made to make provision for setting up a problem automatically. This is for the sake of simplicity and because it is anticipated that the ENIAC will be used primarily for problems of a type in which one setup will be used many times before another problem is placed on the machine."[53]

In January 1944 Eckert had written a three-page memorandum outlining his ideas for a magnetic calculating machine. He proposed that the machine include "automatic programming of the facilities and processes" but made no suggestions about the implementation.[54] Several months later Eckert discovered that a mercury delay line he had worked with on a radar project in 1942 could be turned into a register to store numbers, and he proposed using the delay line for the internal memory in the new computing device.

By late summer the BRL representatives, especially Goldstine and L. Cunningham, had decided they wanted to improve on the ENIAC's clumsy setup procedures and small number (twenty) of internal storage registers. On 11 August Goldstine wrote to Colonel Simon suggesting a new research and development contract for a computing machine that would improve ENIAC's programming and memory facilities.[55] This memorandum evoked considerable discussion in Aberdeen and led to a 29 August meeting of the Firing Table Reviewing Board, which was attended by A. A. Bennett, L. Cunningham, Dederick, Goldstine, Kent, and Sterne from the BRL staff and the mathematical consultants J. McShane, C. B. Morrey, and von Neumann. The board recommended entering into a contract for the construction of a new electronic computing device, which, in comparison to ENIAC, would use fewer tubes in order to cut expense and ease maintenance, be capable of solving a wider range of problems, store larger amounts of numerical data inexpensively and at high speeds, employ simpler and speedier problem setup procedures, and be smaller.[56]

There is no specific evidence of von Neumann's role in the decision; however, his position can be surmised from a statement by J. G. Brainerd, the ENIAC project supervisor, about his conversations with von Neumann (possibly prior to the 29 August meeting):

The progress of work on the ENIAC has led to some rather extensive discussions concerning the solution of problems of a type for which the ENIAC was not designed. In particular, these discussions have been carried out with Dr. Von Neumann, who is consultant to BRL on hydrodynamical and aerodynamical problems associated with projectile motion. Dr. Von Neumann is particularly interested in mathematical analyses which are the logical accompaniment of the experimental work which will be carried out in the supersonic wind tunnels.[57]

In the process of solving the partial differential equations that represented these problems, thousands of intermediate values had to be stored, far in excess of the ENIAC's storage capacity. It is therefore reasonable to assume that von Neumann was a proponent of this new computing device.

Identifying precisely an individual's contributions to a group effort is always difficult, and it is no less so for the contributions von Neumann made in his regular meetings with the Moore School engineers. Without assigning any individual credit, the first EDVAC report described the general content of these meetings:

> The problems of logical control have been analyzed by means of informal discussions among Dr. John von Neumann, Consultant for the Aberdeen Proving Ground, Dr. Mauchly, Mr. Eckert, Dr. Burks, Capt. Goldstine, and others. . . . Points which have been considered during these discussions are flexibility of the use of EDVAC, storage capacity, computing speed, sorting speed, the coding of problems, and circuit design. These items have received particular attention; in addition there has been some discussion of the input and output systems which may be most advantageously used for the EDVAC. Dr. von Neumann plans to submit within the next few weeks a summary of these analyses of the logical control of the EDVAC together with examples showing how certain problems can be set up.[58]

Clearly von Neumann contributed substantially to the discussion of the kinds of problems that could be solved by the computer and the specifications it must have to that end. Eckert and Mauchly credited von Neumann for his work on logical design and coding: "He has contributed to many discussions on the logical controls of the EDVAC, has proposed certain instruction codes, and has tested these proposed systems by writing out the coded instructions for specific problems."[59]

Because there has been so much controversy over von Neumann's contributions to the EDVAC's design, it is useful to examine this topic in as great detail as the written record allows. Notes prepared by Arthur Burks summarizing two of the meetings between von Neumann and the Moore School staff, together with correspondence between Goldstine and von Neumann from this period, indicate that von Neumann's contributions extended beyond scientific applications, coding, and logical control to engineering matters, though the importance of his engineering contributions is difficult to ascertain. For example, in a 14 March meeting he discussed various architectural and engineering issues concerning the connection of the registers to the central equipment and the use of the function table in switching between register tubes. He also discussed architectural and arithmetical issues about converting between the binary and the decimal systems.[60] In a meeting nine days later, he suggested schemes for inhibiting and energizing groups of tubes in adder units and participated in a discussion of the problems of switching.[61] His correspondence with Goldstine touched on many topics: the relative merits of the binary, octal, and decimal systems for use in the EDVAC; a new control scheme for the EDVAC that took advantage of its slow rate of reading information from punched cards to improve precision in certain classes of hydrodynamical problems; Western Electric delay networks, which could be coupled together as an alternative storage device to the mercury delay lines being developed by Presper Eckert; suggestions from Los Alamos about pentodes to use as basic switching elements; and sorting and printing problems.[62]

The capstone of von Neumann's contributions at the Moore School was his "First Draft of a Report on the EDVAC," written in the spring of 1945 and distributed to the Moore School staff in late June.[63] It presented the first written description of the stored-program concept and explained how a stored-program computer processes information. It has also been the focal point of the controversy over von Neumann's role in the development of the stored-program computer.[64]

The stated purpose of the report was to describe the structure of a very high-speed automatic digital computing system and in particular its logical control. Von Neumann had in mind computing devices powerful enough to solve non-linear partial differential equations of two or three independent variables and other problems of similar complexity. In such a computer system, all numerical information and numerically coded instructions for logical and algebraic orders are expected to be given in exhaustive detail, but once the instructions are given, the calculation is expected to be carried through to completion without human intervention (until the production of numerical output). The system is also intended to have some ability to recognize its own malfunctions.

The report organized the computer system into five units: a central arithmetic unit to carry out the four basic arithmetic operations and perhaps higher arithmetical functions such as roots, logarithms, trigonometric functions, and their inverses; a central control unit to control the proper sequencing of operations and make the individual units act together to carry out the specific task programmed into the system; a memory unit to store both numerical data (initial and boundary values, constant values, tables of fixed functions) and numerically coded instructions; an input unit to transfer information from the outside recording medium to the central processing units (the arithmetic unit, control, and memory); and an output unit to transfer information from the central processing units to the outside recording medium.

Von Neumann was interested in presenting a "logical" description of the stored-program computer rather than an engineering description; that is, his concern was the overall structure of a computing system, the abstract parts that it comprises, the functions of each part, and how the parts interact to process information. The specific materials or design of implementation of the parts was not pertinent to his analysis. Any technology, or even any biological organ, that meets the functional specifications can be used with no effect on his results. This explains in part his decision to compare the units of the computer with the associative, sensory, and motor neurons of the human nervous system and to introduce terminology (such as *organ* and *neuron*) and symbolism from a paper by Warren McCulloch and Walter Pitts on neural networks.[65] This approach is illustrated in the discussion of the computer's basic switching elements:

The ideal procedure would be to treat the elements as what they are intended to be: as vacuum tubes. However, this would necessitate a detailed analysis of specific radio engineering questions at this early stage of the discussion, when too many alternatives are still open, to be treated all exhaustively and in detail. Also, the numerous alternative possibilities for arranging arithmetical procedures, logical control, etc., would superpose on the equally numerous possibilities for the choice of types and sizes of vacuum tubes and other circuit elements from the point of view of practical performance, etc. All this would produce an involved and opaque situation in which the preliminary orientation which we are now attempting would be hardly possible.

In order to avoid this we will base our considerations on a hypothetical element, which functions essentially like a vacuum tube—e.g. like a triode element with an appropriate associated RLC-circuit—but which can be discussed as an isolated entity, without going into detailed radio frequency electromagnetic considerations. We re-emphasize: This situation is only temporary, only a transient standpoint, to make the present preliminary discussion possible. After the conclusions of the preliminary discussion the elements will have to be reconsidered in their true electromagnetic nature. But at that time the decisions of the preliminary discussion will be available, and the corresponding alternatives accordingly eliminated.[66]

The general remarks about the overall structure of the computing system were followed by lengthy discussions of the three central processing units. In the section on the arithmetic unit, von Neumann constructed circuits for the four basic arithmetic operations and explained how to handle binary points and round-off.[67] The section on the control unit listed all the machine orders and analyzed the connections between the arithmetic unit and the memory. The section on the memory estimated the storage required for a thirty-digit binary number, as well as the total storage requirements for the numbers and instructions associated with a typical hydrodynamical problem. He estimated that a memory of 2^{18} (~250,000) bits was required and discussed two means for the physical realization of a memory of this size—the delay line and the iconoscope.[68] The memory, he concluded, is the "main bottleneck of an automatic very high speed computing device."[69]

The document is incomplete. Von Neumann left many blank spaces in the text for adding references and gave no detailed discussion of the input and output units. Nevertheless, the document is powerful; a mere 100 pages of mimeographed text gives the fundamentals of the stored-program computer. The report was originally distributed only to the staff of the Moore School and the project's government sponsors, but it soon found its way into the hands of many different groups in the United States and England interested in building high-speed computing devices. In effect, it served as the logical schematic for many of the early stored-program computers.

The initial reception of the report was favorable. Among those at the Moore School, the most positive reaction came from Goldstine: "All of us here have been reading your report with greatest interest and I feel that it is of the greatest possible value since it gives a complete logical framework for the machine. This situation did not obtain for the ENIAC, as you well know, and as a result the ENIAC is full of gadgets that have as their only raison d'etre that they appealed to John Mauchly."[70]

The few criticisms from the Moore School staff passed on to von Neumann by Goldstine were quite mild.[71] The report was regarded as being sufficiently valuable that it was "distributed to the engineers on Project PY in order that they may be familiar with the background for the experimental work which they will do on this project."[72] The response was similarly favorable from the Ballistics Computation Committee at Aberdeen and certain others who received it, notably Stan Ulam and Douglas Hartree.[73]

Over the next two years, however, the document was the focal point of a tension between Goldstine and von Neumann on one side and Eckert and Mauchly on the other, and it led to a severing of relations between them. There were two closely intertwined issues: intellectual credit for the ideas expressed in the draft report and patent rights for the ideas embodied in the EDVAC. Over time it seems that attitudes on both of these issues hardened.

Eckert and Mauchly believed that von Neumann had merely summarized the group's discussions and that they, Eckert and Mauchly, deserved the full credit for discovery of the fundamental ideas.[74] In a July 1945 report Eckert, Mauchly, and Reid Warren wrote that von Neumann "has posed a preliminary draft in which he has *organized* the subject matter of these discussions."[75] The statement is stronger in a report Eckert and Mauchly wrote three months later: "Dr. von Neumann has also written a preliminary report in which most of the results of earlier discussions are summarized. In his report, the physical structures and devices *proposed by Eckert and Mauchly* are replaced by idealized elements to avoid raising engineering problems which might distract attention from the logical considerations under discussion."[76]

Over the years Eckert and Mauchly became harsher in their assessment. Eckert stated in his testimony at the *Honeywell* v. *Sperry Rand* trial, "Dr. von Neumann had translated some of the ideas of Dr. Mauchly and myself into a sort of semi-mathematical logical notation of his own."[77] Mauchly assessed the situation in this way:

Johnny learned instantly of course, as was his nature. But he chose to refer to the modules we had described as "organs" and to substitute hypothetical "neurons" for hypothetical vacuum tubes or other devices which could perform logical functions. It was clear that Johnny was rephrasing our logic, but it was still the same logic. Also, he was introducing different but equivalent symbols; nevertheless the devices still did the same things. Johnny did *not* alter the fundamental concepts which we had already formulated for the EDVAC.[78]

Goldstine and von Neumann had a very different view of the matter. At a meeting held at the Moore School in April 1947 to try to straighten out the EDVAC patent issues, von Neumann argued that the ideas resulting from these discussions he participated in at the Moore School were largely a group effort, so it would be difficult to assign individual credit: "There are certain items which are clearly one man's. . . . The application of the acoustic tank to this problem was an idea we heard from Pres Eckert. There are other ideas where the situation was confused. So confused that the man who had originated the idea had himself talked out of it and changed his mind two or three times. Many times the man who had the idea first may not be the proponent of it. In these cases it would be practically impossible to settle its apostle."[79]

In fact von Neumann disagreed with Eckert and Mauchly's claims to be the sole inventors of the EDVAC. This difference of opinion became more apparent as Eckert and Mauchly pursued their commercial interests in computers. When in late March 1946 they refused to sign a newly imposed University of Pennsylvania patent agreement transferring all inventions made by university employees to the university, they were forced to resign their university posts.[80] The patent issues related to the EDVAC remained unsettled when they left the university, and they continued to make patent claims as they built up a commercial venture to exploit those ideas.

Following common practice, patent lawyers from the sponsoring government agency, the Office of the Chief of Ordnance, processed the EDVAC patent application.[81] Eckert and Mauchly submitted their claims, and the government attorneys began to prepare patent applications on their behalf. Goldstine and von Neumann first learned about these claims in March 1946: "I found that the first attempt by von Neumann to claim any patents on the EDVAC was on 22 March 1946 when Drs. von Neumann and Goldstine had a spur of the moment meeting with Mr. Woodward and Mr. Stevens of the Legal Branch in the Pentagon Building. Dr. von Neumann inquired as to the patent situation and mentioned that he thought he had some patent rights. He was asked to file an Army War Patent Form and to submit any disclosures he might have. He returned the form and submitted as his disclosure his report entitled 'First Draft of Report on EDVAC' dated 30 June 1945."[82] Von Neumann described the situation to his legal counsel in June 1946:

Two of the employees of the University with whom I had very frequent contacts and with whom I discussed freely all my thoughts on this subject of electronic computing machines, have recently left the University to set up a business on their own to build such machines. I had understood while they were employed by the University that all matters pertaining to ownership of patents were to be settled by conferences. I have discovered, however, that these men are making patent applications on matters in which I feel that I am at least a joint inventor and in some cases the sole inventor.[83]

In this letter von Neumann expressed concern that government lawyers were the handling the patent matter. He pointed out that a government lawyer was preparing the patent application on behalf of Eckert and Mauchly, that he had been denied permission to see their application, and that he had been told that his only recourse was to submit materials to the same lawyer, who would decide whether to file patent applications on those items he claimed to have invented. He suggested this might represent a conflict of interest on the part of the government lawyer:

I found the other day that the same Mr. Woodward who is preparing the applications for these other two men is preparing a report determining whether the material I had submitted is sufficient to justify preparation of patent applications.

I am desirous of learning from you whether in your opinion Mr. Woodward is ethically and legally in a position to handle both sides of the matter described above. Inasmuch as he has refused to give me any information with regard to the work he is doing for the other two men, it is difficult for me to understand how he can also, in any fairness, handle my claims which are probably hostile to those of the other persons he is representing.[84]

Goldstine lodged a protest that favoritism was being shown to Eckert and Mauchly, but the government lawyers vigorously disagreed. However, there seems to be compelling evidence to support Goldstine's claim: the government lawyers showed von Neumann's disclosure to Eckert and Mauchly, and in a meeting in 1947 with Mauchly the government lawyer "immediately began offering suggestions to Dr. Mauchly as to how this new situation pertaining to von Neumann's report might be overcome."[85] The representative of the Moore School who attended this meeting between the government lawyers and Mauchly observed, "There is no doubt throughout the entire session that the Patent people were in effect acting as Attorneys for Eckert and Mauchly. They were also accepting help from Mr. Smith [Eckert and Mauchly's private lawyer]. *It is expected that Mr. Smith will prepare certain patent claims and that the Legal Branch will apply for those patents.*"[86]

A meeting arranged by the Office of the Chief of Ordnance (OCO) was held at the Moore School on 8 April 1947 to sort out these patent claims.[87] Eckert, Mauchly, von Neumann, and Goldstine attended, as did representatives of the OCO patent office, the BRL, and the University of Pennsylvania. This "new situation pertaining to von Neumann's report" proved to be the deciding factor. It was judged that the EDVAC report was a publication in a legal sense; that it had been "published" for more than a year before the patent was filed; that this fact rendered all the ideas in the report part of the public domain; and hence that neither Eckert and Mauchly, nor von Neumann, nor anyone else could patent them. As far as ideas developed during the EDVAC project but not contained in the draft report were concerned, it was agreed that no patent would be filed by the OCO but that individual parties were free to apply. Eckert and Mauchly further agreed, contingent upon their lawyer's approval, to show von Neumann any patent claims prior to their filing.[88]

There has been debate about why the patent issue was so important to von Neumann. One scholar has claimed that "recognition and priority were very important to him."[89] It is impossible to rule this out as a factor, but there is abundant evidence that von Neumann had better motives. In a letter of 9 April, the day following the Moore School patent conference, he reported the outcome to his legal counsel with the comment: "This meant, of course, that the situation had taken a turn which is very favorable for us, since we are hardly interested in exclusive patents but rather in seeing that anything that we contributed to the subject, directly or indirectly, remains as accessible as possible to the general public. In addition to this, of course, we have to fulfill our obligations to the Government."[90]

Earlier von Neumann had written, "I would never have undertaken my consulting work at the University had I realized that I was essentially giving consulting services to a commercial group."[91] In a later patent case concerning P. J. Herbst's claims to principles similar to those embodied in the EDVAC, von Neumann had written to a patent attorney at the OCO "I am very happy that this is the case [that the government has license rights under the Herbst patent] since our main interest is to see that the Government and the scientific public have full rights to the free use of any information connected with this subject."[92]

The patent dispute over EDVAC dragged on into 1947, well after the start of the Electronic Computer Project at the IAS. One effect was that von Neumann changed the patent policy for the IAS project. The original plan was to assign patents to individual engineers; instead all ideas were placed in the public domain.[93]

This dispute had further ramifications for the relationship between von Neumann and the Eckert-Mauchly group. In November 1945 von Neumann had offered Eckert a position as the chief engineer on the IAS Electronic Computer Project, and there had been some discussion of joint work among the Moore School, the IAS, and RCA. In January 1946 Eckert and Mauchly's lawyer wrote to Vladimir Zworykin, a senior member of the technical staff at RCA, about this possible collaboration: "Messrs. Eckert and Mauchly are in accord with the building of a machine for the Institute embodying their inventions and, in fact, are quite anxious to cooperate in this project to insure the best possible results by contributing their own knowledge and experience as well as time."[94] Implicit in the tone and content of the letter was the message that all patent rights would be derivative from, and hence the property of, Eckert and Mauchly. This position was so objectionable to RCA that it ruined any prospects for the tripartite arrangement. By March von Neumann realized that he could not reach a common ground with Eckert about commercial interests, and so the job offer was withdrawn.[95]

Von Neumann went on to set a policy restricting the access of Eckert and Mauchly's company to technical information of the IAS Electronic Computer Project. No doubt von Neumann regarded this restriction of the free flow of information about the new computing systems as unfortunate. He explained his policy to Stan Frankel, his wartime associate at Los Alamos, by this time a faculty member at the University of Chicago:

I have the greatest respect for Eckert and Mauchly's ability, for their past achievements and for their future promise. It is no criticism on my part, just an observation of facts, that they are a commercial group with a commercial patent policy. On the basis of the information before me, I have to conclude, that we cannot work with them directly or indirectly, in the same open manner in which we would work with an academic group which has no such interests. I certainly intend to do my part to keep as much of the field "in the public domain" (from the patent point of view) as I can. This is my own inclination, and besides, I owe this to the type of backing that our project has. I can therefore not agree to any pre-publication discussions with a commercial group, directly or indirectly. I can make an exception for R.C.A. only, since they contribute intellectually to our project and since we work on the basis of a clear-cut gentleman's agreement.

For these reasons, and in this sense, anything that we do is open to the University of Chicago and to the members of its staff. It is in this sense that we welcome you and Nick [Metropolis]. If you wish to maintain the same type of close contact with the Eckert-Mauchly group—which is for you and you alone to decide—then you should not put yourself into an incompatible position by communicating with us too. I would appreciate your making your choice in this respect before we continue our discussions further. You will realize that this is the generally accepted practice.[96]

While the planning for the EDVAC, the writing of the EDVAC report, and the controversy over intellectual credit and patents for the EDVAC were occurring, the Moore School staff moved steadily toward completion of the ENIAC. It was not ready in time to serve in the war, but it became usable near the end of 1945 and was dedicated in February 1946. Von Neumann had recognized from the time he first learned of the ENIAC that it would have great value to the work being undertaken at Los Alamos, and at his suggestion arrangements were made to have the first calculation (other than a test) be one for Los Alamos prepared by two of its physicists, Stanley Frankel and Nicholas Metropolis.

The problem was a preliminary study for a hydrogen bomb. The calculation, which amounted to solving a system of three partial differential equations, ran for almost six weeks in December 1945 and January 1946 and involved the transfer of approximately a half-million punched cards of data from Los Alamos to Philadelphia. A publicity release from the Ordnance Department at the time of the first public demonstration of ENIAC in 1946 estimated that this calculation would have required 100 "man-years" at a desk calculator.[97] Many years later by von Neumann's close friend and scientific collaborator, Stan Ulam, described the calculation:

A specific physical arrangement and concrete plans for a thermonuclear weapon had to be calculated more exactly in order to settle the question of whether the scheme would work. The magnitude of the problem was staggering. In addition to all the problems of behavior of fission; that is to say, neutronics, thermodynamics and hydrodynamics, new ones appeared vitally in the thermonuclear problems. The behavior of more materials, the question of time scales and interplay of all the geometrical and physical factors became even more crucial for the success of the plan. It was apparent that numerical work had to be undertaken on a vast scale. . . . It seemed at that time that the feasibility of a thermonuclear bomb was established, according to the opinion of the author. Even though the work was of necessity incomplete and had to omit certain physical effects the results of the calculations had great importance in leaving open the hopes for a successful solution to the problem and the eventual construction of an H-bomb. One could hardly exaggerate the psychological importance of this work and the influence of these results on Teller himself and on people in the Los Alamos laboratory in general. . . . I well remember the spirit of exploration and of belief in the possibility of getting trustworthy answers in the future. This partly because of the existence of computing machines which could perform much more detailed analysis and modeling of physical problems.[98]

Over the next few years von Neumann continued to use the ENIAC in its new home in Aberdeen and to arrange for its use by Los Alamos scientists.[99] In collaboration with Jule Charney, Ragnar Fjortoft, and Nicholas Metropolis, he applied the ENIAC to weather prediction. With George Reitweisner he used it to study statistical properties of numbers. He also used the ENIAC to model the MADDIDA, a digital differential analyzer, prior to its construction, to predict its accuracy in calculating trigonometric functions.[100] Von Neumann was also involved in transforming the ENIAC into a stored-program computer. But most of his attention after the war was directed not to the ENIAC but to the much more powerful computer for scientific research he was building at the IAS.

The war was an education in computing for von Neumann. He learned the principles of machine design from Stibitz at Bell Labs, the ENIAC engineers at the Moore School, and the computing and electronics groups at Los Alamos. He investigated questions of computer-oriented numerical analysis with several mathematical colleagues at Princeton. The military importance of high-speed automatic calculation became clear to him through his work for Army and Navy Ordnance and for the Los Alamos Laboratory. Before long, he had mastered these lessons and become a leading authority on computing machine design and application. The experience changed his career. He was encouraged by the computer's great potential to advance science to reorient his research toward computing and its scientific applications. By early 1945 he was making plans to build and use computers for science, plans that were rapidly implemented after the war.

Planning a Computer for Scientific Research

Von Neumann was confronted with four major problems in his plan to build a computer for scientific research. First there was the question of funding, for the project would cost hundreds of thousands of dollars. The IAS did not have this much money available, and there was little reason to believe that a high-speed computer for science would be of much interest to a commercial firm. The likeliest candidates were the large private foundations, such as the Rockefeller Foundation (which had supported biomedical research in the 1930s), or the federal government (which had paid for a massive mobilization of science during the war). Could the foundations be convinced that a high-price computer would be a good expenditure? Would the government be willing to support computing development in peacetime, especially since it was already supporting the ENIAC, EDVAC, and Whirlwind computer developments and von Neumann wanted a computer to use not for military purposes but for research?

The second problem was who would provide the institutional support. Computing was not regarded as a respectable scientific activity and certainly was not one prevalent in an elite scientific institution, such as the IAS. Moreover, the institute lacked the laboratory facilities needed to build a computer. Could von Neumann convince his colleagues at the institute to accept his computing work, or should he take his new-found interest elsewhere? If so, where was he likely to be received warmly?

Another serious problem was personnel. Unlike his prewar research, he could not carry out this project alone. To build and operate a computer would require a team effort of mathematicians, scientists, and engineers. Where were these people to be found? Some astronomers and statisticians had done computing as part of their research, but few other scientists were numerically oriented. Moreover, numerical analysis had a poor reputation among mathematicians and attracted few specialists. Power rather than control still dominated the training of electrical engineers, though a few had experience in television, communications, or radar that could be applied to computing.

Finally was the question of the computer design itself. As the war ended, von Neumann believed that the computer would be an important tool for scientific research, but his conviction was based on limited experience. Punched-card tabulating systems, analog computers, and electromechanical calculators had been effective in the war effort, but none of them closely resembled the electronic, stored-program, digital computer he had in mind. The most similar device, the ENIAC, was still under construction and had not yet made a single calculation. What features should a computer for scientific research have, and would it be possible to design and construct such a machine? Von Neumann was able to overcome all of these difficulties and establish a computing project at the IAS within a few months after the end of the war.

Postwar Plans

By March 1945, while the Japanese campaign was still underway, von Neumann had begun to consider how to balance his long-standing interests in pure mathematics with his new interests in applications.[1] One problem was that his new interests did not conform with the research traditions of the IAS, which had no laboratories and studied mathematics and physics from a theoretical perspective.[2] Norbert Wiener noted this problem in a pitch to lure von Neumann to MIT: "How does all of this [planning for applied mathematical research] fit in with the Princetitute? You are going to run into a situation where you will need a lab. at your fingertips, and labs don't grow in ivory towers."[3]

Wiener then unveiled an offer, authorized by the dean of science at MIT, George R. Harrison, to make von Neumann chairman of the mathematics department with limited routine administrative responsibilities and ample time for research. As further inducement, Wiener outlined a joint program under negotiation between Harvard and MIT in control science and engineering, a subject he and von Neumann had already been discussing in the context of their mutual interest in biological information processing.[4] The offer attracted von Neumann; he interviewed at MIT in July 1945 and received an offer the following month.[5] Part of his interest in

MIT seems to have been based on its extensive involvement with computing devices.[6]

Leaving the institute was hard for von Neumann, however. He had supportive and extremely able colleagues, and all his time was free to pursue research. He also felt a special commitment to the institute, which had given him his first permanent position and had supported his work so well for more than a decade. Thus, he wrote to Dean Harrison at MIT: "Owing to my long association with the Institute for Advanced Study, and owing to the fact that I had always urged the importance of such a [computer] project, I felt that the Institute for Advanced Study had the first call on my services if it could offer me a promising opportunity to carry out such a program."[7]

Von Neumann was uncertain whether a satisfactory arrangement could be reached at the institute, however, and when in August he met Walter Bartky, associate dean of the University of Chicago, he mentioned his interest in finding a place where he could build a computer and pursue his applied interests.[8] Bartky was encouraging about Chicago because the university's chancellor, Robert Hutchins, was revitalizing the school through a series of senior appointments. Within a couple of months von Neumann was offered a professorship and the opportunity to organize an Institute of Applied Mathematics.[9] At about this same time he also received job feelers from Columbia and Harvard.[10] He was worldly enough to realize the value these expressions of interest from other institutions had in persuading the institute to accept his computer project. His case at the institute was strengthened through support he received from his colleagues James Alexander, Marston Morse, and, especially, Oswald Veblen, as well as from the dean of the Princeton University graduate school, Hugh Taylor.[11]

By November he had convinced the IAS director, Frank Aydelotte, to support the project, which allowed him to decline the other offers and begin to prepare his plans in earnest.[12] The best indication of Aydelotte's attitude toward the computer project is given in April 1947, approximately a year and a half after it began:

The Computer Project initiated during the last two years constitutes the greatest break so far made with our tradition of pursuing merely theoretical studies and not practical laboratory work. Some members of the Institute were opposed to the project on these grounds which I have indicated. However, I do not believe that it is possible to schoolmaster research; an institution of this character must always be willing to gamble, to take long shots. The utility of the electronic computer for such subjects as astronomy and meteorology is obvious. Its value for research in pure mathematics remains to be proved and that will, of course, be its true test. Only time will tell.[13]

Von Neumann proposed to Aydelotte a cooperative venture among the institute, Princeton University, and RCA, which had recently opened research laboratories in Princeton.[14] Under this plan the university would contribute some effort of its physics and mathematics faculty and staff. RCA was called on for information and assistance with vacuum tubes. The bulk of the design, construction, maintenance, and operation was to be provided by the institute. Von Neumann estimated that construction of a computer would take three years and require eight staff members, plus twelve wiremen, a machinist and machinist's assistant, and one or two outside mathematicians or physicists as consultants. He proposed an annual budget of $68,000 for personnel and an additional $30,000 for supplies and test equipment. For the computer's operation and maintenance after construction was completed, he projected a need for a senior and a junior mathematician, three or four clerical personnel, an engineer, and a serviceman, amounting to a postconstruction annual operating budget of $30,000. These estimates did not include rent, which for 3000 square feet of floor and office space cost about $3000 in Philadelphia and up to $30,000 in Princeton. An additional $50,000 was proposed as a reserve fund, primarily for making improvements in the machine as advances were made in component design and "electronic art."

A little more than a week after he first described his plans to Aydelotte, he wrote again to describe the effect that an advanced high-speed computing device could have on basic and applied scientific research:[15]

The use of a completed machine should at first be purely scientific experimenting.... Gradually this should go over into new scientific developments, along the lines suggested by those experiments. It is clear now that the machine will cause great advances in hydrodynamics, aerodynamics, quantum theory of atoms and molecules, and the theory of partial differential equations in general. In fact I think that we are still not able to visualize even approximately how great changes it will cause in these fields. It will also be interesting to see its effects on number theory—I anticipate that they will be considerable.

Finally it should be used in applied fields: it will open up entirely new possibilities in celestial mechanics, dynamic meteorology, various fields of statistics, and in certain parts of mathematical economics, to mention only the most obvious subjects.

Von Neumann was much clearer in identifying the characteristics that such a device should have. It must be fully automatic, digital, and electronic, unlike previous calculating machines:

There are many important problems in hydrodynamics, aerodynamics, celestial mechanics, and in various other fields..., which are practically inaccessible to the present methods of abstract mathematical analysis, and for which the capacity of human computing teams, or of existing, nonelectronic computing machines, is absolutely inadequate. These problems could only be dealt with by machines which possess intrinsic speeds that can only be reached by electronic procedures. Such speeds render any intelligent human intervention, while the machine is working, impossible, and therefore they necessitate a complete automatization of the device. The problems are so varied, and in many cases their details as yet unpredictable, that it would be unwise to build now a "one-purpose" machine for any one problem or closely circumscribed group of problems. An "all-purpose" device should be the aim. Finally, considerable precisions will be required (in many cases 10 decimal digits, in some cases even more). Therefore no "analogy machines", which represent numbers by physical quantities (like the differential analyzer) will be adequate—the contemplated device will have to be strictly digital (like the well-known desk multiplying-machines).[16]

He explained how his machine would differ from the most powerful calculating devices then existing or being planned. The Harvard Mark I, the Bell Laboratory relay calculators, the proposed Harvard Mark II, and the proposed machine of "Womersley (London, National Mathematical Laboratory)" all based their switching on electromechanical relays rather than vacuum tubes and were too slow for the scientific purposes he envisioned. The ENIAC, which did use vacuum tubes for switching, was inflexible, lacked full electronic automation, used too many vacuum tubes (thereby presenting problems of power consumption, air conditioning, and reliability), and had a cumbersome method of problem setup. He also mentioned two projects then underway that incorporated the electronic advantages of the ENIAC, but had none of its disadvantages: the EDVAC and the Harvard Mark II, a computer being built at Harvard for the Navy Ordnance Laboratory. He noted his involvement with both of these projects as an indication of his qualifications to direct a computer project at the institute.[17]

His argument to Aydelotte was crafted carefully to diffuse any objection that such devices were better built by government or industry. He argued repeatedly that to achieve its scientific objectives, the institute must establish its own computing programs before accepting any support from either industry or government:

My reason is that the Government is building such devices for definite Government laboratories, where they are assigned to definite, often very specialized purposes. Any industrial company, on the other hand, which undertakes such a venture, would be influenced by its own past procedures and routines, and it would therefore not be able to make as fresh a start as desirable. All these assertions are based on a considerable body of experience with such situations.

It is, however, very important to be able to plan such a machine without any inhibitions, and to run it quite freely and governed by scientific considerations.[18]

His plans so far left open the question of funding. In January 1946, when he had a better idea of his plans, von Neumann estimated the total cost to be about $400,000.[19] Clearly the project could not be carried through on the $100,000 promised by the institute.[20] An obvious source of funding was the army, but Goldstine and von Neumann were skeptical of its willingness to support another computing project while it still had a large financial obligation to the EDVAC.[21] Von Neumann approached Vladimir Zworykin at RCA and Warren Weaver at the Rockefeller Foundation about funding. RCA pledged $100,000, but support from the Rockefeller Foundation never materialized.[22] Von Neumann also turned to the navy, where he was assisted by Commodore Lewis Strauss.[23] A contract for $100,000 from the navy looked promising, but the negotiations foundered over who would be granted title to the machine on its completion.[24] Then a joint funding arrangement was proposed to the Army Ordnance Department, the Navy Office of Research and Inventions, RCA, and Princeton University.[25] Finally the outside funding was secured. Princeton University provided small in-kind payments, RCA supported the project to its full original commitment by sponsoring the storage tube development, the Office of Naval Research sponsored related mathematical and meteorological research, and Army Ordnance (later with assistance from the navy and the air force) sponsored the bulk of work on engineering, logical design, and programming.[26] During the last few years of the project the military support was partly supplanted by support from the Atomic Energy Commission. By 6 November 1945 representatives of the institute, Princeton University, and RCA decided to go ahead with the Electronic Computer Project, as it was officially known. A scientific advisory committee, chaired by von Neumann, was established that day and met four times in November to discuss design and implementation issues.[27]

Since the different sponsors had different expectations, it was uncertain whether von Neumann could attain the objectives he had outlined to Aydelotte for a machine "without any inhibitions . . . run freely and governed by scientific considerations." RCA requested and received patent control over the storage technology developed but granted a free license to the project and otherwise placed no restrictions on the computer or its use.[28] The IAS's board of directors did not raise objections because Aydelotte sold the project to them on its great scientific potential. He likened the computer to a large-scale telescope, whose position as an experimental instrument important to theoretical scientific advance was widely appreciated: "I think it is soberly true to say that the existence of such a computer would open up to mathematicians, physicists, and other scholars areas of knowldege in the same remarkable way that the two-hundred-inch telescope promises to bring under observation universes which are at present entirely outside the range of any instrument now existing."[29] He emphasized the prestige that would redound from having the most powerful computing device at the Institute to attract "scientists from all over the country": "This means, of course, that it would be the most complex research instrument now in existence. It would undoubtedly be studied and used by scientists from all over the country. Scholars have already expressed great interest in the possibilities of such an instrument and its construction would make possible solutions of which man at the present time can only dream. It seems to me very important that the first instrument of this quality should be constructed in an institution devoted to practical applications."[30]

Meanwhile von Neumann convinced his military sponsors that the computer would have military value even if its use were restricted to experimental scientific research. He explained to Admiral Bowen of the Navy Office of Research and Inventions: "The performance of the computer is to be judged by the contribution which it will make in solving problems of new types and in developing new methods. In other words, it is a scientific and experimental tool, to be used in research and exploratory work, and not in production jobs."[31]

Von Neumann suggested that the institute computer be used to demonstrate the feasibility of militarily relevant scientific calculations and that copies of the computer be built for government installations to carry out these calculations on a routine basis:

Thus, if a new type of problem arises which can not be handled on other existing computing machines, and which this computer may seem likely to solve, then the new computer should be used on the problem in question until a method of solution is developed and tested—but it should not be used to solve in a routine manner further problems of the same type. The policy should rather be, to have further electronic computers of this new type built, which will belong, say, to the Navy, and do the routine computing jobs. The Institute's computer should be reserved for the developing and exploring work as outlined on the preceding page [above], and this should be the objective of the envisioned project and the Institute's function.[32]

This plan was adopted, and several copies were built: AVIDAC at Argonne National Laboratory, ILLIAC at the University of Illinois, JOHNNIAC at the RAND Corporation, MANIAC at Los Alamos Scientific Laboratory, ORACLE at Oak Ridge National Laboratory, and ORDVAC at Aberdeen Proving Grounds.

Once the institute project was approved in November 1945, von Neumann faced two immediate tasks besides working with the advisory group on the design of the machine: recruiting trained personnel and finding adequate office and floor space in Princeton. The first was rather easy.[33] Von Neumann offered Goldstine the position of associate director on 27 November 1945, which he assumed the following February, after the ENIAC was dedicated and his duties at the University of Pennsylvania were largely concluded.[34] Goldstine was not only an administrator but also a major contributor to the mathematical, logical design, and programming groups. The other member of the logical design group was Arthur Burks, who joined the project part time in March 1946. He had previously worked on the ENIAC project and had participated in the logical design of the EDVAC. He contributed to the planning and logical design during the next three summers, when he was free from his teaching responsibilities at the University of Michigan.

Von Neumann first offered the chief engineering position to J. Presper Eckert but withdrew the offer when it became apparent that Eckert's "commercial interests in the automatic computing field on one hand, and the requirements and the stability of the Institute research project, particularly in its phases of cooperation

with our other partners [especially RCA], may not be easily recon-
ciled."[35] Von Neumann tried, unsuccessfully, to hire William Overbeck, an MIT engineer who during the war had developed several
simplified decimal counting circuits and two types of electronic
storage tubes (the Digitron and the Steichotron).[36]

On 7 March 1946, von Neumann hired Julian Bigelow as chief
engineer on the recommendation of Norbert Wiener. Bigelow was
well qualified for the position. After receiving his electrical engineering degree from MIT, he had worked for Sperry Products from
1936 to 1939 and as an electrical engineer at IBM's Endicott
Laboratory from 1939 to 1941. At IBM he came to know Howard
Aiken, who was working in an office two doors away on reading
characters automatically.[37] Bigelow then returned to MIT as a
research associate, where he worked with Wiener on mathematical
and experimental investigations of the stochastic processes involved in the prediction of noise-contaminated flight paths of
aircraft and on a continuous variable computing device he built at
Wiener's request. While at MIT, he also designed a correlation
machine for calculating cross-products of two 1000-ordinate arrays
to be used by a group developing statistical methods of weather
prediction for the air corps. In 1943 he joined the OSRD Applied
Mathematics Group at Columbia University, where he carried
out mathematical and statistical studies and designed a computing instrument for solving certain classes of simultaneous linear
equations.

Three able engineers were on site when Bigelow arrived in June
1946.[38] James Pomerene, who had been working as an engineer at
the Hazeltine Co. of New York, joined the project in April. He became chief engineer in 1951, when Bigelow accepted a Guggenheim Fellowship, and saw the project to completion. Ralph J. Slutz,
a physicist with some electronics experience in a Princeton University laboratory, joined the group in June and participated actively
until he left in 1948 for the National Bureau of Standards. Willis
Ware, an engineer who had worked with Pomerene at Hazeltine,
also joined in June 1946. Pomerene and Ware had experience with
pulse-coded devices; during the war they had worked on Interroga-
tor Friend or Foe antiaircraft devices. They were soon joined by
Robert Shaw and John Davis, who had worked on the ENIAC.[39]
Other engineers joined the project later, though there were never
more than six engineers and a small number of technicians employed at one time.[40]

The Electronic Computer Project was organized into four groups, overseen by von Neumann and managed day to day by Goldstine. Burks, Goldstine, and von Neumann were responsible for logical design; Bigelow (and later Pomerene) led a team of engineers and technicians on engineering development; Goldstine and von Neumann, occasionally in collaboration with other mathematicians, carried out the mathematical analysis and programming design; and the meteorology group was directed for most of its history by Jule Charney.

Finding appropriate space for the computer and the project staff was a more difficult problem. Fuld Hall, the institute's main building, had been completed in 1939 with expansion in mind, but by 1946 little office space remained available, and none of it was suitable for the testing, construction, or operation of a computer.[41] Aydelotte was reluctant to spend institute funds on a building for the project. He first talked with Admiral Strauss about obtaining free of charge from the navy a war-surplus Quonset hut to house the component construction. Aydelotte had in mind a temporary construction located on one of the institute parking lots, with a rough cement floor, portable heaters, and no running water.[42] By April he was still considering a Quonset hut or barracks from the War Department, until he learned it would cost $17,000 to move one of these structures and put it in order for the project. He also considered building a permanent building for the institute that could be used temporarily for the computer, but materials for a permanent building meeting Aydelotte's standards would not be available for a year because of the general postwar shortage. It was possible to erect a temporary building by October, but there loomed the question of who would pay the $45,000 cost.[43] In early June Aydelotte was still wrangling with von Neumann over where the fifteen workers scheduled to arrive in mid-June would work. Aydelotte resisted various suggestions from von Neumann to provide space in Fuld Hall and finally suggested converting a garage on the institute property or applying to the university or RCA for laboratory space.[44] By September an arrangement was finally made. Army Ordnance agreed to pay $63,000 toward a temporary building,[45] overhead was skimmed from the government contracts for the project's mathematical and meteorological programs in order to increase the space to house scientific personnel, and the institute agreed to pay out of its $100,000 contribution for all the features, such as brick veneer, not consistent with a temporary structure.[46]

One final hurdle was the attitude of the citizens of Princeton, who objected to the cheap new housing being built for the institute staff and worried that the computer would generate noise and consume massive amounts of power. At a public meeting several members of the computer project staff allayed the fears about noise, and Julian Bigelow told them that the computer would consume no more electricity than that used by two household stoves.[47] This seemed to settle the matter, and there was no further public outcry.

Designing a Computer for Scientific Research

Throughout 1945 and 1946 while the approval, funding, and hiring processes were occurring, von Neumann gave considerable thought to the features a computer ought to have if it were to be useful in scientific research. He lectured on this subject on several occasions; the most cogent account is given in a paper he wrote with Herman Goldstine, "On the Principles of Large Scale Computing Machines."[48] The stated purpose of the paper was to describe to mathematicians, engineers, and logicians, who plan scientific computing tools, what parts of pure and applied mathematics could be advanced through computers and what characteristics a computer should have in order to meet these objectives.

Goldstine and von Neumann noted that during the late 1930s and the war years, theoretical interest had increased in many topics of applied mathematics (continuum dynamics, electrodynamics, hydrodynamics, and theories of elasticity and plasticity) but that the present analytical methods of mathematics could not be applied to the nonlinear problems central to these studies:

The advance of analysis is, at this moment, stagnant along the entire front of non-linear problems. That this phenomenon is not of a transient nature but that we are up against an important conceptual difficulty is clear from the fact that, although the main mathematical difficulties in fluid dynamics have been known since the time of Riemann and of Reynolds, and although as brilliant a mathematical physicist as Rayleigh has spent the major part of his life's effort in combatting them, yet no decisive progress has been made against them—indeed hardly any progress which could be rated as important by the criteria that are applied in other, more successful (linear!) parts of mathematical physics.[49]

The natural response of the mathematical community had been to emphasize the linear aspects of these subjects in the study of partial differential equations and integral equations and their applications to acoustics, electrodynamics, and quantum mathematics. Goldstine and von Neumann argued that this practice obscured the fundamental regularities of certain nonlinear phenomena, such as shock waves in compressible, nonviscous, nonconductive flows and turbulence in incompressible, viscous hydrodynamics. They noted that many of the advances in these mathematical subjects had been made by physicists. For example, elliptic differential equations had been advanced through the physical insights of Riemann and Plateau. The method of discovery for determining uniqueness theorems or boundary conditions was frequently experimental, but "experimental" in a particular way, as is illustrated by fluid dynamics:

Indeed, to a great extent, experimentation in fluid dynamics is carried out under conditions where the underlying physical principles are not in doubt, where the quantities to be observed are completely determined by known equations. The purpose of the experiment is not to verify a proposed theory but to replace a computation from an unquestioned theory by direct measurements. Thus wind tunnels are, for example, used at present, at least in large part, as computing devices of the so-called analogy type (or, to use a less widely used, but more suggestive, expression proposed by Wiener and [Samuel] Caldwell: of the measurement type) to integrate the non-linear partial differential equations of fluid dynamics.[50]

Because digital devices are much faster, more flexible, and more accurate than analog devices, Goldstine and von Neumann suggested recalculating with digital computers the experiments physicists had previously done with analog devices, such as the wind tunnel. They hoped that digital equipment would give them insight into the nature of nonlinear phenomena and enable them to break the impasse that had stymied mathematicians and physicists for two generations.[51]

Speed was regarded as the main advantage of the computer over past calculating devices. Using the multiplication time of a desk calculator as the basic unit of computing speed, Goldstine and von Neumann estimated that differential analyzers were 10 times as fast, relay calculators 30 times as fast, and electronic computers on the order of 10^4 or 10^5 times as fast. The main mathematical significance of the electronic computer's speed was that it brought into range problems that were only marginally practical or entirely impractical to calculate using earlier devices: large runs of ballistic trajectories, astronomical orbit calculations, and parabolic and hyperbolic differential equations of fluid dynamics.

Von Neumann and Goldstine realized that speed alone could not achieve a breakthrough. Some problems also required changes in numerical methods. To illustrate their point, they showed that computers would be fast enough to carry out all the calculations to solve a large linear system ($n \sim 100$ unknowns) in a practical amount of time but that the solution might be rendered unreliable by the accumulation of round-off errors. So they called for a new line of investigation in numerical analysis oriented to the computer.[52]

One of the first public forums on computers was a summer study held at the Moore School in 1946. In his lecture von Neumann amplified on what he and Goldstine wrote in their paper. His topic was "troubles within mathematical uses of high speed computing, or the probable influence of very high speed computing on mathematical procedures."[53] He argued that the new electronic computing devices would be most effective on problems, such as certain kinds of partial differential equations, that require from 1000 to 1 million times as many calculations as could then be done. He again suggested the heuristic opportunities the computer might afford in replacing physical experimentation, as done in a wind tunnel, for example, and noted that the high cost of a computer might be justified by comparison with the even higher costs of building, maintaining, and operating a supersonic wind tunnel.[54] He held out the greatest hope for advance in areas of mathematics that involve large systems of linear equations, those that approximate solutions with lattice points in multiple dimensions (meteorology, ballistics, aeronautics, and quantum chemistry), and those that are nonlinear, especially hydrodynamical problems involving turbulence. He broached the possibility of computers that could search for mathematical tools to solve currently unsolvable problems and argued that "a computing machine of extremely high speed will probably be used to treat problems which nobody considered computing problems before."[55]

His enthusiasm was tempered by the frailties and limitations of the electronic computers then being planned, however. He noted that the storage of information had become much more expensive in the new computing systems than it had been in any earlier systems that relied on punched cards. He argued that even dramatic increases in computing speed (by the factor of 10^9, which he predicted to occur within the next few years) would not be sufficient to handle certain classes of problems by the most obvious brute force methods. He took the game of chess as his example for extended analysis but claimed that his analysis would apply equally well to many mathematical problems, especially those of a combinatorial nature. Some kind of "intuition" had to be built into any sophisticated chess program, but there was limited knowledge of how to do so. He also mentioned some problems (in particular, some wartime work on the number of bombs needed to saturate a drop zone) that were more readily solved qualitatively, such as with graphs or illustrations, than quantitatively with computers.

In "On the Principles of Large Scale Computing Machines," Goldstine and von Neumann identified factors besides multiplication speed that affect the overall speed of the computing system: problem setup, memory capacity, speed of transfer, logical control, and input-output. This led them to an analysis of the desirable characteristics of each of the constituent units in a scientific computing system.

They found that while the inherently slow speed of mechanical input-output equipment is not disadvantageous in systems with slow arithmetic units, the case for electronic computers is decidedly different. In the ENIAC, for example, the average time to print one output result was equivalent to the time of seventy multiplications, and this speed disparity would compromise the overall performance of the ENIAC or any other electronic computing system. They did not show how to eliminate the problem but did suggest how to ameliorate it by minimizing printing, partly by adding an oscilloscope to display results graphically. The scope could also be used to inspect the smoothness of a curve in an intermediate result, check for errors, or follow the course of a computation. Printing could then be reserved for final results, which could be downloaded from the central processor at high speed on magnetic tape or wire for final printing on demand and yet be retained in machine-readable form for future computations.

The discussion of the memory organ focused on the storage of instructions. They identified two existing methods for storing instructions in computing systems: either all of the connections are made prior to the computation, as in the ENIAC, where one first sets switches and plugs cables, which effectively hard wires the instructions into the machine prior to the computation, or connections are established at the moment in the computation when they are needed, as in the Harvard Mark I and the Bell Labs relay calculator, in which instructions are fed in as needed from an external paper tape. The advantage of the first approach is that, once entered, all of the instructions can be executed at electronic speed; the second approach permits indefinitely long strings of instructions, does not require as much time in problem setup, and can be implemented with less hardware. Goldstine and von Neumann suggested a design that incorporated the best features of each approach, based on storing instructions as numbers in the computer's internal electronic memory.[56]

By early 1946 von Neumann had turned these general principles into basic design specifications, which he summarized in letters written in March to Julian Huxley of UNESCO and M. H. A. Newman, the head of the computer project at Manchester University.[57] Von Neumann had in mind a computer of the digital variety with an elaborate logical control that would allow it to be used on many different scientific problems. Numbers were to be represented in the binary system with forty-digit accuracy. There was to be a 10^{-6} second reaction time with a pass band of up to 2 megacycles.[58] Addition and subtraction were to be carried out in less than 10^{-5} seconds, multiplication in less than 10^{-4} seconds, and division in approximately 10^{-4} seconds. There was to be an internal memory of electronic speed with a capacity of 4000 forty-bit words, which would hold both numerical data (initial data, intermediate results, function tables) and instructions. Switching, clearing, and reading in and out of memory were each to be accomplished in 10^{-5} seconds. Direct input and output to the machine would be done on tapes, probably magnetic, and there was to be a direct graphic output (an oscilloscope). The machine was to have automatic checking facilities to detect and locate most errors. The system, including input-output and program setup, was supposed to be "well balanced" to prevent "bottlenecks." Construction would be completed with between 1000 and 2000 off-the-shelf vacuum tubes (receiving triodes and pentodes), plus 50 to 100 special tubes. These are the general specifications von Neumann passed on to the institute team as they began the detailed work on the logical design, coding system, and hardware engineering.

Logical Design

The first product of the Electronic Computer Project was a report by Burks, Goldstine, and von Neumann, "Preliminary Discussion of the Logical Design of an Electronic Computing Instrument."[59] A first edition appeared in June 1946 and a second edition, giving an expanded account of the arithmetic processes and incorporating some of the experimental work undertaken at the institute in the interim, appeared in September 1947. The report set out the basic logical design known today as the von Neumann architecture, which has been employed (often with modifications) in most computers built during the past forty years. The general-purpose automatic computing system described is composed of units for arithmetic, storage, control, input, and output. Data, intermediate results, and instructions are stored internally in the same memory in an encoded numerical form.[60]

The authors presented detailed analyses of the primary memory organ, the arithmetic organ, and the control organ, but the discussion of the secondary storage unit and the input and output units was incomplete. For this reason, and because the authors anticipated the plans would be modified as the electronic circuits were developed, the report was regarded as preliminary.[61]

The analysis began with the memory device, which the authors argued largely determines the overall logical structure of a computing system. They described the ideal memory organ as one with an unlimited capacity and random access, that is, one in which it is virtually as easy and quick to access, read, and replace the information stored in any one memory location as in any other. They specified a memory system with an access time of 5–50 microseconds in order to be faster than the time (100 microseconds) required by the multiplier to carry out one operation. However, they realized these design goals could not be met with the available technology or that on the immediate horizon, and so they settled for a different design involving a hierarchy of memories, each with greater capacity but slower access time than the former.

The primary memory was designed to be a relatively small unit with rapid random access—its size determined by analyzing the types of data that would be stored when solving a typical differential equation or linear system of scientific research. They found they needed a primary memory with the capacity to hold 4000 numbers—each of forty binary digits (the equivalent of approximately twelve decimal digits).

Previous calculating devices, such as the ENIAC and the Bell Laboratory relay calculators, had used individual components (usually relays or vacuum tubes) for each individual memory element. This practice was not followed in the institute computer design because it was believed it would entail too many memory elements and too much wiring. The designers favored instead a "macroscopic" storage device that incorporated a multitude of "microscopic" memory elements. The EDVAC employed such a device, the mercury delay line, which works by storing individual data elements as acoustical pulses in a trough of mercury. The institute computer designers adopted a different macroscopic device, the Selectron tube developed by RCA, which stores individual data elements as electrostatic charges on the plate of a cathode ray tube. The Selectron tube has random access; the mercury delay line does not because the entire train of pulses in front of the desired pulse must move through the delay line before the desired one can be read. A delay line memory slows the access time and introduces some timing difficulties that result in extra circuitry and more complicated design. In the Selectron, however, one piece of data can be accessed as fast as any other.

The overall design of the EDVAC was serial in order to accommodate its mercury delay line memory. The digits of a number were stored in sequence in the same delay line, and two numbers were added by adding the digits serially, a pair at a time as they emerged from the ends of two delay lines. In contrast, the institute computer had a parallel architecture.[62] It used forty Selectron tubes, each holding one binary digit of a number. In this parallel architecture, all the pairs of corresponding digits of the two numbers were added simultaneously.

The institute computer's secondary memory was designed to hold large quantities of data at a much smaller unit price than the primary memory, accomplished by accepting a slower access time than employed in the primary memory. The purpose of the secondary memory was to transfer information into the primary memory automatically as needed for a computation—at a speed fast enough not to compromise the overall performance of the computing system. The authors identified several features as being desirable in a secondary memory: it should be controllable (the computer should be able to move back and forth through it easily, which makes punched cards unsuitable); it should not require much of the computer's attention in replenishing information (electrostatic charges fade rapidly and are erased when read, so they are not well suited for a secondary memory); it should be rewritable (another disadvantage of punched cards); and the medium should allow the human operator to enter information directly into the secondary storage (thus indicating that the secondary storage can be viewed as part of the input-output organ). Light- and electron-sensitive film, as well as magnetic tape and wire, were identified as meeting these criteria best.

A third level of storage, known as dead storage, was also discussed. It was supposed to meet the same criteria as secondary storage but was not intended to be integrated with the machine; that is, it was permissible to have human intervention in the transfer of information from dead storage into the primary memory. They recommended dead storage for holding tabular data or programs that might be used again but not frequently enough to justify having them occupy primary or secondary storage space.

The discussion of the arithmetic organ considered how to implement the basic arithmetic operations. One issue under debate in the 1940s was whether to use binary or decimal representation of numbers inside the machine. The authors favored binary representation because of the fundamentally binary nature of the storage elements. Also the binary nature of the storage elements makes for simple implementation and faster execution of the elementary operations. Moreover, they argued, binary representation is more economical than decimal representation in the amount of hardware needed to store a given amount of information and it meshes well with the computer's logical operations, also of a binary nature, to provide a more homogeneous design. The main drawback of internal binary representation is that it requires an extra conversion into binary at input and back into decimal at output. However, when a computer is used for scientific purposes, the number of computations per input and output is high, and so overall it is more efficient to pay the extra cost of two conversions in order to carry out the multitude of calculations more efficiently in binary form.

Another design feature under debate in the 1940s concerned the use of fixed-point (having a fixed decimal place for all internal numbers) or floating-point representation (representing numbers in what we today call scientific notation). Unlike their progressive decision about binary-decimal representation, the institute designers conservatively elected the fixed-point architecture.[63] They decided that the extra storage space and the greater complexity of the arithmetic and control circuits required by floating-point representation offset the extra time demanded of a programmer in finding scaling factors that reduce all numbers to the fixed range accommodated by a fixed-point computer.[64] To allow for scientific computations that require more than forty binary digits of accuracy, they introduced a multiple precision feature in which numbers could be represented in multiples of 40 bits.[65]

They considered which elementary arithmetic operations to build into the hardware and selected addition, subtraction, and multiplication. Prior calculating devices realized multiplication by repeated addition commands; however, hard-wired multiplication increases multiplication speed. The decision on whether to hard wire the division and square-root operations was less clear-cut. They decided to build in division since a hard-wired divider is several times faster than a programmed divider, but they chose not to build in the square rooter because it required more equipment than they thought was justified in a prototype computing device.

Addition was carried out much the same way that it had been in IBM counters, relay computers, and the ENIAC. The main component was the accumulator, a storage unit that can receive a number, add it to one already stored there, and send the result to another location. Subtraction was carried out in an already established manner by using the accumulator to add the numerical complements of numbers that are to be subtracted.[66] The logical processes involved in doing multiplication and division were more complicated than in doing addition and subtraction, and so they decided not to implement multiplication and division in exactly the same way as in earlier decimal calculating devices. Multiplication was accomplished by using the accumulator to form and store partial products. The entire multiplicand is multiplied by the successive digits of the multiplier in a serial fashion, and a shifter built into the accumulator adjusts the partial products to the correct digit places. Provision was also made for multiple-precision multiplication, useful in the solution of large linear systems. Division was accomplished by storing the dividend in the accumulator and the divisor in a special forty-bit storage unit in a primary memory known as the selectron register. The quotient is built up from partial quotients stored in another special forty-bit register in the arithmetic organ known as the arithmetic register.

The report concluded with a lengthy discussion of the role of the control unit in the performance of a computation. It explained how a pair of instructions is moved from the memory to the selectron register and the control unit,[67] how first one and then the other of these instructions is executed, and what executive role the control unit plays in performing an arithmetic operation by transferring a number from one place to another, activating input-output equipment, and the like. It described how decoding tables are employed to keep track of actual individual storage locations, freeing the human operators from this task.[68] It also indicated the importance of a clock to time the pulses that initiate actions and thereby synchronize the system's components. They gave various methods for checking computations: making the two halves of the machine carry out the same computation independently and checking one against the other, doing a computation twice in serial fashion and checking the results one against the other, or slowing the clock to a point where one can step through the machine operations one at a time and check the contents of each register. This section also presented each of the individual instructions in the computer's basic instruction set and indicated their function and operation.

This document presented the principal features in the logical design of the institute computer. The design it embodied, known today as the von Neumann architecture, has been supplemented and refined in many ways, but its basic features have not been changed; it continues to be the architectural basis for most computers built today.

Computer Programming

Von Neumann and his associates saw two interconnected classes of problems in the design of a scientific computing device:[69] logical design, addressed in the "Preliminary Discussion" report of 1946, and the design of a system for instructing the machine to carry out specified tasks, addressed in a three-volume report by Goldstine and von Neumann entitled "Planning and Coding of Problems for an Electronic Computing Instrument," which appeared in 1947 and 1948.[70] The authors regarded these three reports as a continuation of "Preliminary Discussion" and reinforced that notion with their organizational structure of the report; for example, they began numbering the sections in "Planning and Coding" where the numbering of "Preliminary Discussion" had left off. They regarded "Planning and Coding" as a preliminary document because it contained no discussion of orders to control the input-output equipment or stop the machine and because they anticipated refinements in their ideas as the engineering work advanced.

Despite the preliminary form, the document was circulated widely in the United States and Europe and was the only major account of programming until the appearance of a book by Wilkes, Wheeler, and Gill in 1951.[71]

The report set out the general principles of coding, described the authors' system of flow diagramming, programmed a number of typical scientific and engineering problems, and discussed a programming methodology built around the use of libraries of subroutines. A lengthy introduction discussed the general principles of coding and flow diagramming and outlined the complexities and subtleties of programming. In particular, the account attempted to disabuse readers of the notion that programming is a straightforward, linear, almost mechanical translation of a mathematical problem into instructions that can be executed by the computer, as programming had been for earlier calculating devices:

We now proceed to analyze the procedures by which one can build up the appropriate coded sequence for a given problem—or rather for a given numerical method to solve that problem. . . . This is not a mere question of translation (of a mathematical text into a code), but rather a question of providing a control scheme for a highly dynamical process, all parts of which may undergo repeated and relevant changes in the course of this process.[72]

The authors pointed out that in the execution of orders, the computer does not simply pass through them a single time in a linear fashion. To gain its full flexibility, the computer must be able to execute transfer orders (which allow it to jump backward or forward to some specified place in the instruction sequence) and substitution sequences (which allow the coded sequence of instructions to be modified in the course of a computation), and these changes may be conditioned on the results obtained earlier in the computation. They described programming as involving two aspects: writing the static code that is entered into the machine and understanding the dynamic process by which the machine executes these orders: "Since coding is not a static process of translation, but rather the technique of providing a dynamic background to control the automatic evolution of a meaning, it has to be viewed as a logical problem and one that represents a new branch of formal logics."[73]

To aid in this dynamic analysis Goldstine and von Neumann invented a logical tool known as a flow diagram: a labeled graph for tracing the dynamic flow as the computer executes orders and changes values of variables. Operation boxes isolate nonrecursive blocks of the computation—sections in which there is a linear execution of the orders during any execution pass. Alternative boxes indicate points of conditional transfer of control, for example, branching based on the sign of a number stored in a particular storage element. Substitution and assertion boxes identify the numerical and logical values of indices used in recursion, as in loops. Storage tables provide partial information about the contents of storage at a given time in a computation. Markers set off the beginning and end of computations and the transition points between different sections of the computation.

The authors described programming as a six-step process:[74]

1. Conceptualize the problem mathematically and physically and give a rigorous but perhaps implicit set of equations and conditions describing it.

2. Select a numerical algorithm, that is, an explicit arithmetical procedure (which may be approximate) to replace these rigorous mathematical expressions.

3. Do a numerical analysis to estimate the precision of the approximation process by means of an investigation of the role of errors introduced by the procedure (truncation errors) and by the machine (round-off errors).

4. Determine scale factors so that the mathematical expressions do not assume values that fall outside the fixed range of the computer at any time during the course of the computation.

5. Do the dynamic analysis by drawing a flow diagram.

6. Write the static code and enter it into the machine.

This report illustrated the programming task by giving typical examples of coding, beginning with simple problems and working up to ones of high complexity "in reasonable didactic completeness."[75] The first few examples encompassed hints about coding. As the authors considered more complicated cases, they showed how to code the binary-decimal conversion and the multiple precision arithmetic they described in "Preliminary Discussion" and provided some general analysis of the effect of these codes on the performance of a scientific computation. They also coded "two problems which are typical constituents of analytical problems, and in which the approximation character of numerical procedures is particularly emphasized:" a numerical integration using Simpson's Rule and an interpolation using a modified version of Lagrange's interpolation formula.[76]

Several combinatorial problems were also programmed, presumably to show that a computer is more than a giant calculator. These problems included the sorting of a sequence and the merging of two sequences in monotone order—tasks that involve almost no arithmetical operations and hence isolate the computer's ability to carry out logical operations. They compared the proposed computer with special-purpose sorting devices, such as the electro-mechanical IBM collators, and showed that the computer outperformed them at combinatorial tasks. They cited three reasons for the superior performance: the computer is 15 to 150 times faster; it requires no human intervention in complex sorting problems, unlike the specialized sorting devices in which intervention introduces a sizable risk of error; and, also unlike the specialized sorters, programs can be written for the computer to carry out complex tasks that involve both sorting and arithmetic operation, which arise in statistical applications. Although the computer could sort on no more than about 1000 numbers in its internal memory, additional numbers could be stored in secondary memory and called in as needed without seriously compromising the computer's performance on the sorting routine. Thus, they concluded that the limited size of the primary memory was not a serious impediment to the performance of logical and combinatorial operations.

The final section of the report described subroutines and the authors' programming philosophy. The ENIAC, the Harvard Mark I, IBM punched-card machines, and essentially all other earlier calculating devices employed a fixed addressing system. Each time any one of these machines was programmed, the program had to be coded anew, even if the new program shared many of the same steps with an earlier one. The incorporation of variable addressing on the institute computer made the programming task more efficient. Frequently used programs, such as routines for producing square roots or trigonometric functions, could be stored on an external storage medium in a subprogram library and called into use by mounting the appropriate tape and assigning parameters in such a way that they agreed with the main body of the program. The authors anticipated that the use of subroutine libraries would provide a methodology for the effective use of the computer: "The importance of being able to do this [write subroutines rather than recode each time] is very great. It is likely to have a decisive influence on the ease and the efficiency with which a computing automat of the type that we contemplate will be operable. This possibility should, more than anything else, remove a bottleneck at the preparing, setting up, and coding of problems, which might otherwise be quite dangerous."[77] The use of subprogram libraries did become common practice but did not entirely remove the programming bottleneck. With their subprogramming plan von Neumann and his collaborators had completed the design not only of the computer and its major units but also of a system for instructing the computer to carry out specified tasks. Meanwhile, the engineers were designing equipment that met these specifications.

Von Neumann succeeded entirely in overcoming the difficulties he faced in establishing a computer project. The funding from the institute, RCA, the military services, and the Atomic Energy Commission was fully adequate for the task. Although the institute did not welcome the Electronic Computer Project with open arms, there was great respect for von Neumann's ability and judgement, and he was allowed to proceed for the most part as he wished. In fact the institute turned out to be a good environment for the project. An excellent laboratory was established, and the space was eventually made satisfactory for both the engineers and the users. The flexibility in the institute's organization simplified the project administration and the hosting of frequent visitors.

The personnel problem was surprisingly easy to resolve. Goldstine's considerable mathematical and administrative talents served the project in many different ways. The engineering staff was able and was assembled in a very short time. The meteorological staff was slower in its development, but the leadership provided by Charney and Phillips was outstanding.

Burks, Goldstine, and von Neumann quickly developed a clear, coherent, and practical plan for the machine's logical design. Although the parallel arithmetic feature was questioned by some outsiders, in the end it proved to be very successful; it was faster, at the expenditure of fewer tubes, than any of the serial computers of its time. The most serious challenges were in engineering adequate memory and input-output units.

4

Engineering a Computer

Burks, Goldstine, and von Neumann had presented a clear and workable logical design for a scientific computer.[1] Supreme engineering challenges nevertheless remained.[2] A body of knowledge about electronics and control engineering had been amassed through the development of radio and television in the 1930s and fire control and radar during the war, but this knowledge, and even that gained from building relay and electronic calculators, was only indirectly applicable to the construction of electronic computers.

The institute computer was intended to have an unprecedented speed and be highly reliable despite its enormous complexity, and this speed and reliability had to be achieved using off-the-shelf components since there was no time to spare for component design. A novel system of control, enabling recursion and other complex, nonlinear sequences of order prosecution, had to be designed.[3] An electronically fast, random access primary memory of lower cost than the vacuum tube storage used in ENIAC was needed. There was considerable skepticism outside Princeton about whether von Neumann's parallel architecture design, especially of the arithmetic unit, could be realized with an acceptably small number of tubes. Finally, a means of input and output needed to be found that would not create a bottleneck when hooked to the other units, all of them operating at electronic speeds.[4]

Early Testing and Design

The original expectation was that the computer could be built by ten people working for three years.[5] A traditional development program, in which the work is carried out in sequential, nonoverlapping stages (exploratory research, experimental component design, operable design, and construction and fault elimination), was rejected as infeasible because of the inchoate understanding of the technology, which von Neumann worried would stall the project in the initial stages too long. He decided instead to construct rapidly a crude machine lacking certain automatic features of the final machine but that would allow experimental computation and refinement of the engineering design prior to construction of the final machine. In the end, however, pressure from users led to this prototype's being transformed into the final machine during the fifth and sixth years of development.

All of 1946 and the first months of 1947 were spent in furnishing a laboratory. The institute had previously housed only mathematicians and theoretical physicists. When the computer project came into being at the beginning of 1946 there were no technical personnel, laboratory equipment, or even laboratory space. A rudimentary machine shop was established in the basement of the institute building, and a small supply of tubes, resistors, and test equipment was requisitioned from army surplus. An adequate supply of tools and parts was stocked by the middle of 1946, and the engineering group moved into the newly constructed computer building in the first months of 1947, where they finally had a machine shop and an experimental laboratory that rivaled those at RCA, Hazeltine, and General Electric.[6] Nevertheless, they still had to construct much of their own test equipment. The only oscilloscope available to them was an A-R Radar Range oscilloscope borrowed from the military, which, like other commercial test equipment of that day, was incapable of tracking electronic events in the required microsecond range. Throughout the project, but especially at first, considerable effort was devoted to the construction of specialized test equipment: pulse sequence generators, regulated power sources, equipment for testing the binary storage capability of magnetic ribbons and high-speed performance of magnetic recording heads, a mechanical drive tester to study the ability of magnetic drums to withstand high acceleration rates, a vacuum tube life and fatigue tester, pulse synchronizers for testing binary elements, and many other devices for testing the control and arithmetic units.

Because of the limited laboratory facilities and the desire to expedite the project as much as possible, large portions of the engineering work were assigned to other organizations. Jan Rajchman at RCA took responsibility for building the primary memory device, a newly designed electrostatic storage tube known as the Selectron. R. D. Huntoon agreed to have the National Bureau of Standards (NBS) develop the original input and output equipment, modified Teletype equipment known as the Inscriber and the Outscriber. A. W. Taylor of Eastman Kodak explored photographic techniques for use as a secondary memory.[7] None of this outside work appeared in the computer as it was finally configured, but these efforts saved the institute staff many hours of design and experimentation, and the NBS equipment was useful as interim input-output equipment.

Perhaps the largest effort in the early years went into the study of secondary memory. The engineers first specified a set of performance criteria for a large-scale memory:[8]

1. It must have sufficient density to store at least 100,000 bits per cubic inch.

2. Digits should be able to be read into memory at any speed up to 0.4 bit per microsecond.

3. Memory should be able to read information to the Teletype output at 40 bits per second.

4. There should be random access—roughly equal time to read or write to any memory location.

5. The memory should be verifiable, that is, readable without clearing the memory elements in the process.

6. Storage should be relatively permanent—measured in periods of months or years.

7. The memory unit should be durable, able to handle millions of operations without wear.

8. The technology should be convenient, not, for example, involving any messy chemical processes.

9. The medium of storage should lend itself to two stable states at low energy levels.

10. There must be a means to hold and clear all memory cells.

11. The memory should be economical.

Using these performance criteria, the group considered and dismissed a number of possibilities: mechanical embossing on wax cylinders, the method used in Dictaphones; storing local thermal, electromagnetic, or electrostatic charges on a sheet; and fluorescence, which Eastman Kodak studied for the project. The engineers settled on magnetic "ribbons" (wires or tapes) as having the most promise. This medium had been used since 1935 for speech and music recording, but a number of problems demanded attention before the ribbons could be used to store digital information.

It was hoped that experimentation on the ribbon and the recording head would find practical resolutions to a number of issues: head orientation relative to the medium, density of information on the ribbon, inscription speed, reproduction speed to the Teletype output, durability, retentivity, and coercive force (the energy per pulse needed to cause erasure). This program of experimental study began in 1946, concentrating at first on the construction of test apparatus, including a low-speed loop comparator to test binary storage capability of magnetic ribbons and a high-speed magnetic performance tester to evaluate the high-speed performance of ribbons and heads.

By the end of 1946 the experimental work had demonstrated the promise of magnetic media for secondary storage.[9] The engineers found that packing densities of 100 bits per inch could be attained using commercial Brush Development speech-recording heads and any of several alloy wires. They believed that modification might allow them to triple the density but decided against following this direction because of the bother of the watchmaker precision and metallurgical research it might lead to and because they saw greater promise in flat paper tapes coated with iron powders. No serious limit on inscription rate was discovered in their tests up to 90,000 bits per second. They attained similarly encouraging experimental rates of 50,000 pulses per second in reproduction speed. The experiments showed that packing density was relatively independent of speed and that the amplification requirements could be met easily. They also found that they could drive the reels of wire as fast as was required without tangling and that automatic control of the memory was not as difficult as they had first imagined.

The only serious problem they faced was head design. There was some trouble obtaining sufficiently vigorous pulses to drive the heads at high inscription rates. Commercially available heads lacked a sufficiently high signal-to-noise ratio to be useful. Moreover, the wire ran in contact with the head, causing many problems: the wire wore deep grooves in the heads, limiting durability; it deposited oil on the heads, fouling their performance; and it created dust, causing information errors. They concluded that the magnetic heads would have to be redesigned to avoid contact between the head and the ribbon.

Throughout 1947 and during the first half of 1948 work continued on the testing and design of secondary memory components. Three models of a high-speed wire tape drive were built; the last was a full-scale model that allayed the group's concerns about wire

tension and the mechanical forces associated with rapid acceleration and change of direction of the tape[10]. However, work on a
magnetic secondary storage was set aside in the first half of 1948 for
more pressing concerns, though this research was later resumed in
the somewhat different context of developing a magnetic drum.[11]

A second area that received early attention was the input-output
equipment. The main development work was carried out at the
NBS, but the institute constructed interim equipment and determined how to integrate the NBS-built equipment into the computer system.[12] Work at the NBS was carried out by C. H. Page in
close contact with Samuel Alexander.[13] The equipment, known as
the Inscriber and the Outscriber, was delivered in January 1948.
The Inscriber, the computer's input device, was a Teletype machine modified to print from the computer's machine code rather
than from Teleprinter code. A Verifier was attached, and the
Teletype machine was modified further to include an electric
clutch and an automatic carriage return and line feed. The data
and instructions were entered twice at Teletype keyboards. If the
Verifier found that the two sets of instructions were identical, it
would unlock the Teletype and send the instruction set to memory.
Otherwise the punched instructions had to be corrected and the
comparison repeated. The output device, the Outscriber, com-
prised some electronic equipment (a high-gain amplifier, a pulse-
shaping circuit, counters, and gating circuits) and a punch to tran-
scribe data from magnetic wire onto punched paper tape, which
could then control the simultaneous printing of output on three
typewriters. The equipment worked well, and the institute staff
modified it only slightly, improving the layout of the keys on the
keyboard, mechanically adjusting the punch, adding a means to
send small amounts of information directly from the keyboard to
the shifting register, and enabling the direct transfer of information from the magnetic memory to the typewriter for printing (the
last two changes made to meet requests of the mathematical users).

In early 1947 the institute worked on a more permanent means
for loading information into memory.[14] They found that it would
take 2 hours to load the planned Selectron memory directly from
the Teletype but only 30 seconds to load the same information
from magnetic wire. Thus they planned to send information typed
on the keyboard to a magnetic wire and use wire to transfer the
input data to the primary memory. This plan stimulated studies of
mechanisms to transfer the information between the Teletype

equipment and the magnetic wire and between the magnetic wire and the Selectron memory.

Chronologically the next area to receive attention was the arithmetic unit. In the first year of the project, many tube varieties were tested to determine their performance as binary switching elements (also known as flip-flops or, as the institute engineers called them, toggles), which were to be used by the hundreds in the construction of the shift register, accumulator, and counter units. The group tested triodes, thyratrons, glow tubes, and crystal rectifiers before settling on the 6J6, a miniature double triode then in mass commercial production.[15]

By the beginning of 1947 the work had turned from the study of binary components to building the best shifting register and accumulator possible with the available binary elements. These were the two units employed in multiplication, which was accomplished through repeated addition and place shifting. Shifting was such a basic operation that a special device, the shift register, was built to shift numbers one place left or right at a rapid rate (in 1 microsecond or less). One design concern was that logical gates might be able to form binary sums so rapidly that they would introduce race conditions and lose information. To avoid this problem a second row of binary switches was added to register the information as the products were formed by the first set of switches rather than relying on transit delays. This double-register design actually simplified the implementation of multiplication and division as well as circumventing the race problem. Research on the shifting registers continued through the first half of 1948 as minor modifications were made to simplify the design, improve the performance, and facilitate the construction, testing, and maintenance of the model for the prototype computer.

The accumulator consisted of the accumulation register, which was a type of shifting register, and adding circuits. The first adder was analog and was based on the principles underlying Kirchhoff's laws to sum three voltages representing the resident digit, the incident digit, and the carry. Tests carried out during 1947 were encouraging, and a series of progressively larger and more complex Kirchhoff adders was constructed. By late 1947 a prototype ten-stage adder had been built and tested, and by June 1948 the full arithmetic unit to be used with the scaled-down computer was assembled, wired, and tested. It worked properly on its first trial, and at this point the arithmetic unit was the most well-developed part of the computer.[16]

Solving the Memory Problem

One of the reasons for von Neumann's original confidence that a computer could be built within three years was RCA's agreement to develop the primary storage unit.[17] He had approached RCA because of its experience in electronics research, including computing, its proximity to the institute, and his prior contacts with some RCA scientific staff. RCA had begun to work on electronic calculating technology in 1939, responding to a request of the Franklin Arsenal in Philadelphia to develop electronic devices designed to improve the aiming of antiaircraft equipment. During the war the company built the analog Typhoon calculator and designed some digital equipment for similar purposes. When the ENIAC contract was awarded, RCA disclosed all of its discoveries to the Moore School. The ENIAC incorporated the resistive matrix function generator and an improved version of a decimal ring counter developed in principle at RCA. RCA also held an NDRC contract to build the Computron, a single tube with multiple electronic beams guided by deflecting electrodes, which was intended to replace the thousands of tubes used to carry out arithmetic operations in a high-speed calculating device. RCA built a small-scale model of the Computron but had difficulties scaling up to a device containing a practical number of switches. Nevertheless, the Computron served as the basis for the Selectron tube being built as the institute's primary memory device.

The Selectron had two sets of orthogonal bars to control the bombardment of electrons on a particular window on the screen. The bombarding electrons would hit a discrete metallic unit and keep it at one of two stable potentials using a secondary emission effect mechanism first employed in the Computron. Von Neumann had visited RCA's research laboratories in Camden, New Jersey, several times in 1942 and 1943 and was familiar with Jan Rajchman and his work on the Computron, so it was natural that he would invite Rajchman and RCA to build the institute's memory device.

By the beginning of 1948 von Neumann was becoming increasingly concerned about RCA's progress on the Selectron. After two years of effort, not a single Selectron tube was working.[18] Bigelow and von Neumann could not predict when these tubes would become available in sufficient quantities to construct their computer, even on a curtailed basis, so they decided to undertake the development of a primary memory device at the institute.[19] Their activity was to be carried out in parallel with the work at RCA in the hope that at the least they could rapidly develop an interim memory device to use in testing the arithmetic and control units. They decided that the underlying technology must be beyond the basic research stage so as to reduce delays and uncertainty about the completion date, be able to be turned into a working memory by one or two engineers within six months, provide storage for at least 500 forty-bit words, have read and write times in the range of a few milliseconds, be simple and reliable, and work without careful maintenance.[20]

They considered three technologies: mercury delay lines, electrostatic storage, and magnetic storage. The Moore School had already determined that mercury delay lines were not fast enough to meet the read and write time specifications of 10–50 microseconds needed to make 2000 to 4000 multiplications per second, so delay lines were not considered further. The institute staff knew that electrostatic storage tubes were being pursued by Project Whirlwind at MIT, the NBS, which was adapting for computer use a tube developed by A. V. Haeff at the Naval Ordnance Laboratory, and the Selectron development at RCA. All three efforts called for special-purpose cathode ray tubes and vacuum tubes, but the institute did not have the laboratory facilities to undertake tube research so they turned to magnetic storage as the most promising avenue.[21] They investigated purchasing a magnetic drum memory from Engineering Research Associates, Inc., of St. Paul, Minnesota, but decided instead to build their own.[22] The goal in the spring of 1948 was not to build the optimal magnetic storage device but rather a workable one that could be completed rapidly.[23]

The institute engineers brought to the magnetic drum work experience with both magnetic ribbons and magnetic cores. In 1947 two of the engineers, Ralph Slutz and Richard Snyder, had applied for a patent on "Parallel Magnetic Memory," which they explained as follows:

In the system under consideration the information is stored in a binary form. . . . Each digit is stored separately as a magnetic charge in a small transformer of rather peculiar construction.

This storage transformer is [as follows]. The primary is wound on a core of laminated permanent magnet material. The secondary is wound on a core of low coercive force material such as permalloy having a small cross section relative to the primary core. The whole unit is very small. In operation, a pulse of current is passed through the primary of the transformer to magnetize the core in one direction. The permalloy section of the core is completely saturated after the pulse. If at a later time a second pulse is passed through the primary in the same direction, the flux through the secondary, being saturated in this direction will not change. Should the second pulse be opposite from the first, the flux in the secondary will reverse and a voltage pulse will develop across the secondary. If the second, or read out, pulse is always in the same direction, the polarity of the first, or read in, pulse can always be discovered at a later time when the second pulse occurs.

A large number of these storage elements are required for a memory large enough to be reasonably useful. In order to systematize the arrangement a multiple matrix array is used. . . . The matrices consist of two sets of wires or busses crossing one another at right angles. A memory element is placed at each intersection.[24]

Other details are similar to the magnetic cores developed at MIT two years later. The patent was not awarded, leading to a mild controversy over development rights in 1953 when Snyder wanted to exploit his idea commercially.[25] Magnetic core storage was not pursued at the institute as a type of primary memory. We can get a clue as to the reason from a letter Goldstine wrote to Mina Rees of the Office of Naval Research in 1947 giving his, Bigelow, and von Neumann's joint reaction to a funding proposal submitted by Dean Wooldridge of Hughes Aircraft to develop a similar memory technology.[26]

There is no doubt that Wooldridge can develop the magnetic unit he describes for remembering a binary digit. In fact, essentially the same idea has been proposed by several other people during the last three or four years. Specifically: J. P. Eckert, Jr., while at the Moore School, Jan Rajchman at RCA, Nordsieck of the Bell Telephone Laboratories, and Richard J. Snyder, while he was at the Institute. In addition, analogous ideas using miniature neon bulbs, small condensors, etc., have been proposed by various people to our knowledge. It would therefore seem that the proposal from Hughes Aircraft does not represent a novel approach to the memory problem.

. . . Since the crux of this approach to the memory problem lies not in the development of a cheap memory element but rather in the development of a satisfactory switch, it would seem that if a contract for a memory organ were to be let the primary objective should be the development of a satisfactory switching mechanism.

This was the reason they did not support the Hughes proposal. Their own report, "Preliminary Design of an Electronic Computing Instrument," had called for a single storage device with "microstorage" elements to avoid the switching problems. This is apparently the reason that magnetic core memory, which worked so successfully at MIT and in many later commercial computers, was not pursued at the institute.

Some of the design features for the magnetic drum were easily established from the general knowledge of magnetics or earlier research on magnetic ribbons: how to code information magnetically as spots,[27] the need to avoid contact between the head and the medium in order to prevent wearing, the need for multiple heads (perhaps ten) to carry out the enormous amount of tracking (an estimated reading of 2 million spots per second), stationary heads with a medium that moves across them, the advantages of a multi-channel drum rotating at high rates of speed on its axis for multiple tracking and high speed, and a standard polyphase induction motor to drive the drum at the required 6000 revolutions per minute.

One of the most difficult problems facing the engineers was the design of the read-write heads. Commercial heads were unsatisfactory because they could not meet the specified times or precision for reading and writing, they interacted with adjacent heads and were sensitive to other outside interferences, and iron traces in the heads created other problems through repeated head action. The institute initiated its own research and development program, building a new head from a single wire filament about 1/4 inch long, which they positioned approximately the same distance from the recording medium. Their tests found this design to be satisfactory: the head recorded with adequate field strength, the magnetic patterns were sharp, the recording performance was acceptable at high repetition rates, pickup from stray sources was low, heads could be densely packed without interference, and alignment was simple.

Another problem they confronted was the coating of the drum surface with magnetic material. They experimented with gluing on a single sheet of magnetic material or coiling a strip around the drum and then using a heat process to transfer the magnetic material to the drum but soon abandoned these methods. At their request Brush Development Company electroplated two brass tubes with an iron compound, while they experimented at the institute with a technique for spraying an iron oxide coating onto a slowly rotating drum.

By the summer of 1948 a prototype drum had been built and tested, made from a brass tube 5 inches in diameter and forty-four single wire heads. It worked well and led directly to the development over the next several years of a permanent drum of similar design but with an 8-inch diameter.[28] The new drum had fourty-five digits spaced to the inch, thus providing 1024 spots around the circumference. There were eighty tracks (two groups of forty, with a switch to move from one group to the other), giving a total drum capacity of 2048 forty-bit words. To expedite development they modified commercial heads (Brush BK-1500 series) instead of fabricating their own; however, they prepared the magnetic surface of the drum by etching the brass with dilute nitric acid, priming it with a spray gun as the drum slowly rotated, baking the drum under infrared light, and spraying on a red iron-oxide coating 1 mil thick. They also prepared all the pulser circuitry, control circuitry, and synchronizer tracks to mark place on the drum.

In the early summer of 1948 the institute learned of a promising electrostatic storage tube developed by F. C. Williams for use in a computer being built at Manchester University in England. It had the great advantage of being constructed from conventional cathode ray tubes, which meant that it could be pursued in the institute laboratory since it involved only circuit design, not tube design. Von Neumann sent Bigelow to England to visit Williams during the summer vacation, and meanwhile James Pomerene began to develop circuits to modify the Williams tube for the institute's purposes. Even before Bigelow had returned from England, Pomerene had created a primitive Williams tube that stored 256 bits—results that were encouraging enough to warrant further extensive testing. A decision was made to continue work on the magnetic drum in parallel with this testing because it was not yet clear whether a reliable Williams tube of at least 1000 words could be built.[29] If not, they proposed to use a 256-word Williams tube memory coupled to a 1000-word magnetic drum subsidiary memory.[30]

A Williams tube stores binary information by charge distributions in the phosphor coating on the inside face of an ordinary cathode ray tube. A fine wire screen is attached to the outside face of the tube, and the phosphor is capacitatively coupled to the screen at the charged spots. By focusing an electron beam at a given point, one can produce a signal on the wire beam. By changing the polarity, one can store either a 1 or a 0. Williams had designed his tube for serial storage: when the beam was deflected to any horizontal row, it read off serially the thirty-two digits stored on that line.[31] Pomerene worked to control both the horizontal and vertical deflection of the beam so as to be able to access every individual storage location directly and thereby transform the Williams tube into a random access memory.

This modification required a total change in the circuitry. Pomerene designed circuits to count through the storage locations to refresh the data stored there, a toggle to switch between regeneration and action modes, a register to store the memory location being accessed, a deflection adder to change the value of the counter and the register in order to deflect the beam correctly, a clock to time the pulse sequence, and a gate circuit to control the operations of the other circuits. Pomerene's work showed that a random-access Williams tube could be built, and then he and Bigelow reworked the design to improve speed and reliability. There were also significant problems with phosphor imperfections on the tubes, and the institute engineers had to build test equipment and test hundreds of tubes in order to find ones suitable for their use. But by the fall of 1949 they were testing a random-access Williams tube memory that met their primary storage requirements, and in this way the Selectron, which was still undergoing development at RCA, was made redundant and was never used on the institute computer.[32] By January 1950 the final Williams tube memory was fabricated and assembled.

The last unit to reach completion was the one for control. Its design depended heavily on that of the other units, particularly the arithmetic unit, and so awaited firm decisions about their designs.[33] The control unit consisted mainly of circuits to produce the appropriate sequence of pulses to conduct an arithmetic operation, direct the memory as to whether an action or regeneration cycle was to be performed, provide a memory address and indicate whether to read from or write to it, and control the input and output devices. Basic work on control components—gates and pulsers—began in early 1947. Work on the control of the arithmetic unit went on in conjunction with the design of that unit in 1947 and 1948, when a variety of pulsers, counters, and multiplier circuits were developed. In the fall of 1949 and throughout 1950 a working control unit was completed and improved. The greatest difficulty was finding a means to control a device that coupled a synchronous memory (since the Williams tube memory had to be restored at fixed intervals) with an asynchronous arithmetic unit, a problem eventually overcome.

Construction and Maintenance

The computer moved steadily toward operational status, especially after James Pomerene became the chief engineer in 1951.[34] Because of the Soviet entry into the nuclear arms race, the project staff was under heavy pressure to complete the computer for use in the hydrogen bomb development and as a stimulus to accelerate the design and construction of clone computers for the Los Alamos and Argonne laboratories. In fact, the computers at these two laboratories, MANIAC and AVIDAC, avoided some engineering pitfalls because of the institute's experience and were actually completed before the IAS machine. Certain emergency measures were instituted.[35] Summer vacations were cancelled for those working on the Electronic Computer Project, and performance bonuses were offered for completion by early fall. High priority was given for military requisition of key components and test equipment.

The demands of the mathematicians to use the computer preempted the plan for separate prototype and final computers. Instead it was decided to make a few modifications to the prototype over a period of several years until it incorporated most of the originally planned specifications of the final computer. Adjustments were made to the Williams tube memory and the logical control in the fall of 1950, and by the end of the year extensive tests and a few trial problems had been run. Although the formal dedication of the computer did not occur until 10 June 1952, by the spring of 1951 the machine was increasingly available for use, and for the first time there were more programming errors than machine errors.[36] The first large problem, which required hundreds of hours of computation, was run during the summer of 1951 for the Los Alamos scientists with only a few machine errors. In 1951 and 1952 numerous improvements were made to the hardware—for example, replacing the Teletype with IBM punched-card equipment to improve input speed by a factor of 10 and output by a factor of 20 and replacing the lead storage batteries being used to power the machine with a regulated power supply. A 2048-word magnetic drum was constructed and tested in June 1953.

The computer was placed in operation two or three shifts a day throughout 1952 and during the first half of 1953 in the experimental area where it had been constructed, next to the engineering laboratory. However, overcrowding and overheating necessitated a move, and the computer was broken down and reassembled four months later, in December 1953, in the mathematical wing of the computer building, where the computer, the IBM punch equipment, and the human operators occupied separate rooms. While the machine was out of operation, small improvements were made to the control system, power supplies, and cooling system to make the computer more reliable and easier to operate. In 1954 a graphical display device used to check the course of computations was installed. It used a 7-inch cathode ray tube to graph 512 coordinates in both the horizontal and vertical dimensions. In 1955 it was decided that additional memory capacity was needed, so a 16,000-word Engineering Research Associates, Inc., Model 1107 magnetic drum was added.[37] The institute staff designed and constructed their own circuitry for the drum, and this task caused them to reassess and redesign the control systems for input-output and secondary memory. At about the same time, they also conducted research on higher-speed circuitry to improve the computer's throughput. Table 4.1 gives the specifications of the institute computer in its final configuration.

A regular maintenance routine of 1 or 2 hours of tests each morning and more extensive tests every several months was established. Unscheduled maintenance decreased to the point that the machine was available 80 percent of the time between July 1952 and June 1953 and 87 percent of the time between July 1953 and June 1954.[38] Except for one bad quarter in 1955, the machine was operable 76 to 91 percent of the time.[39]

Technology Transfer

Determining exactly how much those working on the computer at the Institute knew about computer projects under way elsewhere and what effect this knowledge had is difficult. Julian Bigelow has stated that there was little contact with other organizations: "In the decades since this work was done, several people have asked questions about what we were thinking at the time, when we got our ideas, and in particular what we knew about—and possibly gained from developments taking place at other places such as project WHIRLWIND at MIT and the ex–Moore School team in Philadelphia. The answer is that we had no communication contact except rumors, and as far as I know each of these groups proceeded along its own avenues, directed toward its own goals and developing its own criteria of what constituted excellence."[40] While there is un-

Table 4.1
Specifications of the IAS computer

General	Asynchronous timing
	Sequential operation
	Words handled in parallel
Numerical system	Binary internal decimal system
	40 binary digits per word
	20 binary digits per instruction
	2 instructions per word
	67 decoded instructions
	44 instructions in use
	Fixed-point arithmetic system
	One-address code instruction type
	Number range: $1 > x \geq -1$
Arithmetic unit	31 microsecond add time
	620 microsecond multiplication time
	920 microsecond divide time
	Vacuum tube construction
	4 rapid-access word registers
	Asynchronous operation
	Parallel mode
Storage	Williams tube with 1024 words of 40 digits and 25 microsecond access time
	Magnetic drum with 2048 words of 40 digits and 140,000 microsecond access time (larger drum of 12,288 words of 40 digits and 17,000 microsecond access time added later)
Input	IBM cards, 20 words per second, 12 40-digit words per card
Output	IBM cards, 20 words per second, 12 40-digit words per card
	(Graphical) 7 inch cathode ray tube, 7000 points per second
Circuit elements	Approximately 3000 tubes of 5 tube types
	5 crystal diodes
Checking features	Spill check on division
	Special summation order used to check input-output operations
Power, space, weight	Consumes 28 kilowatts power
	Occupies 36 cubic feet
	Weighs approximately 1000 pounds
	15 tons air conditioning
Personnel requirements	1 engineer and 1 operator for an 8-hour shift
	1 engineer and 2 operators for two 8-hour shifts
	Maintenance staff on call for repairs.
Reliability	Average error-free running period: 4–8 hours
	Good time operating ratio: 70 percent during early 1952–early 1955, 80 percent early 1955

Source: This information is based on a questionnaire filled out by the IAS engineering staff in March 1955 at the request of W. W. Leutert, the chief of the Computing Laboratory at the Ballistic Research Laboratories in Aberdeen, Maryland (IASE).

doubtedly some truth in this statement, it is worth noting that the institute staff had numerous opportunities to read documents from other computer engineering groups and discuss ideas with others interested in building computers.

First, it should be remembered that the institute staff had a good knowledge of computer projects that preceded theirs. Bigelow knew the prewar and wartime work on computing at MIT and perhaps was also familiar with that at the IBM Endicott Laboratories on the Harvard calculator. Von Neumann, Burks, Goldstine, Davis, Shaw, and perhaps others knew about the work done at the Moore School. Von Neumann also had contact with the computer projects at RCA, Bell Laboratories, and Harvard.

In the late 1940s and early 1950s the institute received many visitors interested in the design and construction of electronic computing machines. Among the international visitors during the development stage were Andrew and Katherine Booth and Maurice Wilkes from England, C. E. Froeberg and E. Stemme from Sweden, A. Speiser from Switzerland, Aad von Wijngaarden from the Netherlands, Louis Couffignal from France, and Antonin Svoboda from Czechoslovakia.[41] Engineers and scientists from the United States also visited: Richard Bloch from Raytheon, Leon Brillouin from Harvard, Nathaniel Rochester from IBM, and others.[42] C. V. L. Smith, the head of computing at the Office of Naval Research, was on site for over a year. In fact so many people visited that it began to interfere with work, and von Neumann had to set strict conditions curtailing visits as much as was politically feasible.[43]

Institute personnel, particularly von Neumann, also had opportunities to inspect other computer projects. He visited Jay Forrester at MIT and learned about progress on Whirlwind in late 1947.[44] Bigelow went to Manchester to learn about Williams tubes in 1948. While in England he toured London and Cambridge, where he saw the EDSAC in a more advanced stage of development than any of the American computing machines.

Institute personnel had at least limited access to the progress reports of other computer projects. Von Neumann received a summary report from Whirlwind in December 1947, and one of the IAS progress reports refers to the engineering staff's receiving reports from Engineering Research Associates in 1948.[45] Von Neumann almost certainly had access in the late 1940s to additional information about other computer projects through his membership on computer advisory committees of the Office of

Naval Research and the NBS. The institute also received the Digital Computer Newsletters published by the Office of Naval Research beginning in 1946, which reported the progress on computing devices.[46]

The computer was of great interest to the scientific and engineering communities and was discussed frequently in technical publications. A limited survey of the literature uncovered thirty-four journals that published technical articles on the subject between 1947 and 1949.[47] Some of these concern logical design or applications, and many are somewhat general accounts, but from most of the articles one can obtain a general knowledge of the design of the system, its components, and subcomponents. There are articles describing the computing systems or components under development at Bell Laboratories, Eastman Kodak, Harvard University, IBM, Raytheon, RCA, and the University of Pennsylvania, as well as in Australia, England, France, and West Germany. Most of these publications were readily available in Princeton.

A more certain opportunity for contact occurred at professional conferences. In 1947, the year the institute computer was in its most formative period of engineering development, the staff attended at least five conferences, where they could have learned more about rival computer projects. The first of these was held 7–10 January, when the Navy Department Bureau of Ordnance and Harvard University cosponsored the Symposium on Large-Scale Digital Calculating Machinery at the newly opened Harvard Computation Laboratory. Three people from the IAS attended, including Goldstine, who lectured on "Coding for Large-Scale Calculating Machinery." There were speakers representing six academic institutions, eight government institutions, and five companies. Representatives of over eighty organizations were in the audience, including those of most of the major centers of computer development: Bell Laboratories, Electronic Control Company, Harvard, IBM, MIT, the NBS, and the University of Pennsylvania.[48]

Later that same month, from 20 to 31 January, the American Institute of Electrical Engineers (AIEE) held its winter meeting in New York City. Bigelow lectured on plans for the institute computer, and von Neumann discussed general problems of digital computers. In the same session Howard Aiken described the Harvard Mark I, Jay Forrester the Whirlwind at MIT, T. K. Sharpless the ENIAC and EDVAC, and S. B. Williams the Bell Telephone Laboratories relay calculator. John Mauchly of Electronic Control

Company presented a more general lecture about accuracy in digital computers.

On 4 March at the national convention of the Institute of Radio Engineers (IRE), there was a session on electronic digital computers. Goldstine discussed arithmetic and control circuitry, Forrester presented block diagrams for the Whirlwind computer, Samuel Alexander of the NBS discussed designs and materials for input systems, Jan Rajchman of RCA discussed the work on the Selectron memory tube, and Perry Crawford of the Office of Naval Research discussed applications of digital computers. The interest in this session was so great that the lectures were repeated later in the day.

On 2 September, there was a session on computers at the summer meeting of the Mathematical Association of America held at Yale University. Von Neumann described plans for the IAS computer, and Howard Aiken described the Harvard Mark I and II calculators. Then on 11 and 12 December, at Aberdeen Proving Ground, the Association for Computing Machinery (ACM) held its second meeting, and von Neumann lectured on general principles of coding. In addition to other lectures on coding procedures and applications, there were descriptions of the Raytheon computer by Robert Campbell, the UNIVAC by John Mauchly, and the Aberdeen computers by Franz Alt.

From 1948 on the number of conferences increased. These included the IBM Computation Seminars, conferences sponsored by the Institute for Numerical Analysis at UCLA, more special sessions at the regular meetings of the IRE and AIEE, the regular meetings of the ACM, a second Harvard symposium, and the East and West Joint Computer conferences. Clearly these meetings provided repeated opportunities for exchange of ideas.

The communication channels worked both ways and enabled institute personnel to disseminate knowledge of their progress. This was also accomplished through the progress reports of the Electronic Computer Project, which were distributed widely to government organizations, universities, and government contractors. When the government agreed to fund the project, the institute promised to make available its reports to certain other government organizations interested in building computers. This distribution of logical design and engineering information aided the construction of several early computers with features similar to those of the IAS computer. In fact, the distribution was much wider, but the influence of the institute on computer design can be seen most clearly in these clones.

In 1948 the Los Alamos Scientific Laboratory decided to build a computer, the MANIAC, and brought Nicholas Metropolis back from the University of Chicago to direct the project.[49] Metropolis made arrangements with von Neumann to copy the IAS design; however, there were some differences between the two machines. The institute was having difficulty with its storage units, so Los Alamos designed their own. Their success led them to develop their own control and input-output systems as well. MANIAC was placed in operation in March 1952, several months before the institute computer was dedicated.

Table 4.2
Computers built using the IAS computer design

AVIDAC	Argonne National Laboratory	1953
BESK	Swedish Board for Computing Machinery, Stockholm	1953
BESM	Academy of Sciences, Moscow	1955
DASK	Danish Academy, Institute of Computing Machinery	1957
GEORGE	Argonne National Laboratory	?
IBM 701	IBM Corp.	1952
ILLIAC	University of Illinois	1952
JOHNNIAC	RAND Corporation	1954
MANIAC	Los Alamos Scientific Laboratory	1952
MSUDC	Michigan State University	?
ORACLE	Oak Ridge National Laboratory	1953
ORDVAC	Aberdeen Proving Grounds	1952
PERM	Technische Hochschule, Munich	1954
SILLIAC	University of Sydney	1956
SMIL	Lund University	1956
TC-1	International Telemeter Corp.	1955
WEIZAC	Weizmann Institute, Rehovoth	1955

Notes: AVIDAC: Argonne's Version of the IAS Digital Automatic Computer; BESK: Binar Elektronisk Sekvens Kalkylator; BESM: Bystrodeistwujuschtschaja Elektronnajastschethaja Machina; DASK: Dansk BESK; ILLIAC: Illinois Automatic Computer; MANIAC: Mathematical Analyzer, Numerical Integrator, and Computer; MSUDC: Michigan State University Discrete Computer; ORACLE: Oak Ridge Automatic Computer and Logical Engine; ORDVAC: Ordnance Dicrete Variable Automatic Computer; PERM: Programmgestenerte Elektronenrechenmaschine.

Dates are approximate dates of completion or dedication. The organizations listed are those that operated the machines. In some cases the machines were built by other organizations.

In 1949 Argonne National Laboratory decided to build a computer based on the IAS design, and with Goldstine's assistance they hired Chuan Chu to direct the project.[50] The AVIDAC (Argonne's Version of the Institute's Digital Automatic Computer) was an almost exact copy of the institute machine. Its construction began in 1950 and was completed in 1951, so it was also in operation before the institute computer. When Oak Ridge National Laboratory decided to build a computer in 1950, they chose the AVIDAC engineering staff at Argonne to build it. Their machine, ORACLE (Oak Ridge Automatic Computer and Logical Engine), followed the institute's logical design but used faster circuits, smaller cathode ray tube memory units, a primary memory twice the size of that in the IAS computer, and magnetic tape for secondary storage. Arthur Burks was a consultant on the design of ORACLE, which was completed and installed at Oak Ridge in late 1953.

In early 1949 the University of Illinois and Aberdeen Proving Grounds agreed to share the costs of the construction of two computers to be built at the University of Illinois.[51] The ORDVAC (Ordnance Discrete Variable Automatic Computer) was completed in late 1951 and installed in Aberdeen in early 1952. ILLIAC was completed in the fall of 1952 and served as the principal computing facility at the University of Illinois throughout the 1950s. There was close contact between the construction teams at the institute and the University of Illinois, including visits by the Illinois staff to Princeton, and Illinois received copies of the IAS drawings of the arithmetic and memory units. Both ILLIAC and ORDVAC followed the IAS logical design closely. The Illinois team copied the physical layout of the IAS machine and some of its engineering design features, including the flip-flop, gating, and cathode follower circuits, as well as the registers, complement sets, and clear drivers.

One of the last IAS-class machines to be built was the JOHNNIAC. In late 1950 the RAND Corporation decided it needed new computing equipment to supplement its six IBM 604 calculators. Von Neumann, a consultant to RAND, convinced them that they should have a computer with stored-program capability rather than continue with IBM calculators. After visits to the computers already completed or under development, they embarked on building their own machine based on the IAS design but with a tenfold improvement in reliability. There was extensive discussion with the institute team. Bigelow as well as von Neumann provided suggestions for improving on the IAS design, and one of the IAS engineers, Willis Ware, soon joined the RAND staff. The RAND engineers studied the IAS reports closely and followed the design generally, though they did make a number of modifications: air-conditioning around the circuits, punched-card input and output, octal notation for programming, improved maintenance design (allowing for remote monitoring of tube heater voltages), and improved dynamic checking facilities. The JOHNNIAC began operation in 1953 with a Selectron memory supplied by RCA. Two years later the Selectron memory was replaced by a magnetic core memory from Telemeter Magnetics.

These IAS-class computers in the government laboratories were important tools of atomic energy and ballistics research. The IAS design also had an impact on commercial computer design, most evident in the first computer IBM manufactured for the production line. One of their engineers, Nathaniel Rochester, had studied the logical design reports from the institute and in February 1949 visited the institute to see the computer under construction. This influenced the design of the Defense Calculator, which was marketed commercially as the IBM 701. At a meeting with the Defense Calculator design team in January 1951, Rochester and Jerrier Haddad explained that their goal was a machine "like IAS but with good input-output," and Rochester distributed a four-page report describing the logical design, circuit types, and input-output devices of the institute computer. The final logical design was similar to that of the IAS machine, though the 701 had a different word length, half-word addresses, which simplified branching, and different treatment of number signs. In the engineering area, the arithmetic, control, and memory units were similar to those in the IAS machine, though the Defense Calculator used a more versatile 1-bit electronic storage unit and a pluggable circuit unit, which facilitated servicing.[52] The input-output equipment for the Defense Calculator drew on IBM's extensive prior work in this area and was far superior to that originally used at the institute. In fact, the institute later replaced its input-output equipment with IBM equipment. An engineering model of IBM's computer was completed in early 1952, the first production model was shipped to IBM World Headquarters in New York in December, and other production models of the 701 began to be shipped about one a month beginning in April 1953. The 701 was one of the most important computers of the first generation and helped IBM to obtain its leadership position in the computer field.

In fact, the institute computer had an even wider influence because it was the model for several computers built in other countries, including the BESK built at the Matematikmaskin-namnden in Sweden in 1954, the DASK built at the Regnecentralen in Denmark betweeen 1953 and 1958, the WEIZAC built at the Weizmann Institute in Israel in 1954 and 1955, and the CSIRAC built by CSIRO in Australia between 1947 and 1951.[53] The WEIZAC exemplifies the technology transfer that was involved. It was built by Gerald Estrin, who had been a member of the engineering team at IAS, and was programmed for solving problems of the physical sciences by Chaim Pekeris, who had done similar programming work at the Institute.[54]

The engineering challenges, especially in the design and construction of an acceptable primary memory unit, were more difficult than originally anticipated. The computer took almost twice as long as expected—nearly six years—to complete. However, the finished product was faster and generally more powerful than the other computers of its era, and this power was put to good use in scientific research. The computer itself must be regarded as a prototype—though one that did considerable useful computation. Commercial machines that followed it had much more powerful input-output equipment, unit modularization, and other features to improve throughput, manufacturability, reliability, and maintainability. These advances were possible in part because of the lessons learned from the Institute project. The engineering legacy of the Electronic Computer Project is represented by the many government and commercial IAS-class computers built around the world during the 1950s.

5

The Transformation of Numerical Analysis

Accommodating Numerical Analysis to High-Speed Computers

Although numerical methods for finding approximate solutions to mathematical problems have existed since the time of Newton, the subject of numerical analysis did not receive a thorough investigation until it was taken up by K. F. Gauss in the early nineteenth century. Building on his results, mathematicians of the nineteenth and early twentieth centuries developed practical numerical methods for solving small systems of linear equations, inverting small matrices, approximating integrals, and solving ordinary differential equations. Von Neumann saw the computer's ability to carry out long sequences of calculations rapidly and without human intervention as presenting an opportunity to expand the domain to which numerical techniques could be applied. These new opportunities included the study of larger and more complex systems of linear equations, partial differential equations, and their applications in classical and quantum physics, economics, biology, and the earth sciences.

Von Neumann understood that major changes in numerical methods might be required in order to employ computers effectively and reliably. Computers differ in several crucial respects from the desk calculators and punched-card equipment that had previously driven numerical analyses. Computers could carry out multiplications as much as 10^5 times as fast as hand methods but were seriously limited in their ability to store data, instructions, and intermediate results centrally.[1] Practically unlimited amounts of information could be stored on punched cards and be made effectively available in a punched-card system, but only 20 to 150 numbers could be stored in the first high-speed calculating devices. The computers under construction in the late 1940s, such as the one at the IAS, could store only a few thousand instructions in primary memory. They could store practically unlimited amounts of information on magnetic tape or punched cards (in secondary storage), but the time required to access the secondary storage compromised the overall efficiency of the machine. Memory design involved consideration of not only how much information could be stored but also how rapidly it could be accessed. Information on punched cards could be accessed no faster by punched-card systems than by computer systems, but the ratio between the time for accessing data and calculating with it was much lower in the punched-card systems. Von Neumann described this situation in economic terms:

Thus in an automatic computing establishment there will be a "lower price" on arithmetical operations, but a "higher price" on storage of data, intermediate results, etc. Consequently, the "inner economy" of such an establishment will be very different from what we are used to now, and what we were uniformly used to since the days of Gauss. Therefore, new computing methods, or, to speak more fundamentally, new criteria for "practicality" and "elegance" will have to be developed.

We are actually now engaged in various mathematical and mathematical-logical efforts aiming towards these objectives. We consider them to be absolutely essential parts of any well-rounded program which aims to develop the new possibilities of very high speed, automatic computing.[2]

An analysis of the complexity of numerical problems and the speed of calculating devices convinced Goldstine and von Neumann that new ground could be broken in the areas of partial differential equations, integral equations, and systems of linear equations; however, they worried that problems with numerical stability—that is, the accumulation and amplification of round-off errors—might necessitate substantial changes in the numerical methods developed over the past 150 years. For example, they believed it might be necessary to abandon elimination methods for solving linear systems in favor of successive approximation methods, which often require more multiplications but are intrinsically stable and hence demand less precision to be carried through the calculation. In a 1946 document, "On the Principles of Large Scale Computing Machines," Goldstine and von Neumann set out a research agenda for a computer-oriented numerical analysis. This research began at the time they were designing the institute computer and continued until the end of von Neumann's career.

Matrices and Systems of Linear Equations

The problem of inverting a matrix and the related one of solving a system of linear equations are among the most common in mathematics, and by the 1920s many different methods of solution were in use.[3] These methods were practical only for small systems of equations and matrices of low order, say of order less than 20, because of the limitation on the number of multiplications that could practically be carried out using pencil and paper or a desk calculator. In the 1930s the situation began to change for at least two reasons. Wallace Eckert of Columbia University, L. J. Comrie of the (British) National Almanac Office, and others demonstrated that punched-card sorting and tabulating equipment could be applied effectively to scientific problems, and the use of this equipment eased the practical restrictions on the number of multiplications and therefore the size of linear system open to solution. At the same time, science was finding a need to solve larger problems—for example, in the dynamical analyses of astronomy and aircraft design, the network analyses of electrical engineering, the statistical analyses of agriculture and psychology, and the structural analyses of mechanical engineering. To meet this demand, statisticians and applied mathematicians, including A. C. Aitken, Paul S. Dwyer, R. A. Fisher, Harold Hotelling, and S. S. Wilks, made new investigations of numerical linear algebra.

Until this time many different methods (elimination, partitioning into matrices of lower order, Gram-Schmidt orthogonalization, direct computation of determinants, and other iterative methods) were employed, often with little reason to choose among them. In 1943 Hotelling reexamined the question of matrix calculation and argued that although the availability of punched-card equipment might enable scientists to apply numerical methods in their work, care must be taken about the "neglected question of limits of error in stopping at any point, and . . . the rate of approach to the desired solution."[4] He gave an example of a system of eleven linear equations known to within an absolute value of ε, whose solution, if determined by the standard elimination method, would have an error a million times greater. He concluded (erroneously) that for each decimal place of accuracy in the solution, seven decimal places of accuracy must be carried throughout the computation.

Hotelling advocated using an iterative method on matrices with more than four rows, a method introduced in the nineteenth century by Gauss and Seidel.[5] Its advantage was economy of labor (provided one starts with a good approximation to the variables) and resiliency in the presence of round-off errors. Unlike elimination methods, in which round-off errors build on one another from each stage of the calculation to the next, round-off errors tend to cancel one another out in iterative methods, though perhaps only after additional iterations. Hotelling proposed a new iteration method, which he believed would be particularly effective for large problems, such as those tackled on punched-card machinery.[6] But the main purpose of his paper was to sound a warning about the use of existing elimination methods on large linear systems.

Methods for solving linear systems of high order was one of the first topics von Neumann considered in his investigation of numerical analysis for the computer, perhaps because of the concern Hotelling created. During the war von Neumann had organized a research group at the institute with funds from Navy Ordnance and the NDRC Applied Mathematics Panel to investigate numerical methods for hydrodynamics. Valentine Bargmann and Deane Montgomery were his collaborators. In October 1946 the three of them published a paper analyzing existing methods for their suitability in solving large linear systems and suggesting an iterative method for use with computers.[7] Their paper assumed the correctness of Hotelling's conclusions, apparently the reason for choosing an iteration method.

The first section of the paper compared the complexity of the well-known algorithms for solving linear systems.[8] Using the number of multiplications as a measure of the total time required to solve a linear system, they determined for each computational method an order of magnitude measure of complexity as a function of the order n of the system. They estimated these to be $n^3/3$ for elimination methods, $5n^3/3$ for the Gram-Schmidt orthogonalization process, n^3 for partitioning methods, and $n^4/3$ for direct calculation of determinants. From the complexity analysis they concluded that the determinant method was impractical for systems of high order, and the other methods were about equally practical. This study was perhaps the first to provide systematic estimates of computation times for algorithms, a topic of considerable importance in computer science in later years.

The authors were also concerned about numerical stability. A method of computation is said to be numerically stable if the rounding errors that unavoidably occur at each stage of the computation do not accumulate in a way that vitiates the result.

Numerical stability is not a serious concern when doing hand calculations because of the limits on the number of calculations that can be made. Consequently little was known about this issue in 1946. It became critically important when using high-speed calculating devices, which could carry out thousands of iterations of a numerical procedure. The authors admitted the difficulty of estimating the stability of individual numerical methods but judged the elimination, partition, orthogonalization, and determinant methods all to be unstable and therefore unsuitable for computer use.

From their perspective, the stability was much more important than the complexity of the numerical method. Electronic computing equipment, such as the ENIAC, was thousands of times faster than earlier calculating equipment, so its users were quite willing to increase the complexity or number of calculations in trade for an algorithm that would control round-off errors. With this attitude in mind, von Neumann's group selected an iterative method as the one best suited to high-speed calculating devices. The method was relatively efficient in the number of iterations required to attain a given level of accuracy. More important, it was stable, the number of extra digits carried as a cushion for accuracy was small, and the algorithm could be practically implemented on high-speed calculating machinery.[9]

Von Neumann's interest in numerical linear algebra did not end here, as Goldstine has indicated:

Unfortunately Bargmann, Montgomery, and von Neumann accepted tentatively this very pessimistic conjecture of Hotelling and turned away from the Gaussian procedure to iterative ones. Von Neumann was not at all happy about the situation regarding Gauss's procedure. He and I discussed this many times, and we did not feel it reasonable that so skilled a computer as Gauss would have fallen into the trap that Hotelling thought he had noted.

By the late fall of 1946 or very early 1947 von Neumann and I finally understood how matters really stood. Von Neumann remarked one day that even though errors may build up during one part of the computation, it was only relevant to ask how effective is the numerically obtained solution, not how close were some of the auxiliary numbers calculated on the way to their correct counterparts. We sensed that at least for positive definite matrices the Gaussian procedure could be shown to be quite stable.

With this as our goal, we rapidly satisfied ourselves in a heuristic fashion that for such matrices this was true. It remained then to produce a completely rigorous analysis and discussion of the procedure.[10]

Goldstine and von Neumann took up this analysis in two papers that reexamined the method of elimination.[11]

A few other mathematicians were suspicious of the findings Hotelling and Bargmann, Montgomery, and von Neumann reached because they did not accord with experimental results. Leslie Fox, Harry Huskey, and James Wilkinson, working on desk calculators and punched-card equipment at the National Physical Laboratory in Teddington, England, found the Gaussian elimination method to be stable though it required carrying extra digits to compensate for round-off errors:

Our conclusion is then as follows. If the original coefficients are correct to n places of decimals, computations should be carried out with perhaps one extra figure for every ten equations, these extra figures being the so-called "guarding figures" for the accumulation of rounding-off errors. Then if the first n decimals of the final pivot [using Gaussian elimination, known also as pivotal condensation] contain m significant figures, no answer to better than m significant figures can be obtained from the given equations to the physical problem.

These conclusions have been borne out by experiment on a set of eighteen ill-conditioned equations, whose coefficients were given to five decimals. Several guarding figures were added, and the final pivot had two significant figures in its first five decimals. The coefficients were then rounded off to four decimals, and the elimination process repeated, only one significant figure being left in the final pivot. The two solutions agreed generally to only one significant figure, bearing out the above conclusions.[12]

The experimental results of his colleagues at the National Physical Laboratory also led Alan Turing to reassess Hotelling's claims. Turing was in the midst of these investigations when he traveled to the United States in January 1947. He visited Goldstine and von Neumann in Princeton and had a lengthy discussion of the topic. Afterward the two groups independently pursued their investigations and in the fall of 1947 submitted independent papers presenting similar results.[13] In his paper Turing concluded:

The best known method for the solution of linear equations is Gauss's elimination method. This is the method almost universally taught in schools. It has, unfortunately, recently come into disrepute on the ground that rounding off will give rise to very large errors. It has, for instance, been argued by Hotelling that in solving a set of n equations we should keep $n\log_{10}4$ extra or "guarding" figures. Actually, although examples can be constructed where as many as $n\log_{10}2$ extra figures would be required, these are exceptional. In the present paper the magnitude of the error is described in terms of quantities not considered in Hotelling's analysis; from the inequalities proved here it can immediately be seen that in all normal cases the Hotelling estimate is far too pessimistic.

The belief that the elimination method and other "direct" methods of solution lead to large errors has been responsible for a recent search for other methods which would be free from this weakness. These were mainly methods of successive approximation and considerably more laborious than the direct ones. There now appears to be no real advantage in the indirect methods, except in connexion with matrices having special properties, for example, where the vast majority of the coefficients are very small, but there is at least one large one in each row.[14]

Goldstine and von Neumann responded to Hotelling in the first of their two papers.[15] There they developed the topic of round-off errors systematically from first principles because of the importance they believed it to hold for machine numerical linear algebra.[16] They listed four ways in which incorrect solutions can be obtained through numerical solution: incorrect formulation of the problem, errors introduced from observational data, errors caused by approximation of transcendental functions or truncation of infinite procedures, and errors introduced by the "noise" inherent in calculating devices (in digital computers this noise takes the form of round-off errors). The paper also presented the first account of computer arithmetic—the study of the logical processes that take place when a computer does arithmetic operations (very different from ordinary arithmetic since the computer truncates all digits beyond a certain fixed number).

Their main objective was to examine the cumulative error arising from the noise in a computing device. To isolate the noise effect, they selected a problem that involved no approximation or truncation, required many elementary operations, and had inherently low stability (the noise introduced at one stage was likely to be amplified considerably in later stages). They explained that round-off errors depend on the algorithm used to approximate the solution as well as on the problem. Based on these considerations, they chose the problem of matrix inversion and the method of elimination. Unable to carry out their error analysis in the completely general situation, they restricted themselves to positive definite matrices.[17]

The problem is more explicitly formulated as one of determining the the relationship between the order n of a matrix and the number s of places (base β) that must be carried throughout the computation in order to obtain some specified standard of precision. Their analysis was based on conservative assumptions, which covered the worst possible cases, and resulted in the inequality $n < .15\, \beta^{s/4}$, which under certain plausible precision requirements gives the results in Table 5.1

The general assessment of this first paper is that it was a mathematical *tour de force* but did not give the correct result or serve as the basis for further fruitful investigations. Goldstine and von Neumann recognized that their error estimates were high. On 21 October 1949, as they were reading the final typescript of the second paper, von Neumann received an inquiry from R. Plunkett, a mechanical engineering professor at the Rice Institute, about the error estimates in the first paper. Von Neumann replied:

We have been aware all along that our estimates for the accumulation of errors in inverting matrices are high. It was, however, not our purpose to obtain estimates which are close to optimum, but we wanted rather to make a try to see if it was possible to obtain rigorous error estimates, even at the price of considerable sacrifices. It is clear that our results are less favorable than pure empir[ic]ism because of the superposition of the following three factors:

(a) In almost any form of rigorous estimating one is forced to allow for the most unfavorable combination of individual factors, and in particular, not to make use of such combinations which may in practice be frequent or even universal, but which would require too detailed or too difficult an analysis to establish.

(b) In the case of the superposition of round-off errors at least, there is a reasonably clear-cut way to remove part of the disadvantage described under (a) above: There is some prima facie justification in treating them as independent random variables and to sum them accordingly.

(c) All assumptions about the properties of an "unknown", "typical", "average" matrix are by their very nature questionable. We attempted to bias these assumptions as little as possible toward the favorable side. There are certainly large groups of problems which produce matrices which form a systematically more favorable population than the one we took to be "standard" in our paper. To be specific, correlation matrices in problems in which the correlations are not by nature very strong are apt to be favorably biased in this sense. This is even more true of the "production

Table 5.1
Precision requirements for matrix inversion: Deterministic analysis

Precision level required	Reliable procedure range	Multiplications required
$\beta^s \approx 10^8 \approx 2^{27}$	$n < 15$	3500
$\beta^s \approx 10^{10} \approx 2^{33}$	$n < 50$	120,000
$\beta^s \approx 10^{12} \approx 2^{40}$	$n < 150$	3,500,000

matrices" of W. Leontief's theory. It is quite easy to see in that theory that the overall "profitability" of the economic processes described has the immediate effect of bounding the matrices that are involved considerably away from zero.

I think that the source (a) in general is not terribly serious. It probably does not lead to wrong orders of magnitude. The source (b) is of a certain importance, and it can be accounted for mathematically. This is what our new paper attempts to do. The source (c) is the most important of all, and it is clear that nothing in this respect can be done generally.[18]

In the first paper Goldstine and von Neumann developed their error estimates from a strictly deterministic basis, but they remarked that round-off errors behave essentially like random variables, suggesting that error bounds could be estimated probabilistically. The second paper investigated this approach. Goldstine explained many years later, "In the second paper we raised a question which we thought might become more important than it in fact ever became. We said, let us not worry so much about what might happen in a very small number of pathological cases; instead let us see what occurs on the average, what we can expect if we need to do this task many times."[19]

They began the probabilistic line of investigation in 1947, soon after completing the first paper, but reached a technical impasse they could not overcome until 1949, when some unpublished results of Bargmann, Montgomery, and Gilbert Hunt became available to them. The probabilistic estimates gave considerably better grounds for optimism than the earlier deterministic analysis had.[20] For the same three precision levels as in the deterministic analysis, they arrived at the respective reliability ranges: $n < 19$, $n < 86$, and $n < 400$. But the mathematical community regarded even these results as overly pessimistic. In 1952 the statistician H. P. Mulholland strengthened their technical machinery and improved the estimates to $n < 25$, $n < 113$, and $n < 528$.

Soon after they completed these two papers, Goldstine and von Neumann began to collaborate with Francis Murray, a mathematics professor at Columbia Univeristy, on another problem of numerical linear algebra. They sought a practical numerical method for determining the fundamental invariants of conic sections in n-dimensional space .under rotations of the coordinate axes.[21] Their research had a larger payoff: a general method suited to computers for finding the eigenvalues and eigenvectors of large symmetric matrices with real entries.[22]

The paper began with a survey of methods for determining eigenvalues and an evaluation of their suitability to the computer and then sorted the methods into two categories. One category contained methods to find and directly solve the characteristic equation of the real symmetric matrix A :

$$\text{Det } (A - xI) = x^n + \alpha_1 x^{n-1} + \ldots + \alpha_n = 0 \, ,$$

which involves both finding the $\alpha_1 \ldots, \alpha_n$ and solving the polynomial equation. The authors argued that all of the methods for determining the α_i were impractical because they required either too many multiplications or too many digits to be carried through the calculation. They showed that many digits must be carried in order to ensure even modest precision when solving the characteristic equation by a standard method, such as Newton-Raphson or Graeffe. The other category contained methods for finding the characteristic values serially. They showed that these methods were either unstable for matrices of high order ($n{\approx}100$) or required human intervention during the computation. The upshot of their analysis was that no existing method was satisfactory for using the computer to find eigenvalues of matrices of high order, and they were led to develop their own (rotational) method and give rigorous error estimates for its use. Estimating conservatively, they calculated that the order of the matrix n and the precision requirements (with base β and number of digits s) have the relationship given in Table 5.2. Their analysis was widely accepted, and their rotational method became the standard computer method for a few years.[23]

Partial Differential Equations

Numerical methods for solving ordinary differential equations were well established prior to World War II, but there were few methods for the numerical solution of partial differential equa-

Table 5.2
Precision requirements for matrix analysis: Probabilistic analysis

Precision required	Reliable precision range
$\beta^s{\approx}10^8$	$n < 79$
$\beta^s{\approx}10^{10}$	$n < 500$
$\beta^s{\approx}10^{12}$	$n < 3150$

tions (PDEs). The most important prewar contributions were the work of Courant, Friedrichs, and Lewy on numerical stability and of Southwell on relaxation methods. In the immediate postwar years, problems of fluid dynamics—important to atomic energy, petroleum exploration, and weather forecasting—came to the fore. Von Neumann's involvement in these applications through his consultancies to government and industry led to his interest in the numerical solution of PDEs. Among the many contributions he made in this area are his investigations of numerical stability.[24]

Von Neumann's work on numerical stability built directly on that of Courant, Friedrichs, and Lewy.[25] In a 1928 paper they had introduced this vexing problem by showing that the solution to a set of difference equations chosen in the customary way to approximate a PDE need not approximate the solution of the equation itself. They illustrated their point with a differential equation that described compressible, nonviscous flow, showing that the solutions to the difference equations will converge to the solution of the exact equation just in case the difference equation grid meets certain rigid conditions: that the ratio $\Delta t / \Delta x$ of the discrete time and space intervals is less than a fixed number c; otherwise the errors are amplified beyond control. This result, known as the Courant condition, became a standard concern of numerical analysts in the 1950s.[26]

The Courant, Friedrichs, and Lewy paper presented rigorous stability criteria for hyperbolic and parabolic equations with constant coefficients in one dependent and two independent variables. Von Neumann generalized their result to equations with more than one dependent variable, more than two independent variables, and order higher than 2, but this generality was gained at the sacrifice of rigor.[27] He recognized his method as being heuristic and defended it on empirical grounds, arguing that "as far as any evidence that is known to me goes . . . , it has not led to false results so far."[28]

Von Neumann never published a general account of his stability analysis, though he lectured on his results on several occasions.[29] The best account of his approach is contained in a consultant's report written in July 1948 for the Standard Oil Development Company.[30] The report applies his method to a practical problem of gas-liquid flow around an oil well or along a long oil field being produced at one end.[31] The problem assumes a single, thin, oil-bearing layer, which may be situated on an incline. The layer is treated as two-dimensional but described in terms of a single spatial variable through symmetry considerations. The independent variables are the distance x from the well and the time t. The dependent variables are the pressure p and the liquid saturation s of the semipermeable medium in the oil-bearing layer. This formulation yields a set of PDEs of the parabolic heat conduction type.

Von Neumann's problem is to determine whether there is a practical numerical method for solving these equations on desk calculators or the IBM SSEC.[32] The solution involves setting a two-dimensional grid of approximation points. The company specified the range of the oil field to be 5 miles—$0 \leq x \leq 27{,}000$ (feet), and $\Delta x = 1000$; thus requiring approximately 25 x-netpoints. The time was specified to be 10 years—$0 \leq t \leq 3650$ (days)—and $\Delta t = 30$, thus requiring approximately 120 t-netpoints. With $25 \times 120 = 3000$ netpoints and 50 multiplications per netpoint, 150,000 multiplications were required to solve the problem numerically. Von Neumann regards the problem as beyond the capacity of desk calculators but still within the range of the SSEC. He points out, however, that additional factors must be considered before concluding that a numerical solution is possible. He deals straightforwardly with the discontinuities that arise from a conflict between the boundary conditions and the initial conditions and shows how a special system of ordinary differential equations can be solved to provide initial values. Most of the remainder of the report addresses the problem of error amplification (numerical stability), which he considers "of paramount importance" and "altogether controlling with respect to the stepwise integration methods that can be used."[33]

The question of the amplification of errors is one which receives little or no conscious consideration in the most familiar computing practices. The reason for this is that it is of a subordinate importance in the stepwise integration of total differential equation systems, and these are the subject of the best known and most widely practiced computing procedures. (Error amplification does, nevertheless, play a certain role even for total differential equations. ....) Error amplification is, on the other hand, most critical and decisive in the stepwise integration of partial differential equations (and their systems). Since the application of numerical procedures to any really significant extent to these is of fairly recent date (especially for "non elliptic" equations, and error amplification happens to play no important role in the customary ways of treating "elliptic" equations), the problems of error amplification are not yet well or generally incorporated into the common computing practice. They do, however, play a decisive role in connection with any stepwise integration attack on the system [of equations governing the gas-oil flow] (this system is essentially "parabolic").[34]

Because the problem of numerical stability is little known, von Neumann devotes several sections of the report to a general discussion of error amplification before returning to the problem at hand. He identifies four sources of error in the stepwise numerical solution of ordinary or partial differential equations:[35]

1. Each individual step of the integration process introduces an error by replacing a differential quotient by an approximating finite difference quotient.

2. Within each integration step, arithmetic operations are carried out inexactly because of round-off errors.

3. These elementary round-off errors accumulate since there is one integration for each netpoint in the integration net.

4. In the course of the integration, these elementary errors are amplified as they become multiplied by various factors.

The amplification of errors is most insidious in the solution of PDEs, and consequently it is the source of error on which von Neumann focuses his attention.

His stability analysis begins with a simple PDE that contains the "decisive" terms from the oil-gas flow equations:

$$\frac{\partial p}{\partial t} = m \frac{\partial^2 p}{\partial x^2}$$

Giving an argument explicitly similar to the one in Courant, Friedrichs, and Lewy (1928), he shows that each Fourier component in the error term of the conventional difference equation solution is amplified by the factor

$$A = \left[1 - \frac{4m \, \Delta t}{(\Delta x)^2} \sin^2 \left(\frac{h \Delta x}{2} \right) \right]^{\frac{t - t_0}{\Delta t}}$$

where h is the Fourier frequency. He then could show that the maximum value of A is less than or equal to one (that is, the error term is not amplified) just in case $\Delta t \leq (\Delta x)^2 / 2m$. He also notes that the question of the computational stability is independent from the stability of the PDE itself because it is the heat conduction equation, which was known to be stable.[36]

Taking guidance from this example, von Neumann repeats the stability analysis for the full oil-gas flow equation and demonstrates that it is impossible with existing computing equipment, such as ENIAC or SSEC, to meet the numerical stability conditions if the problem is approximated by difference equations in the conventional way. To meet these conditions and hold $\Delta x = 1000$ as specified by the company, Δt would have to be less than 0.1 for the LP case and 1000 times smaller for the CS—much smaller than the specified $\Delta t = 30$. To satisfy the Courant condition would increase the number of multiplications by factors of 300 and 300,000 in the two cases, removing them from the capacity of all computing machines of this time.

These results force von Neumann to seek a method of stepwise integration for the oil-gas problem that is more stable than the conventional method. He turns to a method, introduced at Los Alamos, that damps out the unstable element in the conventional method.[37] But a price was paid for this stability: extra work to solve an additional system of simultaneous linear equations representing the implicit form of the the solution for every value of t. In the LP (long oil field) case, this amounted to solving a system of twenty-seven linear equations in twenty-seven unknowns for each of 120 values of t. Von Neumann pointed out that although this price initially appeared "formidable," a closer look reveals the situation as more promising because each equation contains only three of the twenty-seven unknowns. Using a slightly improved version of this implicit method, together with a method for solving systems of linear equations optimal for his particular circumstances, he estimates that the oil-gas flow problem can be solved with 170,000 multiplications: 200 weeks of work at a desk calculator, 7 hours on the SSEC if it is working at peak efficiency, or 18 hours on the SSEC if it is working at its average rate of 40 percent efficiency. In a second report, von Neumann gives the details of the flow problem and the computing scheme for the LP case.[38]

The Problem of Shocks

One of the most compelling reasons for von Neumann's interest in numerical analysis was that it was practically impossible to study fluid dynamics in any other way. The PDEs governing fluid flow are analytically intractable and are often impractical to investigate empirically, so often the only recourse in atomic weapons design, aeronautical engineering, weather prediction, and other important flow problems is a numerical approach. These research areas attracted most of von Neumann's attention in the 1940s and 1950s, as well as that of many of his collaborators in Princeton and Los Alamos.

It is impossible to go far in the study of these kinds of flow problems without confronting the problem of shocks. Shocks are endemic in the study of the supersonic flow of compressible fluid.[39] They occur physically on surfaces as discontinuities in density, fluid velocity, temperature, entropy, or some other physical variable. The conditions that apply to plane shocks are well known and are represented by the equations of Rankine and Hugoniot, but dealing with them greatly complicates numerical solution. In the course of his studies, von Neumann confronted shocks many times, and he developed three of the earliest numerical approaches for treating them.

His first treatment is given in a 1944 report.[40] He replaces the full hydrodynamic phenomena with a simple kinetic model that simulates the fluid with a line of beads connected by springs. The beads represent idealized molecules, and the mass of a bead is taken to be the mass of a molecule. To reduce the amount of computation, the number of molecules is reduced from 6×10^{23} (Avogadro's number, the number of molecules in a gram-mol) to between 10 and 100. This scaling down of the number of molecules is compensated for by scaling up the "intramolecular forces." The resulting equations can be solved readily using punched-card equipment. Von Neumann argues informally that this procedure will satisfy the Rankine and Hugoniot conditions and provide arbitrarily good approximations to the full hydrodynamic equations. As evidence, he reports on three successful trial calculations carried out at the Ballistics Research Laboratory under the direction of L. E. Cunningham in March 1944.[41] However, further experience showed that the model was too simplistic to be of great utility.

The second method for dealing with shocks was developed in collaboration with the Los Alamos physicist R. D. Richtmyer and published in 1950.[42] It involves modifying the hydrodynamical equations by adding terms to remove the shocks from the numerical calculation and thus reducing the computation to a size practical to do on existing computing equipment.[43] An artificial viscosity is introduced to dissipate the shocks by giving them a thickness larger than the spacing on the grid points. Then the difference equations can be solved directly, as if there were no shocks at all. These extra terms increase the stringency of the stability conditions but not beyond practical limits. The authors find that the effect of these extra terms can be minimized as far as desired by adjusting the size of the mesh so that the solutions they obtain to the modified problem can be made to approximate as closely as desired the solution to the actual problem. They report the success of their method on one-dimensional flows and express optimism for its application to more complicated flows.

The third approach to the shock problem, undertaken in collaboration with Herman Goldstine, is a direct numerical assault.[44] The problem they consider is the delay and propagation of a shock wave from a strong point-source explosion in an ideal gas. They use an iterative method to calculate the Rankine-Hugoniot conditions across the shock and give the solution, calculated on the institute computer, in graphical form. This is one of the first attempts to solve a complex problem involving shocks directly by numerical means.[45]

Mathematicians tried all of these methods, but only the artificial viscosity method had a lasting impact. Von Neumann's influence in this area goes beyond these three methods, however, as Martin Schwarzschild, one of the early scientific users of computers, witnessed: "I would like to say that my impression was that in all the years after the war whenever you visited one of the installations with a modern mainframe computer, you would always find somebody doing a shock wave problem. If you asked them how they came to be working on that, it was always von Neumann who had put them onto it. So they became sort of the foot print of von Neumann, walking across the scene of modern computers."[46]

Random Numbers and Monte Carlo Methods

Von Neumann's work on numerical linear algebra exemplifies his efforts to modify hand numerical methods for the computer. He also advanced numerical analysis in directions never considered in the hand computing era. His work on shocks is one example, and his contribution to the Monte Carlo method is another. The underlying idea of the Monte Carlo method is to model a complex problem stochastically in a way that admits of a solution's being calculated. The model uses random numbers with an appropriate statistical distribution to replace the complex or seemingly random events under consideration. For example, in the case of neutron diffusion, millions of neutrons might undergo fission, scattering, or absorption at any instant, making it practically impossible to apply established theoretical or experimental techniques of physics to a practical problem. With a Monte Carlo method, the neutrons and their seemingly random behavior are replaced by an appropriately chosen set of "random" numbers that describe the histories of the neutrons over time, and a solution can be calculated without experimental study.

Credit for inventing the Monte Carlo method is generally assigned to Stan Ulam and von Neumann.[47] Ulam has explained how the idea came to him while he was playing solitaire during an illness in 1946.[48] He noticed that it is much simpler to gain an idea of the general outcome of solitaire by making multiple trials with the cards and counting proportions of outcomes than it is to compute all of the combinatorial possibilities formally. It occurred to him that this same observation should apply to his work at Los Alamos on neutron diffusion, for which it is practically impossible to solve the integro-differential equations governing scattering, absorption, and fission: "The idea was to try out by mental experiment thousands of such possibilities, and at each stage, determine by chance, by a random number distributed according to the given probabilities, what should happen, and total all these possibilities and get an idea of the behavior of the physical process."[49]

Computing machines, which were just becoming available, could be used to make the numerical trials and in effect replace the physicist's experimental apparatus. During one of von Neumann's visits to Los Alamos in 1946, Ulam mentioned the method to him. After initial skepticism, von Neumann became enthusiastic about the idea and began rapidly to develop its possibilities into a systematic procedure.[50] Ulam stated that Monte Carlo "came into concrete form and started developing with all its attendant tricks rudiments of a theory after I proposed the scheme to Johnny."[51]

An influential and perhaps the first written account of the Monte Carlo method was given by von Neumann in a letter to Richtmyer at Los Alamos in early 1947. His letter was bound with Richtmyer's reply as a Los Alamos report and distributed within the laboratory.[52] Von Neumann suggests applying the method to trace the isotropic generation of neutrons from a variable composition of active material along the radius of a sphere. He argues that the problem is appropriate for the ENIAC and estimates that it will require 5 hours to calculate the actions of 100 neutrons through the course of 100 collisions each.[53] He also suggests that a more general formulation of the problem, taking into account the energy and momentum exchanges, can be carried out as soon as a more powerful calculating machine, such as the one being built at the institute, becomes available.

The first computerized Monte Carlo calculations were carried out on the ENIAC in 1947 by a team from Los Alamos led by Nicholas Metropolis.[54] These calculations simulated chain reactions in critical and supercritical systems, starting from an assumed neutron distribution in space and velocity at some initial point in time. The Monte Carlo method rapidly spread to a wide variety of applications. It received considerable attention at a conference held in Los Angeles at the Institute for Numerical Analysis (INA) in July 1948. The positive reaction led the INA to organize a symposium devoted entirely to the Monte Carlo method the following summer.[55] The symposium gives an indication of the method's rapid dissemination to many application areas, including atomic physics, statistical mechanics, and materials science (in the aircraft industry), as well as to the solution of PDEs.

The Monte Carlo method was applied initially only to probabilistic problems, such as neutron diffusion, but applications were soon found to deterministic problems. For example, Monte Carlo techniques were discovered to solve both differential equations and operator equations (governing the solution of systems of linear equations). Ulam was particularly fond of a Monte Carlo method to evaluate multiple integrals.[57] One of the first applications of Monte Carlo to a deterministic problem was made in 1948 by Enrico Fermi, Ulam, and von Neumann when they estimated the eigenvalues of the Schrödinger equation.

Von Neumann and Ulam found one of the first Monte Carlo methods for inverting matrices. Their method, particularly well suited to use by a human armed with a table of random numbers, inverted a matrix of order n with only n^2 arithmetic operations in addition to the scanning procedure.[58] Von Neumann also discovered a Monte Carlo method for solving hyperbolic differential equations.[59] He was excited by the method because it provided a solution to a nonlinear problem, seemed capable of wide generalization, and improved on existing Markoffian procedures in that the Monte Carlo analysis applied directly to the differential equation rather than to its finite difference approximant. The lack of further mention of the procedure suggests that it did not fulfill its promise, however.

The Monte Carlo method consumes large quantities of random numbers. Methods for generating random numbers of sufficient quantity and quality for hand computation already existed, but von Neumann believed that the increased use of the computer would lead to a demand for many more random numbers, in particular for ones satisfying much more stringent randomness conditions. He gave some thought to the general question of how to produce a sequence of random decimal digits and identified two general approaches, the physical and the arithmetical.[60] Physical methods use a sensing device to count an ostensibly random physical process, such as the clicks of a Geiger counter, and record the results as a set of random digits. The shortcoming of this approach, as von Neumann saw it, is the irreproducibility of a particular random sequence: unless a sequence is recorded, it cannot be reused to check computational results, but if all these sequences are recorded, they overtax the computer's weakest link, its memory.

Thus von Neumann favored the arithmetic approach.[61] It requires finding a simply calculated function that can be applied iteratively to a fixed number of decimal digits, preferably eight or ten, which is the number of digits that was carried by fixed-point computers of the time. He decided on the middle-square algorithm: square an eight-digit number and take the eight middle digits of the product as the next number in the sequence. He believed that the deterministic relationship between one number and the next in this sequence, and between any two digits within a given number in the sequence, is sufficiently complex that the procedure will generate pseudo-random numbers—those that meet the standard statistical tests for randomness.[62] He realized, however, that since this is a function on a finite domain (the set of eight-digit numbers), the sequence of random numbers must eventually repeat itself. Thus, no such method will generate an infinitely long string of pseudo-random numbers. He hoped to find a procedure that will produce 1000 to 10,000 pseudo-random numbers before cycling.[63] There are several advantages to using an arithmetic procedure like the middle-square method to generate pseudo-random numbers on demand.[64] There is no practical limitation on the number of pseudo-random numbers that can be produced, and the sequence of numbers can be reproduced for checking as needed. Moreover, the ENIAC took 600 milliseconds to read a random number stored on a punched card but only 3 or 4 milliseconds to produce it arithmetically.

Von Neumann was well aware that the pseudo-random numbers produced by this arithmetic process are not truly random[65] and that any determination of their randomness must consider the round-off errors occurring in the algorithm. He regarded all of these procedures as "cooking recipes" that cannot be justified rigorously but must be judged by their results. By this criterion, the middle-square method turned out not to be very good, and other arithmetic methods soon replaced it.

The Monte Carlo method was soon enhanced to extend its applicability. It was apparent from its earliest application that some problems required random numbers that satisfied other than the standard rectangular statistical distribution. Techniques were soon discovered for transforming numbers in a rectangular distribution into some other multivariate distribution. One of the first of these methods that received wide use was von Neumann's rejection technique.[66] Another enhancement of the Monte Carlo process was its customization for special applications, including Herman Kahn's work on the use of expected values and importance sampling techniques developed by Nicholas Metropolis and Edward Teller. Along these same lines von Neumann and others developed variance-reducing techniques by which one stochastic process could be modified to another with the same expectation values but smaller variances, thereby reducing the overall computational task.

The work on the Monte Carlo method interested von Neumann in the properties of randomness. He calculated long strings of decimal digits of real numbers in order to check their statistical deviations from randomness.[67] He wanted to know whether the decimal expansions would remain closer to their expected values than a random sequence of that length should and arranged for the ENIAC to calculate over 2000 decimal digits of e and π during the Fourth of July weekend in 1949. He found that e but not π deviated significantly from the statistical properties of a random sequence of digits.[68] A similar set of investigations was carried out in 1954 when the institute computer was used to calculate decimal expansions of several real algebraic numbers. In collaboration with Bryant Tuckerman, von Neumann generated over 2000 partial quotients in the continued fraction expansion of the cube root of 2. They found no statistical deviations, but the results were inconclusive.

Linear Programming

Linear programming has been one of the most powerful and heavily used mathematical tools of government, industry, and academe in the postwar period.[69] It gives solutions to various kinds of scheduling problems by minimizing or maximizing a linear expression subject to some set of linear restraints. The method was originated in the early nineteenth century by Joseph Fourier. In the late nineteenth and early twentieth centuries a number of mathematicians offered conditions, expressed primarily in the form of duality results, under which a set of linear inequalities could be solved.[70] In the 1930s economists began to build linear economic models which they solved by related methods.

After World War II, the method's great power and applicability was recognized, and a theory of linear programming was developed. The main figure in the development was George Dantzig. During the war Dantzig became the air force's expert in programming planning methods based on the use of desk calculators. In 1946, as mathematical adviser to the U.S. Air Force controller, he was asked to mechanize the planning process for deployment, training, and logistical supply using advanced calculating equipment—at the time, analog computers or punched-card equipment. Brute force methods for solving these planning problems involve so many calculations that they fall beyond the capability even of today's most powerful supercomputers. Thus Dantzig was led to seek alternative methods of solution, and of those developed the most notable was the simplex method. By the end of the 1940s the power of this method was apparent, and it spread rapidly. The driving force in the late 1940s and early 1950s was the air force, through its Project SCOOP and the financial support it gave to the NBS for computing development.[71]

Von Neumann took a strong interest in linear programming after the war, and Dantzig credits him with giving "fundamental insight into the mathematical theory."[72] Von Neumann's interest originated in his economics research in the 1930s and early 1940s, in particular in his 1938 model of general economic equilibrium,[73] which used linear programming methods to give a qualitative description of the economy, and his book with Morgenstern on the theory of games, which presented some important duality results.[74] In October 1947 Dantzig visited von Neumann for the first time to ask for recommendations on solution techniques to use in connection with linear programming. Dantzig recalls that meeting as follows:[75]

I remember trying to describe to von Neumann, as I would an ordinary mortal, the Air Force problem. I began with the formulation of the linear programming model in terms of activities and times, etc. Von Neumann did something which I believe was uncharacteristic of him. "Get to the point," he said impatiently. Having at times a somewhat low kindling-point, I said to myself "O.K., if he wants a quicky, then that's what he'll get." In under one minute I slapped the geometric and the algebraic version of the problem on the blackboard. Von Neumann stood up and said "Oh that!" Then for the next hour and a half, he proceeded to give me a lecture on the mathematical theory of linear programs.

At one point seeing me sitting there with my eyes popping and my mouth open (after all I had searched the literature and found nothing), von Neumann said: "I don't want you to think I am pulling all of this out of my sleeve on the spur of the moment like a magician. I have just recently completed a book with Oscar [*sic*] Morgenstern on the Theory of Games. What I am doing is conjecturing that the two problems are equivalent. The theory that I am outlining for your problem is an analogue to the one we have developed for games." Thus I learned about Farkas' Lemma, and about duality for the first time.

In this way von Neumann discovered the duality theorem that was central to linear programming and suggested the equivalence between game theory and linear programming.[76] A correspondence ensued between them about numerical methods for linear programming, especially about their application to two problems for the air force.[77] One was the minimum cost diet problem in which the air force wanted to find the minimum cost of providing minimum daily requirements of nine nutrients from a selection of seventy-seven foods. The calculations were carried out by five human computers working at desk calculators for 21 days.[78] The second problem, for the air force's Supply Computation Project, concerned the total cost of procurement and repair for each of several classes of equipment. Two calculations of this involved 40,000 and 300,000 punched cards and a total of 800,000 multiplications. Von Neumann estimated that the calculations could be run on the ENIAC in 2 and 12.5 days, respectively.[79]

The computer made feasible the large number of calculations required to solve practical linear programming problems. Von Neumann contributed in this area by providing numerical methods for the computer. The most important one, given in a 1954 paper, is a method for solving optimal linear programming problems that allows one to determine in advance the maximum length of the computation and the maximum size of the numbers that can occur in the course of the computation.[80] At the end of the paper von Neumann compared his method to the simplex method:

> In evaluating the method it ought to be compared with G. Dantzig's "Simplex Method." In the latter method the a priori guarantees for length of calculation and size of numbers are considerably less favorable than ours, but the available practical experience with the simplex method indicates that its actual performance—at least under the conditions under which it has been so far tested—is much better than the limits that can be guaranteed. Limited comparisons of our method with the "simplex method" again indicate that the latter converges faster, but there is reason to believe that our method can be accelerated by various tricks which amount to smoothing the iterative recursive sequence which is involved, and making this recursion dependent on several predecessors. The description of the method is offered here as a first step in this direction, i.e. in order to illustrate the new method, and to furnish a basis for the possible improvements referred to above.

Conclusions

By the 1930s numerical analysis was in a state of decline. It was regarded as an unfashionable subject in the mathematical community and was not attracting much top mathematical talent. The introduction of the computer changed this situation.[81] In the decade immediately following the war, the change can be seen in the increase in the numbers of publications and practitioners, the emergence of specialty professional societies and journals, such as the Society for Industrial and Applied Mathematics (SIAM) and *SIAM Review*, and the origin of related disciplines, including operations research and management science.

The computer opened many new avenues of research in numerical analysis. Some were of a quantitative nature increasing the scale of problems.[82] For the first time mathematical scientists could examine larger systems of linear equations that commonly arise in mathematics or physics. Now there was an engine to drive these calculations, and the numerical analysts had to find efficient and reliable algorithms for the computer to follow. Other changes were qualitative. For the first time there existed practical means to solve PDEs, study nonlinear phenomena, and investigate stochastic models of complex stochastic and deterministic phenomena.

Computers made numerical analysts reconsider the classical methods of their subject. Truncation errors became less significant once there was a machine able to handle more lengthy calculations, but round-off errors and the statistical properties of random numbers took on greater significance. Mathematicians had to reconsider the methods they were using, even for classical problems such as inverting a matrix or finding its eigenvalues, to see how well they could be handled by a computer. Could the methods be fully automated? Did they have numerical stability? What was the relationship between the number of iterations required and the precision that must be carried through the calculation? How many initial data and how many intermediate results must be retained in storage? These and other questions were addressed for the first time.

Von Neumann was aware as early as 1944 that new numerical methods had to be found to fashion the computer into an effective scientific tool. He also understood that the computer, with its different "inner economy" from past calculating devices, would stimulate a thorough reexamination of the discipline of numerical analysis. He began this examination at the same time he began the design of the IAS computer. This early start makes him one of the first scientists to become interested in the new computer-oriented numerical analysis. Some of his results have endured over the past forty years; the methods of Monte Carlo and linear programming are excellent examples. In other cases—such as methods for numerically solving PDEs and large matrices, methods for accommodating shocks, and numerical stability analysis—his work has been largely superseded by later work. But even here his work took the first steps toward a solution, brought into focus the importance of the problems, and suggested an approach.

Under von Neumann's direction, the Electronic Computer Project became an important center for the study of computer-oriented numerical analysis. Herman Goldstine has identified almost fifty people active in the field who benefited from their contact with the project.[83] The institute was by no means the only active center in numerical analysis in the decade following the war. There was major activity in the United States at the National Bureau of Standards in Washington, the Institute for Numerical Analysis at UCLA, and New York University; in Britain at the National Physical Laboratory; and elsewhere in Europe.[84] Von Neumann was a regular visitor and contributor at many of these research centers until his work for the Atomic Energy Commission made him too busy. Almost certainly his elevated status in the mathematical and government communities helped to legitimize this revitalized discipline and improve the flow of research funds.[85] For all of these reasons, von Neumann should be regarded as an originator of modern numerical analysis.

6

The Origins of Numerical Meteorology

The Electronic Computer Project was supported by the IAS on the basis of the belief that the computer would be an important tool of scientific research. At the time the project was conceived, however, there was little basis for this belief. Although electromechanical calculators had made a few practical and theoretical scientific calculations during the war years, none of the much faster electronic calculators, which were expected to yield the real advances, was yet in operation.[1] In order to test this belief, von Neumann chose to study a problem of both theoretical and practical importance: the science of meteorology and its application to weather prediction. He regarded this study as a crucial test because the hydrodynamics of the atmosphere is a prime example of those complex, nonlinear phenomena previously inaccessible to mathematical investigation. The institute's meteorology project was extremely successful at demonstrating the value of the computer to science. It advanced meteorological theory, prepared the first practical numerical method for weather forecasting, and helped to establish the infrastructure for producing daily numerical forecasts.

Early Numerical Meteorology

The subjective method of weather forecasting that prevailed before World War II was more art than science. Vast amounts of data were collected each day from a geographically distributed network of observation stations and recorded on geographical maps. Meteorologists would then manually sketch in isobars and isotherms and identify air masses and frontal systems on the maps. Past weather maps of similar meteorological profile, culled from extensive map libraries, sometimes served as models. Predictions were based on personal experience, a few elementary statistical relationships, and qualitative physical arguments rather than on some general theory of weather phenomena. Forecasters applied different rules of thumb according to their judgment of the prevailing parameters. It comes as no surprise that subjective forecasting was not self-improving or that the quality of forecasts depended primarily on the forecaster's native abilities.[2]

The leading practitioners of the 1940s understood the limitations of the subjective approach, evident from H. G. Houghton's presidential address to the American Meteorological Society in December 1946. It is equally clear that the community did not envision any promising opportunities for change.

Our physical understanding of atmospheric processes is so limited that it is of little utility to weather forecasting. Consequently a forecast is made by the extrapolation of the principal pressure systems in accordance with past trends, as evidenced by previous maps and the pressure-tendency field. To this is added the experience factor which is the fusion of a large number of past situations into a general concept of what constitutes a reasonable pressure configuration under the given conditions. This is largely a subjective process as indicated by the frequent divergences of opinion among equally competent forecasters. Numerous attempts have been made to introduce objective methods based on some theoretical grounds, but it appears that none of these is as effective as the subjective methods practiced by an experienced forecaster. In view of this it is not surprising that many forecasters with little or no formal training are able to compete on equal, or better, terms with the products of our best university training. Such comparisons as have been made indicate that there has been no significant increase in the accuracy of short-range forecasts in the past 30 or 40 years. Such comparisons must be based on forecasts of temperature or precipitation since airway and upper-level forecasting are modern developments. However, I believe that it is mere quibbling to argue the point as to whether forecasting accuracy has improved. The number of elements forecast, the frequency of forecasts, and the types of forecasts have all increased greatly, but it is clear that there has been no corresponding increase in accuracy.

There appears to be no immediate prospect of an objective method of forecasting based entirely on sound physical principles. . . .

Since we cannot foresee an early solution to the forecasting problem on a purely physical basis, it is reasonable and proper for us to attempt to improve present methods. It must always be remembered that such efforts are in the nature of palliatives rather than cures.[3]

Less than ten years after Houghton's address, meteorologists were preparing forecasts every day using a new method of numerical prediction based largely on "sound physical principles." The numerical approach adopted focuses on the laws of hydrodynamics and thermodynamics that govern the behavior of the gaseous atmosphere. By solving these equations, one can predict the dynamic changes in the atmosphere over space and time and apply the information effectively to weather prediction.

Improvements were required in four areas before the numerical approach could become practical. In order to simplify the equations to a degree that their solution was practical, theorists needed to sort through the many hydrodynamic and thermodynamic factors to identify those having the greatest impact on the weather. Even the most simplified set of equations was not amenable to analytic solution, so numerical and graphical techniques were introduced to provide an approximate solution. To supply the initial and boundary conditions for the equations, vast amounts of observational data needed to be systematically collected, communicated, and adjusted to common units. Finally, and perhaps most critically, fast and automatic computing engines were required to carry out the millions of arithmetic operations required in a single daily forecast.

Quantitative physical explanations of atmospheric phenomena were first propounded in the late seventeenth and early eighteenth centuries. Halley gave a partial explanation of the northeast trade-winds using Newton's Second Law of Motion; and Daniel Bernoulli, Laplace, and others investigated the physical basis for the relationship between atmospheric pressure and height above sea level. By the middle of the nineteenth century, all of the hydrodynamic and thermodynamic laws that govern the atmosphere were individually known and widely understood to apply generally to physical phenomena, but no attempt had been made to consolidate these laws and apply them coherently to the large-scale behavior of the atmosphere. The governing laws can be deduced straightforwardly from several basic laws of physics: the Newtonian laws of motion, the Boyle-Charles equation of state, and the First Law of Thermodynamics. The resultant equations can be stated in various ways; all involve a complex, coupled set of nonlinear partial differential equations.

One formulation of the hydrodynamic and thermodynamic laws of the atmosphere, given implicitly by the Norwegian meteorologist Vilhelm Bjerknes in 1904 and stated here in modern mathematical terminology, is the following:[4]

$$\frac{\partial u}{\partial t} = -u\frac{\partial u}{\partial x} - v\frac{\partial u}{\partial y} - w\frac{\partial u}{\partial z} + fv - \frac{1}{\rho}\frac{\partial p}{\partial x}$$

$$\frac{\partial v}{\partial t} = -u\frac{\partial v}{\partial x} - v\frac{\partial v}{\partial y} - w\frac{\partial v}{\partial z} - fu - \frac{1}{\rho}\frac{\partial p}{\partial y}$$

$$\frac{\partial w}{\partial t} = -u\frac{\partial w}{\partial x} - v\frac{\partial w}{\partial y} - w\frac{\partial w}{\partial z} - g - \frac{1}{\rho}\frac{\partial p}{\partial z}$$

$$\frac{\partial \rho}{\partial t} = -u\frac{\partial \rho}{\partial x} - v\frac{\partial \rho}{\partial y} - w\frac{\partial \rho}{\partial z} - \left(\frac{\partial u}{\partial x} + \frac{\partial v}{\partial y} + \frac{\partial w}{\partial z}\right)$$

$$\frac{\partial p}{\partial t} = -u\frac{\partial p}{\partial x} - v\frac{\partial p}{\partial y} - w\frac{\partial p}{\partial z} - \frac{C_p}{C_v}p\left(\frac{\partial u}{\partial x} + \frac{\partial v}{\partial y} + \frac{\partial w}{\partial z}\right)$$

$$\frac{\partial T}{\partial t} = -u\frac{\partial T}{\partial x} - v\frac{\partial T}{\partial y} - w\frac{\partial T}{\partial z} - \frac{RT}{C_v}\left(\frac{\partial u}{\partial x} + \frac{\partial v}{\partial y} + \frac{\partial w}{\partial z}\right)$$

C_p is the coefficient of heat at constant pressure; u, v, and w are the components of the fluid velocity in the x, y, and z directions; ρ is the local mass density of fluid; p is the ambient pressure; f is the Coriolis parameter accounting for the earth's rotation; g is the gravitational acceleration; C_v is the specific heat at constant volume; R is the gas constant related to Avogadro's number; and T is the absolute temperature.

In the second half of the nineteenth century many leading physical scientists attempted mechanical explanations of the earth's atmosphere. Kelvin and Rayleigh applied linear perturbation methods from astronomy to the study of wave motions in the atmosphere. Helmholtz conducted research on the circulation of incompressible media. Oberbeck published on atmospheric currents, and Bezold investigated thermodynamic considerations. Other investigations were conducted by Ferrel, Hagen, Hertz, and Margules.[5]

The program of numerical meteorology was first publicly stated in 1904 by the Norwegian scientist Vilhelm Bjerknes. His work followed closely on the investigations of the dynamical aspects of the atmosphere by his teacher, Heinrich Hertz, and Hertz's mentor, H. von Helmholtz. Bjerknes was also influenced by his father, C. A. Bjerknes, a mathematical physicist who specialized in hydrodynamics. In 1858 Helmholtz had published an important paper stating his laws of the conservation of vortex motion of incompressible media. In 1897 Vilhelm Bjerknes extended these laws to circulation in compressible media, such as air. At the urging of his friend Nils Ekholm of the Swedish weather service, Bjerknes embarked on a systematic study of the application of hydrodynamics to the atmosphere.[6]

Bjerknes believed that observational meteorology had progressed as far as it could without improvements in data collection, and he sought to build up a new theory-based meteorological science by applying the laws of physics to the atmosphere.[7] He states his program at the beginning of his well-known paper of 1904:

If it is true, as every scientist believes, that subsequent atmospheric states develop from the preceding ones according to physical law, then it is apparent that the necessary and sufficient conditions for the rational solution of forecasting problems are the following:

1. A sufficiently accurate knowledge of the state of the atmosphere at the initial time.

2. A sufficiently accurate knowledge of the laws according to which one state of the atmosphere develops from another.[8]

Nine years later, at his dedication lecture for the new chair of geophysics at Leipzig, Bjerknes was still calling for the application of "the equations of theoretical physics not to ideal cases only, but to the actual existing atmospheric conditions as they are revealed by modern observations." He likened the "accurate pre-calculation" problem for meteorology to the one that had been solved centuries earlier for astronomy.[9] He recognized that the most serious impediment was the length of the calculations, which might (under even the most favorable conditions) require three months to calculate three hours of weather. Of course, the length of the calculations was immaterial if he was interested only in establishing a science of meteorology, but he did hold out hope that his approach would eventually lead to a practical method of prediction.[10]

Unfavorable economic conditions in Leipzig during World War I caused Bjerknes to accept a post in Bergen, Norway, where he established an influential school of meteorology that made many contributions. They were the first to differentiate meteorological phenomena explicitly from incidental atmospheric phenomena, such as the Aurora Borealis. They also introduced the key concepts of baroclinic and barotropic and developed the theory of polar fronts. Their approach was to reduce the complex phenomena of the atmosphere to the action of a collection of weather cells at whose boundaries (fronts) weather changes occur. Despite their many contributions to meteorological theory, they had little impact on practical weather prediction, except perhaps on forecasting precipitation.

The main impediment to a practical theory of prediction was the absence of a rapid method of calculation. Vilhelm Bjerknes employed differential geometry and graphical methods instead of direct arithmetic calculation to analyze the data assembled in Bergen from the dense network of observation stations he had convinced the Norwegian government to establish. There was no known analytic method for solving the physical equations, and numerical methods were employed only minimally. Bjerknes described his graphical methods and the importance he attached to visual solutions:

An exact analytical integration of the system of equations is out of the question. Even the computation of the motion of three mass-points, which influence each other according to a law as simple as that of Newton, exceeds the limits of today's mathematical analysis. Naturally there is no hope of understanding the motion of all the points of the atmosphere, which have far more complicated reactions to one another. Moreover, the exact analytical solution, even if we could write it down, would not give the result which we need. For to be practical and useful the solution has to have a readily seen, synoptic form and has to omit the countless details which would appear in every exact solution. The prognosis need only deal, therefore, with averages over sizeable distances and time intervals; for example, from degree of meridian and from hour to hour, but not from millimeter to millimeter or from second to second.

We therefore forgo any thought of analytical methods of integration and, instead, pose the problem of weather prediction in the following practical form:

Based upon the observations that have been made, the initial state of the atmosphere is represented by a number of charts which give the distribution of the seven variables from level to level in the atmosphere. With these charts as the starting point, new charts of a similar kind are to be drawn which represent the new state from hour to hour.

For the solution of the problem in this form, graphical or mixed graphical and numerical methods are appropriate, which methods must be derived either from the partial differential equations or from the dynamical-physical principles which are the basis of these equations. There is no reason to doubt, beforehand, that these methods can be worked out. Everything will depend upon whether we can successfully divide, in a suitable way, a total problem of insurmountable difficulty into a number of partial problems of which none is too difficult.[11]

Although Bjerknes formulated the numerical program, the numerical methods of ultimate significance were introduced by a

British meteorologist, Lewis Fry Richardson. After receiving a broad scientific education at Durham College of Science and King's College, Cambridge, Richardson held various government and industrial scientific positions until his appointment in 1913 as superintendent of the Eskdalemuir Observatory, a geomagnetic and meteorological measurement station in Scotland. As part of his earlier industrial research, he had developed a method of finite differences for the approximate solution of differential equations. The opportunity to explore the application of this method to meteorology was one reason he accepted the position at Eskdalemuir. There, and during the World War I between his trips to the front as an ambulance driver, he refined and applied a numerical method for computing the weather. His results were lost during the war but discovered afterward under a coal heap and published in 1922 as *Weather Prediction by Numerical Process.*

In arguing for his program, Richardson drew an analogy between astronomy and meteorology similar to that drawn by Vilhelm Bjerknes. Richardson opened his book with the following argument:

The forecast is based on the supposition that what the atmosphere did then [at a previous time when the weather conditions were similar], it will do again now. . . . The past history of the atmosphere is used, so to speak, as a full-scale model of its present self.

But—one may reflect—the *Nautical Almanac,* that marvel of accurate forecasting is not based on the principle that astronomical history repeats itself in the aggregate. It would be safe to say that a particular disposition of stars, planets, and satellites never occurs twice. Why then should we expect a present weather map to be exactly represented in a catalogue of past weather? . . . This [fact that forecasts hold good for no more than three days at a time] is sufficient reason for presenting in this book, a scheme of weather prediction, which resembles the process by which the *Nautical Almanac* is produced, in so far as it is founded upon the differential equations, and not upon the partial recurrence of phenomena in their ensemble.[12]

Richardson was sympathetic to Bjerknes's program. He cited Bjerknes's work in his publications and is known to have visited him in Bergen in 1920.[13] Richardson adopted Bjerknes's use of differential equations but not his graphical methods: "But whereas Prof. Bjerknes mostly employs graphs, I have thought it better to proceed by numerical tables. The reason for this is that a previous comparison [Richardson 1908, 1908a, 1910, 1911] of the two methods, in dealing with differential equations, had convinced me that the arithmetical procedure is the more exact and the more powerful in coping with otherwise awkward equations."[14]

Richardson's procedure works in roughly the following way. The equations governing the atmosphere are of such a nature that the time derivatives can be expressed in terms of the space derivatives. Observational data on all independent variables in the equations are collected for an initial time t at each point of a finite grid distributed evenly across a region of the atmosphere. The method of finite differences is then used to approximate the space derivatives, and the time derivatives are calculated from them. Using the initial values and these calculated time derivatives, the value of each variable at each space point is extrapolated for a short period of time later, $t+\Delta t$.[15] This procedure is repeated, using the extrapolated data as the new initial data, to calculate the values at $t+2 \quad \Delta t$, and it can be repeated again as many times as necessary to stretch the predictions to the desired time interval.

With six weeks of intensive labor, Richardson completed the calculations for a "forecast" of a 6-hour period on 20 May 1910 for central Europe. He chose this particular date because it had been an International Balloon Day, and there were unusually complete data available for use as initial condition values and as a check against the calculated values. The numerical "forecast" was a disappointment; it predicted pressure changes (145 millibars in 6 hours) far in excess of what had actually occurred.[16]

Richardson's book, which reported these calculations, received wide attention. It was reviewed in leading American, British, and German journals of general science as well as in specialty journals of meteorology.[17] The reviews were mixed, some praising the promise of his program and others disparaging the failure of his calculation.

Richardson recognized the impracticality of predicting the weather by his method. He estimated that 64,000 human computers would be needed to calculate the entire globe's weather at its rate of occurrence.[18] This impracticality dampened the initial enthusiasm aroused by his book.[19]

While impressive theoretical gains were made by the Bergen School and others and data collection in the upper atmosphere improved rapidly with the introduction of radiosondes and aircraft observations, little attention was paid to numerical weather prediction in the 1920s and 1930s. Some meteorologists even argued that it was impossible.[20] The attitude in the early 1940s toward it is aptly summed up in an anecdote told by Joseph Smagorinsky, one of the leading numerical meteorologists after World War II:

One of the professors at MIT, a man named Bernhard [Haurwitz], was a very distinguished dynamic meteorologist, [a] theoretician. I remember asking him one day [in 1943 or 1944] if anyone had ever tried this [numerical weather prediction]. You see, by this time I knew it wasn't done. But I asked him one day, casually, whether anybody had tried it. And he said, "Well, there's some obscure attempt to do this by a man by the name of Richardson after World War I, in fact it was during World War I, but it wasn't published until after the War." But he said, "That ended in [a] fiasco . . . and convinced me not to try it myself."[21]

The Origins of the Numerical Meteorology Project

World War II created what one leading meteorologist has called a "near discontinuous change" in meteorological practice.[22] Forecasts were important military information, critical for planning military operations and important to balloonists, aviators, and artillery units.[23] Governments had learned the value of meteorologists in World War I and were quick to organize them for action at the beginning of World War II.[24] The U.S. government established training centers at the University of Chicago, the University of California at Los Angeles, California Institute of Technology, Massachusetts Institute of Technology, and New York University, which produced approximately 5000 weather officers during the war.[25] By the end of the war almost every developed country had made some effort toward establishing a national weather bureau. The observations from these bureaus, in addition to those available through the increased use of radio sounding balloons and from ship and aircraft over the Atlantic, substantially enlarged the observational network for the Northern Hemisphere. Of particular importance was the collection of the first adequate data on the upper atmosphere. It enabled researchers to determine that certain physical factors are relatively insignificant in the gross determination of weather phenomena, which in turn allowed them to construct the simpler models of the atmosphere necessary for numerical weather prediction.[26]

Several technological by-products of the war helped to advance meteorology in the postwar period. Rockets and jet aircraft were used extensively to collect data on the upper atmosphere. Radar was used to study clouds, precipitation, cyclones, and fronts.[27]

Improved methods of communication expedited the reporting of meteorological data, and better plotters improved their recording in organized form. Perhaps the most important development was the computer, which through its electronic switching increased computation speed by a factor of 10,000 over the use of desk calculators and through its stored-program capability "broke the human bottleneck of writing out the entire sequence of instructions in advance."[28]

Von Neumann found the problem of numerical weather prediction appealing. During the war he was aware of the military need for improved forecasts.[29] The problem also had a scientific attraction. The physics of the atmosphere was one of those complex, nonlinear problems that he regarded as a particularly fertile area for mathematical research.[30] The computer had the potential to undertake the vast number of computations required to solve the weather problem numerically, and he singled this problem out as the crucial test of the scientific utility of the new computer technology.

How von Neumann became interested in the weather problem is not entirely clear, but a major influence was certainly Carl-Gustav Rossby, one of the leading meteorologists of the period. In the summer of 1942 von Neumann attended a session at the University of Chicago on operations research methods for underwater mine warfare in connection with his work for the Navy Bureau of Ordnance. At this meeting he met Rossby, who introduced him to the weather problem.[31] Rossby informed him about Richardson's work and in early 1946 supplied him with some scientific articles on meteorology, which he read with great interest.[32]

Von Neumann, however, gave credit to Vladimir Zworykin, an electrical engineer at RCA who had made important contributions to the early development of television, for the direct stimulus to use the computer to predict the weather.[33] At a 12 November 1945 meeting to discuss the electrostatic memory device that RCA was planning to build for the IAS computer project, von Neumann learned that Zworykin and others at RCA were already working to develop meteorological instrumentation.[34] Jule Charney has suggested the importance of this contact to the formation of von Neumann's plans: "I remember in late 1945 or early 1946 reading a rather fantastic proposal of Zworkin's for the construction of an analogue computer which would scan two-dimensional distributions of weather data projected on a screen and then compute the future weather by analogue techniques; by varying the input continuously and observing the output one could determine how most efficiently to modify the input to produce a given output. Johnny was in contact with Zworykin at that time, and perhaps his interest in weather computation and weather modification began then."[35]

When F. W. Reichelderfer, chief of the Weather Bureau, learned of RCA's involvement in the computer project and the potential application of the computer to meteorology, he invited Zworykin to visit him in Washington.[36] At Zworykin's suggestion, von Neumann joined the meeting, which was held in Washington on 9 January 1946.[37] The following day an article appeared in the *New York Times* on the planned collaboration of the IAS and RCA on an electronic calculating device and its potential application to weather forecasting and weather modification.[38] The article received wide attention in the meteorological community.[39]

Following a meeting in Princeton in March or early April with von Neumann, Zworykin, and other RCA researchers, Rossby wrote to Reichelderfer that von Neumann was interested in basic meteorological problems but not in many of the practical questions of operational forecasting and that von Neumann was ready to devote up to a quarter of his time to these problems.[40] Rossby made special note of von Neumann's "extremely interesting comments" on the use of the computer as an experimental tool in discovering analytic solutions to the hydrodynamic equations, recommended that von Neumann be encouraged to pursue meteorological research, and indicated that this plan would require finding qualified meteorologists to work with him. Rossby had in mind as von Neumann's collaborators scientists versed in descriptive physical meteorology "with a thorough synoptic knowledge of such thermodynamic factors as ice, clouds and radiation" but also with a "genuine appreciation for the theoretical approach." Most scientists who met these qualifications were already committed to other positions, but Rossby suggested half a dozen names and volunteered to release one of his own staff members, Victor Starr, to the project for a short time as a gesture of goodwill. Rossby observed that the ENIAC could conveniently solve only problems with at most two independent variables but that the general weather problem had four independent variables, so he concluded that a new computer would be required for the general weather problem.[41] Still he believed that the ENIAC could be used profitably in the study of the general circulation problem and other problems of day-to-day forecasting, and he suggested that the Weather Bureau and the armed forces weather services assign personnel to the ENIAC operation. Finally he recommended that an agreement be negotiated between the IAS and some responsible government agency in Washington, such as the Navy's Office of Research and Inventions, to conduct this research.

Within the next week Rossby had conversations with Harry Wexler, research director at the Weather Bureau, and Commander Rex, head of the Office of Research and Inventions. Once their support had been secured, Rossby wrote to von Neumann to encourage him to submit a proposal for a research project at the IAS supported by navy funds.[42] The objective was "to examine the foundation of our ideas concerning the general circulation of the atmosphere, with the intention of determining the steady state of the general circulation of the atmosphere and its response to arbitrarily applied external influences" with the hope that it "might throw some light on the nature of climatic fluctuations."[43]

Rossby suggested a budget of approximately $46,000 per year to cover salaries of five professionals and two clerk-computers, general expenses, travel, and overhead.[44] He argued that success would depend on the presence of a strong senior professional but that none of the present institute staff was qualified for this position and that the only suitable candidate was Wexler (who was available to come to the institute on loan from the Weather Bureau). Rossby recommended that Chaim Pekeris and Paul Queney be hired for two of the other professional positions.

Just prior to submitting a formal proposal as Rossby suggested, von Neumann wrote to Lewis Strauss to ask for his advice on the best approach to the navy for support. The letter summarizes von Neumann's hopes for the meteorology project and shows Rossby's influence on his thinking:

One of the important applications of extremely high speed computing, as we intend to achieve it, lies in the field of dynamic meteorology. It would certainly put the theories of the total planetary atmospheric circulation, of the polar front and of its instabilities, and of the temperate as well as the tropical cyclones, on an entirely new basis. With certain new observations—which, however, are perfectly feasible—it would open up entirely new possibilities for studies of the stratospheric circulation and of atmospheric turbulence, and finally it would make weather prediction a week or more ahead practical. (If such a program were carried out successfully it would also be the first step toward weather control—but I would prefer not to go into that at this time.) These views are shared by some of the best experts in the field, e.g. by Professor C. G. A. Rossby, who is the Director of the Meteorological Institute of the University of Chicago and one of the foremost dynamical meteorologists in the world. Rossby and I have surveyed this field in some detail together, and we are convinced that the entire program indicated above is practical. We feel, however, that the whole body of meteorological theory has to be reviewed and reformulated with these new computational possibilities in mind—since all past and present theory is thoroughly conditioned by the old computing methods, which are about 100,000 times slower than what we propose to make possible. Also certain additional observations will be needed, which are not particularly difficult, but should be carefully planned. He agreed, therefore, that it would be desirable to bring 4 or 5 good, younger theoretical meteorologists to Princeton, who could study these questions in continuous consultation with me and in periodical consultations with an advisory board of some of the leading theoretical meteorologists of the country and certain interested physicists, etc. Rossby and I could bring these two groups together. . . . Rossby and I have formulated the essentials of such a proposal while I was in Chicago, and I will submit the entire matter to Dr. Aydelotte in Princeton.[45]

Von Neumann met with Rex and a navy contracts officer, as Rossby suggested, and a formal proposal was submitted on 8 May 1946.[46] The proposal followed the general lines of Rossby's recommendations: "The objective of the project is an investigation of the theory of dynamic meteorology in order to make it accessible to high speed, electronic, digital, automatic computing, of a type which is beginning to be available, and which is likely to be increasingly available in the future. It is also expected that these investigations will give indications as to what further observations are necessary—both of the laboratory and of the field type—in order to make theoretical work, that is supported by such high speed computing, more fully effective."

Considerable attention was given to the current state of automatic computation. The proposal argued that it was "utterly hopeless" to resolve the equations of the atmosphere analytically and that "it has been recognized for a long time that numerical computational methods are the only ones which offer any prospect of really informative and specific results." An analysis of the time expended in multiplication, logical transfer, and storage led to the conclusion that existing calculation devices (IBM multipliers, relay calculators, and the ENIAC) would be from ten to a thousand times faster at meteorological calculations than human computers working at fast desk calculators and that accelerations by factors of 10,000 to 100,000 over desk calculators would be possible within two to three years on the digital computers under development at the University of Pennsylvania (EDVAC), MIT (Whirlwind), and the IAS. Because "the efforts in meteorological theory were in the main limited by what was practical in actual computing," great promise was seen for advances in meteorology in the near future.

The proposal attempted to make a virtue out of the anticipated two- to three-year lag before these powerful computers would become available. In the meantime, five or six younger meteorologists were to be assembled in Princeton to work with the staff who were designing and constructing the computer. In the first six months the meteorologists were to study the main physical and observational uncertainties in meteorological theory and assist with the investigation of alternative mathematical formulations of the weather problem and their analytical structure.[47] Over the following few months an outside board of meteorologists and physicists would be assembled to evaluate the relative merits of the alternative approaches identified in the first six months and determine the relative experimental and observational difficulties of these approaches.[48] The Princeton group would then devote the last six months of 1947 to working out the analytical details of two or three definite problems. The approximation and computing techniques they required were to be developed in the first part of 1948, and the computations were to be carried out on the IAS computer once it reached completion in late 1948 or 1949. If computing were needed in the interim, they expected to use the ENIAC, at least on simple models. The proposal was accepted by the navy, and funding began in July 1946.[49]

The timetable proved to be too ambitious; not until at least 1953 were all of these goals met. The major delays resulted from problems in recruiting a full and adequately trained staff of meteorologists, difficulties in developing good theories and computing methods, and the slow completion of the IAS computer.

The personnel question arose first. Few meteorologists had both a thorough grounding in the theoretical aspects of dynamic meteorology and a facility for the numerical approach, and even fewer had the qualifications and experience to head the project. Harry Wexler of the Weather Bureau, Paul Queney of the University of Algiers, R. B. Montgomery of Woods Hole Oceanographic Institution, and Bernhard Haurwitz of New York University were all offered the senior position; only Queney was available for more than part-time consultation.[50]

The difficulty created by a lack of available qualified personnel was compounded by a serious shortage of housing and office space in Princeton. The space problem appears to have contributed to Wexler's decision not to join the project full time.[51] Most of von Neumann's effort on the Electronic Computer Project was allocated to the design and construction of the computer, and he was concerned that he would not be able to provide the required administrative attention to keep focus in a large group of meteorologists. Consequently the plan for employing a large staff of meteorologists was revised in favor of a smaller staff of theoretically oriented meteorologists who would work in close consultation with von Neumann. The first meteorologist to join the project was Albert Cahn, Jr., a protégé of Rossby from the University of Chicago. In December 1946, after only a few months, he was replaced by Lieutenant Philip Thompson of the air force. Thompson had received his undergraduate training in meteorology at the University of Chicago and was assigned to the meteorological Divergence Project at UCLA at the time he convinced his commanding officer to transfer him to Princeton.[52] Others associated part time with the project included Chaim Pekeris of Columbia University, Hans Panofsky of New York University, and Captain Gilbert Hunt, an advanced graduate student in mathematics at Princeton University with wartime training in meteorology.[53]

None of these early members of the meteorological group had both the time and the right mix of administrative, meteorological, and mathematical training needed to push the project forward as rapidly as von Neumann desired.[54] Queney soon left for France and Pekeris for Israel. After leaving the service, Hunt turned his attention to mathematics, and he soon accepted a faculty position at Cornell. Thompson, who subsequently enjoyed a distinguished career in numerical meteorology, has characterized himself as "a very young man and rather untutored at this time." He was teaching himself the fundamentals of numerical analysis, with assistance from Goldstine and von Neumann, while continuing to add to his knowledge of the dynamical processes of the atmosphere. He might have developed into the leader von Neumann sought, but he was called away in 1948 to direct the new Atmospheric Analysis Laboratory at the Air Force Cambridge Research Laboratories.[55]

The situation stabilized, and rapid progress ensued, following Jule Charney's appointment in 1948. Charney was the project's principal meteorologist until 1956, when he moved to MIT and the meteorological research ended. He completed his doctoral work in meteorology in 1946 under J. Holmboe at UCLA, writing a dissertation on baroclinic instability that drew heavily on Rossby's work. Charney's office at UCLA was next door to Thompson's, and they frequently discussed the problem of numerical meteorology, including the reasons for Richardson's failure.[56] In 1946 Charney had received a National Research Council Fellowship to study with Professor Solberg at the University of Oslo, but Solberg planned to be on leave that year. Instead Charney accepted Rossby's invitation to spend the year as a research associate in the Department of Meteorology at the University of Chicago. While Charney was at Chicago, Rossby arranged for him to attend a conference in Princeton, which von Neumann organized for the meteorological community in August 1946. Rossby recommended to von Neumann that he offer Charney an appointment at the IAS but nothing came of it at this time, perhaps because of Charney's NRC fellowship.[57] Charney came into contact with von Neumann at least once more before leaving for Oslo for the 1947–1948 academic year, when he visited Thompson in Princeton in late March 1947.[58] As a result of his experiences in Oslo, Charney was eager to be associated with the IAS project: "You may be wondering at all this solicitude for the project.... The main reason is that I have been brooding about the probl[em] of numerical computation ever since coming to Norway, and I think I have come up with an answer to at least one of its most vexing aspects, namely, the practical impossibility of determining the initial vertical velocity and acceleration fields with the necessary accuracy."[59]

Charney asked Thompson to put in a good word for him with von Neumann. He also pointed out that Oslo had two bright young meteorologists, Arnt Eliassen and Ragnar Fjortoft, who were interested in the numerical problem and that Eliassen had a sabbatical coming for the 1948–1949 academic year, which he could spend at the institute. Thompson successfully interceded, and Charney and Eliassen joined the project in the summer of 1948.[60]

Norman Phillips, the other principal meteorologist, was with the project from 1951 until 1956, when he left for MIT with Charney. The remainder of the staff consisted of some forty meteorologists who visited the project for periods ranging from a few weeks to two years.[61]

The Barotropic Model

One of von Neumann's first actions was to call a conference in Princeton for 29–30 August 1946 to inform the meteorological community about the electronic computer being built at the institute and seek their advice and support in designing meteorological research for its use.[62] Eighteen scientists attended, including leading American dynamical meteorologists and several knowledgeable scientists with access to government research funds. The group heard survey lectures on high-speed numerical computing (von Neumann), the state of meteorological research (Rossby), and the Richardson-Elliott approach to numerical forecasting (Cahn), as well as on research needs in dynamic meteorology (B. Haurwitz), synoptic meteorology (H. Willett), and operational forecasting (J. Namias)[63]. A general discussion of the most urgent problems followed. In effect, the conference set an initial research agenda for the Meteorological Project. Charney recalled:

that the response from the established figures was interested but less than enthusiastic. C.-G. Rossby perhaps best voiced their feelings by stating that the mathematical problem was not yet defined: there were more unknowns than equations, for we had not yet been able to express the components of the Reynolds stress tensor in terms of mean flow variables. Citing L. F. Richardson's gallant but unsuccessful attempt to solve the hydrodynamical equations of the atmosphere by hand calculation, Rossby said that computation could not be successful before observation, experiment and analysis had led to a better understanding of fundamental atmospheric processes, in particular of atmospheric turbulence.
His caution had the positive effect of convincing von Neumann of the need for physical as well as mathematical analysis.[64]

The consensus was that six areas merited study: numerical methods for computer solution of important varieties of differential equations (such as the Heisenberg-Lin equation), linearized stability questions that arise under typical meteorological flow conditions, the significance of the stationary and zonally symmetric general circulation of the atmosphere, tropical hurricane theory, diagnostic use of the computer to determine forces not accounted for by the equations (for example, eddy viscosity), and forecasting by direct numerical investigation. Each of these problems was assigned to members of the project or consultants selected from those in attendance.

The first two years of the project, until Charney's arrival in the summer of 1948, can be viewed as a preparatory stage.[65] Uncertain of the dimensions of the numerical meteorology problem or the most promising areas to pursue, the Meteorology Group conducted a parallel series of exploratory investigations.[66]

Working in close contact with a committee from the Weather Bureau and the armed services, Queney investigated perturbations of the atmosphere. His approach was to linearize artificially the inherently nonlinear interactive phenomena of atmospheric change using an established method from astronomy. He developed a theory of perturbation waves of atmospheric flows that took into consideration temperature, vertical stability, Coriolis force, and inhomogeneities in the flow velocity field. He applied the theory to a classification of the waves and their stability properties.

Pekeris undertook a study of instability theory of turbulence in parallel flows. He investigated the stability of the Poiseuille flow (laminar viscous flow through a pipe), modeling his study after a similar study by W. Heisenberg and C. C. Lin of the dynamic stability of laminar viscous flow under small perturbations. With cooperation from Pekeris and Lin, a faculty member at MIT, von Neumann developed a new form of the linear small-perturbation stability equations of the parabolic flow through a channel, which he reformulated as a sixth-order complex linear ordinary differential equation (instead of as two fourth-order equations). Arrangements were made to carry out the computations in New York at the National Bureau of Standards Computation Laboratory and on the SSEC electronic calculator at IBM headquarters.

Von Neumann and Hans Panofsky of New York University sought objective methods for the analysis of weather maps.[67] They believed it was important for both correctness and automation to have nonsubjective, mathematical methods for constructing streamlines and isobars from initial observational data on wind and pressure. Their method analytically represented the initial data by an algebraic polynomial of some forty parameters that had the best least-squares fit respecting initial data. Their method was tested at the Princeton RCA laboratories on their prototype analog, ten-variable, electrical linear equation solver, and also by digital methods at the Mathematical Tables Project in New York. This work was continued for several years under subcontract at New York University.

The investigation that led most directly to the later successes of the project was initiated by Cahn and continued after his departure by Thompson. It concerned the system of hydrodynamic equations of atmospheric flow and their systematic simplification for direct integration. It soon became apparent that the primitive equations were ill suited to numerical as well as analytical solution.[68] In response, Cahn and Thompson simplified the mathematical model of atmospheric flow so that it still reflected important meteorological phenomena but filtered out nonmeteorological phenomena, such as sound and gravity waves: "The phenomena described by the general form of the hydrodynamic equations cover the entire spectrum of events, sonic waves, gravity waves, slow inertial waves, et cetera, and it might simplify matters considerably if those equations were somehow informed that we are interested in only certain kinds of atmospheric behavior—i.e, the propagation of large-scale disturbances. This is tantamount to constructing a 'mathematical filter' to remove 'noise' and otherwise unwanted regions of the spectrum."[69]

The process of filtering had been practiced implicitly by meteorologists when they formulated their theories.[70] In fact, Queney and Thompson offered filter models in the first two years of the project, which they checked against meteorological data.[71] Jule Charney was the first to make this procedure explicit and recommend it as the most promising approach for numerical meteorology.[72] In February 1947 Thompson had written to Charney at Chicago to inquire about how to distinguish among sound, gravity, and planetary waves on the basis of initial conditions and about the factors that govern the speed of travel of mid-latitude cyclones. Charney's response of 12 February explicitly introduced the fundamental concept of filtering and sketched the key idea for the barotropic filter model, which eventually led to the first successful numerical weather prediction.[73] Charney visited Thompson and von Neumann in Princeton in late March, and they discussed these topics at great length.[74]

With Charney's arrival in the summer of 1948, the Meteorology Project assumed a new direction. The wide range of independent, parallel investigations was curtailed, as was the emphasis on solving the primitive equations.[75] Resources were focused on a single approach under Charney's direction, "to consider a hierarchy of 'pilot problems' embodying successively more and more of the physical, numerical, and observational aspects of the general forecast problem."[76] The objective of the project was now clear: "the development of a method for the numerical integration of the meteorological equations which is suitable for use in conjunction with the electronic computing machine now under construction at the Institute for Advanced Study."[77]

The first model that Charney developed evolved directly from his attempts to understand and avoid Richardson's failure. Writing in the third person, Charney recalled this work of 1946 and 1947:

He had previously [to joining the IAS group] devised a method for overcoming the mathematical difficulties responsible for Richardson's failure. His point of departure was the realization that a compressible, stratified fluid held gravitationally to a rotating sphere can support a variety of wave motions, including acoustic and internal-gravity oscillations, which are of little meteorological importance but which impose highly restrictive conditions on numerical algorithms for solving the gas dynamical equations. He proposed to filter out these "noise" motions by imposing certain equilibrium constraints on the primitive equations of motion.[78]

In a paper written in 1948 while in Oslo, Charney made a scale analysis of the dynamic, kinematic, and thermodynamic effects in the hydrodynamical equations. He demonstrated that the problem with schemes like Richardson's resides in the nearly mechanical balance of the slow, large-scale motions of the atmosphere. The pressure, gravitational, centrifugal, and Coriolis forces (each being large-scale and reported with some amount of observational error) nearly cancel one another out, making it exceedingly difficult to calculate accurately the derived values, such as acceleration and velocity divergence, that appear in Richardson's equations. Charney realized he needed to find an approach that avoided this difficulty.

In the 1930s Rossby and others had discovered a class of large-scale and slow-evolving systems in the mid-troposphere known as planetary waves because they were generated by the earth's rotation. Subsequent research showed them to account for much of the large-scale meteorological phenomena. In a paper published in 1939 on planetary waves, Rossby suggested that the atmosphere at the heights between 3 and 6 kilometers behaves like a two-dimensional, homogeneous, incompressible flow.[79] His work inspired investigations by Charney and Eliassen, who came to realize that important atmospheric motions primarily involving horizontal energy dispersion could be studied using a two-dimensional model.

In 1949 Charney presented a simple two-dimensional model of the atmosphere based on the principle of absolute vorticity conservation, known as the equivalent-barotropic or more simply as the barotropic model.[80] The model had two important features: it was based entirely on observable variables, thereby avoiding the difficulty with derived values that occurred in Richardson's method, and it replaced Richardson's primitive equations with a computationally more tractable single equation in a single unknown.[81] The barotropic model filtered out all sound and gravity waves, which travel far more rapidly than atmospheric motions of meteorological significance. This filtering relaxed the Courant condition on the numerical approximation, which allowed longer time intervals to be chosen for the approximations and reduced the number of computations to a point within reach of existing computers.

That same year Charney and Eliassen published a companion article in Rossby's new journal, *Tellus*, that modified the barotropic model in a way that would account for perturbations caused by topographical features of the earth. The paper also presented the results of their first numerical forecasts. The model reduces the three-dimensional atmosphere to a two-dimensional horizontal plane, using initial observational data taken at the height of 500 millibars (about 20,000 feet). To simplify the calculations sufficiently to do them by hand, Charney and Eliassen reduced the model from two dimensions to one by taking data only along a single latitude band in the 500 millibar plane.[82] Using observational data from 12 January 1946, 0400 Greenwich Mean Time for their initial conditions, they calculated the weather map along the 45 degree latitude for 24 hours later. The success was mixed:

The zonal profile of the 500 mb surface may be described as an almost stationary, very long wave pattern, upon which is superimposed a system of shorter, migrating waves. The long wave, stationary pattern consists of two main ridges at the west coasts of Europe and North America, and of troughs over the North American east coast and the western Pacific.

The computed forecast is not bad, as far as the shorter waves are concerned; but the formula gives a rapid propagation of the very long wave pattern toward the west, in contradiction to the observed persistence of this system.[83]

The Meteorology Group employed this method in trial forecasts for different seasons and under different initial conditions. Margaret Smagorinsky hand-calculated over 100 24-hour winter forecasts at one latitude, which proved to be competitive with subjective forecasts.[84] Trial five-day forecasts were generally unsuccessful, however. The one-dimensional model was found to be so simple that its predictive value could be determined in advance and was relegated to use as a supplementary tool in operational forecasting. A two-dimensional model, such as that suggested by Charney and Eliassen, was needed to model nonlinear interactions and give satisfactory operational performance, but it required an electronic computer to drive the calculations.[85]

As late as 30 June 1949, the meteorologists were still anticipating the imminent availability of the IAS computer to test the full two-dimensional barotropic model.[86] By late summer or fall it was apparent that the computer would not reach working order for at least a year. As an interim measure, von Neumann arranged with the Army Ordnance Department to use the ENIAC to test the full barotropic model. ENIAC was already operating routinely in its modified, stored-program mode at Aberdeen Proving Grounds, which simplified the programming and problem setup task for the meteorologists.

Beginning in October 1949 the group concentrated its efforts on preparations for the ENIAC calculations. Von Neumann handled the many aspects of the numerical analysis: determining a method adaptable to the ENIAC for solving the quasi-geotrophic barotropic vorticity equation, investigating the boundary conditions, establishing the computational stability criteria, and identifying the area into which influences from the boundary of the forecast region could propagate.[87] When the numerical analysis was completed, the group set about the programming and coding. These tasks took longer than anticipated, and the schedule to use the ENIAC on 1 December 1949 slipped by over three months. Finally the code was ready, and Charney, Ragnar Fjortoft, John Freeman, George Platzman, and Joseph Smagorinsky operated the ENIAC round the clock for 33 days, beginning 6 March.[88]

After some uncertainty over how best to use the scarce computing resources, Charney had selected two kinds of tests. The first ones tested the barotropic model by using it to produce 24-hour forecasts from observed initial conditions (taken from 5, 30, and 31 January and 13 February 1949). These dates were chosen because their weather maps represented several different important types of conditions—those that are essentially barotropic, essentially baroclinic, and displaying pronounced blocking of the jet stream. The second set of tests was intended to investigate several important hypothetical situations: an isolated vortex in a field of no relative vorticity, an isolated vortex in a field of zonal motion that possesses vorticity, and periodically distributed vortices in a field of zonal motion that is dynamically unstable.[89]

The ENIAC was slower than the Meteorological Group expected; it took 36 hours to produce a 24-hour "forecast."[90] Because the ENIAC did not have floating-point number representation, large blocks of time prior to calculation were consumed in trial-and-error attempts to scale the variables so that they would not underflow or overflow the ENIAC's range. Not unlike today, programming errors took longer than scheduled to locate and correct, and in the end the group had to postpone the hypothetical tests.[91] They did, however, complete two 12-hour and four 24-hour forecasts from observed initial data. The 24-hour forecast for 5 January was not particularly accurate, but the one for 31 January "turned out to be surprisingly good."[92] It was almost a year before the results of the ENIAC calculation were fully analyzed and the paper reporting their results was readied for publication.[93] Long before the paper appeared, however, the results had been circulated through the international meteorological community. The Weather Bureau had introduced the institute's theoretical results into subjective forecasting techniques and began preparatory research on numerical forecasting in anticipation of the completion of the faster IAS computer.[94] The ENIAC calculations were lauded at the time as a "historic event in the science of meteorology" and "the beginning of a new era in weather forecasting."[95]

The Baroclinic Model

The 1950 and 1951 ENIAC calculations, together with further investigations by the Meteorology Group, indicated that the atmosphere behaved barotropically over long periods of time and that the barotropic model performed satisfactorily during these periods. However, everyone recognized that the barotropic model was based on vorticity conservation, which implied that the number of cyclonic and anticyclonic vortices (storms) could not change over time. Stated another way, the barotropic model permitted redistribution of kinetic energy but had no sinks or sources of energy to account for the formation, intensification, or dissipation of storms.

This shortcoming could be rectified by a model that permitted energy transformation between potential and kinetic states. A major source of energy transfer in the atmosphere is the side-by-side juxtaposition of warm and cold air masses. As the warm air masses override the cold ones and the cold air sinks, potential energy is released. It was apparent that predicting storms required a model that could incorporate a vertical component to account for this churning of air and the concomitant release of potential energy, and several groups independently began to develop three-dimensional models simple enough to permit calculation on an electronic computer of that era.

Even at the time of the ENIAC calculations, the Meteorology Group recognized the limited applicability of a two-dimensional model, and in the spring of 1950 they began to prepare for a three-dimensional model.[96] Charney investigated the upper boundary conditions for a three-dimensional model. Meanwhile Fjortoft conducted a theoretical study of a simplified advective three-dimensional model, which gave a significantly better forecast than the barotropic model had in one of the ENIAC calculations.[97]

When the inadequacies of the advective model were discerned in late 1950 or early 1951, Charney and von Neumann tried to solve the general three-dimensional equations. They investigated several relaxation methods, including a modified Liebmann method used in the two-dimensional case. By the end of 1951 they had settled most of the numerical issues associated with this calculation: they had selected a particular Liebmann method with an empirically determined constant of overrelaxation, determined the boundary conditions, and chosen a coordinate system and a finite difference net.[98] As soon as the institute computer became operational, a series of calculations using two-dimensional barotropic and baroclinic models was made to check for coding and machine errors, select the proper time increment for the finite difference equations, and determine how to reduce round-off errors. A programming procedure was devised that automatically checked the machine's results and stopped it when an error occurred, and as a further check, all calculations were performed twice.[99] Because of suspected machine errors, these initial calculations were used only to test the machine.

The first significant baroclinic forecasts were calculated in the summer of 1952. In his dissertation research at the University of Chicago in 1951, Norman Phillips had shown that a model consisting of two homogeneous, incompressible barotropic layers of different densities would provide many of the same features as a three-dimensional model. His model could predict the location of clouds and precipitation if given information on the initial distribution of water vapor. Phillips joined the Meteorology Group in 1951, and it was his model (one of several known as 2 1/2-dimensional models) that was used for the first baroclinic calculations.[100]

Six 12- and six 24-hour forecasts were calculated for each of the two-layer baroclinic models and for the barotropic model.[101] The earlier barotropic forecasts were repeated as a control, though the former ENIAC programs were modified to accelerate the computations. The forecasts "predicted" the Thanksgiving weekend storm of 1950, which had blanketed the eastern coast of North America in snow and during which there was rapid storm formation and intensification.

Twenty-four-hour barotropic forecasts were carried out on a square grid of 361 points spaced approximately 200 miles apart, covering most of North America.[102] Each forecast, made in twenty-four 1-hour time steps, involved approximately 17,000 multiplications and divisions, 54,000 additions and subtractions, and 296,000 executed orders. The institute computer required 90 minutes to complete each forecast. Half of that time was devoted to reading data from and to the Teletype equipment. By replacing the Teletype equipment with IBM equipment, which shortened input-output time by a factor of ten, and introducing other improved methods, the time to calculate a 24-hour forecast was reduced to 10 minutes. The same barotropic forecast would take 36 hours on the ENIAC or 8 years on a desk calculator. The baroclinic forecasts proceeded in half-hour time steps in order to avoid computational instabilities, and each time-step took 2 1/2 hours to compute on the institute computer.

The limitations of the barotropic model were confirmed by these calculations, which showed that it was incapable of fully predicting the rapid and intense development of the Thanksgiving weekend storm. As table 6.1 indicates, the quality of the barotropic forecasts falls off markedly from 12 to 24 hours. In contrast, the baroclinic model gave some indication of storm formation and had a high enough correlation with observation after 24 hours that it was considered to have promise for forecasts of up to 48 hours. The baroclinic model also predicted cloudiness and precipitation with reasonable accuracy.

Table 6.1
Correlation coefficients for predicted and observed changes, IAS, 1952

Date	Initial barotropic forecast (500 mb)		2 layer baroclinic forecast (300,700 mb)	
	12 hour	24 hour	12 hour	24 hour
23 Nov. 0300Z	.89	.72	.89	.90
23 Nov. 1500Z	.81	.77	.86	.87
24 Nov. 0300Z	.88	.75	.86	.73
24 Nov. 1500Z	.74	.51	.77	.62
25 Nov. 0300Z	.61	.61	.58	.56
25 Nov. 1500Z	.81	.59	.73	.87

Charney was not entirely satisfied with the predictive value of the two-layer model and had calculations repeated on the institute computer in early 1953 using a three-layer model. This model led to 24-hour forecast correlation coefficients for the Thanksgiving weekend storm ranging from .80 to .90, which Charney found acceptable. He noted with pleasure that "whereas the [one- and two-layer models] deteriorated from 24 November 15Z, the time the storm began, the [three-layer model] even increased in accuracy."[103] These calculations were repeated in the spring of 1953 for surfaces at 400, 700, and 900 millibars instead of the original 200, 500, and 850 millibar surfaces, and the results were even better. Charney wrote of these calculations as "the first successful attempt to forecast cyclogenesis by purely numerical methods."[104] Additional baroclinic forecasts were made in 1953 with three- and five-layer models, and a seven-layer model was considered in order "to investigate certain kinematical and dynamical effects not taken into account in the simple two- and three-level models initially employed, namely horizontal-vertical vorticity conversion, vertical advection of vorticity, influence of mountain ranges, and vertical propagation of energy"[105] By the end of June 1953, "the trend in the application to short-range prediction of the quasi-geostrophic model equations had become so predictable that this phase of the work had ceased to be—for the Project—a matter of major scientific interest."[106]

The Beginnings of Operational Numerical Weather Prediction

By the summer of 1952, the progress made by the Meteorology Project had stimulated the Weather Bureau and several military organizations to explore operational forecasting using the models developed in Princeton. The IAS group took an interest in seeing an operational numerical weather prediction service established and offered to assist with the training of its staff and cooperate in preoperational research and development.[107] Von Neumann called a meeting in Princeton for 5 August 1952 to discuss this matter with representatives of the Weather Bureau, air force, and navy.[108] The meeting was convened rapidly so that the Weather Bureau could use the findings to support its request during the annual government budget hearings.

Von Neumann opened the meeting with a discussion of the the past and present research in Princeton and the promise and problems of transforming this research into an operational procedure. He suggested using a general baroclinic model, which he believed would be valid for periods of up to 36 hours, to produce 24-hour forecasts for the continental United States.[109] He argued on practical grounds that the initial preparation, computing time, and output preparation and forecast editing must be completed within 12 hours. He also identified two problems facing an operational unit: the lack of synoptic forecasters and mathematicians with an appreciation for numerical prediction methods and the lack of a reliable computing machine.

The first steps toward solving the personnel problem were taken at this meeting. It was decided that the institute was the best place to train the initial group of numerical forecasters for the operational unit—scientists who already possessed most of the qualifications but needed some brushing up—and von Neumann volunteered to accept three of them (one each from the Weather Bureau, navy, and air force) to receive additional training at the institute for a year beginning in December 1952. Over the long term, he looked to the universities to train numerical forecasters. Thus he was heartened by George Platzman's report that the University of Chicago was already offering a course in advanced forecasting techniques, which included some numerical methods, suitable for forecasters having some experience in synoptic meteorology and some knowledge of meteorological theory, and that it, as well as several other leading universities, was beginning to introduce numerical forecasting into the general meteorology curriculum.

The technological questions about computer reliability were tabled when the Weather Bureau reported that funds ($400,000) for their computer would not be available for at least a year. The scientists had done all the planning they could do, and the fate of a numerical prediction service was now in the hands of the government. Responding to a lobbying effort by well-placed scientists and military officers, the Joint Meteorological Committee, a committee under the Joint Chiefs of Staff, which included the heads of the Air Weather Service of the air force, the Weather Bureau, and the Naval Weather Service, formed a subcommittee in late 1952 to study the establishment of an operational numerical weather prediction unit.[110] The subcommittee reported its findings in the summer of 1953: numerical weather prediction had advanced far enough to justify an operational unit, which could best be undertaken by a pooling the resources of the three government weather services, and a research and development group should be established to work in cooperation with the operational unit. The recommendations were accepted, and the Joint Numerical Weather Prediction Unit (JNWPU) was officially established in July 1954 with staffing and support from the three weather services.[111] George Cressman was appointed as director, Philip Thompson as the head of the Development Section, Joseph Smagorinsky as the head of the Computation Section, and Edwin Fawcett as the chief of the Analysis and Operations Section.

The first models used at JNWPU were Thompson's two-dimensional baroclinic model and a simplified barotropic model, both coded under his direction in 1953 at the Air Force Cambridge Research Laboratory and tested in 1954 on an IBM 701 computer at IBM headquarters in New York. Soon after the JNWPU was founded, work began on coding a three-level baroclinic model Cressman had developed in Princeton in 1953. Operational forecasting began on 15 May 1955 on the unit's new IBM 701 computer[112] and has continued to this day with ever more sophisticated models and ever faster computers.[113]

General Circulation of the Atmosphere

From the time of Charney's arrival in Princeton, the Meteorology Project had concentrated most of its effort on developing a model for prediction over short periods of time, generally less than 72 hours. As early as 1951, however, some attention was given to the theoretical aspects of the general circulation of the atmosphere and to the application of this theory to long-range forecasting.[114] In

1952, with aid from John Tukey, the staff calculated power spectra and multiple correlations for a time series of zonal and meridional indices to assist the research on general circulation underway at MIT. As Charney was to report: "By June 31, 1953, the end of the last report period, the trend in the application to short range prediction of the quasi-geostrophic model equations had become so predictable that this phase of the work had ceased to be—for the Project—a matter of major scientific interest. Instead its interest gradually turned to other, more challenging, problems, especially those of long-range prediction."[115]

Work began in earnest on the general circulation problem in 1953. There were both theoretical and numerical issues to consider. A satisfactory model had to account for sources and sinks of energy; the nonhomogeneity of the earth's surface with respect to the transfer of heat, water vapor, and momentum; the processes, such as cyclogenesis, that govern the life cycle of a weather system; and the processes that govern the statistically averaged state of the atmosphere over time. Serious truncation and round-off errors arise in the finite-difference process used to integrate the governing equations when the integrations are carried out for extended periods of time. The first order of business, which lasted through 1953, was to scrutinize existing baroclinic models to understand their limitations for long-range prediction.

From these studies emerged a model completed by Norman Phillips in mid-1955. Building on Charney's work, Phillips constructed a two-level, energetically complete, and self-sufficient quasi-geostrophic model that accorded with actual monthly and seasonal statistics of the atmosphere.[116] Charney described this model as being very simple:

The model consisted of a two-layer atmosphere bounded to the south and north by vertical walls and above and below by horizontal planes. The earth was considered flat except that the effect of the variable coriolis parameter was retained. Provision was made for heating this atmosphere in the south and cooling it in the north and for dissipating its energy by surface friction. The atmosphere was assumed to be at rest initially. To simplify matters still further the motion was supposed to be periodic in the zonal direction with a period corresponding roughly to the wave length of the most unstable of those waves predicted to develop as a consequence of the baroclinic instability engendered by the increasing horizontal temperature gradients. The magnitude of the computation was thereby greatly diminished, but at the expense of ignoring all effects arising from the dispersion of energy from one system to another. Finally the motion was assumed to be constantly in a state of quasi-geostrophic balance.[117]

It was not a predictive model like the one used by the JNWPU because it did not take into account the actual energy sources and sinks or the inhomogeneities of the surface of the earth. The model did, however, consolidate the factors important to the general circulation and demonstrate that the phenomenon could be studied numerically. Charney described the result: "The resultant picture [given by Phillips's model] was remarkably similar to what has been found empirically by V. Starr and collaborators at MIT and J. Bjerknes and collaborators at UCLA. Thus, in one simple mathematical model, most of the important elements which have been proposed to account for the general zonal circulation were brought together. It is for this reason that we now feel that the essentials of the zonal circulation of the atmosphere are understood, and that in a sense a breakthrough has been made which justifies an increased effort to establish a dynamic climatology."[118]

Von Neumann appreciated the significance of Phillips's accomplishment and called a meeting in Princeton in October 1955 on "The Application of Numerical Integration Techniques to the Problem of General Circulation." Experimental and theoretical investigators of the general ciculation problem and scientists studying related questions in radiation physics convened to discuss numerical problems that might be encountered in the future study of general circulation and climatic change.[119] The main topic was Phillips's model, but there was also discussion of the problem of streakiness in the flow known as "noodling," caused by truncation errors from the extended use of long-range models, meteorological applications of von Neumann and Richtmyer's artificial viscosity method for shock waves, and the prediction of precipitation.[120]

In his remarks at the conference, von Neumann made some predictions about future research in numerical meteorology, which were borne out by experience.[121] He separated the motions of the atmosphere into three categories, depending upon the time scale of the prediction. Short-term motions—those of a few days' duration—he characterized as being dominated, if not entirely determined, by their initial values. Long-term motions—those of more than 30 to 90 days' duration—he argued are dominated by "traits of the circulation which, on the average, will always be present" and relatively little affected by initial conditions. Intermediate-range motions, he claimed, are affected but not dominated by both initial conditions and general circulation parameters. He predicted that progress would be made first in short-range prediction, then long-range prediction, and only much later in intermediate-range prediction: "The approach is to try first short-range forecasts, then long-range forecasts of those properties of the circulation that can perpetuate themselves over arbitrarily long periods of time [such as climate simulations], and only finally to attempt to forecast for medium-long time periods which are too long to treat by simple hydrodynamic theory and too short to treat by the general principles of equilibrium theory."[122]

Progress in the international community on short-range prediction followed rapidly on the work of Charney and the JNWPU. By the mid-1970s substantial progress had been made on the long-range prediction problem, following on the work of Phillips and the General Circulation Research Section.[123] Intermediate-range prediction began to make real progress only in the 1980s.

In late July 1955, after the value of Phillips' model had become apparent but before the conference on general circulation was held, von Neumann and Harry Wexler of the Weather Bureau drafted a proposal for a project on the dynamics of the general circulation.[124] The proposal called for the Weather Bureau, air force, and navy jointly to support a group of scientists in Suitland, Maryland, who would be given access to the JNWPU's IBM 701 computer in order to continue the study of the general circulation along the lines of approach taken in Princeton.[125] A scientific advisory committee consisting of Charney, Phillips, von Neumann, and Wexler was proposed. The first year the group intended to organize personnel and facilities, determine the computing methods for the general circulation problem, and carry out sample calculations. During the second year the study was to be expanded to consider kinematic effects of geography and topography, acquisition of humidity in the atmosphere by evaporation, delay relationships between oversaturation, cloud formation, and precipitation, the effects of atmospheric humidity on the solar irradiation of the earth and on long-wave radiation from the earth and atmosphere, and other pertinent factors. The proposal called for a staff of four meteorologists, four programmers, and five other computer operators, meteorological aides, or clerks, supported by a budget of almost $200,000 for the first nine months of operation.

The Weather Bureau, air force, and navy agreed to fund the proposal, essentially without modification. Joseph Smagorinsky was chosen to head the General Circulation Research Section, as it was called, and by the end of 1955 the section had five employees.[126] After a slow start because of lack of qualified personnel, an active and fruitful research program was established.[127]

This was the last major contribution von Neumann and the IAS project made to numerical meteorology.[128] By 1955 von Neumann was living in Washington and devoting himself to his duties for the Atomic Energy Commission. No other faculty member at the institute had an interest in the project. Charney and Phillips were intensely aware of this fact, and they soon departed for positions at MIT, where they helped to build a robust research and training program in numerical meteorology.[129] With their departure, the institute closed the Meteorology Project. Its legacy resided in the programs continued by JNWPU, the general circulation project, and others, and also in the people trained at the institute who spread across research centers and universities worldwide and became the leaders of the new, numerically oriented meteorology.

The Computer as Meteorological Tool

Von Neumann had high expectations of the computer as a scientific research instrument. He regarded its application to meteorology as the crucial test of its scientific value, in large part because the hydrodynamics of the atmosphere is a prime example of those complex, nonlinear phenomena that were previously inaccessible to mathematical study. The work at the institute in the decade following the war proved the computer's scientific value beyond question. Indeed it may be fair to say that the computer has transformed meteorology into a mathematical science. In a lecture to the National Academy of Sciences in 1955, Charney eloquently expressed the promise of the computer for his discipline:[130]

The advent of the large-scale electronic computer has given a profound stimulus to the science of meteorology. For the first time the meteorologist possesses a mathematical apparatus capable of dealing with the large number of parameters required for determining the state of the atmosphere and of solving the nonlinear equations governing its motion. Earlier, for want of such an apparatus, both the forecaster and the investigator were forced to content themselves with such highly oversimplified descriptions or models of the atmosphere that forecasting remained largely a matter of extrapolation and memory, and dynamical meteorology a field in which belief in a theory was often more a matter of faith than of experience. Needless to say, the practicing meteorologist could ignore the results of theory with good conscience.

The radical alteration that is taking place in this state of affairs is due not merely to the ability of the machine to solve known equations with known initial and boundary conditions but even more to its ability to serve as an inductive device. The laws of motion of the atmosphere, especially as they concern the dynamics of the large-scale motions and their energy-exchange processes, are very imperfectly known. The machine, by reducing the mathematical difficulties involved in carrying a physical argument to its logical conclusion, makes possible the making and testing of physical hypotheses in a field where controlled experiment is still visionary and model experiment difficult, and so permits a wider use of inductive methods.

Charney's comments have been borne out by the events of the past thirty years. The work at the institute attracted international attention. By the mid-1950s groups interested in numerical weather prediction had been formed at the Napier Shaw Laboratory of the British Meteorological Office, the Institute of Meteorology at the University of Stockholm, the Deutscher Wetterdienst, and the Japanese Meteorological Agency.[131] The first educational programs in numerical meteorology were established at about this time at the University of Chicago, MIT, New York University, and the University of California at Los Angeles in the United States, as well as in Norway and other countries. By the 1970s the use of the computer in meteorological education had become the rule rather than the exception, a change characteristic of all the geophysical sciences. The change has been so complete that Philip Thompson, a pioneer in the numerical approach, has rued the lack of synoptic training for meteorologists being educated today.[132]

Because of the computer's speed and programmability, it was employed in ways different from earlier calculating technologies; it was not used simply as a giant calculator. Charney has identified four types of computer use in fluid geophysics over the period 1945-1972, which he labeled synthetic, experimental, heuristic, and data analytic.[133] According to his classification, a computer's operation is synthetic when it is used to predict or simulate large-scale phenomena. Experimental use occurs when the computer simulates an individual phenomenon, in isolation from its environment, so that the user may infer its physical causes. The computer is used heuristically to build highly simplified models as a means to discover new relationships within complex phenomena, such as the nonlinear relationships in the atmosphere. Finally the computer can be used to reduce and analyze observational data. Not mentioned by Charney, a computer might also be used to control a system of scientific apparatus, such as one that includes operational recording equipment or data communication equipment.

In the institute project the work on general circulation can be classified as synthetic and that on simple baroclinic models to determine the physical basis of cyclogenesis as experimental. Von Neumann and Panofsky's early work on least-squares fitting of data falls under the data-analytic category, but it is one of the few instances where early computers received this type of use. The computer was never used substantially as a heuristic device in the institute Meteorology Project despite von Neumann's being the leading promoter of the computer's heuristic value in scientific research.[134] The fact that the computer did not receive heuristic use, at least as far as can be gleaned from the documentary evidence of the Meteorology Project, is understandable. In those years time on a high-speed computer was a scarce commodity, problems for calculation were selected with care, and there was little opportunity to use the computer for these high-risk exercises. When computers became more readily available and the cost of calculation decreased, these heuristic uses became more prevalent.[135]

The meteorologists experienced a common phenomenon when they came to use the computer in their research; they found that it was not an instrument that could be used productively in isolation but only as part of a technological system. Where computing was once the primary bottleneck, the process of data collection, communication, and reduction subsequently took on that role. The numerical approach to forecasting required upper air data where they had not been important or collected before.[136] The computer was more sensitive than subjective forecasters to imperfections in the grid of observation stations and the data they reported, and automated methods of reporting, checking, and reducing observational data had to be developed in order for the computer to produce timely forecasts.[137] A conference was called at the institute in May 1955 to discuss the needs of the meteorological community for collecting, processing, transmitting, and storing observational data.[138] Some progress was made in these areas in the early years, but it was slow because of the enormous cost of massive and systematic collecting and because of the difficulties in getting governments to move in international concert.[139]

7

The Computer as a Scientific Instrument

The IAS computer had been more than six years in the making, but finally it was completed, and a gala dedication ceremony was held on 10 June 1952. Like most other prototype computers, it had been in partial operation for quite a few months before the dedication, but large blocks of the machine's time were reserved for engineering changes, repairs, and maintenance and much of the remaining time for learning about machine operation, identifying appropriate numerical algorithms, and determining the range of mathematical and scientific applications within the machine's capacity. As the staff gained experience and as less time was required for hardware improvements, the computer came into increasing use for scientific research. The research program was actively pursued from 1952 to 1957, when the project was ended and the computer was given to Princeton University, where it was used for three more years before being decommissioned.[1]

Long before the computer was operable, von Neumann had established the basic guidelines for its scientific use, as he explained to the Indian physicist Homi J. Bhabha:

I am in essential agreement with your remarks about the "philosophy" of using in the future high-speed calculating machines. They will at first necessarily be rather rare and, therefore, the ones which exist should be used on as broad and as varied a basis as possible. From every possible point of view, it would be a great mistake to tie them down to any kind of routine production. The theory and practice of solving non-linear partial differential equations, in hydrodynamics as in other fields; the execution of large statistical experiments, especially in the kinetic theory of matter; some parts of astro-physics and the theory of stellar systems, as well as in a number of problems connected with cosmic ray showers; calculation of atomic and nuclear energy levels and wave functions, both in "quantum chemistry" and nuclear theory; analysis of theories of statistical significance; various problems related to but going considerably beyond Fourier analysis in connection with crystal and molecular structure determinations in X-ray crystallography—these are the main problems which now come to mind, but I am sure that the list will prove to be incomplete once the machines are actually available and we will be able to do things instead of planning for them. I think that it would be very desirable to have the machine run under a system or organization which makes it accessible to many scientific groups and guarantees a wide and varied use.[2]

Problems were selected for both their intrinsic scientific merit and the opportunity they presented the staff to learn about the computer as a scientific instrument. The computer was used not only by the project staff but also by the IAS and Princeton faculties, members of government laboratories (especially Los Alamos), and a few other scientists (most of them acquaintances of von Neumann).[3] All applications to use the computer were given serious consideration, and funds were made available to individual researchers to pay for numerical analysis, coding, computer time, and travel to the institute.[4] The coding was sometimes done by the scientists themselves but more often by members of the computer project staff or the wives of Princeton scientists.[5] This chapter describes the most important scientific applications outside meteorology carried out on the institute computer.[6]

Table 7.1
Applications of the IAS computer

---

adiabatic pulsation of an originally isothermal atmosphere

angular distributions for deuteron-proton reactions

astronuclei-thermonuclear evolution and gravitational contraction

Bessel and cylinder functions

binomial probabilities

bionumeric evolution

blast wave calculation

cavity flows

continued fractions and random properties

cubic diophantine equations

distribution of a proton charge in electron scattering cross-sections

eigenvalues of bordered matrices with infinite dimensions

eigenfrequencies of order 3 matrices

electronic structure of iron

electronic wave functions

Table 7.1 (continued)

errors involving use of Runge-Kutta method
ferromagnetism theory
ground state of the helium atom
historical ephemeris
hyperbolic differential equations (with and without shocks)
Kummer conjecture
magnetohydrodynamic theory of solar spicules
mathematical decision procedure for additive arithmetic
middle-squares random number generator
mixing problem
molecular integrals
multiple integrals in meson theory
Navier-Stokes equations for compressible fluids
network analysis
particle accelerator orbit stability
pulsational stability of stars with convective envelopes
rational approximations of transcendent functions
red giants
slipping stream amplifier
solar model with carbon cycle
solid diffusion in fixed beds
stellar evolution
stripping reaction
Taylor instability nonmixing problem
total differential equations
traffic simulation
traveling wave amplifier
vibration frequencies of a crystal
wave equation for crystals
wave propagation in the earth's crust
X-ray diffraction

Experimentation on Numerical Methods

The first applications of the computer were made more to learn about numerical methods than to solve problems of inherent scientific importance. This was the justification for an early set of computations to solve ordinary differential equations,[7] which taught the staff about the efficiency in machine time of the several established numerical methods and enabled them to examine the error estimates for linear differential equations in the neighborhood of singularities of the coefficients. Among the first of these calculations was a set of solutions to the wave equation using the Runge-Kutta method, but the results were not very revealing. Slightly later the staff tried a modified Heun method in a calculation on the wave equation in connection with a problem on crystals for Eleanor Trefftz of Ohio State University. The Heun method was also used in an astrophysical problem involving the integration of three first-order, nonlinear differential equations, and the results were checked by an inspection of their smoothness properties. With this experience behind them, the staff returned to the Runge-Kutta method to solve a more complicated problem, a modified form of the Bessel equation, which gave them experience with singularities in coefficients and floating-point calculation.[8] They also tested the Milne method of integration on a problem from electromagnetic theory involving the solution of a second-order differential equation and the location of its proper values in the complex plane.[9]

These numerical experiments identified the Runge-Kutta method as the preferred one since it was more efficient in machine time than the Heun method and gave an answer superior to that given by the Milne method, except in a small number of cases. The staff also discovered that classical error estimates could be used only with caution and that singularities significantly lowered precision.[10]

Not all calculations of ordinary differential equations were merely numerical experiments; some were made for their scientific applications as well. A good example is a set of calculations made for Professor M. White of Princeton University on the design of a particle accelerator. These calculations tested the effect on particle orbits of imperfections in the accelerator's construction, such as variations in the magnetic field gradient from one focusing magnet to the next or in displacements of the focusing magnets from their ideal positions. Mathematically the problem involved solving a pair of second-order differential equations. The calculation was mathematically interesting because the integration path was broken into segments, and in each segment the integrand had a different form. Random numbers were used to introduce small random perturbations as a means of simulating the gradient and alignment variations.

Numerical linear algebra also received considerable attention. Goldstine, Murray, and von Neumann had rediscovered Jacobi's method for calculating the eigenvalues of symmetric matrices, and they experimented with it on symmetric matrices of up to order 16.[11] The method was applied in February 1953 to calculate the eigenvalues and eigenvectors of an 18×18 matrix in a model of the U.S. economy for Oskar Morgenstern. That same month, the staff also calculated some eigenvalues in the design of a slipping-stream amplifier.[12]

The staff increased their knowledge of numerical linear analysis in carrying out two other scientific applications. The first was made in 1954 on the energy band structure of iron as a test of a theory of ferromagnetism.[13] The energy values and wave functions for the body-central form of iron were calculated using the Hartree-Fock equations as the theoretical basis. The problem's mathematical interest lay in finding matrix elements and simultaneously diagonalizing two Hermitian matrices.

The second problem was set by G. L. Squires, a visitor to the institute in 1955. It concerned the relation between the vibration frequencies of a crystal and the scattering of slow neutrons.[14] Starting with 2792 third-order matrices whose entries were linear combinations of products of trigonometric functions, the staff calculated the eigenvalues and their square roots (the eigenfrequencies), used these to calculate the distribution function of the eigenfrequencies, and then calculated the average of some thirty functions over the distribution function. The problem required them to develop fast square-root subroutines. They also had difficulties in finding an appropriate smoothing procedure to apply in calculating the frequency distribution function—a procedure that would remove the noise in the calculated values of the eigenfrequencies but retain the true discontinuities of the distribution curve. In the end they decided the challenge was too great, so they graphed the eigenfrequencies on the cathode ray tube output scope and did the smoothing by manual inspection. This procedure, carried out in April 1955, was the institute's first major use of the graphical output device.

Another area of mathematical interest was tabular functions—those for which values were given by or calculated from mathematical tables. The first such calculation was of a set of Bessel and cylinder functions made for S. Chandrasekhar of Yerkes Observatory.[15] The problem held mathematical interest because of the propagation of round-off and truncation errors at one of the singularity points of the differential equation. This calculation gave the institute mathematicians a better understanding of the use of the Runge-Kutta method and enabled them to find some errors in the standard tables of Bessel functions.

A second example was a table of cumulative binomial probabilitites coded for John Tukey of the Princeton University Mathematics Department.[16] Calculating these probabilities is an enormous task—too large if the standard interpolation procedures are applied. As a replacement, the staff found a means to produce a short table and a simple interpolation procedure that work reasonably well for most values.

The last important area of experimentation for the purpose of improving numerical methods was a set of calculations seeking rapidly calculable rational approximations, quotients of polynomials, for certain classes of transcendent functions, which are time-consuming or even impossible to calculate directly.[17] The staff experimented with both the power series expansions and continued fraction expansions of transcendent functions. They succeeded in finding somewhat adequate approximations for $(\arctan x)/x$, $(\log\cosh x)/x^2$, and $(\tan x) - x$.

Mathematical and Statistical Research

At least three sets of calculations concerned not the investigation of numerical methods but rather their application to research problems in pure mathematics or mathematical statistics. The first was carried out at the request of Princeton University mathematician Emil Artin.[18] In 1846 the mathematician E. E. Kummer had sought to generalize to the cubic case a famous result of Gauss about quadratic sums. Kummer showed that for all $p \cong 1 \pmod 3$,

$$x_p = 1 + \sum_{v=1}^{(p-1)/2} \frac{p-1}{2} \Diamond \cos\left(\frac{2pv}{p}\right)^3$$

satisfies the cubic equation $f(x) = x^3 - 3px - pA = 0$, where A is uniquely determined by the requirements $4p = A^2 + 27B^2$, $A \equiv 1 \pmod 3$. Since $f(x)$ has three real roots for all such p, Kummer classified each x_p according to whether it was the largest, intermediate, or smallest root of $f(x) = 0$. He conjectured that the asymptotic frequencies for these classes are $1/2$, $1/3$, and $1/6$, respectively. Artin calculated the first 45 x_p by hand, and his results seemed to confirm Kummer's conjecture, but not enough x_p had been calculated to convince Artin. The institute computer was used to calculate all x_p where $p \equiv 1 \pmod 3$ and $p < 10,000$. The densities were found to be .4452, .3290, and .2258, which Artin took as a strong disconfirmation of Kummer's conjecture. These calculations involved 20 million multiplications and 6 hours of computing time.

The second example of a mathematical research computation was made for Ernst Selmer, a visitor to the institute in 1952.[19] He was making a complete classification of the cubic Diophantine equations and had been able to calculate all but a few cases by hand. The institute computer was sufficiently slow at multiplication that the integer cubic polynomials were not evaluated by the customary numerical approach of nested multiplication,

$$f(x) = x(x(px + q) + r) + s,$$

but instead by the method of finite differences. Selmer remembers these computations:

I am really a number theoretician, and wrote my Dr. philos. thesis on the indeterminate equation $ax^3 + by^3 + cz^3 = 0$. By manual computations, I had made large tables of solutions, but a few unsolved equations remained. They were all solved by means of the computer. As far as I know, this was the first number theoretical problem ever that was solved by large scale computation. At least, my programs were the first large ones to go through on the IAS computer at the first attempt, without any programming errors.[20]

A statistical research computation originated in von Neumann's interest in random numbers and Monte Carlo methods.[21] In 1953 the staff made experimental calculations to test the middle-squares method for generating pseudo-random sequences of numbers.[22] The next year they ran a sequence of continued fraction expansions of algebraic numbers to check "evident peculiarities" in the expansions as compared to random sequences. They calculated the cube root of 2 to 2232 terms and the cube root of 3 to 500 terms, finding no "peculiarities" in either expansion. They took this occasion to write subroutines for taking third and larger roots and for doing multiple precision arithmetic, devised more sophisticated error-checking methods (to combat a persistent memory error whose source they never identified), and developed methods for breaking long computations into pieces so that they could be printed onto punched cards and verified before proceeding to the next stage of computation.

Astrophysics

Unquestionably the largest use of the institute computer, after the meteorological calculations, was for the astrophysical research of Martin Schwarzschild and his associates at the Princeton University Observatory.[23] These computations continued over the operating life of the computer, including the time in the late 1950s when it was under the control of Princeton University. During some periods this group accounted for up to half the computer time. Schwarzschild has explained why von Neumann was willing to assign so much time to these astrophysical problems:

Then von Neumann developed the MANIAC here in Princeton. We had occasional contacts and he became more and more interested in one or two examples of highly non-linear problems for which a lot of hand computations were available. He wanted ones that were sufficiently complicated so that they couldn't be analytically solved, so that the numerical job wasn't just to check something that was completely understood analytically. He wanted a real problem that you really needed computers for. It just happened that these stellar interior problems were exactly of the kind that was important for von Neumann. We had computed numerical solutions with which you could check, and you at least knew exactly how you could solve it the tedious way with desk computers. That was why he encouraged me to work initially with Herman Goldstine and then later very extensively with Heddie Selberg, who was one of the members of this group, to get the equations onto the MANIAC and start using the MANIAC. Actually, von Neumann assigned a lot of time to the stellar interior problem.[24]

Another explanation was given by Goldstine following the successful completion of some of these computations: "Astrophysics differs from other physical sciences by the circumstance that its objects of study can be observed but cannot be experimented with. This impossibility of physical experimentation can be compensated for to a remarkable degree by numerical experimentation. It is for this reason that the numerical research plays such an unusually important role in astrophysics."[25]

When Schwarzschild arrived in Princeton in 1947, he started a major investigation of stellar interiors, in particular of red giant stars. Recent contributions to nuclear physics had made it possible to calculate the reaction rates (as functions of temperature and density) of the nuclear processes that provide the main energy sources in the stellar interior. The most basic stellar interior problem is represented by four highly nonlinear, first-order differential equations in one variable (the distance from the center of the star along a radius) with two boundary conditions at the surface and two more at the center. Because analytical methods of solution for even the simplest physical cases are unknown, Schwarzschild adopted a numerical approach. In the late 1940s, he and his collaborators laboriously produced solutions on a desk calculator. To get one data point, a solution for one particular star at one particular time in its life cycle, would take two to three months usually and up to a year in complicated cases. The problem was computationally challenging because of the wide range of values assumed by the variables. Moreover, the energy release from gravitational contraction made the governing equation similar to the heat conduction equation, which was numerically unstable. For all these reasons, Schwarschild was eager to find a way of improving the computational process.

There were actually two classes of astrophysical calculations.[26] One main class investigated the internal structure and evolution of stars. These calculations traced the changes in luminosity and radius as the star evolved through a series of configurations caused by changes in the chemical composition of the deep star interior from internal burning. Mathematically this calculation required solving highly nonlinear, high-order eigenvalue problems, which demanded efficient new trial-and-error methods. The early models applied best to dwarf stars, and a later model also took into consideration the conversion of hydrogen into helium through the carbon-nitrogen cycle, which generates the energy for more massive stars.

Schwarzschild's group did another class of astrophysical calculations on the perturbations of stars, including stellar pulsations and hydromagnetic waves. One study by D. A. Lautmann, a doctoral student at Princeton University, examined the periodic variation of brightness in Cepheid stars as explained by adiabatic pulsations of originally isothermal atmospheres. A study initiated by Schluter, Schwarzschild, and Lautmann investigated solar spicules, which are small disturbances of the solar chromosphere. According to the theory under investigation, spicules begin as a pressure variation at the base of the chromosphere and, under the influence of a strong magnetic field, give rise to magnetohydrodynamic waves. These were important because they were thought to transport energy to the corona. The problems computationally involve finding efficient algorithms, free from numerical instability, for integrating the governing partial differential equations, which may have as many as three independent variables.[27]

Fluid Dynamics

Meteorological problems were not the only fluid dynamics problems calculated on the institute computer. In 1954 a major blast wave calculation was made of the decay and propagation of a spherically symmetric shock wave generated by a strong point source in an ideal gas.[28] As with many of the other early calculations, it was a test of both science (in this case, hydrodynamics) and computational methods (comparison of approximation techniques, test of an iterative shock-fitting procedure to satisfy the Rankine-Hugoniot conditions, extensive study of error analysis).

As a companion study to the spherical shock problem, the computer was applied to a hydrodynamical problem in which shock considerations were not important.[29] The problem chosen is a two-dimensional mixing problem in which two fluids, one heavier than the other, are separated by a common interface. It is assumed that the walls of the container are rigid, gravity is the only external force, and the presssure has an initial uniform distribution. A small perturbation of the interface is introduced, and the motion is studied as a problem of Lagrangean hydrodynamics. The first numerical experiments assumed that the lighter fluid starts on top (though parameters such as the compressibility of the fluid and its initial velocity distribution were varied from one calculation to the next), but later experiments reversed the position. These later experiments introduce the further complication of Taylor instability. A von Neumann–Richtmyer artificial viscosity was applied in all of these experiments to remove the shock.[30]

Atomic and Nuclear Physics

The institute computer was applied to a number of problems in atomic and nuclear physics.[31] One example is a calculation of the ground state of the helium atom made for Toichiro Kinoshita.[32] Improved measurements of the energy level became available at about the time Kinoshita came to the institute, which enabled him to carry out a new and much more elaborate computation of the ground state. The problem involved using a set of coordinate functions to give an approximate solution to a three-body system consisting of the nucleus and two electrons. Mathematically it was essentially an eigenvalue problem, and preliminary computations, involving up to ten coordinate functions, were carried out on the institute computer. The work was completed, with the full complement of 39 coordinate functions, on the AEC-UNIVAC computer at New York University.[33] This calculation exemplifies the philosophy of the Electronic Computer Project: to use the institute computer to demonstrate the feasibility of a computational approach by making some preliminary calculations and then to relegate the detailed computational work on the full solution to another organization and computer.

Another example of nuclear physics research was a calculation made for Princeton University physicist Eugene Wigner of nucleon-nucleus interaction.[34] Wigner had concluded that the properties of the wave functions of quantum mechanical systems are so complex that they are most productively studied by statistical methods. The institute computer was used to solve an integral equation representing the density function of the distribution of eigenvalues of infinite bordered matrices, together with a recurrence formula for the moments of the distribution.

For a number of years, hand calculations had been made of the energy levels of atoms from the Schrödinger equation and certain atomic constants in order to learn about the electron shell and the magnetic moments of nuclei. However, the analysis of molecular spectra is beyond the capacity of hand calculation. R. C. Sahni of Cambridge University, with assistance from J. W. Cooley, made an extensive numerical analysis and then used the computer to calculate a large number of multicentered integrals that occur in the computation of molecular orbitals.[35] These values were then used to compute the ground and excited state energies and the corresponding molecular wave functions for biatomic particles.

A fourth problem, involving the calculation of complicated double and triple integrals, was solved for Hiroshi Suura, a visitor to the institute in the 1955–1956 academic year.[36] Suura wanted to test the extended structure of the proton, as predicted by meson theory, against recent experiments on high-energy electron scattering by hydrogen. The calculations were an attempt to find a distribution of a proton charge that would match the measured magnetic moment and the electron scattering cross-sections.

Finally, in 1955 and 1956, calculations were done for W. Tobocman, a visitor to the institute, on a scattering problem of nuclear physics, the theory of the stripping reaction.[37] Mathematically the problem requires calculating several hundred integrals over triple products of hypergeometric functions, about 1000 associated Legendre polynomials, and vector addition coefficients for each case. The problem appears to have overwhelmed the institute computer because of the widely varying range of parameters and the demanding storage requirements.

Automating Applications Research

Beginning in 1955 the computer was used in a more sophisticated manner. Rather than employing it as a brute-force calculator, albeit one with great speed and stored-program capability, as they had in the past, the staff began to use it in a way we would regard as more modern. Modifications were made to automate many routine functions that had previously been the concern of the programmer or operator. The change was made possible partly by the mounting experience of the machine's capabilities and partly by improvements in the hardware, especially additional storage space to accommodate these auxiliary programs.

The new systems programs fall into two categories: machine-language service routines and floating-point interpretive routines.[38] Among the former were an assembly routine to compile subroutines with relative addresses into a running code with absolute addresses, two programs to check the operation of the Williams tube memory, control cards to aid in debugging code, and a general-purpose binary-decimal conversion routine. Two floating-point interpretive subroutines were also written. One was designed for use in combination with machine coding. The other, known as FLINT (floating point interpretive routine), was a complete programming system in which one did not have to know anything about machine orders. FLINT was used to write many of the later applications programs and was used effectively even by students with no programming experience.

The automated application tool that received the most development was a network analyzer.[39] In the first half of the twentieth century, many special-purpose analog network analyzers had been built to analyze complicated electrical networks of direct and alternating current. The use of those machines was limited by the considerable amount of time required to set up new problems. In 1955 a program was written for the institute computer to simulate an automatic network analyzer with the objective of showing that a stored-program digital device could effectively replace analog equipment and markedly reduce the setup time. The user did not have to know anything about coding a computer to use the network analyzer program but needed only to specify the nodes of the electrical network and the connections among them. The computer would then automatically transform those specifications into the appropriate set of equations. The analyzer was tested on a direct current resistive network problem and on a short-circuit analysis for an electrical distribution system. The success on these problems showed clearly the practicality of a digital machine for network analysis.

Another automatic applications tool was designed for use in molecular physics.[40] There was a search for a general method that would not require extensive mathematical knowledge on the part of the user to calculate electronic wave functions automatically. The program was intended to calculate functions of the ground state as well as of the excited and ionic states. However, no evidence has been found that the program was successfully completed.

From History of Science to Traffic Simulation

A number of other problems were accepted for computation on the institute computer, problems that did not fit into any larger program of computation but were chosen either because of their scientific importance or because they allowed the staff to test the value a computer might have in a particular research area. One of the earliest such calculations concerned a traveling wave amplifier; it was carried out in 1953 for W. R. Beam of the RCA research laboratories in Princeton.[41] The propagation of waves of space charge from an electron beam collinated by a large magnetic field was well understood in the case where the beam is assumed to have constant cross-section, uniform density, and uniform velocity. But where the space charge is high, the velocity varies over the cross-section and the waves are of a more complicated and less well understood form. This calculation treated the wave form in the case where the velocity of electrons was given as a single-valued function of the radial distance from the center of the beam. The calculation resulted in a better understanding of the wave form rather than in any definite theoretical or practical result, and so this might be regarded as an example of a heuristic use of the computer.

Another calculation from 1953 gives another example of a heuristic computation. Garrett Birkhoff of Harvard University and E. Zarantonello of the University of Maryland suggested a problem related to a theory they had developed for plane cavity flows past curved obstacles.[42] Calculations were made for the symmetric case in order to give Birkhoff and Zarantonello insight into asymmetric flows. The problem was mathematically stated as an integral transformation, which was handled using Fourier transforms and an inductive method of solution for the integral equation.

A computation was performed for J. B. Rosen of the Princeton University Forrestal Research Center who was studying diffusion processes in fixed-bed chemical systems, such as ion exchange columns and adsorption columns.[43] The computation concerned the saturation problem, where a fluid of constant concentration enters at one end and one wants to know the concentration flowing out at the other end. The problem had numerical interest in that the integrand oscillated infinitely often in one region, so in order to keep the length of the calculation practical, a method had to be found to avoid integrating too many oscillations.

In 1955 the institute computer was used for some historical research, perhaps making this the first time a computer was so applied. The problem, suggested by O. Neugebauer and A. Sachs of Brown University, was to prepare an Ephemeris—a table of positions at regular intervals of time—for the sun, the moon, and the planets observable by the naked eye. The Ephemeris was to be used in the dating of astronomical records, and thereby of historical events, from the period 600 B.C. to 1 B.C.[44] Because this was considerably different from the other problems being solved, the staff felt the need to justify it in the report to their funders, and in their justification they explained the criteria used in selecting problems for the institute machine:

This problem was thought appropriate for the Electronic Computer Project for several reasons. Primarily, it was an example of a novel and useful application; while the amount of computation involved was of such magnitude as to be completely impractical without an electronic computer, it was of considerable but not excessive size on our computer. Secondly, it presented a number of interesting problems in high-precision calculations, error analysis, information handling, and methods of checking. Finally, the results were of a non-commercial nature and would be of permanent scientific value.[45]

The tables, published in 1962, were used subsequently by historians of ancient astronomy.[46]

Another unusual application, programmed by S. Y. Wong of the institute staff, was a traffic simulation.[47] The objective was to determine whether a digital computer could be applied effectively to the study of traffic flow and highway design. A very simple model was built that carried out all computations in multiples of unit car length (18 feet, 4 inches) and unit speed (12.5 miles per hour) and in which the entry of cars into the traffic flow, their speeds, and their lane switching were governed by random numbers generated according to a specified probability distribution. The results demonstrated that the model resembles observed traffic behavior reasonably well but that longer runs would be needed for a more realistic test. They would require faster computers with larger memories, as well as a method for determining and entering the input parameters (such as the expected flow of traffic at all points and under various conditions such as holidays and weekends). The investigators also hoped to extend the model to include such factors as the psychological behavior of drivers and the mechanical properties of cars.

It is fitting to close this discussion of scientific computation with an application of special interest to von Neumann because of its similarity to his own work on cellular automata.[48] This is a model of bionumeric evolution that was programmed for Nils A. Barricelli, a visitor to the institute in 1955–1956 from the Mathematics Institute of the University of Oslo. The model simulates evolution with organisms composed of numerical genes. A linear array of N locations is studied through successive generations. At each location in each generation a number represents the presence of a particular type of gene. Reproduction and mutation rules describe how the genes change from one generation to the next. Using hand methods, Barricelli had exhibited the formation and growth of numerical organisms—linear sequences of genes that reproduce themselves from one generation to the next, as well as further biological analogs such as "parasites." The institute computer enabled Barricelli to study a larger number of generations (512) and more types (40) of numerical genes, as well as more complex mutation rules (which determine what happens when two or more genes collide in a given location, since his model forms mutations through the collision of genes). The computations showed that if a single mutation norm is used for the entire universe, then after fewer than 500 generations, uniform conditions (either disorganization or single species population) are reached across the universe. In multinorm universes, in which different mutation norms apply in different regions, Barricelli observed a vitality principle: that certain kinds of gene combinations are more fit and become dominant in some regions of the universe. He noted that these numerical organisms behave much like low-level biological organisms, such as bacteria. He also observed several kinds of cross-breeding, which he noted play a significant role in bionumeric evolution. The computer models also exhibited chains of evolution, which had not appeared in any of the hand experiments.

Limitations on the Computer as a Scientific Instrument

The mathematical group in the institute's computer project concentrated its attention in two broad areas: investigations intended to improve numerical techniques and calculational experiments designed to test the practicality and scientific importance of computational procedures.[49]

The institute computer was applied to an impressive range of scientific problems. The work in meteorology and astrophysics had direct influence on the development of these fields. The computations also showed that the computer could be an effective tool in solving ordinary differential equations and certain kinds of partial differential equations, in numerical linear algebra, and in modeling complicated processes through the use of random numbers. Finally the work demonstrated the value of the digital computer for network analysis, a wide range of hydrodynamical applications, and many problems of nuclear and atomic physics.

Goldstine and von Neumann recognized that current limitations on the technology seriously restricted their investigation of realistic scientific problems.[50] Using the blast wave calculation as an example, they estimated that one-dimensional hydrodynamical problems would require approximately 25 hours of calculation on the IAS computer, a two-dimensional hydrodynamical problem would require 1250 hours and a three-dimensional problem as much as 50,000 hours. Yet, they noted, the two- and three-dimensional problems are those of the greatest import in physics. Another example, the mixing problem with Taylor instability (with the heavier fluid on the top and a sinusoidal perturbation introduced at the interface), showed that some problems could not be solved on the insititute computer. To stay within the capacity of the IAS computer, a coarse mesh had to be chosen—but then the higher harmonics in the motion, which were the decisive ones, were not resolved. To capture the effect of the higher harmonics, by using a smaller mesh, would require 10^{11} multiplications, or 50,000 hours of machine time on the IAS computer. Similarly the solution of a simple three-dimensional elliptic differential equation would require 10^8 multiplications and more than 50,000 words of storage. Many common matrix inversion problems were estimated to have similar memory requirements. These calculations were clearly beyond the capacity of computer technology at the time, and this limited the computer's utility as a practical scientific instrument. In the end, the institute project demonstrated that the computer could be a useful scientific instrument, but the current technology did not entirely satisfy the computing needs of von Neumann and his scientific colleagues.

8

A Theory of Information Processing

In the 1945 EDVAC report von Neumann did not describe the stored-program computer as being built from vacuum tubes, electromechanical relays, or even mechanical switches but instead from the idealized neurons presented in a 1943 paper by Warren McCulloch and Walter Pitts. It may seem anomalous to capture the design of a technology in biological terms; it certainly did seem that way to Eckert and Mauchly.[1] But this practice allowed von Neumann to separate the logical design from the engineered components used to implement the logical structure. From the full body of articles and correspondence he left, it is apparent that von Neumann had a further reason for using the McCulloch-Pitts neurons: to emphasize the similarities between the stored-program computer and the human nervous system as information processing systems. In the report he drew the analogy between the associative, sensory, and motor neurons of the human nervous system and the respective central processing, input, and output units of the computer. He also contrasted the synchronous timing of the clocked ENIAC circuits with the asynchronous firing of neurons.[2]

Unlike most of the other engineers and mathematicians involved with high-speed computing in the 1940s, von Neumann brought to the subject substantial experience of scientific disciplines in which information is a key concept, which shaped his approach to computing, especially his attempts to build a theoretical discipline that allied computing with biological information processing.

Early Experiences with Information

Von Neumann's earliest experience with information as a scientific concept came in the late 1920s through his work on the mathematical foundations of quantum mechanics. The information concept had been introduced into this science much earlier, in 1871, when James Clerk Maxwell put forth his famous Demon paradox:

A being whose faculties are so sharpened that he can follow every molecule in his course, and would be able to do what is at present impossible to us. . . . Let us suppose that a vessel is divided into two portions, *A* and *B* by a division in which there is a small hole, and that a being who *can see the individual molecules* opens and closes this hole, so as to allow only the swifter molecules to pass from *A* to *B*, and only the slower ones to pass from *B* to *A*. He will, thus, without expenditure of work raise the temperature of *B* and lower that of *A*, in contradiction to the second law of thermodynamics.[3]

Several generations of physicists had puzzled over this paradox until 1929 when it was resolved by one of von Neumann's senior Hungarian colleagues, Leo Szilard, who showed that the answer lay in the relationship between entropy and information.[4] The entropy the gas loses from the Demon's separation of low and high energy particles is compensated for by the information the Demon gains about the motion of the gas particles. In order to obtain this information the Demon introduces negative entropy into the system, which explains the paradoxical net loss of entropy.

Szilard's explanation was accepted by the physicists, and subsequently information became accepted as a scientific concept defined by its statistical-mechanical properties as a kind of negative entropy that introduces order into a system. Von Neumann employed Szilard's idea in his own account of quantum thermodynamics in 1932.[5] In answer to a thought experiment similar to Maxwell's Demon, von Neumann proposed "the intervention of an intelligent being in thermodynamical systems."[6]

Von Neumann returned to the statistical definition of information and its connection with entropy in the 1940s in his discussions with Claude Shannon on communication engineering.[7] Their conversations related to the mathematical theory of communication Shannon published in 1948, which built on work of the 1920s and 1930s by Harry Nyquist, R. V. Hartley, and other communication engineers.[8] Shannon gave abstract definitions of the components of a communication system (source, transmitter, channel, receiver, destination) and general theorems about the theoretical limits on the capacity of information flow along a channel subject to noise. He was the first to distinguish carefully between the

concepts of information and meaning. His collaborator and popu-
larizer, Warren Weaver, explained the concept:[9]

The word *information*, in this [Shannon's] theory, is used in a special sense
that must not be confused with its ordinary usage. In particular, *information*
must not be confused with meaning.

In fact, two messages, one of which is heavily loaded with meaning and
the other of which is pure nonsense, can be exactly equivalent, from the
previous viewpoint, as regards information. . . .

To be sure, this word *information* in communication theory relates not
so much to what you do say, as to what you could say. That is, information
is a measure of one's freedom of choice when one selects a message. If one
is confronted with a very elementary situation where he has to choose one
of two alternative messages, then it is arbitrarily said that the information,
associated with this situation, is unit. Note that it is misleading (although
often convenient) to say that one or the other message conveys unit
information. The concept of information applies not to the individual
messages (as the concept of meaning would), but rather to the situation
as a whole, the unit information indicating that in this situation one has an
amount of freedom of choice, in selecting a messsage, which is convenient
to regard as a standard or unit amount.

Shannon knew that his definition of information closely resembled
the concept of entropy from statistical mechanics in its conception
as a measure of the orderliness of the message set and in its
mathematical formulation as

$$H = -(p_1 \log_2 p_1 + \ldots + p_n \log_2 p_n),$$

where the possible messages have probabilities $p_1, \ldots, p_n$.

Quantities of the form $H = -P_i \log P_i \ldots$ play a central role . . . as measures
of information, choice and uncertainty. The form of H will be recognized
as that of entropy as defined in certain formulations of statistical mechanics where P_i is the probability of a system being in cell i of its phase space.
H is then, for example, the H in Boltzmann's famous H theorem.[10]

But apparently it was von Neumann who had made Shannon aware
of the historical antecedents of his ideas:

Dr. Shannon's work roots back, as von Neumann has pointed out, to
Boltzmann's work on statistical physics (1894), that entropy is related to
"missing information," inasmuch as it is related to the number of alternatives which remain possible to a physical system after all the macroscopi-
cally observable information concerning it has been recorded. L. Szilard
(*Zsch. f. Phys.*, Vol. 53, 1925) extended this idea to a general discussion of

information in physics, and von Neumann (*Math. Foundation of Quantum Mechanics*, Berlin, 1932, Chap. V) treated information in quantum mechanics and particle physics.[11]

These ideas were developed further by Shannon, Robert Fano, Denis Gabor, Richard Hamming, and others into the rich modern engineering discipline of communication theory.[12]

Another of von Neumann's early involvements with information came through his contact with the mathematician Alan Turing.[13] As an undergraduate at King's College, Cambridge, Turing enrolled in the spring term of 1935 in a course on the foundations of mathematics taught by M. H. A. Newman. The course introduced Turing to some of the current research on the logical foundations of mathematics, in particular Hilbert's formalist program for providing a foundation for mathematics and Kurt Gödel's incompleteness results of 1930 and 1931, which destroyed Hilbert's program. Newman showed how Gödel's results still left open one important question that had been formulated by Hilbert, known as the decision problem or, as it was commonly referred to in German, the *Entscheidungsproblem*: is there a procedure that, for every formally statable mathematical assertion, will determine the truth value of the assertion?[14]

The problem attracted Turing's interest, and in 1936 he wrote a paper that answered it in the negative. He framed his answer in terms of theoretical machines able to carry out the decision procedures. These Turing machines, as they were later known, subsequently had great significance in the theory of computing. Turing believed, as do many computer scientists today, that the numbers that can be calculated by any purely effective or mechanical procedure in mathematics are exactly those that can be calculated by one of his Turing machines.[15] He showed there is a single machine, known as the universal Turing machine, that can have instructions encoded in it to make it behave like any of the other Turing machines. In effect, the universal Turing machine is a mathematically precise, theoretical model of the stored-program computer (developed eight years later).

Turing intended his machines to model how humans carry out computations. Each machine was supplied with "a tape (the analogue of paper)" divided into squares that are "scanned" for symbols. The square being scanned at a given time, he wrote, is the only one of which the machine is "directly aware." The machines are designed so that the internal configuration can be altered, allowing them to "remember" some of the symbols they had previously "seen." Turing's anthropomorphic description concludes:[16]

We may now construct a machine to do the work of this [human] computer. To each state of mind of the [human] computer corresponds an "m-configuration" of the machine. The machine scans B squares corresponding to the B squares observed by the [human] computer. . . . The move which is done, and the succeeding configuration, are determined by the scanned symbol and the m-configuration. . . . A computing machine can be constructed to compute . . . the sequence computed by the [human] computer.

In 1936, with Newman's assistance, Turing received a fellowship to study with Alonzo Church in the mathematics department at Princeton University. Church was pursuing a similar line of investigation, which he formulated in a very different way from Turing, in terms of what is known as the lambda-calculus. Turing refined his computability results in Princeton and eventually decided to return for a second year and write a doctoral dissertation under Church's direction. Turing, Church, and others in the Princeton mathematical community (including Stephen Kleene, J. Barkley Rosser, and Gödel) were largely responsible for developing the subject of Turing and Church's investigations into the mathematical theory of recursive functions, which has been of continuing interest to mathematical logicians and theoretical computer scientists.

Turing and von Neumann probably first met in April 1935, when von Neumann came to Cambridge at Newman's invitation to lecture on almost periodic functions. Only several weeks earlier Turing had submitted for publication a minor improvement to a result of von Neumann on this subject, and although there is no firm evidence of their meeting, it is likely that Newman introduced them. Turing and von Neumann certainly came into contact in Princeton, for at the time of Turing's graduate study the IAS was housed in the building with the Princeton University mathematics department. The earliest contacts between Turing and von Neumann apparently involved their mutual interests in almost periodic functions and the theory of continuous groups, though by 1938 von Neumann knew of Turing's work on computable numbers.

Von Neumann's actions suggest his high regard for Turing and his theoretical machine model. In the spring of 1938 von Neumann offered Turing a position as his assistant at the institute, but Turing declined it to return to his fellowship at Cambridge and his war-threatened homeland. Stan Ulam has reported that von Neumann played with Turing machine-like mechanical descriptions of numbers while they toured Europe in the summer of 1938 and that von Neumann spoke highly of Turing's work several times during 1939.[17] After the war, von Neumann had the employees of his computer project read Turing's paper as part of their education in the theory of computing.[18]

An important episode in von Neumann's intellectual development was his correspondence from 1939 to 1941 with the Hungarian physicist Rudolf Ortvay.[19] Ortvay played an important role in the Hungarian scientific community by following current trends in science, suggesting research problems to other scientists, and organizing international symposia. He became interested in what quantum theory could illuminate about the brain and contacted von Neumann, presumably because of von Neumann's earlier work on quantum mechanics. Ortvay found a responsive correspondent, for von Neumann admits that he had been thinking "extensively, mainly from last year [1938]" about the nature of the "observer" in quantum mechanics as a kind of "quasi-physiological concept."[20]

In the course of their correspondence Ortvay tutored von Neumann on the anatomy of the brain and suggested a program of brain study closely resembling the one von Neumann later followed. In a letter written on Christmas day 1939, Ortvay returned to a topic "I have already brought forward many times before, namely to the theory of the operation of the brain." He predicted that science was on the verge of a rapid advancement in the study of the brain as a "switching system" and argued that the fundamental breakthrough would not be made by physicians or physiologists but by mathematicians or physicists, who are better able "to see the simple and theoretical structure of a complicated complex." In a letter of 30 March 1940 Ortvay first made explicit the comparison between the brain and electronic calculating equipment, if only to deny the similarity:

Of course I don't think that the mechanism of the brain is very similar to a computing equipment consisting of electronic valves but I do believe it is a complicated and very specialized equipment, which may be very simple in terms of basic properties! . . . I am ready to believe that a less detailed treatment, that with the mechanism for the brain, whereby the cell would be the unit and some idea for the interconnection, is perhaps even now timely.

This is startlingly early for the discussion of any electronic calculating equipment. Perhaps Ortvay had in mind the cosmic ray counters, which were internationally available in the late 1930s. Von Neumann concurred with Ortvay about the importance of having the theory be simple, entirely in keeping with his own previous efforts to provide axiomatic regularity in set theory, quantum mechanics, and the theory of games: "I cannot accept that a theory of prime importance, which describes processes which everybody believes to be elementary, can be right if it is too complicated, i.e. if it describes these elementary processes as being horribly complex and sophisticated ones. Thus I feel instinctively horror of the present day quantum chemistry and especially biochemistry."[21]

The imminent breakthrough in the understanding of the brain was a recurrent theme in Ortvay's letters.[22] In a letter of 29 January 1941 he went a step further and suggested von Neumann as the appropriate person to carry forward this research program. Ortvay also amplified on a suggestion in his 30 March 1940 letter about the mathematical approach to be taken, and his outlines resembled closely the program that von Neumann developed after the war:

I liked your paper [on the theory of games] very much at the time and it gave birth to the hope that, if I could succeed in drawing your attention to the problem of brain cells, you may succeed in formulating the problem. The problem seems to be this: The brain can be conceived as a network, having in its nodes the brain cells. These are interconnected in a way that each cell can receive from and transmit to several other cell impulses. As to which of these impulses are taken in from or passed on to the other cells may depend on the state of the cell which in turn is dependent on the effects previously affecting the cell in question. For the cell it may perhaps be enough to have a limited number of potential states? (Although it is genetics which shows us how differentiated a cell can be since we know many hundreds of genes in the chromosomes.) The actual state of cells conceived as numbered ones could characterize the state of the brain. There would be such a distribution corresponding to every spiritual state and the state would be relevant to every reaction, e.g. that which is the way of transmitting a stimulus to a nerve. It may recall an automatic telephone center where there is a change however after every communication in the connection. Perhaps the ever refining techniques in the switching equipment would prove a fertile analogy.

The big trouble is that the physicians, who know the facts, are so hostile towards the more abstract way of thinking.

In a final letter of interest, dated 16 February 1941, Ortvay suggested a program of study strikingly similar to Wiener's cybernetics:

Now I wish to mention another matter: these days everybody is talking about organization, totality. Today's computing machines, automatic telephone exchanges, high-voltage equipment like cascade transformers as well as radio transmitter and receiver equipment, but also an industrial plant or an office are all technical examples of such organizations. I think there is a common element in all these which is capable of being axiomatized. I don't know if there has been an attempt in this direction? I am interested in knowing this because I believe that if it is possible to sharply accentuate the essential elements relevant to the organization, as such, this would give an overview of the alternatives and would facilitate the understanding of such systems as, for instance, the brain.

It was not his correspondence with Ortvay, however, but instead his reading of a paper by Warren McCulloch and Walter Pitts that triggered von Neumann's active interest in information processing.[23] At the recommendation of Norbert Wiener and Julian Bigelow, von Neumann read the paper, "A Logical Calculus of the Ideas Immanent in Nervous Activity," soon after its publication in 1943. He was impressed by its potential for bringing mathematical regularity to the ill-understood phenomena of information processing in the human brain.[24] The paper presented a simple logical calculus of neural nets, using as axioms rules that McCulloch had developed in an earlier research project to describe psychons and as a logical framework a combination developed by Pitts of Rudolf Carnap's logical calculus and Bertrand Russell and Alfred North Whitehead's *Principia Mathematica.*[25]

The McCulloch-Pitts model did not describe the structure or internal operation of the individual neurons. Instead these neurons were treated as "black boxes," about which it was known only that they obey certain mathematical rules governing the input and output of signals. Networks of neurons cooperate to calculate, learn, store information, and carry out other information processing tasks. McCulloch and Pitts argued for the universality of their networks to carry out any information processing task and claimed to have "proved, in substance, the equivalence of all general Turing machines—man-made or begotten,"[26] which they took as a fundamental relationship between artificial and biological information processing. Working at times in collaboration with Pitts, McCulloch continued these investigations. For example, in a 1945 paper he used a related model to explain how humans believe universal ("for all") statements.[27] Pitts accepted a position at the MIT Research Laboratory of Electronics in 1943, and McCulloch joined him there in 1952. At MIT their work came under the influence of

Norbert Wiener, who regarded it as contributing to his research in cybernetics.[28] Meanwhile, von Neumann began to build on their work in his own direction as he developed his theory of automata.[29]

Psychologists and physiologists were less than enthusiastic about McCulloch and Pitts's axiomatic model of neurons, objecting (correctly) to its great simplicity and in particular to its inability to model some important physiological features.[30] Von Neumann himself recognized the primitive character of the model: "Following W. Pitts and W.S. MacCulloch [*sic*]... we ignore the more complicated aspects of neuron functioning: Thresholds, temporal summation, relative inhibition, changes of the threshold by after effects of stimulation beyond the synaptic delay, etc."[31] Nonetheless, von Neumann appears to have been attracted by the fundamental unity of the biological and man-made worlds he found in their model. He made their neural nets and Turing's machines the two pillars of his theory of automata and in doing so brought McCulloch and Pitts's work to a wider recognition in the biomedical community.[32]

Contacts with the Biomedical Community

Following his reading of the McCulloch-Pitts paper and his first involvement with high-speed calculating equipment, von Neumann took an active interest in the scientific work on what might be called biological information processing. He began to read extensively on neurophysiology, establish contacts in the biomedical community, and participate in topically related interdisciplinary conferences.[33]

His scientific interchanges on biological information fell into two categories. There were his regular discussions over a period of years with several close friends and associates: Julian Bigelow, Herman Goldstine, Stan Ulam, Norbert Wiener, and Eugene Wigner and, to a lesser degree, Warren McCulloch and Abraham Taub. These interchanges generally occurred in informal conversation and are mostly undocumented; however, there were also other scientists with whom von Neumann had brief, but occasionally intensive, contact, such as when he inquired about biological phenomena or engaged in discussion following one of his public presentations. These kinds of interchanges left a more permanent record and enable us to sketch a picture of his interests and intellectual development.

His interaction with the biomedical community began at about the same time as the IAS computer project. The first contact seems to have been in December 1946, when he corresponded with Sol Spiegelman, a biochemist from Washington University in St. Louis, following a meeting that Spiegelman and Edward Teller had attended in Washington, D.C., at which von Neumann lectured on the possible role of servomechanisms in chromosome pairing.[34] In this correspondence, von Neumann provided references to the literature on servomechanisms, and Spiegelman sent information about the literature on biophysics and discussed his ideas for "self-duplication."[35] Von Neumann continued to discuss his ideas on biological information processing with other scientists in the late 1940s. In this period he corresponded with the population biologist A. J. Lotka of Metropolitan Life Insurance Company in New York about the similarities between Lotka's results on reproduction and multiplication in biological populations and the wartime work at Los Alamos on neutron multiplication in near-critical states.[36] In 1948 or 1949 he met twice in Princeton with Heinz von Foerster, later the director of the Biological Computer Laboratory at the University of Illinois, about a theory of memory Foerster was developing.[37] He had an interesting correspondence with the German physical chemist K. F. Bonhoeffer.[38] Through the California Institute of Technology scientist Max Delbruck, Bonhoeffer sent von Neumann a copy of his 1948 paper presenting a theory of nervous excitation and conduction based on his investigation of an iron-wire analog of the nerve that had been developed by Ostwald, Heathcote, and Lillie.[39] In response, von Neumann provided Bonhoeffer with a lengthy analysis of the results of McCulloch and Pitts, explained his ideas for building counters and learning automata out of idealized neurons, recounted plans for a probabilistic theory of automata, and gave his reasons for not studying humans, rats, or even army ants for learning about biological information processing.[40] That same year K. S. Lashley of the Yerkes Laboratory of Primate Biology sent von Neumann suggestions about a physiological research program to test his ideas on the general and logical theory of automata as they had been presented at the Hixon Symposium.[41]

These contacts continued through the 1950s while von Neumann was healthy. In 1950 he agreed to participate in a study by Alejandre Arrellane of Massachusetts General Hospital, who was collecting electroencephalographs of "privileged brains."[42] In 1951

R. Lorente de No, a physiologist at the Rockefeller Institute, encouraged him to continue with his work on the reliability of automata with unreliable organisms as a means of improving the general understanding of the cerebral cortex.[43] In August 1955 he corresponded with the University of Wisconsin geneticist Joshua Lederberg about the adequacy of von Neumann's model of self-reproduction for explaining biological reproduction.[44] Later the same year, von Neumann was in contact with the physiologist C. M. Williams, who, together with Graham Weddell, carried out a research project at Oxford in the years from 1952 to 1954 on the innervation of ear hairs in a rabbit. Williams and Weddell discovered an information mechanism they regarded as similar to the multiplexing technique von Neumann developed to improve reliability in computing machinery.[45]

Von Neumann also participated in two interdisciplinary organizations dating from near the beginning of his work on high-speed computing. In late 1944 von Neumann, Howard Aiken, and Norbert Wiener decided that there was sufficient interest in the broad subject of information processing to convene a small group of scientists to discuss the future development of this field of effort, which they pointed out "as yet is not even named."[46] They did not hold an open meeting because so many of the projects involving information processing were connected to the war effort and remained classified. Those who received invitations were scientists and engineers with an interest in "communications engineering, the engineering of computing machines, the engineering of control devices, the mathematics of time series in statistics, and the communication and control aspects of the nervous system."[47] Aiken and Wiener proposed that the group be known as the Teleological Society, for as it was explained to Herman Goldstine: "Teleology is the study of purpose of conduct, and it seems that a large part of our interests are devoted on the one hand to the study of how purpose is realized in human and animal conduct and on the other hand how purpose can be imitated by mechanical and electrical means."[48]

The group, which met in Princeton 6–7 January, 1945, included Leland Cunningham (Aberdeen Proving Ground), W. E. Deming (Census Bureau), Goldstine (University of Pennsylvania), R. Lorente de No (Rockefeller Institute), McCulloch (University of Illinois Medical School), Pitts (Kellex Corporation), E. H. Vestine (Carnegie Institution), and Samuel Wilks (Princeton University), in addition to the three organizers.[49] On the first day, von Neumann lectured on computing machines and Wiener on communication engineering. On the second day, Lorente de No and McCulloch described the organization of the brain.[50] According to the agenda, they discussed the publication of a journal, steps to take to form and support a research center in this discipline, a patent policy for the group, measures to bring the work to public attention (such as through the American Association for the Advancement of Science), and "how to protect the researches of the group from dangerous and sensational publicity."[51] The outcome was the formation of four study groups reflecting the principal interests of the participants: filtering and prediction problems (Pitts, Wiener), applications of fast computing methods to statistical problems (Deming, Vestine, Wilkes, von Neumann), applications to differential equations that arise in astronomy, hydrodynamics, and ballistics (Aiken, Cunningham, Goldstine, von Neumann), and neurology (No, McCulloch, Pitts). The study groups agreed to prepare within three months memoranda about research they would be interested in pursuing, with the understanding that another meeting would be called within six months to formulate a final memorandum on a research program. Correspondence about the Teleological Society tailed off rapidly, no second meeting was ever convened, and no research memorandum was written.[52] Julian Bigelow attributes this failure in part to a clash of personalities among the organizers.[53]

Although plans for the Teleological Society fell apart, von Neumann continued to ponder the character of biological information processing and discuss his ideas with other scientists. A good indication of his thinking in late 1946 can be gleaned from a long letter he wrote to Wiener describing topics for a meeting they planned for the coming December.[54] The first part of the letter was highly pessimistic and expressed doubts that von Neumann stated he had felt "for the better part of a year." It argued that the results of Turing, McCulloch, and Pitts were too general to be informative about the working of the neural mechanism:

What seems worth emphasizing to me is, however, that after the great positive contribution of Turing-cum-Pitts-and-McCulloch is assimilated, the situation is rather worse than before. Indeed, these authors have demonstrated in absolute and hopeless generality, that anything and everything Brouwerian can be done by an appropriate mechanism, and specifically by a neural mechanism—and that even one, definite mechanism can be "universal." Inverting the argument: Nothing that we may know or learn about the functioning of the organism can give, without "microscopic", cytological work any clues regarding the further details of the neural mechanism.... I think you will feel with me the type of frustration that I am trying to express.

The problem he foresaw with microscopic work was that the complexity of the brain is "overawing":

To understand the brain with neurological methods seems to me about as hopeful as to want to understand the ENIAC with no instrument at one's disposal that is smaller than about 2 feet across its critical organs, with no methods of intervention more delicate than playing with a fire hose (although one might fill it with kerosene or nitroglycerine instead of water) or dropping cobblestones into the circuit. . . . And our intellectual possibilities relatively to it are about as good as some bodies vis-vis [*sic*] the ENIAC, if he has never heard of any part of arithmetic.

He discussed alternative approaches, such as studying the nervous systems of frogs or employing Gestalt theory, but dismissed them all as not leading to any direct knowledge of the human nervous system. He also dismissed the axiomatic study of multicellular organisms in which cells are chosen as the undefined basic elements, arguing by analogy that the cell is too refined an object to be taken as elementary:

To be more par terre: Consider, in any field of technology, the state of affairs which is characterized by the development of highly complex "standard components", which are at the same time individualized, well suited to mass production, and (in spite of their "standard" character) well suited to purposive differentiation. This is clearly a late, highly developed style, and not the ideal one for a first approach of an outsider to the subject, for an effort toward understanding. For the purpose of understanding the subject, it is much better to study an earlier phase of its evolution, preceding the development of this high standardization-with-differentiation, i.e, to study a phase in which these "elegant" components do not yet appear. This is especially true, if there is reason to suspect already in that archaic stage mechanisms (or organisms) which exhibit the most specific traits of the simplest representatives of the above mentioned "late" stage.

The second half of the letter was more upbeat; von Neumann suggested a program of empirical research involving the study of the bacteriophage, which he hoped "may be the first relevant step forward and possibly the greatest step that may at all be required."[55] His optimism was based on the fact that these organisms are simple enough to be studied yet complex enough to orient themselves in an unorganized milieu, locate and appropriate food, and reproduce. He suggested high-precision X-ray analysis and advanced electron microscopy as the most promising methods of investigation.

The ideas in the second half of the letter had arisen through his discussions with Irving Langmuir, associate director of General Electric's Research Laboratory in Schenectady, New York. In October 1946 von Neumann and Langmuir had met to discuss the study of proteins by chemical and crystallographic analyses, and Langmuir had introduced him to the work of the crystallographer Dorothy Wrinch.[56] Von Neumann found X-ray crystallography of proteins unsuitable for his purposes because of concomitant problems with data analysis, for he estimated that analysis of some proteins would require 1000-term Fourier analyses and involve millions of multiplications.[57] Thus he began to search for other procedures to use, at least until high-speed computers became available.

The plan he settled on was to scale up the existing "linear" and "cyclol" models of proteins by a factor of 10^8 and use similarly scaled-up electromagnetic centimeter waves to simulate X-rays in order to study medium- and large-sized proteins.[58] This provided a kind of analog replacement that avoided the large amounts of calculation required in X-ray crystallography.[59] He discussed the engineering aspects of the plan with RCA scientist Vladimir Zworykin and then submitted a funding proposal (which was unsuccessful) to Mina Rees that called for an engineering group with radar experience, an X-ray crystallographer, a group of physical chemists, and a theoretical coordinator.[60] He mentioned that Zworykin and the RCA engineers had agreed to serve as the engineers, H. S. Taylor and J. Turkevitch of the Princeton University Chemistry Department to serve as crystallographers, the trained British crystallographer A. D. Booth who was coming to the Institute as a visitor in 1947 could handle the physical chemistry, and he would assume the duty of theoretical coordinator. He asked for initial funding of $50,000 and annual continuing support of $15,000. When the proposal to ONR failed, von Neumann seems to have abandoned this avenue of research.

The Macy Conferences on Feedback Mechanisms and Circular Causal Systems in Biology and the Social Sciences, or as they were later known, the Conferences on Cybernetics, provided a substitute for the Teleological Society.[61] The Josiah Macy, Jr. Foundation was a regular sponsor of conferences, especially in the biomedical sciences, which brought together by invitation groups of up to twenty-five distinguished scientists to discuss narrowly focused, often interdisciplinary problems. Frank Fremont-Smith of the Macy Foundation initiated a series of conferences in which mathematicians, neurophysiologists, psychiatrists, psychologists, and sociologists could discuss with one another "mechanisms underlying purposive behavior," and he recruited Warren McCulloch to chair the meetings.[62] The work of Wiener and others on cybernetics was the stimulus for the organization of the meetings, as McCulloch explained:

Our meetings began chiefly because Norbert Wiener and his friends in mathematics, communication engineering, and physiology, had shown the applicability of the notions of inverse feedback to all problems of regulation, homeostasis, and goal-directed activity from steam engines to human societies. Our early sessions were largely devoted to getting these notions clear in our heads, and to discovering how to employ them in our dissimilar fields.[63]

The first meeting was held in New York in March 1946, with subsequent meetings initially scheduled at six-month intervals. After the fifth meeting it was decided that a full year was needed between meetings in order to give the participants enough time to make observations and explore ideas arising at the meetings. The tenth and last meeting was held in April 1953.[64] The core of people who participated in the majority of meetings included the mathematicians Pitts, von Neumann, and Wiener, the electrical engineer Julian Bigelow, the physiologists Freemont-Smith and Ralph Gerard, the anthropologists Gregory Bateson and Margaret Mead, the psychologist Hienrich Kluever, and the psychiatrist McCulloch. A few other people, notably the biophysicist Heinz von Foerster and the philosopher F. S. C. Northrop, attended several conferences. Quite a few other scholars were invited to attend a single meeting when a topic close to their interests was under discussion.

Von Neumann was a central figure and a regular lecturer, especially at the early meetings. At the March 1946 meeting he lectured on "Computing Machines: Their Formal Behavior including Memory, Learning, and Recording." At the third meeting, in March 1947, he presented his ideas on the connection between entropy and information and compared feedback and memory systems in biological and artificial information processing systems.[65] At the fourth meeting, in October 1947, he lectured on "Circuits for Typical Logical Tasks." After this meeting, the number of formal talks was reduced, and he made no more presentations. Outside obligations caused him to miss several of the later meetings, and he resigned at the ninth meeting to make room for other participants. His resignation and that of Wiener may have been a primary reason for terminating the conferences.

Two examples illustrate the interdisciplinary nature of these meetings and suggest the context in which von Neumann developed his ideas about automata. The first example is from the March 1947 meeting, which McCulloch described as follows:

The second day, at von Neumann's request, began with a discussion of consciousness, as to whether there is an anatomical substrate for what everybody has [called] "knowing things." Von Bonin held it was probably not [the] cerebral cortex that determined awareness but more likely something in the vicinity of the midbrain, the cortex determining what we know rather than that we know; and I suggested the importance of the thalamus as suggested by experiments with strychnine. Fremont-Smith went into the different degrees of consciousness from full attention through twilight states to sleep and hysterical amnesias. Molly Harrower described the stimulation of the cortex as not disturbing patients even when it induced all sorts of sensations, but throwing them into a panic when it caused vocalization resembling speech. Fitch sharpened the distinction between consciousness and awareness, and I tried vainly to help him with Spinoza's definition of consciousness as the idea of ideas, or else awareness of awareness, but was unable to tie it to the mid-brain. I then presented my scheme of how we know universals, including diagrams that had the circuit action I expected in the auditory and visual cortex. Their likeness to the known anatomy was self-apparent, but I had difficulty in formulating the process of averaging over a group of transformations . . . . Von Neumann was disturbed by these notions for there was too much chaos instead of exact connections in the cortex and I failed to make clear, but Pitts succeeded, that the beauty of these circuit actions was that they only required statistical regularity, which is all I thought I had a right to expect of the tissue.[66]

The other example is from the eighth meeting, held in March 1951, on the topic of communication. Karl von Frisch spoke on communication among bees, the literary scholar I. A. Richards on human communications, Claude Shannon on the theory of communication, and the philosopher Suzanne Langer on the problem of symbols. Von Neumann was scheduled to talk about communication among machines but was called away on government business.

These repeated excursions into biological information process-ing and the interdisciplinary study of cybernetics have been ig-nored in previous accounts of von Neumann's computing, yet they clearly shaped his ideas.

The General and Logical Theory of Automata

Von Neumann began his study of the theory of automata at about the same time that work began on the Electronic Computer Project.[67] By the spring of 1946 he was already developing his first model of a self-replicating automaton, and in June he presented informal lectures in Princeton covering many of the topics he discussed two years later at the Hixon Symposium. This Hixon Symposium lecture, "The Logic of Analogue Nets and Automata," was delivered 20 September, 1948 at a symposium in Pasadena, California, on cerebral mechanisms in behavior and published in 1951. It is the earliest published account of von Neumann's theory of automata.[68]

The objective of the Hixon Symposium was to assemble a small group of distinguished scientists to discuss cerebral mechanisms from the behavioral, as opposed to the biochemical or genetic, viewpoint. The audience consisted mainly of knowledgeable fac-ulty from California Institute of Technology and a few surrounding universities, including such distinguished scientists as G. W. Beadle, Max Delbruck, and Linus Pauling.[69] It was Pauling who first ap-proached von Neumann about participating.[70] McCulloch, who was also an invited lecturer, encouraged von Neumann to speak on "the evolution of order out of chaos," but instead von Neu-mann took as his subject an analysis of logical switching elements and their integration into digital machines (both biological and artificial).[71]

His lecture called for a theory of natural and artificial automata based on mathematical logic. He discussed the significance the work of Turing and McCulloch-Pitts might have for such a theory and outlined a number of issues meriting further investigation, including a probabilistic theory of automata, complexity and self-replication in automata, and comparisons between the computer and the brain. Von Neumann did not explicitly define "automata," but from his usage we can infer its application to any system that processes information as part of a self-regulating mechanism. His prime examples were the human central nervous system and the

computer, but his remarks suggest that he regarded other homeostatic systems within biological organisms, as well as radar systems
and telephone and other communication systems, as examples of
automata. What he had in mind is akin to what is known today as
a control system.

Von Neumann expressed hope that the theory of automata
would both provide a greater understanding of the functioning of
the human nervous system and guide improvements in the design
of computing machinery:

Automata have been playing a continuously increasing, and have by now
attained a very considerable, role in the natural sciences. During the last
part of this period automata have begun to invade certain parts of
mathematics too—particularly, but not exclusively, mathematical physics
or applied mathematics. Their role in mathematics presents an interesting
counterpart to certain functional aspects of organization in nature.
Natural organisms are, as a rule, much more complicated and subtle, and
therefore much less well understood in detail, than are artificial automata.
Nevertheless, some regularities which we observe in the organization of
the former may be quite instructive in our thinking and planning of the
latter; and conversely, a good deal of our experiences and difficulties with
our artificial automata can be to some extent projected on our interpre-
tations of natural organisms.[72]

Attention is paid to the complexity of the two prime examples of
automata. Fast computing equipment, he noted, contains at least
10^4 basic switching components and routinely carries out calculations involving 10^6 multiplications (10^9 binary operations), at least
30 percent of which he believed were critical to the correct
outcome; he estimated (correctly) that the human central nervous
system has approximately 10^{10} basic switching elements (neurons).
To handle the complexity he believed to be endemic in the important examples of automata, he suggested dividing the study of
automata into two parts. One part was to study the structure and
functioning of the individual elements that the system comprises,
which is the province of physiology in the case of the human nervous system and electrical engineering for the computer. The other
part was to study how these elements are organized into a whole and
how the functioning of the whole is expressed in terms of its
elements. This he regarded as the province of automata theory.

In order to dispose of the first type of study and get on to the
theory of automata, von Neumann resorted to axiomatics. He
treated the individual elements of automata, whether neurons or

vacuum tubes, as "black boxes" having "certain well-defined, outside, functional characteristics" and "assumed to react to certain unambiguously defined stimuli, by certain unambiguously defined responses."[73] The electrochemical processes within the neuron or the electrical processes in the vacuum tube that underlie the external behavior of these elements are not disclosed by the axioms.

Because of the centrality of the neuron and the vacuum tube to his theory, von Neumann gave a direct comparison of them as "digital, electrical" organs, by which he meant ones that give all-or-none responses and transmit their stimulus and response by electrical impulses.[74] He explained that in both cases his characterization was an idealization because both types of organ exhibit some analog (non-digital) behavior: neurons have fatigue, summation, self-oscillation, and subliminal stimulation, and in some circumstances vacuum tubes have continuous or nonlinear phenomena caused by properties of solid state physics, thermodynamics, and mechanics. However, the neuron and the vacuum tube are both taken as digital, electrical organs because of their digital behavior under normal operating circumstances.

He carried the comparison of the physical constitution of the neuron and the vacuum tube further in order to explain what "prevents us from attaining [in computers] the high degree of complication and the small dimensions which have been attained by natural organisms."[75] From a brief analysis of the size and spacing of elements and the electrical properties of the materials used in the computer and the brain, von Neumann concluded that artificial automata use materials that are "marginal and inferior to the natural ones."[76] At places his analysis was quite prescient, as when he suggested that within a few years computers would not be using vacuum tubes as their computing elements and that other logical designs for computing machines would eventually become possible.[77] The same is true of his argument (based on the ratio of neurons to vacuum tubes in the respective systems, their switching speeds, and their space and electrical potential requirements) that 10^4 was an appropriate number of switching organs for a computer system, a number he suggestd would not vary greatly without a change in the materials used to build computers. Indeed, computing systems never did use many more than 10^4 vacuum tubes; only after transistors and integrated circuits were introduced into computing systems did the number of switching components increase beyond this figure.

Von Neumann moved next from the physical to the intellectual problems of building better computing devices. He described two entirely different philosophies for finding errors and treating component malfunction, which he attributed to the human central nervous system and the computer. The natural system, he explained, tries to make errors as inconspicuous as possible: it detects them as they occur, adjusts to minimize their effect, and repairs or blocks the faulty components while allowing the rest of the automaton to continue to function. In contrast, the artificial system attempts to make errors as conspicuous as possible so that they will be brought to immediate attention, the machine be shut down, and repair or replacement be immediately commissioned:

> With our artificial automata we are moving much more in the dark than nature appears to be with its organisms. We are, and apparently, at least at present, have to be, much more "scared" by the occurrence of an isolated error and by the malfunction which must be behind it. Our behavior is clearly that of overcaution, generated by ignorance.[78]

The reason given for this ignorance is the lack of a "properly mathematical-logical" theory of automata. The theory, von Neumann maintained, should incorporate formal logic because it studies discrete, all-or-none properties, such as digital switching, and because Turing and McCulloch-Pitts had already shown how to apply it effectively to automata. Von Neumann identified some shortcomings in formal logic that limit its applicability to automata. One is that logic (as it was then practiced) considers only whether a result can be achieved in a finite number of steps—no matter how many—but the length is a practical consideration in the theory of automata since tasks must be completed in a practical amount of time and the cumulative effect of errors is more likely to render an effort unreliable when it involves many steps. To rectify these shortcomings von Neumann called for two modifications in logical theory as it is to be applied to automata:[79]

1. The actual length of "chains of reasoning," that is of the chains of operation, will have to be considered.
2. The operations of logic (syllogisms, conjunctions, disjunctions, negations, etc., that is, in the terminology that is customary for automata, various forms of gating, coincidence, anti-coincidence, blocking, etc., actions) will all have to be treated by procedures which allow exceptions (malfunctions) with low but non-zero probabilities.[80]

He believed that these modifications would result in a mathematical theory less combinatorial and more analytical (in the mathematical sense) than formal logic, one that would resemble "thermodynamics, primarily in the form it was received from Boltzmann, . . . that part of theoretical physics which comes nearest in some of its aspects to manipulating and measuring information."[81]

Von Neumann clearly had in mind the McCulloch-Pitts and Turing contributions as the foundation for his new theory. He lauded McCulloch and Pitts's formal logic of neural networks as "probably the most significant result obtained with the axiomatic method up to now" and cited its value for the scientific understanding of the human nervous system:[82]

It has often been claimed that the activities and functions of the human nervous system are so complicated that no ordinary mechanism could possibly perform them. It has also been attempted to name specific functions which by their nature exhibit this limitation. It has been attempted to show that such specific functions, logically, completely described, are per se unable of mechanical, neural realization. The McCulloch-Pitts result puts an end to this. It proves that anything that can be exhaustively and unambiguously described, anything that can be completely and unambiguously put into words, is ipso facto realizable by a suitable finite neural network. Since the converse statement is obvious, we can therefore say that there is no difference between the possibility of describing a real or imagined mode of behavior completely and unambiguously in words, and the possibility of realizing it by a finite formal neural network. The two concepts are co-extensive.[83]

The analysis up to this point left open the question of what can be "completely and unambiguously put into words." Taking visual analogy as an example, von Neumann admitted that this type of information processing is not covered by existing logics, that perhaps "the connection pattern of the visual brain itself is the simplest logical expression or definition of this principle," and that logic may "have to undergo a pseudomorphosis to neurology" to provide an adequate analysis of visual processing.

A discussion of Turing's contributions enabled von Neumann to introduce two of the themes central to his automata research: complexity and self-replication.[84] He formulated his analysis in terms of a paradox involving self-replication: one expects the complexity of a species to increase (or at least remain constant) through evolution, yet it is hard to understand how an automaton can produce anything more complicated than itself. Von Neumann first considered Turing's universal machine, which itself can imitate the behavior of a wide array of complex automata when supplied with their descriptions; however, he regarded the example as not entirely pertinent since Turing machines do not self-reproduce in the sense that biological automata do.

Therefore his goal was to derive an "equivalent" of Turing's result for automata with the ability to self-reproduce. He sketched plans for a kinetic model—an automaton that floats in a reservoir of liquid filled with a virtually unlimited supply of the dozen or so elementary parts from which it is built. Once given a set of instructions, the kinematic automaton will sort through the parts, locate those it needs, and assemble its progeny according to the instructions.[85] Von Neumann never presented the mechanical details to elaborate how the automaton will move in the reservoir, recognize components, grasp parts, or position or assemble them. These shortcomings presumably explain in part why he abandoned the kinetic model in favor of a series of progressively more complex, abstract, mathematical automata, the last of which is self-reproductive.[86]

The Hixon Symposium lecture closed with an explanation of the genetic function in terms of the theory of self-reproducing automata.[87] Von Neumann showed how some of the instructions he defined could be regarded as modeling the functions of a gene and how one of his automata "performs the fundamental act of reproduction, the duplication of genetic material."[88] He even suggested how, by altering one of his sets of instructions, one "can exhibit certain typical traits which appear in connection with mutation, lethally as a rule, but with a possibility of continuing reproduction with modification of traits."[89] Finally he considered a model of a gene that can both self-reproduce and produce select "enzymes." But his models fell short in that they did not describe the new automaton completely but offered only "general pointers, general cues." With all of this as preparation, he presented a solution to his evolutionary paradox: that there is a certain minimum level of complexity below which automata are degenerative (can only produce less complex automata than themselves) but above which some automata can reproduce equally or more complex progeny.

Complicated Automata

In December 1949, a little more than a year after the Hixon Symposium, von Neumann made his second public presentation on the theory of automata. The occasion was a series of five lectures, "The Theory and Organization of Complicated Automata," delivered at the University of Illinois.[90] In them he amplified on many of the points in the Hixon Symposium and discussed "the behavior of very complicated automata and the very specific difficulties caused by high complication."[91] The first lecture introduced his audience to the basic facts of modern computing machinery, the second and third lectures described the logical and probabilistic theories of automata, and the final two lectures explored in greater depth the issue of complication.

The first lecture mainly repeated the material in the Hixon Symposium on the computer and the brain as information processors and the distinction between analog and digital devices. But von Neumann broke new ground when he asked the "not completely obvious" question of how to measure the complexity of automata.[92] He suggested measuring the complexity by the number of vacuum tubes, the speed by the number of multiplications per second, and the efficiency by the percentage of code-ordering manipulations.[93]

The second lecture examined the contributions of McCulloch-Pitts and Turing in greater mathematical detail than did the Hixon Symposium. Von Neumann contrasted McCulloch and Pitts's "synthetic" approach of building automata from axiomatically defined simple components to Turing's "integral" approach of giving an axiomatic presentation of the whole system without defining the individual components. Von Neumann seemed to favor the synthetic approach in the study of simple automata and the integral approach in cases of higher complexity.[94]

The McCulloch-Pitts model had received an unenthusiastic reception from the biomedical community, but von Neumann promoted it with fervor because of its potential value for dealing with the great complexity in biological information processing organs.[95] He demonstrated the potency of McCulloch and Pitts's simple, idealized building blocks by constructing from them some networks that could have useful applications: a simple memory, a counting mechanism, and an elementary learning circuit (one that counts the number of times when a stimulus a is followed by a stimulus b and fires a pulse when the count reaches 256).

The discussion of Turing's contributions focused on the universal machine, the halting problem, and their significance for the study of complication.[96] After having shown how the universal Turing machine can imitate any other Turing machine, even one much more complicated, von Neumann argued that "a lesser degree of complexity in an automaton can be compensated for by an appropriate increase of complexity of the instructions"—provided that the imitating automaton is not below the level of complexity needed to carry out this imitative process.[97] Applying the halting result to the universal machine, he concluded about complication in automata:

The feature is just this, that you can perform with the logical type that's involved everything that's feasible, but the question of whether something is feasible in a type belongs to a higher logical type. It's connected with the remark I made earlier: that it is characteristic of objects of low complexity that it is easier to talk about the object than produce it and easier to predict its properties than to build it. But in the complicated parts of formal logic it is always one order of magnitude harder to tell what an object can do than to produce the object. The domain of the validity of the question is of a higher type than the question itself.[98]

The fourth lecture, "The Role of High and Extremely High Complication," resumed the analysis of complication in automata. (The third lecture, "Statistical Theories of Information," bore mainly on the question of reliability in automata, so discussion of it is deferred to the next section.) Von Neumann returned to the direct comparison of computing machines and the human nervous system as information processing automata, which he had begun in the Hixon Symposium, but added some new information and some numerical comparisons. For example, he compared the complexity and efficiency of these two types of automata according to several different measures. He calculated that there are a million times as many neurons as there are vacuum tubes (in the typical respective systems) and that by the most generous measure (on a logarithmic scale) the computer is not half as complicated as the brain. Even after noting that vacuum tubes can switch 5000 times as fast as neurons, however, he gave the overall advantage to the nervous system by a factor of 200.[99] The computer fared even less well in other comparisons, when his analyses showed that it occupies 10^9 more volume, dissipates 10^9 times as much total energy, and is 200,000 times less efficient in energy dissipation per binary act.[100]

Von Neumann repeated most of his Hixon discussion about the analog and digital nature of neurons and vacuum tubes, though he gave several new examples of the analog aspects of digital computers (such as their input and output when embedded as control devices in more complex systems, such as missiles and airplanes). He closed the discussion by judging digital methods as the far more effective ones in complex situations: "Also, it appears that digital mechanisms are necessary for complicated functions. Pure analog mechanisms are usually not suited for very complicated situations. The only way to handle a complicated situation with analog mechanisms is to break it up into parts and deal with the parts separately, and alternately, and this is a digital trick."[101]

The final Illinois lecture addressed the topics of hierarchy and evolution in complicated automata. Von Neumann repeated his Hixon Syposium remarks about the paradox of complication in evolution and his belief in a minimum threshold of complication needed for automata to be able to produce other automata as complicated as themselves. Then he extended his argument and quantified the threshold as being at a million or more elementary parts. Out of this discussion arose the closest statement to a definition of complication von Neumann ever gave:

There is a concept which will be quite useful here, of which we have a certain intuitive idea, but which is vague, unscientific, and imperfect. This concept clearly belongs to the subject of information, and quasi-thermodynamical considerations are relevant to it. I know no adequate name for it, but it is best described by calling it "complication." It is effectivity in complication, or the potentiality to do things. I am not thinking about how involved the object is, but how involved its purposive actions are. In this sense, an object is of the highest degree of complexity if it can do very difficult and involved things.[102]

Much of the lecture was devoted to a more thorough description of the kinematic model of self-replication than was he gave in the Hixon Symposium.[103] The twelve to fifteen elementary components, he explained, are intended as the analogs of neurons, muscle, connective tissue, and a producer of metabolic energy.[104] The purpose of the kinematic automaton is to produce other automata, including ones like itself. As originally envisioned in 1948, the kinematic automaton was designed to build copies from patterns, but by the time of the Illinois lectures, he wanted to build the offspring from a set of instructions in order to model more exactly the biological process of self-replication:

To proceed in this matter one must have axiomatic descriptions of automata. You see, I'm coming quite close to Turing's trick with universal automata, which also started with a general formal description of automata. If you take those dozen elements I referred to in a rather vague and general way and give exact descriptions of them (which could be done on two printed pages or less) you will have a formal language for describing automata unambiguously. Now any notation can be expressed as a binary notation, which can be recorded on a punched tape with a single channel. Hence any automaton description could be punched on a piece of tape. At first, it is better not to use a description of the pieces and how they fit together, but rather a description of the consecutive steps used in building the automaton.[105]

Von Neumann concluded with an explanation of how to build a kinematic version of Turing's universal machine by constructing out of rigid elements both a binary tape and a "constructing automaton," the latter with the ability to read the tape and build the automaton specified by the tape's instructions. Von Neumann also showed how to introduce random changes as a way to model mutations in the progeny.

Building Reliable Automata from Unreliable Parts

In the third Illinois lecture, "Statistical Theories of Information," von Neumann described his ideas for extending the logical theory of automata to a probabilistic theory.[106] The main motivation was to make automata more reliable in the face of component failures. No physical component can be expected to work faultlessly over long periods of time, so he proposed to examine the effect of component error on the overall functioning of the automata in which they occur and to develop a probabilistic logic that takes reliability into account. His discussion of the probabilistic theory was more schematic than that of the logical theory. He indicated various research that could be assimilated into the new probabilistic theory, as well as stating some of the objectives the new theory should have, but he set forth no formal theory.[107]

He introduced two theories of information, "which are quite relevant in this context although they are not conceived from the strictly logical point of view."[108] These are the work of thermodynamicists on entropy and information and the work of the electrical engineers on communication theory.[109] From communication theory, he showed how Shannon provided a quantitative approach to measuring the capacity of a communication channel and how redundancy can be used to increase channel capacity in the presence of noise. He used Hamming's work on error-detecting codes to begin an analysis of the value of digitalization in producing precision in imprecise devices.

He suggested the connection to thermodynamics by giving several analogies. He compared bottlenecks in computing systems—notably small memories and slow input equipment—to heat engines that have excessive temperature differentials that make them run inefficiently and then continued:

Thermodynamical concepts will probably enter into this new theory of information. There are strong indications that information is similar to entropy and that degenerative processes of entropy are paralleled by degenerative processes in the processing of information. It is likely that you cannot define the function of an automaton, or its efficiency, without characterizing the milieu in which it works by means of statistical traits like the ones used to characterize a milieu in thermodynamics. The statistical variables of the automaton's milieu will, of course, be somewhat more involved than the standard thermodynamical variable of temperature, but they will probably be similar in character.[110]

Von Neumann continued his analysis of the issue of reliability in a series of five lectures he presented at the California Institute of Technology in January 1952, "Probabilistic Logics and the Syntheses of Reliable Organisms from Unreliable Components."[111] The approach in these lectures was generally the same as in the earlier ones: "Error should be treated by thermodynamical methods . . . as information has been, by the work of L. Szilard and C. E. Shannon. The present treatment falls short of achieving this, but it assembles, it is hoped, some of the building materials, which will have to enter into the final structure."[112]

In contrast to the two previous sets of public lectures, these concentrate not on descriptive analysis but rather on building up the requisite mathematical machinery for a detailed analysis. He presented the automata as networks of idealized neurons, linked by lines that carry pulses, in which the output of one neuron becomes the input of another neuron. Input lines can be either inhibitory or excitatory, and each neuron has associated with it a threshold function $\phi(x)$ that describes the input conditions under which it will fire an output. The system is timed so that the output of a neuron becomes excited at time $t+1$ if and only if at time t the number k of excitatory inputs and the number j of inhibitory inputs satisfies the formula $k \geq \phi(j)$.

Von Neumann then gave an analysis of the logical character of the single-output automata. He showed a one-to-one correspondence between the class of single-output automata and the polynomials of the propositional calculus. A reduction theorem is proved, which states that any single-output automaton can be replaced by a network built from three basic single-output automata that correspond to the logical compositions "*a* or *b*," "*a* and *b*," and "*a* and not-*b*." This reduction theorem is strengthened by showing two ways in which every network can be built up from a single type of automaton, using either organs corresponding to the well-known Sheffer Stroke "not-(*a* and *b*)" or from majority organs $m(a,b,c)$ which represent the logical composition "(*a* and *b*) or (*a* and *c*) or (*b* and *c*)."[113] Thereafter he assumed automata to be composed of either Sheffer or majority organs, whichever was more convenient to the analysis at hand. He also claimed that if feedback loops are allowed and an unlimited memory is added, the class of automata is equivalent to intuitionistic logic.[114] Finally he gave some examples of the kinds of automata that can be constructed from these basic organs: a memory organ that recalls whether *a* or *b* was the last input to be stimulated, a scalar organ that counts input stimuli by twos, and a simple learning automaton that learns to anticipate that stimulus *a* is followed by stimulus *b*.

With these preliminaries concluded, von Neumann turned to the question of error. The problem with unreliable components, he claimed, is not that they will occasionally cause the automaton to give an incorrect result but rather that they degrade the performance such that the reliability of all results is called into question. To illustrate this point he showed that when the memory organ he had just defined is modified to incorporate unreliable components, it has a probability of giving the correct answer, which approaches one-half over time; in other words, the organ loses its memory over time. With the problem carefully specified, he set his problem mathematically as follows: given any fixed probability of error $\varepsilon < 1/2$ in the basic components (Sheffer organs or majority organs) and $\delta > 0$, can an automaton be built from these basic components that will perform the desired function and commit an error in the output of the automaton with probability less than δ?[115]

The method he offered to answer the question affirmatively is known as multiplexing.[116] The basic idea is to carry each message simultaneously on a bundle of N lines instead of on a single line. Each neuron has a bundle of lines entering and exiting it, where it had a single line before. A "fiduciary" level θ, $0 < \theta < 1/2$, is set such that the stimulation of $\geq (1-\theta)N$ lines is interpreted as a stimulated state for the bundle, the stimulation of $< \theta N$ lines is interpreted as the nonstimulation of the bundle, and the stimulation of an intermediate number of lines is interpreted as an undecided result. Von Neumann explained how to refine the neurons to accommodate bundles instead of single lines by using an executive organ to perform the basic operations on the input signals and a restoring organ to restore the stimulation to an appropriate level.[117] He sketched a statistical argument showing that the use of a sufficiently large bundle of lines will give any desired degree of accuracy. He estimated that multiplexing at the level $N = 20,000$ ($\pm 40\%$) will be required to ensure suitable reliability in either the computer or the human nervous system.[118]

Von Neumann appreciated the theoretical value of multiplexing but had no illusions about its practical applicability to computing machinery: "This implies, that such techniques are impractical for present technologies of componentry (although this may perhaps not be true for certain conceivable technologies of the future), but they are not necessarily unreasonable (at least not on grounds of size alone) for the micro-componentry of the human nervous system."[119] He knew, in fact, that the human nervous system does not use a simple multiplexing technique like the one he described, and he reviewed some of the ways in which the nervous system uses a combination of analog and digital techniques (he had already discussed many of these in his Hixon and Illinois lectures). It is not so clear that he understood another limitation of his analysis: that there is no accommodation for a feedback mechanism, which is important in the human nervous system.[120] Nonetheless, his technical mathematical results served as the starting point for the study of reliable computation with unreliable components, a subject that has received steady, if modest, attention to this day.[121]

Cellular Automata

Von Neumann's most extensive work in the theory of automata was his investigation of cellular automata; the results are contained in an incomplete manuscript, "The Theory of Automata: Construction, Reproduction, Homogeneity," edited and completed by Arthur Burks.[122] According to von Neumann's wife, Klara, work on this manuscript began in late September 1952 and continued until 1953.[123] Two chapters were completed in draft form, as were fragments of several other chapters. There is evidence that work on at least one additional chapter was planned but never started.

It is possible to gain additional information about von Neumann's ideas on cellular automata from John Kemeny's essay, "Man Viewed as a Machine." In March 1953 von Neumann delivered the Vanuxem Lectures at Princeton University. The information in the first three of these lectures, "Machines and Organisms," was largely repeated in *The Computer and the Brain* (and is discussed in the next section). The final lecture described four of his models of automata: kinematic, cellular, excitation-threshold-fatigue, and continuous. Because of his plans to describe these models, together with a probabilistic model, in his manuscript, "Theory of Automata: Construction, Reproduction, Homogeneity," which he had promised to the University of Illinois Press, he declined an invitation to write up the Vanuxem Lectures for publication.[124] Instead John Kemeny would write up a general account of von Neumann's ideas based on both the Vanuxem Lectures and the two completed chapters of von Neumann's manuscript. The result was published in *Scientific American* in 1955 and became publicly available many years before Burks completed von Neumann's own manuscript.

Kemeny discussed many of the topics included in von Neumann's other publications on automata. He compared the computer and brain with respect to energy consumed, number of switching units, switching speed, memory capacity, and method of retrieving information from the memory. He described McCulloch-Pitts neural nets and Turing machines and indicated their importance for automata theory. He also gave the first detailed description in print of the cellular automaton capable of self-reproduction. The self-reproducing automaton is constructed from three types of cells: McCulloch-Pitts–style neurons to provide logical control, transmission cells to provide the channel and mechanism for carrying messages between the constructing automaton and the construction area for the new automaton, and muscles for enacting the new construction. The constructing automaton is estimated to fill a central unit of rectangular size 80 cells by 400 cells, with a tail holding an instruction tape 150,000 cells long. Kemeny's diagrams illustrate how the neural nets carry out conjunction, disjunction, negation, delay, counting, and memory. They also show the automaton in the process of self-reproduction.

The Vanuxem Lectures give the most detailed presentation of von Neumann's models of self-reproducing automata. The kinematic model, developed in 1948 or earlier, has already been described. Stan Ulam convinced von Neumann to abandon this approach in favor of cellular models, which have the advantages of avoiding many physical considerations (such as the fusing together of physical parts) and being more amenable to rigorous mathematical examination.[125] The cellular approach has the added advantage of reducing the spatial complexity of the self-reproducing automata from three dimensions to two through the use of a signal-crossover design.

Von Neumann called these structures "crystalline regularities" but also "cellular automata," using modern terminology. They are homogeneous, two-dimensional arrays of square cells, each containing the same twenty-nine-state finite automaton.[126] Any cell can assume at a given time the unexcitable state (representing the presence of no neuron), one of twenty quiescent (resting, but excitable) states, or one of eight sensitized (excited) states. Quiescent cells can respond to ordinary stimuli from adjacent cells; unexcitable cells respond only to special stimuli, which initiate the construction or growth of new cells. The state of a given cell at a given time is determined, according to a set of transition rules, by the states of that cell and its four nondiagonal neighbors at some fixed earlier time.[127] At time 0 a cellular automaton has a given initial cell assignment consisting of a finite distribution of excited and quiescent cells. Self-replication is said to occur if the initial cell assignment is copied in a different region of the cellular array.

The excitation-threshold-fatigue model is a refinement on the cellular model. It is a cellular array in which each cell contains a finite automaton, as before, but the cells are modified to incorporate a fatigue mechanism with a designated threshold and two refractory periods, which models the fatigue pattern of human neurons. When the cell is not fatigued (having not been fired recently), it will fire (with a suitable time delay) if the input stimulus attains the threshold. From the time of firing and for a fixed finite period thereafter, the cell will be in an absolute refractory period and will not fire no matter how great the input stimulus. When the absolute refractory period ends, the cell enters a relative refractory period for another fixed finite amount of time. During the relative refractory period the cell can fire (with suitable delay) but only if the input stimulus attains a higher (but fixed) threshold than its threshold during periods of nonfatigue.[128]

The continuous model was planned as a further refinement, modeling not the discrete but the continuous case. The idea was to provide a set of partial differential equations that govern the diffusion process in a fluid—presumably intended to model the process in the human nervous system by which ion diffusion from the cell body triggers neuronal firing. The details of this model were never worked out.[129]

Even less work was completed on the probabilistic model, which was intended as a major topic of the unfinished portion of the manuscript. The idea involved determining the transitions in cell states probabilistically rather than deterministically, based on the prior states of the cell and its neighbors. It is easy to imagine how this model might extend the ideas developed in von Neumann's California Institute of Technology lectures on probabilistic automata. Von Neumann hoped that this model would enable him to investigate the nature of mutations and evolution.

Von Neumann wrote that the theory of automata is "a subject lying in the intermediate area between logics, communication theory, and physiology."[130] The interdisciplinary character is apparent in the five main questions he focused on:[131]

• *Logical universality*—When is a class of automata able to perform all of those logical operations that can be performed with finite means?

• *Constructibility*—What is the class of automata that can be constructed from "raw materials" by a suitably given automaton?

• *Construction-Universality*—Does there exist an automaton that is able to construct every other automaton?

• *Self-Reproduction*—Is there an automaton able to construct an automaton entirely like itself?

• *Evolution*—Can the construction of automata evolve to increasingly complicated types?[132]

He answered the question of logical universality by explaining how Turing's machine model can be reformulated in terms of cellular automata and also gave definitive answers to the middle three questions. He showed how to transform his version of the universal Turing machine into a constructor of other automata, using special stimuli to initiate growth by changing unexcitable into excitable cells. This constructor is then transformed into a universal constructor, which can construct other automata upon being supplied with their description on the equivalent of Turing's infinite tape. The universal constructor is embedded into a two-dimensional cellular array.[133] Finally, he indicated a method by which the universal constructor could be made to reproduce itself.

He discussed briefly the final question (regarding evolution) but gave no definitive answer. In an effort to avoid kinematic considerations, von Neumann replaced the ability of automata to move with the ability to change from a quiescent to an active state. Being fixed in place, there is a potential conflict among automata over room to grow, and this is a basis for the discussion of genetics and mutations:

There is no difficulty in incorporating logical devices into automata of [a certain general type he has described] . . . which will modify . . . [the description] areas in their [infinite tapes] . . . depending on outside stimuli which they may have received previously. This would amount to a modification of the mass of heredity that they represent by the occurrences (experiences) of their active existence. It is clear that this is a step in the right direction, but it is also clear that it requires very considerable additional analyses and elaborations to become really relevant. . . .

In addition to this it must be remembered that conflicts between independent organisms lead to consequences which, according to the theory of "natural selection," are believed to furnish an important mechanism of evolution. . . . Our models lead to such conflict situations. Hence this motive for evolution might also be considered within the framework of these models. The conditions under which it can be effective here may be quite complicated ones, but they deserve study.[134]

A large portion of the manuscript was devoted to working out the detailed operation of the automata—for example, showing that the twenty-nine states are sufficient to accommodate all logical and construction circumstances that may arise and establishing all of the transition rules for moving from one state to another. He gave considerable attention to building a constructing arm that can travel across the cellular two-space, sense the states of cells in another region, report this information back to the constructing automaton, return to the instruction site with instructions, and implement them. The construction arm is composed of pulser organs for sending signals from one point to another, decoding organs for receiving and understanding messages sent as coded pulses, counters for sending pulses around the embedded tape that stores instructions about automata to be built, heads for reading information on the tape, timing loops to adjust for the length of the tape, and other components.

Clearly von Neumann was attempting to prove feasibility rather than maximize efficiency in his designs.[135] The immensity of the task must have surprised him. When he first began the project, he believed that two chapters would suffice.[136] A year and four lengthy chapters later, he had still not achieved his objective.[137] The details of the self-reproducing automaton were left incomplete and in fact included many inaccuracies.[138] He had intended to return to this manuscript upon completion of his term as an Atomic Energy Commission (AEC) commissioner, when he expected to have more time, but did not live to do so.

The Computer and the Brain

Von Neumann's last sustained intellectual effort was his work on the Silliman Lectures, a comparative study of the computer and the brain.[139] In the preface to these lectures, his wife, Klara, explained his heroic efforts to complete them. In early 1955 he was invited to give these distinguished lectures at Yale University during the spring term of 1956 and agreed to give a week of lectures despite his heavy schedule at the AEC. Work proceeded on the lectures even as his cancer progressed and he became confined to a wheelchair, until he entered the hospital for the last time. He relinquished all of his other research projects to pursue this one but never completed or delivered the lectures. In his posthumously published book, *The Computer and the Brain*, we have two partially completed lectures of what was originally planned as a longer series.

The material for the Silliman Lectures grew out of a talk he delivered to a meeting of the American Psychiatric Association in Atlantic City, New Jersey, on 12 May 1955 on the topic "Fixed and Random Logical Patterns and the Problem of Reliability."[140] At the encouragement of Warren McCulloch, one of the invited discussants in his session, von Neumann agreed to write up the lecture for publication.[141] We do not know the exact content of the Atlantic City talk, except that von Neumann spoke of the Silliman Lectures as "a very expanded version of my Atlantic City talk"[142] and that McCulloch later said about it:

Neurophysiologists are indebted to John von Neumann for his studies of components and connections in accounting for the steadiness and the flexibility of behavior. In speaking to the American Psychiatric Association (1) he stressed the utility and the inadequacy of known mechanisms for stabilizing nervous activity, namely, (a) the threshold of non-linear components, (b) the negative feedback of reflexive mechanisms, (c) the internal switching to counteract changes—"ultrastability"—(2), and (d) the redundancy of code and channel. He suggested that the flexibility might depend upon local shifts of thresholds or incoming signals to components that are more appropriate to computers than any yet invented.[143]

The address was largely concerned with the differences between biological systems and computers in whose activity the logical patterns were largely fixed, but which, once perturbated, became rapidly unreliable. You will remember that he had examined the possibility of bundling axons all carrying the same information, and had come to the conclusion that such a redundancy could not explain the reliability to be sought in biological systems of components as unreliable as real neurons. He suggested that, while there might be special ways of designing circuits of constant input-output functions under common shifts of threshold, no such circuits had been described. He thought at that time that the crucial problem was to develop a proper probabilistic logic to cope with the uncertainty of the functions computed and above all he emphasized his disbelief in mere redundancy of similar components. He closed by discussing the retina, which from a hundred million photoreceptors at the input reduced the channel to a scant million ganglion cells for the output to the brain. This he would not attribute to mere redundancy, but suggested that in this small logical depth photoreceptor—bipolar—ganglion cell there must be precalculated functions before transmission to the brain. He remarked of the axons from the brain to the retina that they probably instructed it what functions were to be computed, and he closed with the statement that this suggested that neurons were much cleverer components than the Eccles-Jordan circuits of manmade computers. . . . .

Sofar as I know this address contained the only public statement of his interest in what he called in conversation: "logically stable nets under a common shift of threshold", but on several occasions he talked about them to several of us of the old Macy group on cybernetics.[144]

The Atlantic City lecture was intended for publication in *Scientific American*.[145] By October von Neumann was reconsidering this arrangement because the manuscript was becoming too lengthy[146] and in November told *Scientific American* he planned to use the material as the basis for his Silliman Lectures, which had committed him to a publication, but that he would try to write up an abbreviated version for the magazine. He never found the time.[147]

In the introduction to *The Computer and the Brain* von Neumann described his work as "an approach toward an understanding of the nervous system from the mathematician's point of view . . . [or rather as] merely a somewhat systematized set of speculations as to how such an approach ought to be made."[148] He made it clear that his findings were only the beginnings of a logical and statistical investigation of information processing automata, especially of complicated examples like the computer and the brain: "It would

be very satisfactory if one could talk about a 'theory' of such automata. Regrettably, what at this moment exists—and to what I must
appeal—can as yet be described only as an unperfectly articulated
and hardly formed 'body of experience'."[149]

The first lecture, on the computer, gave an articulate popular
overview of the principles of modern computing. It discussed the
differences between analog and digital procedures and the existence of mixed procedures even in machines, such as the computer, that are usually regarded as being purely digital. The lecture
reviewed several ways in which computers can be controlled,
ranging from plug-board instructions to stored programming. It
also described at length the organization of the computer into a
central processing unit and memory and presented the various
technologies employed in their construction (relays, vacuum tubes,
and solid state devices; magnetic tape, magnetic core, magnetic
drum, etc.). The lecture concluded by introducing several of the
important technical concepts of digital computing: direct and
indirect addressing, hierarchical memories, and access times.

These descriptions were undoubtedly instructive to the general
audience, but they did not add any new knowledge about the
organization of modern computing machinery. One noteworthy
feature of this account, however, is that the descriptions were given
in a way that invites comparisons to be drawn between digital
machinery and biological information processors. For example,
rather than give the standard account of the logical organization of
the computer, von Neumann presented it in terms of active and
memory elements, which enabled him to compare the arithmetic
unit of the computer with the neuron and at another to ask where
memory is located in the human nervous system.

The second lecture, on the brain, is more instructive to us today.
It gives von Neumann's most detailed description of the human
nervous system as an information processor and offers several
comparisons of the computer and the brain not found in his earlier
writings: speed, energy consumption, size, efficiency, and number
of basic switching components. He calculated that the computer
requires greater volume, consumes more energy, and is 10,000
times less efficient than the brain (in binary actions per unit either
of energy or volume) but that the computer compensates by its
considerable advantage (a factor of approximately 5,000) in speed.[150]
He argued that the brain and the computer are logically organized

in rather different ways: the brain favors more but slower-switching components while the computer favors fewer but faster components. He concluded that the computer is organized for serial operation and the brain for parallel operation, and he predicted some of the problems that must be confronted in moving from one mode of operation to the other (finding efficient algorithms to make use of parallel facilities, for example, or adding extra storage for intermediate results in a serial operation). He anticipated that computer designers could profit by modeling features of the human nervous system in their designs but sounded a cautionary note on possible difficulties.[151] He took these simple comparisons about as far as he could without better knowledge of the nervous system or improved materials and architectures for building computing systems.

The Cybernetic Program

Von Neumann's research in the theory of automata was part of a larger scientific interest in information in the postwar period. At war's end the scientific community began to assimilate the monumental advances in communications, computation, and the control of systems that were all by-products of the war. Physicists and electrical engineers had introduced a mathematical definition of information, which they were applying to communication engineering. Physiologists and psychologists were seeking mathematical models emphasizing feedback information loops to explain the nervous and other biological systems. Mathematicians were investigating the theoretical limits of computability and the meaning of these limits for the new electronic computing devices. Others were studying the possibilities of intelligently controlled machinery as models of human behavior.[152]

Some scientists believed there was a unity among all these investigations. In 1948 Norbert Wiener sounded the rallying cry with his book *Cybernetics,* staking out a new science based on "the essential unity of the set of problems centering about communication, control, and statistical mechanics, whether in the machine or in living tissue."[153] Contributions to the cybernetic program came from many directions, but in the end Wiener's hope for a unified science of control and communication was not fulfilled. As one participant in these events explained, cybernetics had "more extent than content."[154] It ranged over too disparate an array of subjects, and its theoretical apparatus was too meager and cumbersome to achieve the unification Wiener desired.

The cybernetic program may be best understood as an intermediate stage in a larger historical process. The process began when established scientific and engineering disciplines developed similar collections of problems involving many of the concepts later central to cybernetics—among them information, control systems, communication channels, and feedback. These problem areas developed independently of one another, at different rates and at different times, with vocabularies specific to the scientific discipline in which they were formulated. Some examples are the work described at the beginning of this chapter by Hartley, Nyquist, and others on the theory of information transmission in communications engineering and of Church, Turing, and other mathematicians on limits of computation for the foundations of mathematics.

The middle stage of this historical process is characterized by a movement toward interdisciplinary study of similar scientific problems—in this case, those involving information, control, and communication. World War II was a catalyst, bringing together scientists from many different disciplines to work on large, complex problems of national importance that cut across traditional scientific boundaries. Von Neumann, Wiener, and a few others who were conversant in more than one science found their war work especially stimulating, and they continued to straddle the traditional scientific disciplines after the war. Their efforts attracted like-minded scientists, and for a few years the results were encouraging for establishing a grand science of cybernetics.

In the end, however, the successes came not through interdisciplinary study but instead through revitalization and growth of new subdisciplines within the traditional scientific and engineering disciplines (artificial intelligence, automata theory, biological modeling, coding theory, communication theory, homeostasis, information theory, recursive function theory, robotics) that in some way involve the study of information, control, and communication. These subdisciplines use methods and concepts appropriated by cybernetics, but they specialize and apply them to the particular needs of their parent scientific discipline (computer science, electrical engineering, mathematics, physiology, or psychology).

Given their contemporaneous appearance, what is the relationship between computing and cybernetics? The evidence suggests that the computer stimulated the growth of cybernetics. For example, Wiener credits his wartime design of computing equipment as a source of his cybernetic ideas; and the computer, a machine designed specifically to process information and control systems, is at the very least a powerful ideograph of the cybernetic program. The relationship also cuts the other way. Many of the powerful concepts of control, statistical information, and neural networks that Wiener appropriated for cybernetics were ones that von Neumann and others subsequently used for computer science. Von Neumann worked in the interdisciplinary spirit of cybernetics, though his final results fell more squarely in computer science and neurophysiology.[155]

It is in the light of these remarks that we are best able to understand the reception, diffusion, and impact of von Neumann's work on the theory of automata. In the end, no theory of automata ever materialized that coordinated the design of computing machinery and the study of information processing in the biological realm. Von Neumann's work, however, moved in the general direction of the post-war scientific disciplines, which had a decreased emphasis on motion, force, energy, and power and an increased emphasis on communication, organization, programming, and control.[156] A number of von Neumann's ideas were taken up by later researchers and worked into the fabric of neurophysiology and computer science.

The Silliman Lectures continue to be reprinted and read in the biomedical community more than thirty years after their publication; nevertheless, von Neumann's influence on this community is somewhat difficult to trace directly. There were a few instances of experimental work based directly on his theoretical predictions. For example, J. T. Allanson and I. C. Whitfield's empirical investigation of the auditory nerve demonstrated that the information content of an auditory signal is conveyed by the totality of responses in the fibers of the auditory nerve rather than by the response of a single fiber, confirming a prediction von Neumann made in his 1952 paper on probabilistic logics.[157] A wider effort has been made to apply the theoretical results of von Neumann, Shannon, and Wiener to biological information processing by Bremermann, Quastler, and others.[158]

The biomedical community has undertaken theoretical investigations building on von Neumann's work to provide more realistic models of biological information processes than those offered by

McCulloch-Pitts and von Neumann.[159] For example, McCulloch and others examined the question of logical stability—the ability of the brain to function normally under abnormal circumstances—by building neural networks that can reliably carry out logical functions under environmental changes (as represented by changes in neural thresholds).[160] Inspired by von Neumann's models of self-replication, the British geneticist L. S. Penrose built a simple model of genetic replication.[161]

Von Neumann's research also contributed to the origins of theoretical computer science. Various researchers have drawn on his results in their work on switching theory and the theory of automata.[162] One area in which he was highly influential is the design of reliable computing equipment with unreliable computing elements, and this work has increasing practical importance as computing machinery becomes larger and faster. Particularly important has been his multiplexing technique, on which there have been many variations.[163] Others have tried to apply information theory to von Neumann's ideas in order to formulate a more general theory of computing in the presence of noise.[164]

Von Neumann almost single-handedly initiated the study of cellular automata. For many years it was regarded as a subject of only theoretical interest, and it attracted only a small number of practitioners, the most important being Arthur Burks and the faculty and students of the Logic of Computers group he founded at the University of Michigan. In recent years these studies have become of more central importance for what they can tell us about the design and limitations of massively parallel computing systems and so in the 1980s became an active research field. It is clear that the results of this field have been built directly on the work of von Neumann.[165] In these many different contributions we find the legacy of von Neumann's theoretical work on computing.

Von Neumann with Cuthbert Hurd, director of IBM's Applied Science Department, in front of the IBM Naval Ordnance Research Calculator, probably at the time of the NORC dedication in 1954. (Courtesy of Marina Whitman)

The Atomic Energy Commission. (Front, from left) William Mitchell (General Counsel), Commissioner von Neumann, Commissioner W. F. Libby, Chairman Lewis L. Strauss, Hon. Herbert B. Loper (Chairman of MLC), Major General Herbert B. Thatcher, and Major General Alvin R. Luedecke (Chief of AFSWP). (Back, from left) Brigadier General Thomas M. Watlington, Rear Admiral George C. Wright, Rear Admiral Paul H. Ramsey, Colonel Alfred D. Starbird, Brigadier General John P. Daley, E. E. Fields (General Manager, AEC), Major General Leland S. Stranathan, and Paul C. Fine. Washington DC, probably 1955 or 1956. (Courtesy of Marina Whitman)

The April 1953 meeting of the Josiah Macy, Jr. Foundation Conference on Cybernetics, New York City. (Front, from left) T. C. Schneirla, Yehoshua Bar-Hillel, Margaret Mead, Warren S. McCulloch, Jan Droogleever-Fortuyn, Yuen Ren Chao, W. Grey-Walter, and Vahe E. Amassian. (Middle row, from left) Leonard J. Savage, Janet Freed Lynch, Gerhart von Bonin, Lawrence S. Kubie, Lawrence K. Frank, Henry Quastler, Donald G. Marquis, Heinrich Kluver, and Frank S. C. Northrop. (Back, from left) Peggy Kubie, Henry Brosin, Gregory Bateson, Frank Fremont-Smith, John R. Bowman, G. E. Hutchinson, Hans Lukas Teuber, Julian Bigelow, Claude Shannon, Walter Pitts, and Heinz von Foerster. (Courtesy of Marina Whitman)

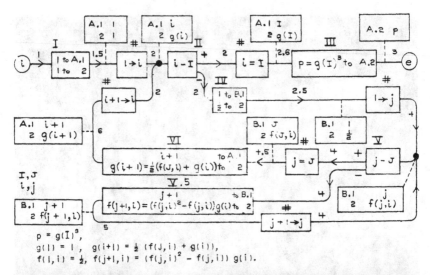

$$p = g(I)^3,$$
$$g(1) = 1, \quad g(i+1) = \tfrac{1}{2}(f(J,i) + g(i)),$$
$$f(1,i) = \tfrac{1}{2}, \quad f(j+1,i) = (f(j,i)^2 - f(j,i))\,g(i).$$

(Top) The first complete flow diagram published by Goldstine and von Neumann. It describes the procedure for calculating a doubly inductive function p. From *Planning and Coding Problems for an Electronic Computing Instrument*, Report on the Mathematical and Logical Aspects of an Electronic Computing Instrument, part II, volume I. Princeton, NJ: Institute for Advanced Study, 1947, p. 18. (Courtesy of the Charles Babbage Institute)

(Bottom) Moore School computer projects staff, University of Pennsylvania, 1946. (From left) James A. Cummings, Kite Sharpless, Joseph Chedaker, Robert Shaw, John Davis, Chuan Chu, Harry Huskey, J. Presper Eckert, Herman Goldstine, Arthur Burks, C. Bradford Sheppard, F. Robert Michaels, and John Mauchly. (Courtesy of the Charles Babbage Institute)

Treavor Pearcey operating the CSIRAC, Australia's first computer, which was a copy of the IAS computer. Circa 1950. (Courtesy of the Charles Babbage Institute)

(Facing page, top) An eleven-stage binary accumulator of the experimental Kirchoff summation type. This was one of the early research and development accomplishments of the IAS engineers. From the *Second Interim Progress Report* of the Electronic Computer Project, IAS, 1 July 1947. (Courtesy of the Charles Babbage Institute)

(Facing page, bottom) Ruth Freshour, programmer, and two students at the AVIDAC console. Carl Bergstrom, maintenance engineer, is at the blackboard. The AVIDAC, an almost-exact copy of the IAS computer, was built at Argonne National Laboratory in 1950 and 1951. (Argonne National Laboratory photograph #401-621; courtesy of the Charles Babbage Institute)

(Below) The STRETCH supercomputer built by IBM for Los Alamos Scientific Laboratory. Completed in 1961, it was the most powerful computer of its day. Von Neumann advised in the planning of the computer on account of his connections with both IBM and the AEC. (Courtesy of the Charles Babbage Institute)

(Above) The ENIAC, circa 1946. Betty Jennings and Francis Bilas are setting switches and plugging cables for a computation. Along the back wall on the right side is the Master Programmer unit. In the foreground, far right, is the portable function table. (Courtesy of the Charles Babbage Institute)

(Facing page, top) An IBM 701 computer installed at General Electric's plant in Evansville, Indiana, mid-1950s. The 701 was based largely on the design of the IAS computer. Note the five-ton room air conditioners. (Courtesy of the Charles Babbage Institute)

(Facing page, bottom) Robert Hawkins, Howard Aiken, and Robert Bloch in front of the Harvard Mark I calculator (also known as the IBM Automatic Sequence Controlled Calculator), circa 1944. (Courtesy of Cruft Laboratory, Harvard University)

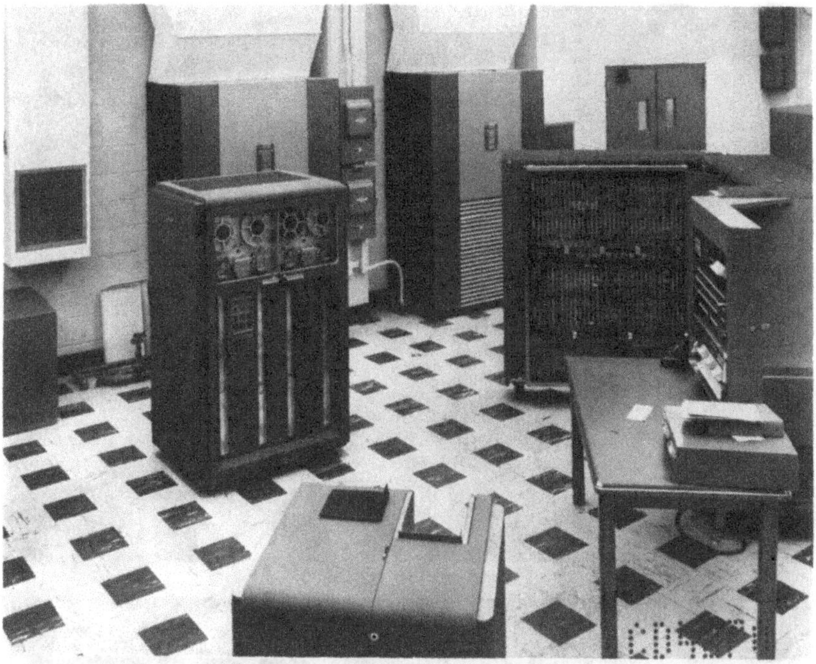

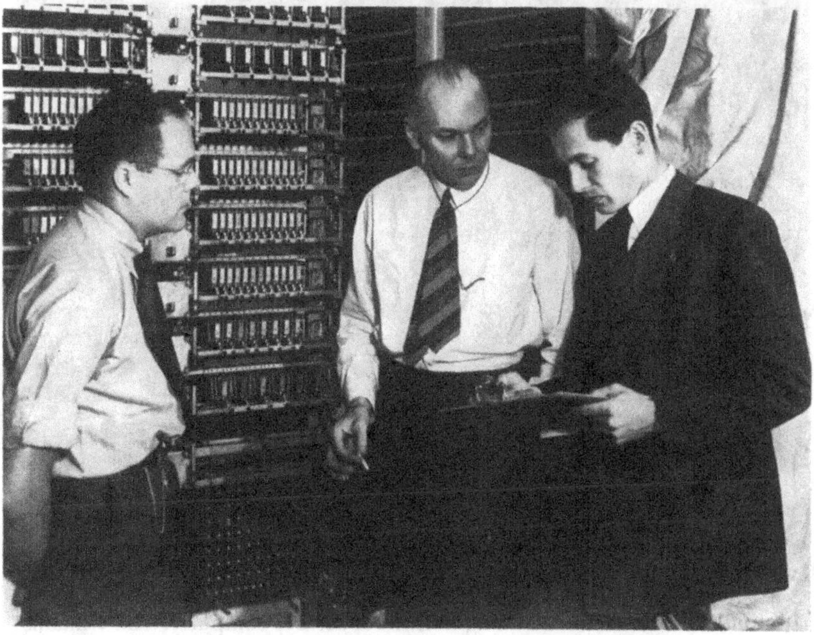

(Top) Thomas J. Watson, Sr. showing the Harvard Mark I to Navy personnel who operated the machine during the war. Circa 1944. (Courtesy of Cruft Laboratory, Harvard University)

(Bottom) Von Neumann standing in front of the IAS computer. The Williams memory tube is in the row of cannisters to his left. The oscilloscope output is in the foreground. Probably taken at the dedication ceremony in 1952. (Courtesy of the Institute for Advanced Studies, Historical Studies—Social Science Library)

James Pomerene holding the Williams memory tube in front of the IAS computer, circa 1952. (Courtesy of the Institute for Advanced Study, Historical Studies—Social Science Library)

(Facing page, top) The leaders of the IAS Electronic Computer Project, circa 1952. (From left) James Pomerene, Julian Bigelow, von Neumann, and Herman Goldstine. (Courtesy of the Institute for Advanced Study, Historical Studies—Social Science Library)

(Facing page, bottom, from left) Julian Bigelow, Herman Goldstine, IAS Director Robert Oppenheimer, and von Neumann in front of the IAS computer, circa 1952. (Courtesy of the Institute for Advanced Study, Historical Studies—Social Science Library)

(Below) Von Neumann in his home in Princeton, New Jersey, circa 1954. Note the fine nineteenth-century painting in the background, brought by von Neumann from Hungary. (Courtesy of the Institute for Advanced Study, Historical Studies—Social Science Library)

(Above) Oskar Morgenstern and von Neumann at Spring Lake, New Jersey. (Courtesy of the Institute for Advanced Study, Historical Studies—Social Science Library)

(Facing page, top) IAS Director Robert Oppenheimer and von Neumann in front of the IAS computer, circa 1952. (Courtesy of the Institute for Advanced Study, Historical Studies—Social Science Library

(Facing page, bottom) Leon Harmon holding paper tape from the IAS computer's input unit. (Courtesy of the Institute for Advanced Study, Historical Studies—Social Science Library)

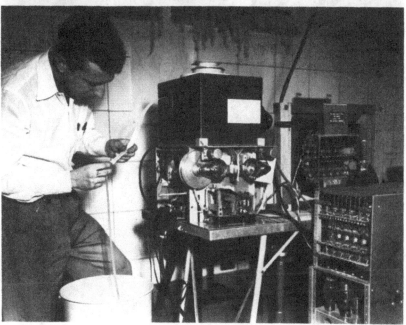

IAS Electronic Computer Project staff members (from left) Joseph Samgo-rinsky, Norman Philips, Herman Goldstine, and Gerald Estrin. (Courtesy of the Institute for Advanced Study, Historical Studies—Social Science Library)

Staff of the IAS Electronic Computer Project. (Courtesy of the Institute for Advanced Study, Historical Studies—Social Science Library)

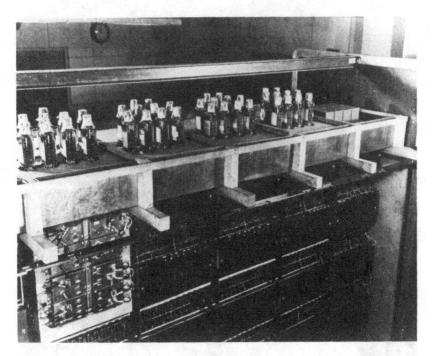

(Above) JOHNNIAC computer at the RAND Corporation, early 1950s. JOHNNIAC, an IAS-class machine, was the only computer ever to employ the Selectron memory developed by Radio Corporation of America. (Courtesy of Willis H. Ware, the RAND Corporation)

(Facing page) Notes made by von Neumann in 1943 in association with his first experience at programming a calculating machine, the National Cash Register Model 3000 Accounting Machine of the Nautical Almanac Office of Britain. (Courtesy of John Todd)

$$x_i \Rightarrow x'_{i+1} + \sum_{i+2}^{n} a_{ij}\, x'_j =$$

$$= x''_{i+2} + \sum_{i+2}^{n}\left(a_{mn} + \sum_{i+j}^{n} a_{ij}\right)x'_k$$

$$= x''_{i+2} + \sum_{i+3}^{n} a_{m+1}x''_k +$$

$$+ \sum_{i+2}^{n} a_{ij}\left(x'_{j+1} + \sum_{j+2}^{n} a_{j k}x'_k\right) =$$

$$= x''_{i+2} + \sum_{i+3}^{n}\left(a_{i+1,k} + a_{i,k+1} + \sum_{i+2}^{k+1} a_{ij}\,a_{jk}\right)x'_k$$

$$a_{1n}$$
$$a_{2n} + a_{1+n} + \sum_{3}^{n-2} a_{ij}\,a_{jn}$$

$$v_i = x'_{i+1} + a_i\,x'_n$$
$$= x''_{i+2} + a_{i+1}\,x''_n$$

$$\mathbf{4}.$$

(Top) Inscriber unit used originally for input on the IAS computer, circa 1948. (Courtesy of the Charles Babbage Institute)

(Bottom) AEC Commissioner von Neumann (far left) visits at Redstone Arsenal, Alabama, 9 November 1955. Others (from left) are Brigadier General H. N. Toftoy (Redstone Arsenal commander), Wernher von Braun (chief of the Guided Missile Development Division at Redstone), Brigadier General J. P. Daley (representing the office of the chief of Army Research and Development), and Colonel Miles B. Chatfield (chief of Research and Development at Redstone). (Courtesy of the Library of Congress [John von Neumann papers])

(Top) Von Neumann with his friend and collaborator, Stanislaw Ulam, and Ulam's daughter, Claire, 1954 or 1955. (Courtesy of the American Philosophical Society [Ulam papers]

(Bottom) Speakers and panelists at the Hixon Symposium on Cerebral Mechanisms in Behavior, Pasadena, California, 1951. Seated are (from left) Ward C. Halstead, K. S. Lashley, Heinrich Kluver, and R. Lorente de No. Standing are (from left) H. W. Brosin, Lloyd Jeffress, Paul Weiss, Donald B. Lindsley, von Neumann, J. M. Nielsen, R. W. Gerard, and H. S. Liddell. Only Warren McCulloch is missing. (Courtesy of the American Philosophical Society [Warren McCulloch papers])

C. B. Tompkins repairs the tire on a car borrowed from Albert Tucker to attend a mathematics conference in North Carolina, circa 1937. Neumann and Marshall Stone look on. (Courtesy of Albert Tucker)

Scientific Consultant and Statesman

After the war von Neumann spent less time in mathematical research and more in research management, consulting, and scientific statesmanship. Most of the leaders in the new computing field, such as J. Presper Eckert and Jay Forrester, were young men who had not yet established their scientific reputations, while most senior members of the American scientific community who had an interest in computing, such as Vannevar Bush and Samuel Caldwell, were wedded to the analog technology. Von Neumann was unusual among the scientific elite for his knowledge of and dedication to digital computing technology.[1] His international scientific stature gave credence to the computer as a technology worthy of scientific attention. His contacts at high levels in the federal government, particularly within the military community, opened up channels of funding for computer purchase and development. He was in great demand as a lecturer and adviser to the scientific societies, industry, and the federal government, and everywhere he went, he preached about the importance of the digital computer. For all of these reasons, he was an effective catalyst for the development of computing in America in the decade following the war. This chapter describes some of his work as a scientific consultant and statesman, not only in computing but also in atomic weapons and their delivery systems.

Government Consulting

Von Neumann's postwar career as a scientific adviser and statesman has its origins in his wartime service to the Army and Navy Ordnance departments and the Manhattan Project.[2] During the war the Navy Ordnance theoretical group in high explosives was making numerous computations.[3] They did not own computing equipment but instead had their calculations done for them by the NDRC Applied Mathematics Panel, the Harvard Computation Laboratory, the Bureau of Ships, and the Tabulation Division of the Bureau of Ordnance. In April 1945 the group became convinced that it would be more efficient to establish its own centralized computing facilities at some place like the Naval Ordnance Laboratory in Maryland. They envisioned a facility that would serve not only their own needs but those of the entire research and development division of the Navy Department Bureau of Ordnance as well.[4]

The group turned to von Neumann for advice about computing equipment. His response came in late August in the form of a long memorandum, which began with an assessment of the computing facilities needed by the high explosives group to solve a problem they would typically confront: a hyperbolic or parabolic differential equation in two variables.[5] He noted that hand computing facilities would "remain a necessity for the foreseeable future" but that only computing machines much faster than the relay computers or the ENIAC would widen the range of problems able to be solved computationally: "Generally speaking, really fast machines would educate the theoretician not to be afraid of complicated computations and of extensive surveys, and they would provide easy ways to obtain the very considerable benefits which will necessarily result from such possibilities. It is probably true that the greatest value of such machines will be found in connection with problems which are not considered to be practically computable at all at present."

He then presented a detailed analysis of the strengths and weaknesses of every type of calculating machine he knew about: differential analyzers, standard IBM punched-card machines, enhanced IBM machines (such as experimental High Speed Multipliers), Bell Telephone Company relay computers, Harvard Marks I and II, ENIAC, EDVAC, and analog fire control equipment.[6] Not surprising to us today but probably not evident to the navy in 1945, he recommended the construction as soon as possible of an EDVAC-like electronic computer and a concurrent program of studies in high-speed computing methods. The navy followed his advice and contracted for IBM to build the powerful NORC computer.[7] The Naval Ordnance Laboratory also pursued a program of study on computing methods, and ONR soon became a leading funder of academic computer science research.[8]

Von Neumann had a similar effect on the computing program at Army Ordnance.[9] His contributions as a BRL consultant to the EDVAC project have already been recounted. What is less well known is that during this same period and for a few years after the war he continued to consult at Aberdeen. His report to IAS director Frank Aydelotte describes these activities: "Since early 1945 I have been taking part in advising the [Ballistics Research] Laboratory on its development program on various high-speed computing devices, and quite particularly in planning a new electronic machine."[10]

In January 1945 von Neumann wrote a memorandum on mechanical computing devices, which he sent to Colonel Leslie Simon at the BRL with the request that it be placed on the agenda for discussion at the next BRL Scientific Advisory Committee meeting.[11] The memorandum argued that computing machinery was crucial to the mission of the BRL. It pointed out that the BRL had already become a heavy user of computing equipment, apparent from the differential analyzers installed at BRL and the Moore School, the commercial IBM punched-card equipment and the enhanced IBM multipliers used in the preparation of ballistics and firing tables, and the Bell Laboratory relay calculator and the ENIAC being applied to general aerodynamic and shock research. The memorandum mentioned the importance he expected these last two machines to have on shell, bomb, and rocket research, but it also noted that those machines had difficulties solving partial differential equations—in contrast to the EDVAC, which offered great promise though it had so far received only a preliminary development grant. The memorandum highlighted three reasons for supporting the EDVAC: its ability to solve entirely new classes of problems (three-dimensional aerodynamical problems), its applicability to the design of better fire control devices, and its capacity to make other BRL facilities (such as the supersonic wind tunnel and the ballistic and shock wave ranges) more effective.

The navy turned to von Neumann for advice on computing matters on many occasions. In the autumn of 1945 it solicited his and Goldstine's advice on ways to improve the BRL's Bell Telephone relay calculator. They made several suggestions for improving its setup procedures and computational speed: ways of wiring the function tables, an increase in the number of storage tapes, and the addition of a device to transfer data automatically from Teletype tape to punched cards.[12]

Von Neumann also played a leading role in selecting the final design for the EDVAC and ensuring that the final funding was made available by BRL. In October 1946 the BRL held a meeting to consider three alternative versions of the EDVAC, which the staff of the Moore School was prepared to build, known as EDVAC I, II, and III. Von Neumann convinced those present at the meeting to adopt none of the three plans but instead to support construction of a machine designated as EDVAC 1.5, a modification of EDVAC I that incorporated built-in binary-decimal conversion hardware. The EDVAC 1.5 was the version that was built.[13]

Von Neumann suggested the plan by which the BRL staff transformed the ENIAC into a (read-only) stored-program computer. As originally designed, the ENIAC had no central control organ. It was operated by setting switches and plugging cables between units of the machine as a means to establish circuits to move numbers from one point to another within the computer. This procedure made it difficult and time-consuming to code and set up the machine for a new problem.

About the time when Goldstine and von Neumann completed the first volume of "Planning and Coding of Problems for an Electronic Computing Instrument" in April 1947, von Neumann found a means of applying to the ENIAC the coding methods described in this report.[14] Cables were plugged and switches set to allow the ENIAC to function as a centralized machine with a single arithmetic unit and a single computation stream directed by a single instruction stream. The remaining accumulators were used only for storage, not for computation. The function table was used to store up to 1800 "orders"—two-digit numbers each representing a different instruction for the machine to execute. The execution was sequential except when a transfer order caused a discontinuity. Fifty of the orders caused numbers to be transferred from one register to another (so-called listen and talk orders). There were orders for conditional and unconditional transfers and also ten operational orders (multiply, divide, square root, drop sign, change sign, shift, halt, etc.).

In March von Neumann discussed this idea with Herman Goldstine and his wife, Adele, and the Goldstines worked out a system of fifty-one orders.[15] In April von Neumann discussed the new coding scheme with R. F. Clippinger, head of the Computing Laboratory at Aberdeen, who worked out the refined sixty-order system. Later the system was modified to include ninety-two orders.[16] The operators identified four advantages of the new system: it was easier for novices to learn, one could code more complicated problems, a shorter time was needed for problem setup, and checking was systematized and expedited.[17] The ENIAC was first used in the stored-program mode on a problem for the Los Alamos Laboratory code-named Monte Carlo.[18] Thereafter the ENIAC was always operated as a stored-program computer because the programming advantages more than compensated for the reduced operating speed in this mode.[19]

Even after the ENIAC had been modified for stored-program operation, von Neumann was not entirely satisfied because he was eager to see the technique formalized and disseminated:

So far, all this work has been done in a rather informal, non-literary form; that is, it exists only in the minds of those concerned, in viva voce discussions between them, and in very sketchy notes for intra-group use. I think that this has already [only four weeks after discussing the idea with Clippinger and Kent!] gone further than optimal, and that it would be most desirable to have a "permanent," "literary" record. In fact, I think that the whole "art" of setting up complicated computing machines, of programming and of coding, would be much less of an "art," and much more of a communicable and expoundable scientific technique, if we all took the trouble to put our ideas, insofar as they are likely to be of interest over any extended period, into a "publishable" form sooner and more conscientiously than we do now. . . .

I think that a report of the type which I suggest would also be very useful outside Aberdeen. I am convinced that the ENIAC already presents an opportunity for mathematical physics which very few people appreciate . . . . The sooner we lay the foundation for a "literary" method by which the properties and potentialities of the ENIAC can be made known to the general scientific public, the better.[20]

Von Neumann's mark on government computing can also be seen in his war work for the NDRC. His research on gas dynamics for the Army and Navy Ordnance programs convinced him that there were additional problems concerning shock collisions, problems of both a theoretical and a computational nature, that deserved attention. In early 1944, with the assistance of Warren Weaver and Richard Courant, von Neumann obtained a contract from the NDRC Applied Mathematics Panel to do research in Princeton on shock collisions. His contract covered research that was not part of his army or navy work and that was preparatory to both.[21] Although he and his assistant, Valentine Bargmann, did some computation, they concentrated their investigations on numerical methods.[22] By the spring of 1945 the NDRC had become seriously interested in computers, and Warren Weaver asked von Neumann to write a report for the Applied Mathematics Panel surveying past, present, and future computing machines. Initially there were objections that this report, which was to contain sections written by the major centers of computer development, would deflect the Moore School staff from their primary responsibility of completing the construction of the ENIAC and EDVAC and that it might divulge classified information about their electronic circuit designs. However, these objections were overcome, and permission was soon granted.[23] Using his earlier report to Navy Ordnance as a basis, von Neumann prepared a much longer survey, but he never completed it to his satisfaction. He presented it orally to the Navy Office of Research and Inventions in May 1946. The content gave the most complete account of von Neumann's requirements for a computer for scientific research (it was described in chapter 3).[24]

In the fall of 1946 R. C. Gibbs of the Physical Sciences Division of the National Research Council established the Committee on High-Speed Computing. Von Neumann was appointed chairman, and the other members were Howard Aiken, Walter Bartky, Samuel Caldwell, E. U. Condon, John Curtiss, George Stibitz, and Warren Weaver.[25] The committee's objective was to assist in the rational development of the high-speed computing field, which it did not do particularly effectively. They did, however, make two contributions. First, in 1947 they improved the dissemination of information about the new computing technology by reorganizing and expanding the journal *Mathematical Tables and Other Aids to Computation* to include news and articles on high-speed computers.[26]

Their second contribution was to advise the NBS in 1948. Standards was charged with the responsibility of contracting for five computers to be built for government agencies: the army air forces, the Office of Naval Research, and the Bureau of the Census. John Curtiss of the NBS requested that the committee review the technical merits of the proposals received by NBS, and a subcommittee of Aiken, Stibitz, and von Neumann was formed for this task. The subcommittee reviewed proposals from Electronic Control Company, Raytheon Manufacturing Company, and the Moore School. They judged that all three proposals were feasible from an engineering standpoint, that all of the designs would result in computers that could be applied usefully to mathematics, and that there was no significant technical basis for choosing among them. They recommended awarding more than one contract since the state of the art was not sufficiently settled to rely on a single design. They also suggested that it would be more profitable to award contracts for components design first and for systems development later and that research and development (as opposed to simple construction)was needed in order to meet the desired technical specifications. Their advice was largely followed.

The committee remained in existence until 1952 but took no significant action after 1948. Nevertheless, it had served a useful function in improving the dissemination of information and in providing the government with advice about the design specifications for this new and unsettled technology.

IBM

Industry too was anxious to secure von Neumann's expert advice after the war. Although he was also under contract with Rand, Ramo-Woolridge, Sandia, and Standard Oil, attention is restricted here to his work for IBM.[27] IBM first offered him a consulting contract in 1945, before he had even completed the draft report on EDVAC. The retainer agreement drawn up by IBM on 1 May 1945 called for him to spend 10 percent of his time in New York: "to assist IBM's engineering divisions, particularly the Watson Scientific Computing Laboratory, in problems of research and inventions pertaining to IBM machines, more especially in the matter of the application of advanced mathematical knowledge to the problems of machine calculations and mechanical or electrical devices for statistical, analytical or computation purposes."[28] By August he had received permission from Frank Aydelotte, IAS director, as well as from government representatives, to enter into this agreement.[29] Once he had decided to build a computer at the IAS, however, he dropped the idea of consulting for IBM.[30]

Late in 1951 von Neumann did enter into a consulting arrangement with IBM at the encouragment of his friend Cuthbert Hurd, director of the company's Applied Science Department. Thomas Watson, Jr., then IBM's executive vice-president, favored this appointment as a means to ensure that IBM would move in a proper direction with its computer program.[31] The contract called for von Neumann to devote thirty days a year to IBM, for which he would be compensated with the generous sum of $12,000 plus expenses.[32] His time was divided among the IBM laboratories in Endicott and Poughkeepsie, New York, and the Scientific Computing Laboratory and World Headquarters in New York City.

One of his earliest tasks was to work with Hurd to set up and solve by computer a linear programming problem to improve shop floor scheduling at the Endicott plant in an effort to expedite manufacturing of calculating equipment. They set up the problem but found that it was too large to solve on any existing computing machine. The 701 computer was used, however, to simulate the collator production line. The simulator arranged and rearranged the flow of parts through the machine tools, and the resulting reorganization of the production flow led to a 10 percent increase in efficiency.

One of the most critical problems facing the computer industry in this period was the development of reliable and cost-effective memory systems. Von Neumann participated in a number of discussions at IBM about the strengths and weaknesses of various configurations of primary and secondary memory. In early 1952 he met with Harry Polachek and L. H. Thomas to consider the desirability of a drum memory for the NORC, a computer that the company was building for the navy.[33] Von Neumann argued that it would be important for IBM to incorporate a magnetic drum storage unit into the NORC. He thought that drums would be easier to manufacture reliably than fast tapes or large CRT stores and that the efficiency of their present storage system could be improved using a drum of 20,000-word capacity to replace six to eight of the magnetic tape units and perhaps also some primary cathode ray tube memory.[34] The NORC was ultimately delivered with a cathode ray tube primary memory (later supplemented by magentic cores) and magnetic tape secondary memory, but IBM did offer the 701 with a drum for auxiliary storage.

IBM called upon von Neumann's knowledge of numerical analysis. With Arthur Samuel, von Neumann solved some differential equations for a project on optical character recognition. He worked with John Sheldon, manager of the company's Technical Computing Bureau. Sheldon remembers meetings with von Neumann to discuss numerical methods for linear algebra and differential equations.[35] Von Neumann was involved with evaluating the 701 computer system, which he used to solve the Schrödinger equation and test five-layer meteorological models. He described the importance of the meteorological calculations:

The purpose of the IBM calculations was to establish how much greater precision could be obtained by a further increase in the number of layers [of the numerical model], with five being considered the greatest number that will still yield an increase in precision. Neither the speed nor memory capacity of the Princeton machine were deemed adequate for these computations. Calculations with the five-level model required that a number of its mathematical and physical properties be explored. This exploration, utilizing the IBM 701, extended over three separate versions of a five-layer model. It was established that one, and only one, of these three versions was suitable. Its precision was found to be higher than that of the three-level model, but a residual error remained even then. As a result of these calculations, we know how to proceed with multi-layer models of the most general type and we have established, in the shape of the residual error mentioned above, the inherent error of all geostrophic models. . . . Also, as a result of the IBM calculations, we know that it will be necessary to perform computations with both the geostrophic and non-geostrophic models.[36]

To a small degree von Neumann participated in planning new IBM computer products.[37] In 1954 Stephen Dunwell and Werner Buchholz began planning a new computer system, named Datatron, to replace the scientifically oriented IBM 704 and the commercially oriented IBM 705 computer systems. Von Neumann, who attended at least one meeting on this topic held in November, influenced the evaluation of the changes required to make a 704 perform the data processing tasks typically carried out by a 705 and the changes required for a 705 to perform the extensive numerical computations typically carried out by a 704. His conclusion was that a 704 equipped with the input-output equipment usually found on a 705 system could perform a wide range of accounting applications as quickly as a 705 but that a 705 could not match the speed of the 704 on any problem involving extensive calculation and so was not suited for modification into a universal machine. This finding was potentially of great value to the company because the 704 and 705, despite being built from many of the same components, required two separate manufacturing lines and some extra sales effort over what would have been needed if there were a single, universal product. If a single line of machines could have been designed for both accounting and scientific applications, there would have been tremendous potential for economy of scale. However, resistance from the engineering groups for the 704 and the 705 to the idea of a single line of general-purpose computers, together with a major reorganization at IBM soon after, caused the idea to be set aside until the introduction of the System/360 computers in the 1960s.[38] Nonetheless, some of the planning for the Datatron was influential on the design of the Stretch computer that IBM delivered to the Los Alamos Laboratory in 1958.

Just three weeks after this meeting, at the invitation of IBM chairman Thomas Watson, Sr., von Neumann delivered the main address at the dedication of the NORC.[39] After making a few comments about the value of the NORC to the navy ordnance computations for which it had been designed, he turned to another class of problems, from geophysics and logistics, that would require computers far more powerful than the NORC or any existing computer and called for the design of computers that would advance the state of the art as much as possible.[40] His remarks were perhaps addressed mainly to the two Watsons, who sat in the audience, because he knew that only they were in the position to authorize the company's expenditure for cutting-edge computer development that would meet the needs of the scientists at the Los Alamos and Livermore Laboratories.[41]

Von Neumann applied for only one patent in his career, but this patent is associated with both the beginning and the end of his IBM consultancy. When Hurd first approached von Neumann about being a consultant, he learned that von Neumann had an idea for generating high-speed signals that could be applied to increasing the speed of computers. Von Neumann had made an extensive Fourier analysis showing that two fast wave signals could be merged in such a way that their subharmonics formed discrete signals suitable for use in a computer at a rate approximately 1000 times faster than those employed at the time.[42]

Hurd realized that IBM did not want to become entangled in von Neumann's patent case and advised von Neumann to file for a patent prior to joining IBM as a consultant. Von Neumann followed this advice and selected a patent attorney from a list supplied by Hurd. Once the patent application had been filed in von Neumann's name and the consulting contract was signed, meetings were held at the Watson Laboratory to discuss the patent idea.[43] IBM contracted with the electronics firm of Dean Watkins and Robert Johnson to build a prototype. In the end, however, the idea was superseded by the introduction of transistors, and it was never employed in an IBM product in the United States.

In 1954, when Lewis Strauss wanted to appoint von Neumann to the AEC he was worried about the financial impact on von Neumann's family of the appointment, which would not pay as much as his IAS salary and would require him to sever his lucrative consulting contracts. Strauss called Thomas Watson, Jr., to ask if IBM would acquire von Neumann's patent as a way to ease the financial burden. The matter was examined by a technical committee within IBM, and the patent was purchased for $60,000.[44]

This action had an unexpected benefit for IBM.[45] In 1954 the Japanese government passed the Foreign Investment and Foreign Exchange Laws of Japan. Under this legislation, the Japanese government argued that for IBM to do business legally in Japan it must reorganize as a joint venture with a Japanese company, disclose all of its know-how to its Japanese partner, not take its customary 10 percent royalty for use of patents, use all Japanese parts, and do all its manufacturing in Japan. IBM wanted to avoid these conditions and assigned James Birkenstock to represent the company in the validation negotiations. IBM delayed the negotiations until 1957, which allowed it time to strengthen its patent position in Japan. Birkenstock learned that the Japanese were using subharmonic devices in their computers that very likely would fall under the von Neumann patent, and he used this patent, together with some others, as leverage in his bargaining with the Japanese government. Birkenstock was ultimately successful at avoiding all of the conditions sought by the Japanese government, and IBM-Japan was validated as a totally owned IBM subsidiary.

Final Plans

Von Neumann consulted in many areas besides computing. At the height of his consulting activity, in 1954, he was under contract to over twenty government and industrial organizations (table 9.1). His other major consulting area besides computing was the design of nuclear weapons and their delivery systems.

Von Neumann was an important adviser to the Manhattan Project; he participated in the development of the implosion device, helped to move the design work from full reliance on testing to the use of numerical modeling, and influenced the advancement and procurement of computing facilities to drive these models. He was also a member of the scientific-military committee that decided on the strategy and sites for the atomic bombing in Japan.

His interest in nuclear weapons continued after the war. In 1946 he testified at a hearing of the Senate Committee on Atomic Energy

Table 9.1
Biographical data on von Neumann

Government and industrial consultancies
  1940–1957 Scientific Advisory Committee, Ballistics Research Labs, Aberdeen Proving Ground, MD
  1941–1955 Navy Bureau of Ordnance, Washington DC
  1943–1955 Los Alamos Scientific Lab, Los Alamos, NM
  1947–1955 Naval Ordnance Laboratory, Silver Spring, MD
  1948–1955 RAND Corporation
  1949–1953 Research and Development Board, Washington, DC
  1949–1954 Oak Ridge National Laboratory, Oak Ridge, TN
  1950–1955 Armed Forces Special Weapons Project, Washington, DC
  1950–1955 Weapon Systems Evaluation Group, Washington, DC
  1951–1957 Scientific Advisory Board, U.S. Air Force, Washington, DC
  1952–1954 Member, General Advisory Committee, U.S. Atomic Energy Commission, Washington, DC
  1952–1955 Central Intelligence Agency, Washington, DC
  1952–1955 Radiation Laboratory, University of California, Livermore, CA
  1953–1954 Strategic Missiles Evaluation Committtee, U.S. Air Force
  1953–1955 Sandia Corporation, Albequerque, NM
  1953–1955 Ramo-Wooldridge Corporation, Inglewood, CA
  1953–1955 National Security Agency Advisory Board, Washington, DC
  1953–1957 Nuclear Weapons Panel, Scientific Advisory Board, U.S. Air Force, Washington, DC
  1953–1957 Technical Advisory Panel on Atomic Energy, Department of Defense, Washington, DC
  1955 Ad Hoc Panel on University Computing Facilities, National Science Foundation, Washington, DC

Awards
  1926 Rockefeller Fellowship
  1937 Bocher Prize, American Mathematical Society
  1947 Medal for Merit (Presidential Award) and Distinguished Civilian Service Award, U.S. Navy
  1955 Science Award, Air Force Association
  1956 Medal of Freedom (Presidential Award)
  1956 Enrico Fermi Science Award, U.S. Atomic Energy Commission
  1957 American Meteorological Society Award for Extraordinary Scientific Accomplishment

Honorary societies
  Academia Nacional de Ciencias Exactas, Lima, Peru
  American Academy of Arts and Sciences
  American Philosophical Society
  Instituto Lombardo di Scienze e Lettere, Milan, Italy
  National Academy of Sciences
  Royal Netherlands Academy of Sciences and Letters, Amsterdam, Netherlands

Honorary degrees
  1947 Princeton University
  1949 University of Pennsylvania
  1949 Harvard University
  1952 University of Istanbul

Table 9.1 (continued)

Honorary degrees
  1952 Case Institute of Technology
  1952 University of Maryland
  1953 Polytechnics Institut, Munich
  1954 Columbia University
Honorary positions
  1937 Gibbs Lecturer, American Mathematical Society
  1937 American Mathematical Society Colloquium Lecturer
  1951–1953 President, American Mathematical Society
  1953 Vanuxem lecturer, Princeton University
  1950–1957 member, Board of Advisors, Universidad de Los Andes, Colombia
Society memberships
  American Mathematical Society
  American Physical Society
  Econometric Society
  International Statistical Institute, The Hague, Netherlands
  Sigma Xi

Source: The information comes from biographical statements prepared by von Neumann: an application prepared on 10 April 1942 to do work for NDRC Section B1b, the questionnaire he filled out on 18 December 1956 for *Who's Who in World Aviation*, and a slightly annotated copy of his vita. All of these documents can be found in the von Neumann Papers, Library of Congress.

that $500 million was needed for continuing atomic research.[46] In the late 1940s and early 1950s he spent two or three months each year at Los Alamos and often visited the national laboratory in Livermore, California. He aided Edward Teller and Stan Ulam in their design of a thermonuclear bomb and arranged for a computer modeling associated with this work to be the first major calculation made on the IAS computer.[47] That same year, 1952, he joined the AEC General Advisory Committee, on which he served until September 1954. By this time he was devoting half of his time to government work, at least half of it for the AEC. He explained his willingness to participate in these activities as an outgrowth of his political views: "I am violently anti-Communist, and I was probably a good deal more militaristic than most. . . . My opinions have been violently opposed to Marxism ever since I remember, and quite in particular since I had about a three-months taste of it in Hungary in 1919."[48]

Because of his political views, his overall scientific abilities, and his past contributions to nuclear weapons design, it is not surprising that he was invited in 1954 to become a member of the AEC. His name was apparently suggested by his old acquaintance Lewis Strauss, the commission chairman.[49] President Eisenhower supported the appointment, perhaps because it helped to mend fences with the scientific community following the infamous Oppenheimer security hearing.[50] Von Neumann did not personally like Oppenheimer or share many of his views about politics or atomic weapons development, but he had nevertheless testified in Oppenheimer's defense in June 1954. Because of this testimony there was some speculation about whether von Neumann would be confirmed by the Congress, but the five-year appointment was approved without incident.[51] When asked why he would want this appointment, which required relocating to Washington, doing extensive detailed administrative work, working long hours that cut into his research time, and taking a considerable financial loss, he replied that it was "quite important . . . [to have scientists on the commission] for a rapid evaluation of the developments which might open up and the direction which they might go."[52]

For a little less than a year, while his health held out, he was an effective commissioner. He spent several weeks in Washington each month that the commission was in session and the rest of his time visiting the national laboratories. After he was hospitalized for cancer in 1956, he continued his duties by a direct telephone line to the commission offices and was driven by ambulance to meetings, which he attended in a wheelchair. He used his position to lobby for greater support of computing technology. As he said, "It seems to me that high-speed computers are just as vital to the AEC's development programs as, e.g., high-speed particle accelerators."[53] AEC computing requirements, he noted, had doubled every year since 1945. He worried that private industry would not develop computing technology as fast as the AEC wanted it developed and argued that it was incumbent on the government to support and foster the necessary research and development through liberal subventions to companies and through programs to encourage universities to train students in computing.

For all these reasons it seems to be absolutely imperative that the AEC spend yearly increasing and very substantial amounts of money in the computer field. I would view the $1 million proposed for next year as just a starter—an experimental amount which may, and I think will, prove to be too low and which we should immediately increase when the justification for this appears. I think it would be a grave mistake to cut it down or to eliminate it from the budget. In no matter how tight budgetary squeezes we are, we are compromising our developmental effort if we neglect to invest in the development of faster and better computing machines, and in the training of students to handle them and to invent new ones. I think that this is as vital as any of the componentry development or machinery development that we are supporting, including obviously vital fields like those of high explosives, high-speed particle accelerators, manufacturing processes for fissionable materials and other materials vital in the AEC program.[54]

There was an internal battle during the next several years over the extent of the AEC's future role in funding computing and computer education. Because of his illness and then death, von Neumann was not there to argue in support of extensive involvement, and the AEC never became the leader in computing he had hoped it would become.[55]

The AEC did, however, undertake an active program of computer development and acquisition for the national laboratories, and for a while von Neumann influenced the direction of this program. For example, he recognized that the era of research groups' building their own computing machinery was past and that the commercial era had begun. He cancelled a plan by New York University to build its own computer, suggesting that instead it buy or rent one.[56] He was a vigorous proponent of and an occasional participant in the design discussions of the Stretch and LARC supercomputers being built, respectively, by IBM and Remington Rand for the Los Alamos and Livermore laboratories.[57] Interestingly he disagreed with the designers of the LARC on one technical issue: the size and use of the memory. His position was representative of what was increasingly being seen as an old school, which advocated use of only small amounts of primary memory and overcoming the limitation by having scientists write their own code in a way that optimized use of the available space.[58] He argued that the LARC design had too many magnetic drums (twelve, where he thought only eight were justified), too much primary memory (10,000 to 20,000 words were planned), and too much primary memory (2500 words) allocated to input-output and machine administration.[59]

During the 1950s von Neumann, increasingly concerned about the Soviet Union's building a nuclear arsenal, was one of the first to turn his attention from the task of building bombs to that of delivering them.[60] He became an early leader in the U.S. program to develop intercontinental ballistic missiles (ICBMs).[61]

On 1 November 1952, in the MIKE experiment, the AEC successfully tested its first thermonuclear device on Eniwetok Atoll in the Pacific Ocean. The test demonstrated that an operational hydrogen bomb missile warhead would be technically and economically feasible within a few years. Air Force Secretary Harold E. Talbott named a civilian, Trevor Gardner, as his special assistant, and Gardner began to champion the ICBM concept. The development of the ICBM was felt to be more urgent after August 1953 when the Soviets exploded their first hydrogen bomb. That fall, in order to obtain technical validation for the ICBM concept and prevent the Pentagon from curtailing its support, Gardner formed the Strategic Missiles Evaluation Committee, with von Neumann as its chairman and a group of distinguished scientists as its members.[62] The von Neumann committee (as it was commonly known) reported in February 1954 that an effective ICBM could be readied within six years and that a new organization should be established to move the program forward rapidly. During 1954 von Neumann oversaw several study groups that resolved many of the technological problems involving guidance, miniaturization of components, and heat resistance that stood in the way of a productive ballistic missile.

When von Neumann was appointed by President Eisenhower to the AEC in late 1954, the air force and several key senators insisted that he be permitted to continue to lead the air force committee on ballistic missile design. This he did though he gave up almost all of his other work for government and industry. Apparently von Neumann was influential in gaining the president's support for the ICBM program, visiting him in connection with this work on several occasions at the White House and at least once by ambulance at his home in Gettysburg, Pennsylvania.[63] The program moved ahead quickly. Brigadeer General Bernard Schriever took command of the program in June 1954, and by the middle of the following year the ICBM was a high national priority. The Ramo-Wooldridge Corporation was formed to give technical assistance to the Strategic Missiles Evaluation Committee. A 2500-mile test flight of the Atlas missile was successfully completed in 1958, and by 1962 the more advanced Titan missile had been deployed. These missiles had been proposed by the von Neumann committee in 1954 and 1955.

Von Neumann had taken a leave of absence from the IAS in 1955 in order to join the AEC. He knew that the AEC position would end in 1959, at which point his government commitments would ease, so he began to give serious thought to what he wanted to do afterward. He was uncertain about returning to the IAS, though he was grateful for the opportunities it had afforded him.[64] The Electronic Computer Project was rapidly coming to an end, and there was little interest among the institute faculty in retaining the meteorologists Jule Charney and Norman Phillips, who had become von Neumann's closest scientific collaborators, together with Goldstine. Nor were von Neumann's mathematical colleagues at the institute very interested in his continuing a personal research program in computing and scientific computation.

Von Neumann had long had a great fondness for the climate, geography, and cuisine of the southwestern United States, particularly southern California. He was especially attracted to Los Angeles, home of the burgeoning aerospace (and with it computer) industry and not too far from the Los Alamos and Livermore laboratories. With the assistance of Lewis Strauss, von Neumann made contact with the University of California. He reached agreement with them in March 1956 to assume a position, following completion of his AEC duties, as professor at large to the University of California.[65] He was to be located on the Los Angeles campus.[66] His duties were to provide consulting advice to any department on any campus of the University of California system that needed advice, including departments of computing, earth sciences, economics, business, and engineering. He also wanted to have computing facilities available to him in order to continue his research on "high-speed computing machines and, especially, in their application to problems of geophysics and meteorology."[67] There was some discussion of bringing Charney and Phillips to UCLA as faculty in the Meteorology Department, though in the end they decided to go to MIT.[68]

These plans were all for naught. Surgery had removed only a secondary lesion, and the cancer spread rapidly. He was soon confined to a wheelchair and in April 1956, only a month after his negotiations with the University of California, entered the hospital for the last time. His health steadily deteriorated, and he died in the hospital on 8 February 1957. The scientific and government communities, as well as family and friends, mourned the early loss of this great man.

Notes

Introduction

1. Von Neumann to Oswald Veblen, 21 May 1943, OVLC.

Chapter 1

1. It may be contested whether the discipline of computing was new in the 1940s. There had been calculating in business and science since antiquity. Desk calculators were invented in the seventeenth century, and an industry for their mass production and distribution arose in the late nineteenth century in response to the industrial revolution and the rise of big business. A long line of analog computing devices (tide predictors, differential analyzers, gunnery computers, etc.) for use in engineering and the military began to appear in the late nineteenth century with the increasing mathematization of the engineering disciplines. Punched-card tabulating systems, first developed for the 1890 U.S. Census, became valued tools of large business and government in the first half of the twentieth century and were used in the 1930s for several important scientific applications. There is some continuity from these calculating technologies to the electronic stored-program computers of the postwar period, especially among equipment manufacturers and users. All that said, however, the differences created by the electronic speed and stored-program capability were so great that component and systems design, numerical methods, algorithms, applications, manufacture, and sales almost had to be entirely rethought. For more information on computing before computers, see Aspray (1990) or Williams (1985).

2. Nyce and Kahn (1989, p. 218) have cited Bush's own comments about the new digital computing technology: "For example, in a letter to R. C. Gibbs, who chaired a postwar National Research Committee on high speed machines, Bush writes 'I would like very much to discuss the subject with him [von Neumann] even though I know I cannot contribute to a field that is moving as rapidly as this one without much study.' (September 19, 1946). 'If I mixed with it' Bush wrote later, 'I could not possibly catch up with the new techniques and I did not intend to ... become a patriarch emitting dull generalities on the subject.' (Bush 1970, p. 208)."

3. In addition to the information provided by Nicholas A. Vonneuman, I have drawn on Heims (1980) and Ulam (1958a). There are some factual inaccuracies in both accounts, and I have tried to corroborate their material with other published and archival sources wherever possible. These sources include informa-

tion gleaned at three conferences held in honor of von Neumann: one in Budapest in February 1987 in honor of the thirtieth anniversary of his death; a related one at Arizona State University in May 1987, "The Computer and the Brain"; and a third, "The Legacy of John von Neumann," sponsored by the American Mathematical Society and held at Hofstra University in May 1988.

4. Max was awarded the von Margitta title of nobility by Emperor Franz Joseph in 1913 for his contributions to the economic development of Hungary. Max went by the name Margittai Neumann, which he passed on to his sons. When John went to Zurich, he used the name Johann Neumann von Margitta, which the German-language publishers shortened to von Neumann. I use anglicized given names in cases where they have been used by family and friends; thus I use John instead of Janos or Johann, John's father Miksa becomes Max, and John's mother Margit becomes Margaret.

In 1920 Max left this bank for another bank, Adolf Kohner's Sons, which was influential in financing the Hungarian industrial reconstruction after World War I.

5. *Allgemeine Geschichte in Einzeldarstellungen* by Wilhelm Oncken.

6. Regarding his abilities in mental arithmetic, see his memorandum to the National Academy of Sciences of 26 March 1954, Re: Autobiographical facts concerning John von Neumann, VNLC; also see an unpublished manuscript by Stephen White and Stan Ulam, "Bio I," SUAP.

7. For example, in the von Neumann conference held in Budapest in February 1987, von Neumann's classmates at the Lutheran Gymnasium spoke with warmth about the teachers: one taught the students about Nietzsche's writings as a sidelight to his lectures on geology; another, who was a linguist, took his students on trips around Europe; a third, whose father was a professional philosopher, taught John about philosophy and classical culture; and a fourth shared his poetry with his students as he published it.

8. Wigner, his good friend, coauthor, and later winner of the Nobel Prize in Physics, was one year ahead of John. Four years behind him were the famous musician Anatol Dorati and John's brother Michael. The younger brother, Nicholas, attended a Lutheran Gymnasium four years after that.

9. Von Neumann's grade reports are held in the National Technical Information Center and Library (OMIKK), Budapest. Except for handwriting, his grades were uniformly in the highest categories. One subject that did not interest him particularly was music; apparently he was too impatient to attend concerts.

In 1920 von Neumann won the Eotvos Prize, a Hungarian national competition for the best graduating secondary student in mathematics and science.

10. Even after the tutoring was arranged, Racz continued to teach John mathematics at the Lutheran Gymnasium. Racz was a gifted teacher and was known internationally for his contributions to the study of mathematical education.

11. Von Neumann said that his real mathematical interest began at age thirteen and that he remembered being given mathematics books by his father as a reward for being a "rapid calculator" in his Gymnasium class. See the interview of 28 May 1955 with von Neumann in Washington, DC; also see a memorandum written by von Neumann on 26 March 1954 to the National Academy of Sciences, "Re: Autobiographical facts concerning John von Neumann," both in VNLC.

12. Fekete and von Neumann (1922).

13. See the account of this decision in Von Karman (1967, pp. 106–107).

14. Ulam, "Recollections concerning Johnny's studies," SUAP, which is material intended for use in Ulam's uncompleted biography of von Neumann. Ulam was not in Zurich but presumably learned this information directly from von Neumann. Polya was a fellow Hungarian, and Weyl, like Erhard Schmidt, was a student of David Hilbert. Thus they represented the two most important connections in von Neumann's early career: Hungary and Göttingen.

15. This account of von Neumann's mathematical career in Europe is drawn from many sources, including Legendi and Szentivanyi (1983), Ulam (1958a), and various accounts of von Neumann's contributions to specific research areas. On his decision to leave Hungary for a career in Germany, see his testimony in the Oppenheimer security hearing (U.S. Atomic Energy Commission, 1954).

16. Reid (1976, p. 336) explains how David Hilbert and Richard Courant interceded to get von Neumann a Rockefeller Fellowship to work with Hilbert on the foundations of mathematics. Courant is quoted as stating, "Mr. von Neumann, in spite of his youth, is a completely exceptional personality . . . who has already done very productive work . . . and whose future development is being watched with great expectation in many places." It is quite likely that von Neumann was recommended to Hilbert by Erhard Schmidt.

17. For example, a 1928 paper solves a problem of Steinhaus on the decomposition of the interval into countably many disjoint, congruent sets. A 1928 paper, discussed in detail later in this chapter, introduces his theory of games. A 1929 paper shows how to extend the decompositions of the Banach-Tarski paradox from Euclidean space to general non-Abelian groups.

18. For additional background on the history of logic and foundations of mathematics in this period, see Moore (1986) and van Heijenoort (1967).

19. Hilbert (1904). The formalist program attempts to reduce mathematics to a collection of formulas, about which one tries to show that certain elementary formulas are free from contradiction and that rules allowing one to form more complex combinations of elementary formulas do not introduce contradictions.

20. Notes by Ulam for the biography (SUAP) suggest that as early as 1925 von Neumann had some inkling of problems with the formalist program, along the lines Gödel suggested, and that it was a great disappointment to von Neumann not to have discovered the incompleteness results himself.

21. See, for example, the account in Fraenkel (1922).

22. Von Neumann (1928a). This is the publication of his doctoral dissertation written for the University of Budapest.

23. These papers also discuss models of set theory, questions of categoricity, and the Lowenheim-Skolem theorems for set theory.

24. Succinct descriptions of von Neumann's contributions to quantum mechanics, at a higher technical level than the one presented here, can be found in Mackey (1957) and van Hove (1958).

25. See Hilbert (1912, 1935, 3: 217–289). Birkhoff and Bennett (1987) describe Hilbert's work in axiomatizing geometry and other areas of mathematics and physics.

26. Another attempt was made by Max Born, a Göttingen physics professor, and Norbert Wiener, an MIT mathematician who visited Göttingen in 1924, 1925, and 1926. This is apparently when von Neumann first met Wiener.

27. This account is taken from Heims (1980), who states that his source is a private communication from Lothar Nordheim dated 24 July 1978.

28. The introduction to Hilbert, Nordheim, and von Neumann (1927) credits Hilbert's influence.

29. See von Neumann (1932b, chs. 5, 6). His theory of measurement had epistemological ramifications, which it would take us too far afield to discuss.

Von Neumann and Garrett Birkhoff (1936) also developed a model for quantum logic closely related to the Hilbert space formalism in the 1932 book and closely tied to von Neumann's other research on operators and lattice theory.

30. This account of the Princeton University and IAS appointments is drawn largely from Aspray (1988) and Porter (1988).

31. Letters from Veblen of 15 October and 10 December 1929 and replies by von Neumann of 13 and 19 November 1929, OVLC, describe the invitations to von Neumann and Wigner.

32. Ulam (1958a) tells how von Neumann rationally calculated that there were approximately forty Privatdozents, each hoping for a mathematical professorship, while only three or four professorships were likely to become available within the next few years. Princeton University was already one of the three strongest mathematical centers in the United States but was by no means a match for Göttingen or Berlin.

Many years later, at the hearing to approve him as a member of the Atomic Energy Commission, von Neumann explained his reasons for coming to America: "I must say that the main reason was partly because conditions in Hungary were rather limited, and I thought the thing I was doing had a better field in America and to a considerable extent because I was much more in sympathy with the institutions of America; and, lastly, because I expected World War II, and I was apprehensive that Hungary would be on the Nazi side, and I didn't want to be caught dead on that side." "Nomination of John von Neumann to be a Member of the United States Atomic Energy Commission", 8 March 1955, VNLC. It is difficult to determine how much this explanation, particularly regarding the war, was shaped by hindsight.

33. Albert Tucker (private correspondence 6 January 1989) has indicated that he believes the physicists objected to giving von Neumann the chair.

34. "I had a feeling that, as this is an American institution, the staff must be recruited as far as possible with Americans, provided men of sufficient promise and ability could be secured." Meeting minutes, FASC.

35. A form that von Neumann filled out on 10 April 1942 to do work for NDRC section B1b describes his travel: to Germany, Austria, Hungary, Italy, and France in 1930 and 1931; to Germany and Hungary in 1932; to Hungary and Italy in 1933; to Hungary alone in 1934, 1937, and 1938; to England and Hungary in 1935; and to France in 1936. VNLC.

36. See Birkhoff (1958) on von Neumann's research in continuous geometry, Halmos (1958) on the ergodic theory, Kadison (1958) on the ring of operators,

and Murray (1958) on the spectral theory. Also see the accounts in Dieudonne (1976), Halmos (1973), and Ulam (1958a).

37. Contributions to operator theory are made in von Neumann (1929a, 1929b, 1931e, 1932e, 1935a,c).

38. See Birkhoff and Koopman (1932), which gives an explanation of the historical sequence of events and the differences between the Birkhoff and von Neumann results. The fact that Birkhoff had proved a stronger, more interesting, and more self-contained ergodic theorem led von Neumann to doubt his abilities, according to Ulam. In fact, Ulam claims, von Neumann felt quite a bit of self-doubt about his abilities and about the importance and reception of his mathematical work in the 1930s. "Johnny's MATHEMATICS and mine," study for his aborted von Neumann biography, SUAP.

39. See, for example, Hopf (1937).

40. The most important papers on rings of operators were Murray and von Neumann (1936, 1937, 1943) and von Neumann (1929a, 1936a,b, 1940, 1949a).

41. This work was announced in three notes—von Neumann (1936a, 1936b, 1937a)—and described in detail in mimeographed lecture notes, *Continuous Geometry* (Princeton Mathematical Notes, Spring 1936) and *Continuous Geometry, 1936–1937* (Edwards Brothers, 1937). They were later published in a revised and enlarged edition as von Neumann (1960) by his student, Israel Halperin. I am grateful to Halperin for his explanations of continuous geometry and its spread. Private communication, May 1989.

42. To simplify somewhat, Hilbert's Fifth Problem asks whether Lie's concept of a continuous group of transformations can be formulated without assuming the differentiability of the functions defining the group. For Hilbert, this was a problem in the foundations of geometry, and he believed that continuity was a natural geometric assumption but that differentiability was not. For further discussion of the problem, see Kaplansky (1977).

43. Von Neumann (1933b) proves that every compact and n-dimensional topological group is continuously isomorphic to a closed group of unitary matrices of a finite-dimensional Euclidean space.

44. Von Neumann (1934b, 1936f).

45. Von Neumann (1934a), Bochner and von Neumann (1935b).

46. This account is drawn largely from Kuhn and Tucker (1958), Morgenstern (1976), Ulam (1958a), and Weintraub (1983).

47. There is some controversy over the origination of the theory of games. Frechet (1953) credits Borel. In a note appended to Frechet's article, von Neumann does not deny that he had learned the concept of a game from Borel but points out that Borel had not proved any theorems, whereas he had given the strict formulation and proof of the Minimax Theorem, the central result in the theory of games.

48. The Minimax Theorem states: for any finite, zero-sum, two-person game in a normalized form, there exists an optimal strategy, given in terms of a unique number (known as the "minimax" value of the game), which represents the minimum gain and maximum loss each player can expect.

49. Weintraub (1983, p. 13). See Kuhn and Tucker (1958) and Weintraub (1983) for details. Morgenstern (1968, p. 386) argues that this paper "together with that

of Abraham Wald, marked the beginning of a new period in mathematical economics." Von Neumann's contributions to economics are also assessed in Thompson (1987), Rubinov (1987), and Makarov and Rubinov (1987).

50. See Hurwicz (1945) and Marschak (1946).

51. The literature on the theory of games has grown so extensively that it would take us too far afield to trace its development from von Neumann's ideas. A well-received popular account of the theory is given in McDonald (1950).

52. Von Neumann's interest in econometrics also continued. During and after the war he often stopped in Chicago at the Cowles Commission on his way to Los Alamos in order to discuss econometric research. He gave advice on the theory of games and on solving large systems of nonlinear simultaneous equations by iterative methods. Lawrence R. Klein, "Implications of the Electronic Computer for Economics," manuscript for the von Neumann Anniversary Conference, NWMI. Kuhn and Tucker (1958) list von Neumann's writings on the topic, including Hartley Rodger's transcription of a seminar presented by von Neumann at Princeton, 26 October 1951, which is printed as von Neumann (1953).

Chapter 2

1. This period in the history of computing is the subject of Ceruzzi (1983). It is also discussed in Aspray (1990) and Williams (1985).

2. This remark deserves qualification. Bell Laboratories, which supported Stibitz, and IBM, which built Aiken's machine, were certainly respected organizations with capital to expend, but at the time neither company had a strong commitment to the design and construction of fast computing equipment.

3. The account of von Neumann's war work presented here is drawn primarily from a letter von Neumann wrote to IAS director Frank Aydelotte on 11 October 1945 (VNLC) in reply to Aydelotte's request to account for his wartime activities. The information has been corroborated by other archival materials and testimonies of von Neumann's scientific colleagues. Of particular interest is von Neumann to Aydelotte, 14 September 1942, LANA, answering a similar request.

4. Kent Symposium, December 1955, VNLC.

5. Colonel Paul Gillon remembers the original (July 1940) appointments to have been: Hugh Dryden, Albert Hull, Bernard Lewis, I. I. Rabi, Henry N. Russell, Harold Urey, Theodore von Karman, and Von Neumann. Gillon to Herman Goldstine, 24 July 1970, HGAP. Also see R. H. Kent, "Historical Sketch of the Ballistic Research Laboratories," BRL Report, June 1954, HGAP.

6. A number of minutes of meetings, as well as von Neumann's reports to the Subcommittee on Detonations and Shock Waves, can be found in the archives of the Los Alamos Scientific Laboratory.

7. Actually von Neumann's work on shaped charges was not entirely successful. The problem was solved in the United States by Garret Birkhoff and in England by G. I. Taylor. See Birkhoff et al. (1948).

8. Von Neumann's interest in computing seems to have been stimulated directly by his work on ordnance. I have extensively, and unsuccessfully, sought any evidence that von Neumann was aware of the work being undertaken on cryptol-

ogy at Bletchley Park. Von Neumann was well acquainted with M. H. A. Newman and Alan Turing before the war, as chapter 8 indicates. There is no evidence, however, that von Neumann saw Turing during the trip to England or in 1944 when Turing visited the United States for his cryptologic work. Von Neumann does report in a letter to Veblen (30 March 1943, OVLC) an impending visit with Newman. The late Marshall Stone, an American mathematical colleague of von Neumann who did war work related to cryptology and visited Bletchley Park, believed strongly that von Neumann was unaware of the British work on codebreaking machines. Private communication, 2 June 1988.

9. Letter, 21 May 1943, OVLC.

10. This account is based on Todd (1974).

11. Details of the program are given in ibid., which indicates that it was a fixed program involving substantial human intervention but that it did present von Neumann with perhaps his earliest experience of selecting sequences of operations and operands, registers into which the operand is added or subtracted, and tabulations.

12. Letter, 17 November 1947, quoted in ibid. (p. 526).

13. This account is drawn largely from Goldstine (1972), Metropolis (1980), and Metropolis and Nelson (1982); oral histories the author conducted with Charles Critchfield (OH 134, 29 May 1987, OHCB) and Nicholas Metropolis (OH 135, 29 May 1987, OHCB); and a lecture given by Edward Teller on 2 June 1988 at a symposium, "The Legacy of John von Neumann," in Hempstead, New York.

14. Von Neumann explained in his testimony at the Oppenheimer security hearing how Oppenheimer had approached him in early 1943 about joining an important war project but could not tell him what it was. Von Neumann was obligated to go to England on other war work and joined the Los Alamos project only in the autumn, shortly after his return from England (U.S. Atomic Energy Commission 1954).

15. Neddermeyer is generally given credit for originating the implosion idea, but possibly it originated with Richard Tolman at the California Institute of Technology. Edward Teller, James Tuck, and others also worked on the implosion device. Tuck claims to have arrived at the implosion idea independently in England, before coming to Los Alamos. Critchfield credits von Neumann as an important catalyst for this work. See the Critchfield and Metropolis interviews already cited and Rhodes (1986).

16. Nicholas Metropolis (private communication, 7 December 1989) has indicated that the initial concern at the laboratory was for quick assembly because of predetonation but that von Neumann stressed the added advantage in an increase of material density resulting from the implosion.

17. Many other distinguished scientists participated in the computing activities at Los Alamos, including Richard Feynman, Richard Hamming, John Kemeny, and Peter Lax.

18. According to Metropolis and Nelson (1982), Los Alamos ordered three 601 multipliers and a single 402 tabulator, reproducer summary punch, verifier, key punch, sorter, and collator.

19. Metropolis oral history (OH 135).

20. Metropolis and Nelson (1982, p. 351).

21. Letter, 14 January 1944 (University of Pennsylvania Archives), cited by Stern (1981, p. 71).

A remembrance by Ulam many years later in his paper, "The Role of Los Alamos Laboratory Work in the History of the Modern Computing Machines," 1969(?), SUAP, addresses this same period of January 1944 when von Neumann was learning about computing: "I participated, in January 1944, in some of these discussions with von Neumann and [the mathematician Jack] Calkin and I well remember the schematized and over-simplified way by which one first tried to compute the course and results of implosions. From the beginning the schematizations seemed to me too crude and unreliable. I remember discussions with von Neumann in which I would suggest proposals and plans to calculate by brute force very laboriously—step by step—involving an enormous amount of computational work, taking much more time but with more reliable results. It was at that time that von Neumann decided to utilize the new computing machines which were "on the horizon."

22. See Weaver to E. L. Chaffee, 22 March 1944, and to von Neumann, 22 March 1944, VNLC; also von Neumann to Weaver, 27 March, 28 June 1944, HSRC.

23. The best sources on Aiken's machine are two forthcoming books, one a biography of Aiken by I. Bernard Cohen and the other a set of collected essays written by Aiken's students and colleagues and edited by Cohen. Useful accounts can be found in Ceruzzi (1983) and Williams (1985).

24. There is some confusion over when the problem was run, how many problems were run, and whether all of the extant correspondence relates to the Los Alamos calculation described in the text. Weaver provided introductions for von Neumann to the groups with high-speed computing equipment with the statement that von Neumann needed this computing service for his work with NDRC Division 8 and the Applied Mathematics Panel (AMP). Weaver never referred directly to the Los Alamos work, but this is understandable given the secrecy of the project. It is difficult to sort out the sequence of events because von Neumann was also pursuing computing applications in connection with his Applied Mathematics Panel project at the IAS. From the archival record we know that Weaver wrote to E. L. Chaffee, director of Harvard's Cruft Laboratory and Aiken's academic superior, on 22 March 1944, asking if Aiken would show von Neumann the Harvard machine. On 29 March von Neumann wrote to Chaffee about his discussions with Weaver and asked if he could visit in April. The next day Chaffee wrote, inviting him to visit Harvard then. In a letter of 26 June Weaver tells Captain T. A. Solberg of the Navy Bureau of Ships of recent conversations between Aiken and von Neumann in which they agreed that von Neumann's problem was suitable for the Harvard machine but in which Aiken declined to accept the job because of his manpower shortage. Letters of 1 July from von Neumann to Weaver and 6 July from Solberg to Weaver indicate that von Neumann and Aiken had come to an understanding and that the problem would be run. Von Neumann offered to have Valentine Bargmann, his assistant on the AMP project at IAS, and Charles Loewner, a Brown University mathematician also under AMP contract, do the problem preparation. In the end, however, the programming was carried out by one of Aiken's staff,

Richard Bloch. Oral history with Bloch conducted by author, 22 February 1984, OH 66, OHCB. All letters cited here are from VNLC except for the 29 March letter, which is from HSRC. Also see the interview of Bloch conducted by Henry Tropp on 12 May 1972, OHSM.

25. Metropolis and Nelson (1982, p. 351).

26. Von Neumann to Jesse W. M. DuMond of California Institute of Technology, 14 April 1944, VNLC. Some of this work was carried out under a contract the IAS received from the Applied Mathematics Panel in 1943 following a conversation among von Neumann, Weaver, and Richard Courant. The work involved both theoretical and computational aspects of shock collisions. Valentine Bargmann joined the project as von Neumann's assistant in 1944. Von Neumann to Weaver, 23 August 1943, 15 January 1944, VNLC.

27. Weaver to von Neumann, 22 March 1944, VNLC.

28. Von Neumann to Weaver, 10 April 1944, VNLC.

29. Weaver to von Neumann, 1 April 1944, VNLC. Consolidated Edison had cooperated extensively with the Applied Mathematics Panel in the past by providing access to their IBM machines at night for bombing calculations.

30. Fry to von Neumann, 28 March 1944, and von Neumann's reply the following day; Schilt to von Neumann, 7 April 1944, VNLC.

31. Von Neumann to Schilt, 1 July 1944; von Neumann to Stibitz, 6 July 1944, VNLC.

32. A memorandum, dated 24 April 1945, almost a year later, from J. A. E. Hindman of the Navy Department Bureau of Ordnance to von Neumann refers to computing work done as a courtesy by the Applied Mathematics Panel, Harvard University, Bureau of Ships, Tabulation Division of the Bureau of Ordnance, and others.

33. LANA.

34. Von Neumann to Oppenheimer, 1 August 1944, pp. 1, 6, LANA.

35. For more information see Eckert (1948).

36. Von Neumann to Oppenheimer, 1 August 1944, p. 7, LANA.

37. The questions are listed in a document entitled "Questions About Proposed Bell Relay Calculator" attached to ibid. It is not clear whether von Neumann had assistance from Stanley Frankel in preparing this list. The draft of this letter in the Los Alamos archives states "the 21 questions Stanley Fraenkel [*sic*] and I formulated," but Frankel's name is crossed out.

38. These points are distilled from von Neumann's list of questions and answers. Although many of them are taken directly from von Neumann's list, there is no direct one-to-one correspondence between his list and the one given here.

39. The number of arithmetic units in his plan was flexible, depending on the intended application of the calculator.

40. Lyle Johnson and John Palmer of the IBM Technical History Project (private communication, 20 November 1989) have suggested that the distinction here may be between arithmetic-by-counting (the wheels in IBM's ordinary tabulators) and arithmetic-by-logic (as in most relay calculators and electronic computers, in which registers are just storage elements and addition is performed by switching

circuits, which act to transfer the contents of two registers into one). Von Neumann would probably have agreed that this distinction is a useful one, and it may have been what he had in mind, but there is no evidence that his thought had developed so far by this time.

41. For example, a single instruction would cause the machine to take the contents of registers *a* and *b*, multiply them, and store them in register *c.*

42. Subroutines were described in terms of auxiliary tapes for storing frequently recurring subcycles.

43. However, there was discussion of a second tape for entering operational instructions common to all problems of a given type.

44. Conditional branching was described in terms of "alternate orders" based on the sign of the number located in a specified register.

45. We can round out the account of von Neumann's early wartime knowledge of calculating machines and methods. By May 1941 he had been receiving circulars from the Mathematical Tables Project established in New York by the Works Administration Project in the 1930s and later taken over by the National Bureau of Standards. They were using desk calculators to do their calculations. Arnold N. Lowan, head of the Mathematical Tables Project, to von Neumann, 7 May 1941, VNLC. Von Neumann replied (22 May 1941, VNLC): "I am very glad—and I think that the same goes for every mathematician who has been in contact with these questions—that this work [of the Mathematical Tables Project] has already progressed so far under your supervision. I think that this is a really worthwhile enterprise, and fills an important need both for applied mathematics and physics and for certain types of research work. I hope that your program will continue in the future, and that you will find it possible to include other functions in your program, like elliptic integrals and elliptic functions, confluent hypergeometric functions, Bessel functions of large integral orders, non-periodic solutions of the Mathieu differential equations, and error functions for complex arguments." After the war, von Neumann used the services of the Tables Project for some of his meteorological calculations. He was also familiar with nomographic techniques. He apparently knew of the work of Maurice d'Ocagne, and Robert Kent had recommended to him a book on nomography by Hewes and Seward (1923). Kent to von Neumann, 17 February 1941, VNLC.

46. Background for this account, in addition to archival sources, is taken from Burks and Burks (1981), Goldstine (1972), and Stern (1981).

47. This description of the ENIAC is taken from Goldstine and Goldstine (1946).

48. Stern (1981)

49. Goldstine (1972, p. 182).

50. Ibid. (p. 185). A letter of 5 September 1944 from R. A. Line, the Ordnance Department security officer, to the Moore School (HSRC) granted permission for von Neumann and J. W. Alexander, one of von Neumann's mathematical colleagues at the institute who was also doing work at Aberdeen, to visit the Moore School for two months beginning 7 September. A letter from J. G. Brainerd, project supervisor of the ENIAC project, to Colonel Paul N. Gillon at the Office of the Chief of Ordnance, 13 September 1944 (HGAP), suggested that von Neumann

had visited earlier than 7 September, for it talks of "extensive discussions . . . with Dr. Von Neumann" about using the ENIAC on scientific problems. In a private communication (June 1989) Arthur Burks concurred with this assessment. He indicated that the 7 September letter was intended to give security clearance to Alexander and that von Neumann already had clearance from Aberdeen so did not need a letter of permission. Burks also recalled clearly von Neumann's first visit to the Moore School, on which he came alone. Close dating is especially important here, for it bears on von Neumann's role in the decision to award a contract to build the EDVAC.

51. This is not to say that the ENIAC design was then complete. For example, most of the design work on the divider–square rooter remained.

52. A letter from Goldstine to von Neumann of 20 October 1944 (VNLC) explained that Colonel Schurig had approved this arrangement.

53. As quoted in Stern (1981, p. 75) from the University of Pennsylvania archives.

54. "Disclosure of a Magnetic Calculating Machine," HSRC.

55. Goldstine (1972, p. 155). The timing of this letter is interesting. If Goldstine remembers correctly the date of von Neumann's first visit to the Moore School, Goldstine's letter was written only four days later. This suggests strongly that von Neumann was a catalyst in the application for funds for a new research and development contract for EDVAC.

56. Minutes of the Meeting of the Firing Table Range Board, 29 August 1944, HSRH.

57. J. G. Brainerd to Colonel Paul N. Gillon, Office of the Chief of Ordnance, 13 September 1944, HGAP.

58. J. P. Eckert, J. W. Mauchly, and S. Reid Warren, Jr., "PY Summary Report No. 1," 31 March 1945, HSRC. "PX" refers to the ENIAC project and "PY" to the EDVAC project.

59. "Automatic High-Speed Computing: A Progress Report on the EDVAC," 30 September 1945, Report on Contract No. W-670-ORD-4926, Supp. 4, HSRC.

60. Arthur W. Burks, "Notes on Meeting with Dr. von Neumann, March 14, 1945," HSRC.

61. Burks, "Note on Meeting with Dr. Von Neumann, March 23, 1944," HSRC.

62. See von Neumann to Goldstine, 10 December 1944, 12 February 1945 [dated 1944 incorrectly], and Goldstine to von Neumann, 24 February, 13 April 1945. Also see Goldstine to Colonel P. N. Gillon, 14 December 1944. (All are in HSRC, except the 24 February letter, which is in HSRH.) According to Nicholas Metropolis (private communication, May 1987), von Neumann consulted with W. Higginbotham and his electronics group at Los Alamos in 1945 about electronic technology and its utility to computing equipment.

63. In a private communication (June 1989) Arthur Burks indicated that the report was distributed to him and some others on the staff (probably Eckert, Mauchly, Goldstine, and Reid Warren) in May. The June distribution was much wider.

64. Von Neumann gives his account of the history and summarizes the contents of the EDVAC report in a draft of a deposition written in 1947, IASD.

65. This topic is discussed in detail in chapter 8.

66. Von Neumann (1945b, pp. AB 29–30).

67. The computer was assumed to employ binary arithmetic internally in order to take advantage of the inherently binary switching nature of the basic elements.

68. An iconoscope is the viewing tube, originally developed at RCA, used in a television camera. A bit of information would be stored by an illumination at a particular location on the face of the tube.

69. Von Neumann (1945b, p. AB 59).

70. Goldstine to von Neumann, 15 May 1945, HSRC.

71. The Moore School criticisms were that the report should (1) consider number systems, perhaps including the ternary system, other than the binary one; (2) consider whether multiplication should be a programmed operation rather than an elementary one, as von Neumann has it; (3) describe the adder being patented by Eckert and Mauchly; (4) should have minor modifications made to the notation for delays and input-output lines; (5) reiterate where in the machine checking procedures should be established; and (6) modify the 2^n-way switch so as to reduce the number of elements needed to realize it. (Goldstine to von Neumann, 15 May 1945, HSRC.

72. J. P. Eckert, J. W. Mauchly, and S. Reid Warren, Jr., "PY Summary Report No. 2," 10 July 1945, HSRC.

73. The only criticism from Aberdeen was of von Neumann's choice of terminology (Haskell Curry to von Neumann 10 August 1945, VNLC). Von Neumann responded: "I am in complete agreement with your remarks about the lack of a unified terminology in the field of computing devices. This defect applies to the entire subject and is certainly a considerable nuisance—but I am rather pessimistic whether we can cure it in the immediate future. It will probably take a lot of work and the formation of considerable cooperating research establishments before we can get an even approximately universally accepted set of notations." Von Neumann to Curry, 20 August 1945. VNLC. See Hartree's response in a letter to Goldstine, 24 August 1945, HSRH.

74. These opinions were shared by T. K. Sharpless and Reid Warren of the Moore School. Sharpless wrote: "In general [von Neumann] discussed the problem from the point of view of a neurologist. This paper [the Draft Report] was of considerable philosophic interest although not of much practical help towards the development of EDVAC. . . . I believe all the organs which von Neumann mentions in that paper already had an existing counterpart here in ENIAC or in proposed plans for EDVAC." Memorandum, "Subject: Von Neumann's report of EDVAC—June 1945," 2 April 1947, HSRH. Warren wrote of the draft report as presenting "a summary of the conclusions—both definite and tentative—that had arisen from these discussions [with the Moore School staff]." Deposition, 2 April 1947, "Notes on the Preparation of 'First Draft of a Report on the EDVAC' by John von Neumann," HSRC.

75. PY Summary Report No. 2, 10 July 1945. Emphasis added. University of Pennsylvania archives as cited by Stern (1981, p. 77).

76. "Automatic High-Speed Computing: A Progress Report on the EDVAC," 30 September 1945. Report on Contract No. W-670-ORD-4926, Supp. 4, HSRC.

77. As quoted in Stern (1981, p. 78). In an oral history interview (28 October 1977), Nancy Stern asked Eckert if von Neumann had made any contribution to the stored program concept. Eckert replied: "He brought up questions that we evaluated but he didn't answer them . . . he came in with some ideas on circuits . . . which influenced my thinking on BINAC and UNIVAC. . . . But I found out that he got that idea from Willy Higgenbotham [of Los Alamos]. . . . I found him a great sounding board to talk to because he understood what you were saying to him, and he could sound ideas out but I didn't really find him terribly inventive." (OH 13, OHCB).

78. Quoted in Stern (1981, p. 78).

79. "Remarks from Minutes of Conference held at the Moore School of Electrical Engineering on 8 April 1947 to discuss Patent Matters," HSRC.

80. Whether the patent agreement was only intended to apply to subsequent inventions or also to prior ENIAC and EDVAC inventions is unclear. Either way, such an agreement would have seriously undermined the viability of Eckert and Mauchly's commercial venture.

81. There is a far more extensive correspondence concerning the patent dispute than is cited here. Copies of this material can be found in IASD, HSRH, and, especially, HSRC.

82. J. Warshaw, Report on Trip to Patent Branch, Legal Division, Office of the Chief of Ordnance, 3 April 1947, HSRC. Warshaw was representing the Moore School in preparation for the meeting to discuss patent claims held there on 8 April 1947.

83. Von Neumann to Aaron Townshend, 6 June 1946, HSRC. He does not make clear here what these inventions are. Other sources suggest that he believed he deserved credit for the new code enabling the operation of the EDVAC, certain switching arrangements, the serial adder, the system design of the arithmetic unit, the use of the iconoscope as a memory device, and the use of an oscilloscope as an output device. This list does not include his theoretical contributions. See Goldstine (1972, pp. 223–224); Remarks from Minutes of a Conference held at the Moore School of Electrical Engineering on 8 April 1947 to Discuss Patent Matters; and a memorandum from Mauchly to Eckert, 10 April 1947, outlining the outcome of that this meeting (all in HSRC).

84. Von Neumann to Aaron Townshend, 6 June 1946, HSRC.

85. J. Warshaw, Report on Trip to Patent Branch, Legal Division, Office of the Chief of Ordnance, 3 April 1947, HSRC.

86. Ibid. Emphasis appeared in the copy available to me, though it may not have appeared in the original.

87. See Minutes of Conference Held at the Moore School of Electrical Engineering on 8 April 1947 to Discuss Patent Matters; also see Mauchly to Eckert, memorandum, 10 April 1947, and von Neumann to his lawyer, Aaron Towshend, 9 April 1947, giving their synopses of the outcome of the meeting (all in HSRC).

88. There is no evidence the lawyer ever agreed or that Eckert and Mauchly ever showed von Neumann any patent documents.

89. Stern (1981, p. 99).

90. Von Neumann to Aaron R. Townshend, 9 April 1947, HSRC.

91. Von Neumann to Aaron Townshend, 6 June 1946, HSRC.

92. Von Neumann to M. Libman, 25 November 1947, HSRC.

93. In a memo to the Electronic Computer Project staff (Bigelow, Hildebrandt, Melville, Pomerene, Slutz, Snyder, and Ware) dated 6 June 1947 (VNLC), Goldstine described the new patent policy as turning over to the government most patentable ideas—though he held out the possibility that a different course of action could be followed for "the probably few exceptional developments that give rise to extremely valuable commercial applications." In practice, all the ideas were placed in the public domain. See the oral history conducted by Nancy Stern with James Pomerene, 26 September 1980 (OH31, OHCB). Also see Goldstine's letter to Colonel G. F. Powell of the OCO, 10 May 1947, VNLC.

A similar situation caused Goldstine and von Neumann additional worry in 1949 over patent rights to the Williams tube memory. They were concerned that the British government, which held the patent rights in England to the Williams tube, would license it to a sole American company and that "such a move might militate against free research in the field of electronic computation and might even prove a source of embarassment to the [Atomic Energy] Commission" Goldstine to Holbrook McNeille of the AEC, 5 August 1949. The reason for the comment about embarassment was that the IAS computer, which was being supported by the AEC, used a modified form of Williams tube. Also see a letter from Mina Rees of 24 March 1949 and von Neumann's reply the following day (all in HSRC).

Von Neumann had begun to be concerned about a patent policy earlier. He wrote to MIT president Karl T. Compton about the MIT policy on 23 February 1946, VNLC. In a letter of 1 April 1946, VNLC, to the IAS mathematician Marston Morse, von Neumann had already begun to call for an IAS patent policy and writes: "I think that the patent policy I suggest strikes a reasonable middle route between leaving everything to the employee or taking everything for the Institute. I am not in favor of the former procedure since it may lead to commercially minded control of the inventions developed with our money."

94. George A. Smith to Zworykin, 26 January 1946, HSRC.

95. Von Neumann to J. Presper Eckert, 6 March 1946, VNLC, as quoted in Stern (1983, pp. 84–85).

96. Von Neumann to Frankel, 29 October 1946, HSRC. Eckert and Mauchly do seem to have a point here in that von Neumann's attitude toward RCA as expressed in this quotation does seem inconsistent.

97. Noted in H. Halladay's memorandum, "Re Honeywell vs. Sperry Rand—Los Alamos Problem," 6 February 1970, SUAP. For further information on this calculation, see "Operation of ENIAC in Philadelphia," HGHC.

98. "The Role of Los Alamos Laboratory Work in the History of the Modern Computing Machines," SUAP. In an interview, Frankel claimed that in hindsight this calculation was ill advised, that it was vastly beyond the scope of the ENIAC, and that even though it was carried out successfully the answer was too crude (interviewed by Robina Mapstone, 5 October 1972, OHSM). Nicholas Metropolis (private communication, 7 December 1989) disagrees with the assessments of Ulam and Frankel: "I think the whole spirit of that first calculation on the Eniac is missed. Whenever any theory or calculation is evaluated in retrospect, it is trivial to be

superficially critical about it" and "Frankel's thought twenty-seven years later (surprisingly) misses the whole point in referring to the Eniac work as 'ill-advised'—it ushered in a new era in science!"

99. Von Neumann also arranged in 1948 for the ENIAC to be used for a Los Alamos problem, code name Monte Carlo, on "a very important and urgent AEC problem." The calculation was carried out in eight weeks of full-time computation in 1950. Von Neumann to Colonel Leslie Simon of BRL, 5 February 1948; von Neumann to Carson Mark of Los Alamos, 19 April 1950, VNLC.

100. Problems run by and for von Neumann and others on the ENIAC in its operation at Aberdeen are described in W. Barkley Fritz, "A Survey of ENIAC Operations and Problems 1946-1952," Ballistics Research Laboratories Memorandum Report No. 617, August 1952, HGAP.

Chapter 3

1. See Norbert Wiener to von Neumann, 24 March 1945, VNLC, in which von Neumann's postwar plans for hydrodynamics research are mentioned.

2. For further information about research style at the institute, see Aspray (1988). See von Neumann to Veblen, 28 August 1945, VNLC, about faculty support at the Institute for his computer research plans.

3. Letter, 24 March 1945, VNLC.

4. This topic is discussed in greater detail in chapter 8. Apparently the control science aspect appealed to von Neumann, for he wrote expressing a desire to meet Wiener's Mexican collaborator Arturo Rosenblueth and learn more about their program of research. Von Neumann to Wiener, 18 May 1945. Wiener wrote to Rosenblueth 11 July 1945 (NWMI) that he thought von Neumann's appointment and acceptance are "in the bag," that von Neumann was enormously interested in their joint paper, and "it is quite clear that if the appointment comes through, all of our ideas concerning an organized collaboration between physiological and mathematical subjects will follow as a matter of course."

5. In a letter to Gretel [last name not given], 11 July 1945, (NWMI), Wiener wrote, "Johnny has been and gone and it looks as though he is in the bag. Everybody is delighted and we are going to go places." The formal offer from Dean Harrison to be professor of mathematics and, upon the retirement of Professor Phillips, chairman at a salary of $15,000 was made in a letter of 14 August. In a letter of 23 August (VNLC) Harrison tried to convince von Neumann to accept an MIT appointment even if the IAS could find the money for the computer because MIT had the experience in computing and "you would find yourself immersed here in a 'potential field' which could only be built up over a long period of time."

6. In a letter to Wiener of 21 April 1945 (NWMI) in which von Neumann discussed his conversations with Dean Harrison about an MIT appointment he also mentioned MIT's computing work: "I was in Cambridge and saw R. Taylor and the Tech mechanico-electronic analyzer, we spent two days together. It was very interesting, particularly considering what Taylor might do in the future. We should by all means have a talk á trois.' I think there is more to learn from Taylor than from Aiken—and not on analyzers only or mainly."

7. Von Neumann to Harrison, 20 November 1945, VNLC.

8. Bartky referred to this conversation in a letter to von Neumann dated 13 August 1945. Also see von Neumann to Bartky, 19 August, VNLC.

9. Von Neumann discussed the offer in his letter to Hutchins, 20 November 1945, VNLC. Von Neumann's interest in Chicago was heightened by the presence of its Institute of Nuclear Studies, where many of his Los Alamos colleagues held appointments.

10. The approach by I. I. Rabi and J. F. Ritt of Columbia was referred to in von Neumann to IAS director Frank Aydelotte, 25 August 1945, VNLC. His appointment at Harvard had been pushed by Marshall Stone and perhaps others. See the letters to von Neumann from Stone dated 22 November 1945 and the mathematics department chairman, David Widder, dated 26 November 1945, VNLC. It is possible that the work taking place under the direction of Howard Aiken in the Harvard Computation Laboratory was also attractive to von Neumann.

11. See Taylor to Aydelotte, 29 October 1945. Also see Goldstine (1972, p. 241). Von Neumann described his various offers to Aydelotte in a letter of 25 August 1945 (all of these letters are in the VNLC).

12. Von Neumann wrote diplomatically to Wiener on 20 November 1945, "I need not tell you how much I regret that this means that I cannot join you at Tech, especially since I am sure that without the decisive encouragement that I received from you and from the Tech authorities I would hardly have had the perseverance and the strength of conviction which are the minimum requirements in this project."

13. Report of the Director, 18 April 1947, FASC.

14. Letters of 25 and 27 August 1945 describe the plan, VNLC.

15. Memorandum, 5 September 1945, VNLC.

16. Ibid. Von Neumann pointed out that concurrent with machine design and construction a group of mathematicians and engineers should be working together in one place to develop and test new computing methods that would make efficient use of the new machine.

A subsequent interchange with Aydelotte shows that von Neumann already clearly understood the differences between analog and digital devices and that the differences were decisively in favor of digital technology. On 30 October 1945 Aydelotte sent von Neumann a clipping from the *New York Herald Tribune* describing the MIT differential analyzer then being commissioned. Von Neumann replied two days later (VNLC): "I think that it [the differential analyzer] is very far behind the fast digital devices now contemplated: it does not have their precision, nor their flexibility (e.g. it can handle partial differential equations in only a few simple cases) and even the fastest relay devices now under development will outdo it in speed. The electronic device which we are planning would of course surpass it in speed, precision and flexibility (all-purpose character) and will be at least as easy to 'set up' or 'program.' In speed our device should be better by the factor 100 even in the most unfavorable cases—and on problems which require a reasonable amount of computing this factor should be well above 1000. Furthermore, I would like to repeat that those problems which offer the most interesting and important uses for future computing machines, and in particular for the device which we plan, cannot be done at all on any differential analyzer with practicable characteristics."

17. Von Neumann to Aydelotte, memorandum, 5 September 1945, VNLC.

18. Ibid.

19. Von Neumann to Weaver, 22 January 1946, VNLC. The estimated expenditures break down as follows: $68,000 for a building, personnel at $69,000 per year, supplies at $9,200 per year, laboratory and shop at $7,000 per year, and construction $22,500 per year—all for three years. Thereafter, $34,500 was budgeted per year for staff, maintenance, power, and supplies (e.g., magnetic wire and punched cards). These figures are based on a computer sketched out by von Neumann, V. Zworykin, and J. Rajchman. See von Neumann to Weaver, 2 January 1946, VNLC. Weaver believed (correctly) that these figures were unrealistically low (letter to von Neumann, 12 March 1946, VNLC).

20. Aydelotte wanted to reserve the institute funds for development work that extended beyond the three years in von Neumann's development budget, redesigning and rebuilding any units that did not work originally, and the first two years of experimental application of the computer. The $100,000 did not include the part of von Neumann's salary paid by the institute. How the institute funds were ultimately expended is not clear. See Aydelotte to Weaver, 16 January 1946, VNLC.

21. This account of early funding is drawn largely from Goldstine (1972, pp. 242–246) and is corroborated by various documents in the VNLC: excerpt from the Minutes of the Meeting of the Executive Committee of the Institute for Advanced Study held at 125 Park Avenue, New York City, Tuesday, 18 December, 1945, at 4:00 P.M.; Aydelotte to von Neumann, 1 January 1946; von Neumann to Herbert S. Maass, president of the institute, 6 February 1946, and his reply of 8 February.

22. Von Neumann already knew Vladimir Zworykin, Jan Rajchman, and others at RCA who had been involved with building computing devices and components in the Camden, New Jersey, laboratories of RCA during the war. (This wartime research is described in chapter 4.) See the interview of George W. Brown conducted 15 March 1973 by Richard Mertz. In another interview conducted by Mertz, Jan Rajchman (26 October 1970) stated that von Neumann had been impressed by RCA's war work on digital techniques for fire control and that the discussions about the computer project came directly out of von Neumann's conversations with Zworykin near the end of the war about their mutual interest in weather prediction. (Both interviews are in OHSM.)

   In a letter of 26 December 1945 (VNLC) Weaver indicated to von Neumann that other demands on Rockefeller resources, particularly from the "ravaged European countries," would swamp their budget and probably not permit them to fund the computer project. There is additional correspondence between Aydelotte and Weaver and later between Weaver and von Neumann continuing through March 1946. The decision was delayed by Weaver's illness, and it was not until 21 March 1946 (VNLC) that Weaver wrote to von Neumann with the decision not to provide support. Weaver held out the possibility (never realized) that the Rockefeller Foundation might later provide funds for modification, improvement, maintenance, and the basic scientific program. Also see the minutes of the 19 March 1946 Institute Board of Trustees meeting, FASC.

23. See von Neumann to Strauss, 16 March 1946, VNLC, 21 March 1946, HSRC, in which he credited Strauss with initiating the subject with the navy.

Von Neumann's first contacts with Strauss about this matter were in person on 16 and 18 October. On 20 and 24 October (VNLC) von Neumann wrote Strauss a two-part letter about his plans for a computer.

In the 20 October letter, von Neumann indicated what he thought were the more challenging tasks. Engineering problems, he believed, were not great: "As you know, it is possible at present to accelerate the automatic performance of the elementary arithmetical operations (addition, multiplication, etc.) by a factor of about 10,000 against what is ordinary practice today, and a factor of 1000 against the most advanced device in actual use. This can be done by electronic counting methods and by using various television and radar techniques which have been developed in the course of the last five or ten years—and it can be done without inventing anything very new from the engineering point of view, just by combining and properly 'organizing' existing components." Later in the letter he explained that it was is "technically quite clear that very considerable mathematical and logical changes will have to be effected in this field" and that these were best done "experimentally" by constructing such a computing device.

The 24 October letter described problems from aerodynamics, hydrodynamics, elasticity and plasticity, optics, electrodynamics, and dynamic meteorology, as well as large sorting problems.

24. E. W. Engstrom, vice-president for research at RCA, put Aydelotte in contact with key navy personnel in Admiral Bowen's office. Aydelotte to von Neumann, memo, 9 November 1945, VNLC; von Neumann to Admiral Bowen, 23 June 1946, VNLC. The letter was apparently not sent; its purpose was merely to confirm a telephone conversation von Neumann had had earlier that day with Bowen.

In a long letter of 4 May 1946 (VNLC), von Neumann explained to Strauss the problems that he and Aydelotte had with the prospective navy contract: the institute was pursuing contracts for the project with the Navy and Army Ordnance at the same time and for the same amount of money ($100,000). The institute believed the contract would be approved by the army but was worried that the comptroller general's office would void the contract less favorable to the government. The proposed navy contract was clearly less favorable to the institute since it called for matching funds from both the institute and RCA and also for a certain amount of time on the machine. Engstrom and von Neumann were both strongly opposed to this last condition, the reason that von Neumann wrote to Strauss to see if the navy support could instead be given in the form of support for mathematical and meteorological work associated with the computer project, in this way avoiding a direct competition between army and navy funds.

25. Princeton University agreed to construct certain components at no charge in its Palmer Physical Laboratory. The institute trustees hoped never actually to expend their $100,000. They hoped first to replace it with the Rockefeller money, which never appeared, and then to use it solely as a contingency fund.

26. On the army's involvement see Major General G. M. Barnes to Aydelotte, 9 January 1946, and Aydelotte's reply of 16 January. This resulted in contracts DA-36-034-ORD-1023, DA-36-034-ORD-1330, and W-36-034-ORD-7481. The navy was already supporting a limited amount of mathematical research under Navy Department Bureau of Ordnance contract NOrd-9596, dated 1 September 1945, whose Task 1 was "Analysis and Development of Methods for High-Speed Automatic Computing." A new contract with the Navy Department Office of Research

and Inventions, contract N-6-ori-12, was awarded for mathematical and meteorological analysis. The rationale of this work was described in a letter and an attached memorandum from von Neumann to Admiral Bowen (draft in VNLC). Numerical analysis, programming, and coding were carried out under navy contract N-7-ONR-388.

Contracts and various correspondence in VNLC document the support in the period 1949–1954 from the Ordnance Corps, the Office of Naval Research, the Air Research and Development Center, and the Atomic Energy Commission. The best summary is given in AEC 553/5, Atomic Energy Commission, Past Support and Present Relationship of AEC to Maniac Installation at the Institute for Advanced Study, 6 January 1953, Report by the Director of Research, DOEA. Because of Argonne and Los Alamos interest in this kind of computer, in 1948 the AEC authorized transfer of $150,000 to Army Ordnance to support the project for two years. In 1949, when the IAS computer building had to be expanded to add research space in part for the visitors from the AEC laboratories, AEC paid $51,000 of the $85,000 extension. In December 1949 AEC authorized another $150,000 to support the project through 1952 and in January 1952 authorized $85,000 through June 1953. There was discussion of withdrawing AEC support then, provided that it would not jeopardize the continuity of the project, because Argonne and Los Alamos had already gained what they could from the project. However, von Neumann wrote Goldstine on 3 January 1955, HGAP, to suggest that this was the time to eliminate AEC support altogether, so it must have continued until then.

An undated note in von Neumann's hand (VNLC) summarizes costs of the Electronic Computer Project from the beginning of 1946 through June 1950. A total of $772,000 was expended, including $90,000 from ONR ($40,000 for the computer and $50,000 for related mathematical research), $82,000 from IAS ($30,000 for the building, $40,000 for von Neumann's salary, and $12,000 for disallowances), and $600,000 from Army Ordnance, the three military services jointly, and AEC (including $200,000 for the building). Costs after June 1950 are not so easily compiled.

27. See Goldstine (1972, p. 244). Memorandum of the program of the high-speed computer project, 8 November 1945, von Neumann to Aydelotte (IAS), E. W. Engstrom (RCA), and H. S. Taylor (Princeton University) (HSRC) gives von Neumann's original plan for the computer. This memorandum served as the basis for the meetings at RCA. Also see von Neumann's ten-page letter of 2 November 1945 (VNLC), which describes some of his early thinking about the binary system, memory size and speed, order codes, library of subroutines, and feasible scientific applications.

The minutes of the four "E.C." meetings at RCA (held 12, 19, 21, 29 November 1945) can be found in HSRC. These meetings were attended by G. W. Brown, J. Rajchman, A. W. Vance, and V. Zworkyin of RCA, Goldstine and von Neumann of the IAS project, and J. Tukey of Princeton University. Presper Eckert attended the last of the four meetings. Von Neumann led a discussion that ranged over all aspects of the computer design and implementation. A list of some of the topics covered illustrates the overall nature of the discussion: basic machine configuration, choice of vacuum tubes, speed requirements, the iconoscope and delay line as memory units, how to distinguish coded numbers from instructions, magnetic tape input-output and oscilloscope output, precision levels, selection of primitive arithmetic operations, and block diagrams for the computer system.

28. See the unsigned letter from the RCA Laboratories to IAS Director Frank Aydelotte, 7 December 1945, IASD, proposing the patent policy.

29. Minutes of the Regular Meeting of the Board of Trustees, Institute for Advanced Study, 19 October 1945, quoted in Goldstine (1972, p. 243).

30. Aydelotte, minutes of the Meeting of the Committee on the Electronic Computer held in the Director's office, Institute for Advanced Study, November 1945, quoted in Goldstine (1972, pp. 243–244). Portions of this section are reprinted, with permission of the Mathematical Association of America, from Aspray (1987).

31. Letter, 23 January 1946, VNLC.

32. Von Neumann to Admiral Bowen (Navy Office of Research and Inventions), 23 January 1946, VNLC.

33. On the backgrounds of the Electronic Computer Project staff, see the Report of Computer Project, I. Progress to date, n.d. (probably March 1946), HSRC.

34. This account is drawn largely from Goldstine (1972, pp. 245–246, 252–255). It is supplemented and corroborated from primary sources in the VNLC.

35. Von Neumann to Eckert, 6 March 1946. Also see Eckert's response of 15 March 1946 and the letter of offer from von Neumann dated 27 November 1945, all in VNLC. This offer was presumably withdrawn with regret. According to Mina Rees, head of ONR's Mathematical Section and a mathematician with whom von Neumann frequently discussed computing, von Neumann admired Eckert and thought he was "a real genius." Interview with Henry Tropp, 20 October 1972.

36. See letters from von Neumann dated 28 November 1945 and 26 February 1946 and letters from Overbeck dated 16 December 1945, 14 February 1946, and 18 March 1946, all in VNLC. In these letters the two men exchanged substantial information about their design plans and experience. Von Neumann described his thinking much along the lines indicated in this chapter. In his 14 February letter Overbeck described how the Steichotron and Digitron tubes could be used in a computing machine, and in his letter of 18 March he described his plan for a computing machine at MIT, including a discussion of the logical design of the totalizer, multiplying and dividing matrix, temporary storage, permanent storage control, storage selection, master control, and function tables.

37. Bigelow, private communication, 6 November 1987.

38. Von Neumann described in a letter of 21 November 1948 to L. G. Smith of the University of Michigan (VNLC) what he was looking for in the way of engineers: "If you know of a good electrical engineer—or a physicist or applied mathematician with some leaning to PF techniques and a present or potential interest, or at least a lack of hostility, for electronic computing—junior or medium senior, please let me know."

39. By January 1946, when it was understood that a computer project was to proceed at the institute and that the Army Ordnance Department was to be a sponsor, it was deemed appropriate that there be cooperation between the projects at the University of Pennsylvania and the IAS. This cooperation was intended to include free visits of varying lengths between staff members of the two projects. See, for example, Frank Aydelotte's letter of 16 January 1946 to University

of Pennsylvania president George W. McClelland, and McClelland's reply of 22 January. One agreement reached that month was that the institute would not make further raids on the EDVAC personnel. (IAS had previously made offers to Burks, Eckert, and Goldstine.) The fragile cooperation was strained over the offer of an appointment to another engineer, Robert Shaw, in May 1946. Irven Travis, supervisor of research, wrote an angry letter to von Neumann on 8 May about Shaw. Von Neumann replied the following day to point out that Shaw had already informed the Moore School that he was departing to join Eckert and Mauchly's commercial venture and had only subsequently decided that he wanted not to join Eckert and Mauchly's company but instead the institute project, that von Neumann had in no way solicited or enticed Shaw to leave the Moore School for the institute, and that "under these conditions, it would seem quixotic of us not to attempt to secure so valuable a man" (all letters from VNLC).

40. Bigelow (1980, p. 310) lists the following people as working at some point as part of the engineering group: J. Bigelow, A. Bliss, H. Crane, J. Davis, G. Estrin, D. Gillies, L. Harmon, T. E. Hildebrandt, G. Kent, R. Melville, J. Pomerene, P. Panagos, J. Rosenberg, M. Rubinoff, R. Shaw, J. Sims, D. Slotnick, R. Slutz, R. L. Snyder, and S. Y. Wong.

41. Von Neumann also asked Colonel Paul Gillon of Army Ordnance, whom he knew well from Aberdeen Proving Grounds, about two army barracks for the computer project. Gillon to von Neumann, 5 March 1946, VNLC.

42. Aydelotte to von Neumann, 1 January 1946, VNLC.

43. Ibid., 13 April 1946, VNLC.

44. Ibid., 4 June 1946. Aydelotte's carping continued in a letter of 10 June (VNLC), this time about salt tablets, electric fans, and lack of appropriate administration of the computer project.

45. The "temporary" building was made of concrete since wood was hard to obtain just after the war.

46. See Ames Bliss to Aydelotte, memorandum, 20 August 1946, VNLC, and von Neumann to Aydelotte, memorandum, 6 September 1946, VNLC.

47. A town meeting on this topic is described in the 15–21 June 1952 edition of *Town Topics*, the local community newspaper. There is another, unattributed newspaper article in VNLC.

48. Von Neumann did not publish this paper, but it is printed in both Taub (1961) and Aspray and Burks (1987). A footnote to the paper indicates that it contains material from several lectures but in particular from one that von Neumann presented to the Mathematical Computing Advisory Panel of the Navy Office of Research and Inventions on 15 May 1946. See a transcript of this lecture with the title "A Survey of Large Scale Automatic Computing Machines," VNLC. The transcript discusses many of the same points as the paper; however, the paper has the ideas entirely reorganized, the arguments tightened, and the examples more carefully chosen and worked out.

Von Neumann discussed similar ideas in his Moore School Lecture of August 1946 (an unedited transcript is also available in VNLC).

There is an additional section at the end of the paper that is not reprinted in either of the volumes. The missing section discusses flow diagrams and the steps in the preparation and coding of problems similar to that appearing in "Planning and Coding of Problems for an Electronic Computing Instrument." Here von Neumann described the nonlinear sequence by which code is executed more mathematically in terms of the motion of the control unit on a Riemann surface projected over a memory surface.

49. Goldstine and von Neumann (1946?, pp. AB 318–319).

50. Ibid. (p. AB 320). Von Neumann expanded on this point in a letter of 3 April 1946 to Howard Emmons of Harvard University, VNLC: "I have always believed that very high speed computing could replace some—but of course not all—functions of a wind tunnel. That is, that an appreciable fraction of the work done in a wind tunnel is not a physical experiment, nor a physical measurement, but that it is performed under conditions where there is absolutely no doubt about the physical factors which intervene essentially, nor about the mathematical laws which describe them, and then the wind tunnel is simply used as an 'analogy' computing machine. This latter use of the wind tunnel is a peculiar thing: It is superior to ordinary computing, because the wind tunnel as an 'analogy' computer is much faster than the existing digital computing facilities, and it can handle, in its own limited field, much more complicated problems than those facilities can. On the other hand the 'analogies' used are of limited validity, the 'noise level' is high, and the precision correspondingly low.

"We are in the process of developing an electronic digital computer with a very high intrinsic precision, which will be able to handle problems of very high complexity—actually of much higher complexity than that of the typical wind tunnel—or flow-problems. . . .

"I would like to add, that such a machine would be much smaller and cheaper than a conventional wind tunnel."

51. See Pasta and Ulam (1959) for a discussion, based on their experience at Los Alamos, of the use of a computer as a heuristic tool—one for giving insight rather than proving results.

52. These investigations are the subject of chapter 5.

53. Unedited transcript of lecture, 13 August 1946, VNLC.

54. It is interesting to compare von Neumann's vision in the 1940s with the situation in 1988: "Someone coined the expression 'von Neumann's Dream of the Digital Wind Tunnel'. I have heard estimates that we are perhaps 10–20 % down this Dream Tunnel. We have the NAS, the National Aerodynamic Simulator, at NASA-Ames, we have the Navier-Stokes machine at Princeton, with N-S software built in. We have large projects on turbulence. We have the DDWT (DARPA Digital Wind Tunnel, still a dream)." Davis 1988, p. 18.

55. Unedited transcript of the Moore School lecture, 13 August 1946, VNLC.

56. This section also repeats the discussion of the value of having random access memory, the parallel architecture that takes advantage of its operation, and the possibilities of the Selectron memory for physically realizing these principles.

57. Letter to Newman 19 March, to Huxley, 26 March, VNLC.

58. The specifications given to Newman in March 1946 are one to two orders of magnitude faster than the ones von Neumann was considering only five months earlier in a letter to Ulam: "With the device I contemplate a multiplication takes

1 millisecond, a division 1–2 ms, a single transfer .5–1 ms, finding a definite object in the memory and transferring it 2–3 ms, if such transfers are performed in sequences of 2–30 successive transfers, the whole sequence need only exceed the above estimate by about 5–10% per extra transfer. These are crude estimates, but probably roughly right." Letter, 25 October 1945, SUAP.

59. Original copies of the report are available in the Charles Babbage Institute archives and elsewhere. References here are to the second edition as reprinted in Aspray and Burks (1987). Because I am not particularly concerned here with the progression of the logical design ideas from 1946 to 1947, I will review the second edition. This report thanks John Tukey for his assistance with its content.

60. See Aspray and Burks (1987, pp. 13–16) for Burks's description of the institute computer in modern terminology. Also see Burks (1986) for a description of the von Neumann architecture, a list of the main advances over the past 40 years leading to modifications in the von Neumann architecture, and some examples of radically non–von Neumann architectures that have been tried.

61. For example, the report mentions that the National Bureau of Standards Ordnance Development Division was modifying standard Teletype equipment for their use.

62. James Pomerene (private communication, 18 November 1988) recalled the arguments put forth in the 1940s in favor of serial memory: a serial memory already existed in the form of the mercury delay line, the arithmetic carry operation was of a fundamentally serial nature, and a parallel memory would require too many tubes to implement. The institute computer was the first to employ a parallel memory architecture. The result belied these arguments. The institute computer, which employed only 3000 tubes, worked well and at a higher speed than any of the serial computers of the period.

63. Judging the design decisions about binary versus decimal and fixed point versus floating point as progressive or conservative based on the later history of computer design would be Whig history, except for the fact that von Neumann's discussions of his design choices suggest that he understood that future designers would choose binary and floating point. In reviewing this manuscript, Arthur Burks noted that both of von Neumann's design decisions were conservative in the sense of minimizing equipment and that both binary-decimal conversion and floating point could be programmed.

64. Von Neumann later amplified on the decision to build a fixed-point machine: "Our decision to make all numbers in the machine lying [*sic*] between −1 and +1 was due to the fact that it seemed to us that no automatic arrangement can wholly eliminate the necessity of previously considering changes in size or losses in significance, which might occur in the course of a long problem. Some machines, built in the last decade, contained automatic arrangements to move the decimal point (or the binary point), that is, they represented a number as a product of an appropriate power of 10 (or of 2), a sign, and a number between 0 and 1—the last-mentioned number being kept away as much as possible from null. This arrangement removes the worries on account of size. It seems to us, however, that this gain is in part spurious, because in really vicious problems this is only achieved in conjunction with a corresponding uncertainty regarding significances. To put it another way: If the problem involves the risk of having to divide by a number which

might be close to zero, then no formal arrangements can remove this risk, only a thorough mathematical penetration of the problem can help. Our other objection is, that to the extent to which this 'floating decimal point' helps, it does so at a rather high price: It increases the memory requirements, slows down the simplest arithmetical operations (addition and subtraction) very considerably, and, last but not least, in problems where a real loss of significance threatens it makes the use of 'double precision' methods rather difficult" von Neumann to Hans Bueckner, Instituto Nazionale Per Le Applicazioni Del Calcolo, Rome, 14 April 1950, VNLC.

65. The multiple precision feature was implemented at an early date because of von Neumann's interest in number theory.

66. The account in this report differs from the reports of other early computer design groups in its detailed mathematical analysis. An extensive mathematical analysis of the carry mechanism demonstrates that it can be speeded up from its apparent worst possible case. There is also a sophisticated mathematical analysis of the rules for rounding off digits in the computer. Every multiplication and division of two forty-digit numbers introduces an error, due to the round-off of the result to a forty-digit number. Although these errors are uniquely and rigorously determined, it is impractical to treat them rigorously, so they are analyzed statistically. The excluded digits are regarded individually as random variables with equiprobable digital values, and any two such digits are generally treated as statistically independent so that standard methods of mathematical statistics can be applied. This is perhaps the beginning of the subject of computer arithmetic.

67. Instructions are encoded, like other data, as numbers; however, because instructions can be represented by a string of fewer than twenty binary digits, a pair of them is encoded in a single forty-bit word to save space.

68. The authors noted that decoding tables had been independently developed by Jan Rajchman at RCA and Perry Crawford at MIT. Burks, Goldstine, and von Neumann showed how this concept could be implemented with the Selectron memory using a special twenty-bit control register.

69. The modern word *programming* is used anachronistically here. Von Neumann and his associates discussed these matters in terms of "planning" and "coding."

70. The three volumes appeared on 1 April 1947, 15 April 1948, and 16 August 1948. A fourth volume was promised but never delivered. Burks, who had coauthored the "Preliminary Discussion" document with Goldstine and von Neumann, had left for the University of Michigan by the time these reports were being prepared; nonetheless, he contributed to their content. As he indicated to me (private communication, July 1989), when he first arrived at Princeton in 1946: "Herman [Goldstine] told me about von Neumann's great ideas on programming, flowcharts and a library of subroutines. . . .

"Starting from Johnny's ideas I set out on my own to write some routines, designing them so that they had standardized parameter regions such that another routine could easily substitute parameter values to be computed and could later find the result of the computation. The idea was to write most [of] a library subroutine so it would be independent of its context when used, and to gather all its free variables (for input to it and output from it) into one area so as to get a standard structure which would be convenient to work with. I worked on an example and described the structure in an incomplete manuscript, which I gave to Herman when I left at the end of the summer of 1946."

Burks continued to work on this manuscript, which was published (Burks, 1950). There are a few differences, such as in the flow diagrams, between his 1950 programming system and that in the Goldstine and von Neumann reports. At Goldstine's request, Burks returned to Princeton during his spring vacation in 1947 and met with Goldstine and von Neumann to comment on their *Planning and Coding Problems for an Electronic Computing Instrument* (pt. II, vol. I). Burks's contributions are noted at the beginning of that volume.

71. See Wilkes, Wheeler, and Gill (1982) and its historical introduction by Martin Campbell-Kelly.

72. Goldstine and von Neumann (1947b, p. AB 155).

73. Ibid. (1947b, p. AB 154).

74. Burks (1950) and Goldstine (1953) are interesting accounts of programming in the early days of stored-program computers.

75. Goldstine and von Neumann (1947b, p. AB 151).

76. Goldstine and von Neumann (1948a, p. AB 224).

77. Goldstine and von Neumann (1948b, p. AB 287).

Chapter 4

1. This account of engineering development is written largely from the interim and final progress reports prepared under Army Ordnance contract W-26-034-ORD-7481. A complete set of these reports is available in the archives of the Social Sciences–Humanities Library of the Institute for Advanced Study. This set of reports was not available to me, nor was any complete set available in one location, when this chapter was written. The first reference to each of these reports will indicate another place where a copy is located. The account here is supplemented by information from the monthly progress reports and from Bigelow (1980) and Rajchman (1980).

It is hard to obtain an accurate picture of the distribution of these reports since I found no distribution lists or relevant correspondence. However, they did become widely known within a year or two of their preparation because many of them were reviewed in *Mathematical Tables and Other Aids to Computation*.

I make no claim here to the uniqueness of the engineering work done at the IAS. Rather, this IAS work should be viewed as exemplary of that of many groups in the late 1940s and early 1950s.

2. Von Neumann did not play a major direct role in the engineering aspects of the Electronic Computer Project. Bigelow (1980, p. 293) states that he gave von Neumann verbal progress reports on engineering each week but that von Neumann entered the laboratory only every few months and that von Neumann asked penetrating questions but made few suggestions about engineering matters. Goldstine has a somewhat different impression (private communication, June 1989). He indicated that he briefed von Neumann about the project almost every day and that they had frequent discussions about engineering matters. In an oral history (OHCB, OH 31, 26 September 1980, conducted by Nancy Stern) James Pomerene corroborated Goldstine's account by mentioning that von Neumann

followed the engineering progress, especially of the memory units, quite closely. Pomerene indicated that it was Goldstine who handled day-to-day administration of the project and that Goldstine was also deeply involved in making the engineering decisions.

3. The ENIAC allowed for some recursion but could not match the logical complexity of control on the IAS computer.

4. James Pomerene has identified (private communication, 18 November 1988) as the main engineering challenges of the project (approximately in decreasing order of difficulty): an adequate memory, circuits reliable over wide-range degradation, an adequate cooling system, direct-couple control, adequate input-output, stability in the Williams tube, shift registers with a minimum number of tubes, and the master flip-flop to connect the synchronous with the asynchronous parts of the machine.

5. "Interim Progress Report on the Physical Realization of an Electronic Computing Instrument," 1 January 1947, CBIA.

6. James Pomerene (private communication, 18 November 1988) made this assessment and stated that only IBM's research facilities were clearly superior to those at the institute (from its third year on).

7. Eastman Kodak had succeeded by 1947 in storing 3000 forty-bit words per linear foot of 16 mm film and reading it at up to 250 feet per second. Von Neumann rejected this technology for secondary memory because developing the film took too long, the film was not erasable, and access time was too slow (on average 1.33 milliseconds to retrieve a word). Von Neumann to J. B. Reid, Programme Specialist for Scientific Literature, UNESCO, 4 April 1949, VNLC.

8. Interim Progress Report, 1 January 1947, pp. 20ff.

9. Ibid., p. 40.

10. There are discussions of these tape drives in the "Third Interim Progress Report on the Physical Realization of an Electronic Computing Instrument," 1 January 1948, pp. 25ff., AONA, and the "Fourth Interim Progress Report on the Physical Realization of an Electronic Computing Instrument," 1 July 1948, pp. II–22ff., CBIA.

11. Bigelow (1980, p. 299).

12. In early 1947 the institute built an interim input device by modifying a Type 19 Teletype machine. Proofreading was done by printing on a tape the instructions entered on the keyboard. Data were entered into the computer prototype by punched paper tape. Interim Progress Report, 1 January 1947, pp. 62ff.; Second Interim Progress Report, 1 July 1947, pp. 17ff.

13. Fourth Interim Progress Report, 1 July 1948, sec. II.

14. Third Interim Progress Report, 1 January 1948, pp. 10ff.; Fourth Interim Progress Report, 1 July 1948, sec. II.

15. Immediately upon their development in 1948, von Neumann took an interest in transistors, though there is no evidence he seriously considered their use in the institute computer. This is not surprising since transistors were not very reliable or available in sufficient quantities at that time. On 27 July 1948 L. A. Delsasso of Aberdeen Proving Ground wrote to inform von Neumann that an effort was being

made to pressure Bell Laboratories into giving Aberdeen twenty-five transistors to experiment with in flip-flop circuits, some of which would be sent to the institute for examination. Von Neumann replied on August 6 (VNLC): "Many thanks for your intention to get us some Bell 'Transistors'. It would certainly be an excellent thing, if we could start trying them out, and I don't know about any other channels through which we could get them in the immediate future. If you can get us some, it will be very greatly appreciated. I did, of course, read Bardeen and Brattain's articles in the Phys. Rev. of July 15. I only wish that they were more detailed, gave more facts about the characteristics, noise levels, and a less cryptic theory."

There is no evidence whether von Neumann received these or other transistors to examine, though there are other undated notes in his papers (VNLC) in which he made calculations about the properties of transistors.

16. See, for example, the successful life tests reported in the "Fifth Interim Progress Report on the Physical Realization of an Electronic Computing Instrument," 1 January 1949, AONA. The circuit designs for the arithmetic and other units are described in detail in the "Sixth Interim Progress Report on the Physical Realization of an Electronic Computing Instrument," September 1951, written by C. V. L. Smith, head of the Computer Branch of the Office of Naval Research and a visitor at IAS from July 1950 to February 1951, CBIA.

17. The information given here is taken largely from Rajchman (1980) but confirmed wherever possible from archival sources: Jan Rajchman, Highlight Report, Electronic Computers, n.d. (probably 1946), Plaintiff's Trial Exhibit No. 5417, HSRC; von Neumann to Rajchman, 7 January 1946, HSRC.

18. Bigelow (1980, p. 303) has noted that he and von Neumann believed part of the problem was that RCA was too ambitious in its effort to store 4096 bits on a Selectron tube, that 128 bits was a more practicable figure, and that this belief was borne out by the fact that the working Selectron tubes delivered to Rand Corporation for the JOHNNIAC in the early 1950s stored only 256 bits per tube. Von Neumann also speculated that the Selectron development might have been completed on time if RCA had been able to retain the services of the engineer George Brown. Von Neumann to John Williams of RAND Corporation, 26 October 1951, VNLC. John Williams, head of RAND's Mathematics Division, attributed RCA's delay to its preoccupation with television, thus not allocating the resources to complete the Selectron satisfactorily.

Williams noted that RCA was not interested in supplying Selectrons, even after the development work was completed: "So we [RAND] abandoned plans for Williams tubes and placed a sizeable order for Selectrons in the expectation that, thus encouraged RCA would lean into the harness, push development and production, and prepare to welcome all the frustrated people who had been living (reluctantly) on Williams tubes and delay lines. There was a high level confab at this juncture between RCA and IBM regarding Selectrons, which made it look as though they might hit a really big market. So RCA took its engineers off black-and-white television and put them on color television, and hired the mothers-in-law of two deserving employees (the Chairman of the Board and the President) to make Selectrons for us. Besides wanting to sell us the rejects, the price of the tubes was remarkably arranged so that the more we bought the higher the unit cost became. There is even some question that the tubes really meet RCA specifications (and they are not bound because it is a development contract)." Memorandum, 12 June 1953, to RAND Vice President J. R. Goldstein, quoted in Gruenberger (1968, p. 26).

As Rajchman (1980) points out, the progress of the three people assigned to the Selectron tube development was impressive. What he does not point out is that, by not allocating enough resources to the project, RCA missed out on an important new business opportunity.

19. This account of magnetic drum development is based largely on "First Progress Report on a Multi-Channel Magnetic Drum Inner Memory for Use in Electronic Digital Computing Instruments," 1 July 1948, which is appended to the Fifth Interim Progress Report on the Physical Realization of an Electronic Computing Instrument," 1 January 1949.

20. Note that this requirement on read and write time made the interim memory one hundred times slower than the specifications for the final memory.

21. One alternative was to couple a cathode ray tube to an iconoscope, but this solution was considered too elaborate and expensive (Bigelow 1980, p. 334).

22. See the memorandum of 18 March 1948 from J. M. Coombs to R. I. Meader (SRHM) concerning a visit the previous day by Julian Bigelow and Morris Rubinoff of the IAS to determine whether Engineering Research Associates could build a drum to their specifications within three months. Since the drum was to be used as an interim replacement for the Selectron memory, which the IAS personnel expected to be completed in nine months, the timetable was critical. Perhaps this was the reason that the IAS decided not to enter into a contract with ERA. For a description of the visit to ERA and a discussion of drum design and construction at the two organizations, see a forthcoming book by Arthur L. Norberg, *Computers and Commerce*.

23. At the time the institute began development of the magnetic drum, it had access to Andrew Booth's report, "General Considerations in the Design of an All Purpose Electronic Digital Computer," in which he claimed that a magnetic drum for parallel operation could be built with a cylinder capable of rotation at more than 1000 rotations per second and a read and write time of less than 10^{-4} seconds per complete number. Herman Goldstine informed Mina Rees of ONR's Mathematics Section that he believed that Booth was too optimistic by an order of magnitude, that a more modest magnetic drum would not be a big development, but one attaining Booth's specifications would require perhaps six months or a year of intensive development. Goldstine was aware that the National Bureau of Standards and General Electric had already held discussions about building a magnetic drum in line with Goldstine's more modest specifications. Reed to Goldstine, 30 June 1947, and Goldstine's reply, 2 July 1947, HGAP.

24. "Parallel Magnetic Memory." The application was dated 17 June 1947 and witnessed 10 November 1947, VNLC.

25. The Snyder patent dispute is heavily documented in both HGAP and VNLC. For an account of the context of Slutz and Snyder's idea, see Pugh (1984).

26. 7 October 1947, Goldstine Papers, HGAP.

27. "Progress Report on a Multi-Channel Magnetic Drum" refers to commercial products of Brush Development Company and the reports of Engineering Research Associates as evidence.

28. As their plans matured, the institute had at least some knowledge of other drum developments. For example, in early 1950 Bigelow and others at IAS received information about the drum that was being developed at the University of California, Berkeley, by D. H. Lehmer and Paul Morton. Descriptive materials about this equipment and Bigelow's rather negative appraisal (in a memorandum to L. A. Delsasso, Goldstine, and von Neumann, 23 February 1950) can be found in HGAP.

29. James Pomerene recalls (private communication, 18 November 1988) that his first tests showed that the Williams tube would work in principle but that initially he could not get it to work reliably for more than a few minutes because it picked up and "remembered" noise. He improved the shielding and made other adjustments for noise isolation, so that by late June 1949 he was able to complete a successful 33-hour endurance run. This test apparently encouraged IBM to develop an electrostatic storage device.

30. The institute personnel seemed to be relieved at the prospect of the Willams tube memory; however, it was not as good a solution as the Selectron would have been, as pointed out by von Neumann's friend, John Williams, head of the Mathematics Division at RAND, in a memorandum of 12 June 1953 to RAND Vice-President J. R. Goldstein (reprinted in Gruenberger [1968, pp. 25–26]: "The Princeton machine was conceived about the notions of reliability and speed. The original intent was to couple the present type of arithmetic unit with a high speed Selectron memory of 1024 words. However, RCA became interested in television and never put in the development time needed to debug the tube, so the builders of Princeton-type machines were put in an unhappy position: they could choose between Williams tubes and mercury delay lines. Both were messy technologically and neither was satisfactory logically; they chose Williams tubes as the lesser evil and wore a silly grin so people would judge them to be happy. How happy they really were may be inferred from the advantages they had to forego: In the Selectron a particular slot in the memory is selected by digital (rather than analog) means, and the output signals are a thousand times larger than those in Williams tubes and delay lines—facts intimately related to sensitivity to noise and therefore to reliability."

31. In an article the institute staff read, Williams and Kilburn (1948) described how the tube might be used as a random-access storage device.

32. C. V. L. Smith describes the circuitry of the Williams Tube memory in detail in the Sixth Interim Progress Report, pp. 30ff.

33. There was some initial concern about the control unit. The report on logical design emphasized how much more complex this control unit must be than those in previous computing devices, and the Second Interim Progress Report, 1 July 1947, p. 45, mentions the "formidable" theoretical problem of building a pulser. However, the British and Americans had worked extensively on pulse circuits during the war in connection with radar. There was also work on pulse circuits for ENIAC and EDVAC, which was revealed in the 1946 summer lectures at the Moore School.

34. Bigelow appears to have been a capable engineer but also stubborn and insistent on design perfection. Although he made many correct decisions, his work style slowed the overall design and construction process and at times exasperated

Goldstine and von Neumann. This is presumably part of the reason that von Neumann contacted Henry Allen Moe to help arrange for Bigelow to be awarded a Guggenheim Fellowship at a time when the computer was not yet completed. Pomerene was promptly chosen to replace Bigelow during his absence. Private communication, Herman Goldstine, 19 May 1989.

James Pomerene gives a further perspective on Bigelow: "Bigelow was a perfectionist, and he wanted to do things only a certain way, or not at all. And Herman was considerably more of a pragmatist, and he wanted to get things done. At some point he wanted to get things done in whatever way he could. And Julian, being a New Englander, and one who might be considered a stubborn New Englander, could not be moved. He wanted to keep working out—keep trying to solve a problem in a certain way. He was not easily induced to do it more pragmatically. And that perhaps was the source of the friction. Viewed in retrospect, we were a prototype machine for a number of other machines; we were not the first machine to become operational. And the reason was that it took a while to work out the particular kind of control circuits that we used. And that was done by Bigelow in a certain way that he highly insisted on. We could have built those controls in a different way much earlier. So we probably could have gotten the machine out— we *probably* could have been the first one to become operational, for whatever that's worth" (OHCB, OH 31, interviewed by Nancy Stern, 26 September 1980).

35. See Goldstine to Mrs. Bradley, memorandum, 13 July 1950; von Neumann to Norris E. Bradbury (director, Los Alamos Laboratory), memorandum, 18 July 1950, DOE Archives.

36. See Boardman (1952) for a journalistic account of the opening.

37. Final Report on Contract No. DA-36-034-ORD-1646; Part I (Engineering), Electronic Computer Project, 1956, NMAH.

38. Effective operating time was defined as the ratio of operating time divided by the sum of operating time and unscheduled maintenance. This formula disregards time devoted to scheduled maintenance and engineering improvements in the equipment. From July 1953 to June 1954, total time was divided as follows: 10 percent for routine maintenance, 17 percent for engineering improvements, 9 percent for unscheduled maintenance, and 64 percent for productive operation. This information and the other details on the period beginning in 1952 are from "Final Report on Contract No. DA-36-034-ORD-1023," April 1954, and "Final Report on Contract No. DA-36-034-ORD-1330," December 1954, AONA.

39. Final Report on Contract No. DA-36-034-ORD-1646, Part I (Engineering), Electronic Computer Project, 1956, NMAH.

40. Bigelow (1980, p. 308).

41. This information is taken from ibid. and correspondence of Herman Goldstine. For example, Goldstine explained how he had just spent a day discussing machines and the coding of problems with Couffignal and then taken him to see the ENIAC. Letter to von Neumann, 20 September 1946, VNLC. In another letter Goldstine describes a ten-day visit by Svoboda, who was sent to the institute by Ralph Phillips. Letter to von Neumann, 12 July 1947, VNLC.

42. Bloch and Goldstine spent a day discussing Raytheon's plans for realizing arithmetic in a delay line machine and also the problems of using a relay device to

carry out binary-decimal conversion. Goldstine to von Neumann, 12 July 1947, VNLC.

There was also a visit in June 1947 by ten representatives of the National Bureau of Standards and the Office of Naval Research to discuss the advantages of delay line machines. The ONR representative from Boston, Harry Goheen, informed the institute staff of the progress on the Harvard Marks II and III and on MIT's Whirlwind. Goldstine to von Neumann, 27 June 1947, VNLC.

43. Von Neumann to Goldstine and Bigelow, memorandum, 15 March 1949, VNLC. The restriction on visits even applied to groups building copies of the institute machine.

44. Von Neumann to Forrester, 2 December 1947, VNLC).

45. Ibid.; "First Progress Report on a Multi-Channel Magnetic Drum Inner Memory," 1 July 1948.

46. Copies of most of these newsletters are held in CBIA.

47. These journals are: *Actuarial Society of America Transactions, American Journal of Physics, Army Ordnance, Atomes, Bell Laboratories Record, Comptes Rendues, Discovery, Electrical Engineer, Electrician, Electronic Industries, Electronics, Federal Science Progress, Future, Instruments, Iron Age, Journal of Applied Physics, Journal of Scientific Instruments, Journal of the Acoustical Society of America, Journal of the Franklin Institute, Journal of the Optical Society of America, Mathematical Tables and Other Aids to Computation, Mechanical Engineer, National Underwriter, Nature, Proceedings of the Institute of Radio Engineers, Proceedings of the Royal Society of London, RCA Review, Review of Scientific Instruments, Revue des Questions Scientifiques, Scientific American, Science Monthly, Tele-Tech, The Engineer,* and *Transactions of the American Institute of Electrical Engineers.*

48. The symposium has been reprinted in Aspray (1985) with an introduction analyzing in various ways the organizations represented at the symposium.

49. This account is taken from Metropolis (1980).

50. This account is taken from Chu (1980).

51. This account is taken from Robertson (1980).

52. James Pomerene has stated (private communication, 18 November 1988) that the institute computer was built for speed and without concern for manufacturability, which was, of course, a paramount consideration for IBM. Given the institute's objectives, the design succeeded, for it was as fast as any other machine of its time and much faster than any serial machine.

Pomerene's observation is reinforced by Martin Schwarschild's experience as a user of the institute computer (OHCB, OH 124, 18 November 1986, interviewed by the author): "The Institute machine I think it is fair to describe as marvelously designed, fundamentally by von Neumann's logic but also by very, very good electronic engineers. . . . But it was not designed by anybody who thought about the serviceability, the maintainability, the repairability of the machine. And in that regard, from our modern point of view the machine could hardly have been more difficult. If you remember, they were all tubes, not yet transistors. If something went wrong and they identified which tube it was, to get at that tube usually meant cutting a whole slew of wires, not just the ones to the tube. Just to get at the tube you had to cut dozens of wires, keep track of them, get at the tube, replace the tube, and resolder the wires. It was a major undertaking whenever a tube went bad, particularly those that were really in the main body of the computer. So the down time was high because the failure rate was still very high and in part because the repair time was very high."

53. Further references to most of these machines can be found in Aspray (1986).

54. See, for example, Pekeris (1972) for an account of some of the problems solved on the WEIZAC.

Chapter 5

1. Von Neumann argued that multiplication required approximately the same amount of time as division and that it dominated the time required for addition or subtraction, so that multiplication time was the appropriate measure of speed of arithmetic operation for a calculating device. In fact, multiplication was adapted as the standard measure of calculating speed in the computer industry.

2. Goldstine and von Neumann (1946, p. 6).

3. See, for example, the methods listed in the standard source of that era on numerical and statistical analysis, Whittaker and Robinson (1924).

4. Hotelling (1943, p. 3).

5. To solve a system of linear equations by the Gauss-Seidel method, an initial guess is made at values for each of the unknowns. The value of the first variable is then changed so as to satisfy the first equation, then the value of the second variable is changed so as to satisfy the second equation, and so on. The procedure is repeated using these new values for each of the unknowns. The procedure is iterated until consecutive values of the unknowns are sufficiently close to indicate that the process has converged on a solution to within the desired error bounds. The method converges if the matrix of coefficients is positive definite.

6. Hotelling (1943, p. 15). Hotelling probably regarded problems involving more than about 20 parameters as large.

7. This report (Bargmann, Montgomery, and von Neumann, 1946) was prepared under Navy Bureau of Ordnance contract NORD-9596. Also see the account given in Goldstine and von Neumann (1946, pp. 14–15). In a private conversation, Montgomery told me (6 November 1987, Princeton, NJ) that von Neumann was convinced by the end of this project that round-off errors would not be a very great problem in solving linear systems.

8. The word *complexity* is used in the modern sense of that branch of computer science known as complexity theory.

9. The details of the algorithm are summarized in section 19 of the paper (pp. 473–476), and examples for inverting matrices with $n=20$ and $n=50$ are given in section 20 (p. 477). An empirical study by Birkhoff and Gulati (1979) indicates that the error term was much smaller than Bargmann, Montgomery, and von Neumann estimated.

10. Goldstine (1972, p. 290).

11. Von Neumann and Goldstine (1947a) and Goldstine and von Neumann (1951). The papers are written as sequels.

12. Fox, Huskey, and Wilkinson (1948, p. 155). It is not surprising that this group was the source of the criteria because it was the leading research center for numerical analysis in the United Kingdom, and the British were well ahead of the Americans in this subject at the time.

13. Goldstine (1972, p. 291) wrote: "The significant fact shown by Turing and by us [Goldstine and von Neumann] was that the total error in finding the inverse of a positive definite matrix A was proportional to the ratio of the largest to the smallest eigenvalue and to the square of the order n of A. This made clear where the difficulty lay since the ratio of those two eigenvalues in effect measured how nearly parallel the hyperplanes represented by the linear equations were. Thus Gauss's method was shown to be very good indeed provided the original problem was not 'ill-conditioned'; in other words, the procedure was stable."

An account of the contributions of Turing, Goldstine and von Neumann, and others to the modern theory of error analysis is given in Wilkinson (1963).

14. Turing (1948, p. 287). Turing is referring to the paper of Bargmann, Montgomery, and von Neumann (1946), among others, in the reference to indirect methods in the second of the quoted paragraphs.

15. For an assessment of Goldstine and von Neumann's work on error analysis by one of the leading numerical analysts of the computer era, see Wilkinson (1971).

16. See Goldstine (1972, p. 290). Von Neumann provides further explanation of the reasons for this paper in a letter of 14 April 1948 to E. Bodewig of the Hague, who had published a review of the paper in *Mathematical Reviews* that von Neumann and Goldstine thought misrepresented their results. This letter and related correspondence among von Neumann, Bodewig, and R. P. Boas, Jr. (representing the editors of *Mathematical Reviews*), written between March and May 1948 can be found in VNLC. In the 14 April letter von Neumann wrote: "We discussed the inversion of matrices of high order (n~100) for the following reasons:

"First, the introduction of new procedures and new devices makes it quite important to consider the inversion of matrices of much higher order than were ever discussed in the past.

"Second, we wanted to exhibit and analyse the problems that arise in extremely long calculations, in which processes that amplify the early round-off errors occur. We wanted to isolate and to display these difficulties 'in vitro', that is, separate from the usual problems of approximation, which are due to more ordinary analytical causes. We, therefore, selected a problem which contained none of the difficulties of 'transcendentality,' like differential equation problems, but which had a maximum of round-off-accumulation and of round-off-amplification difficulties. Inasmuch as there exist at present very widely diverging opinions concerning the precision requirements for the calculations in inverting high order matrices, it seemed desirable to produce absolutely rigorous estimates, not depending upon quasi-empirical and heuristic considerations that are so often used in this field.

"In considering this problem, we concentrated on the elimination method because it requires relatively few multiplications . . . as compared to other schemes. . . .

"The statistical estimates made at the end of the paper were given with a desire to orient the reader as to what he had to expect with matrices of order n, when no more specific *a priori* information is available than the order of magnitude of n."

17. A matrix is (symmetric) positive definite if the entries are such that $a_{ij}=a_{ji}$ and the inner product $(A\Theta,\Theta)>0$ for all Θ. As the authors point out, many important types of matrices, including all correlation matrices, are positive definite.

18. Von Neumann to R. Plunkett, 7 November 1949, VNLC. The other letter is also in VNLC.

19. Goldstine (1990, p. 13).

20. The authors claim that the results have probability greater than 99.9 percent for matrices of order ten or greater.

21. See the account given by Goldstine (1972, p. 294).

22. As Goldstine (1972, p. 294) points out, the method in this paper was superseded in 1954 and 1958 by methods of Wallace Givens and Alston Householder, respectively. Others using some variation on the rotational method proposed by Goldstine, Murray, and von Neumann between the time of their first public presentation in 1951 and the paper's appearance in 1959 were George Forsythe and Peter Henrici (1960), R. T. Gregory (1953), and D. Pope and C. Tompkins (1957). Wilkinson (1965) gives a good account of the state of the field a few years later.

23. For a historical overview of the modern history of linear algebra, see Birkhoff (forthcoming).

24. A discussion of these topics would go beyond the bounds of this study. A good account of von Neumann's contributions to numerical fluid dynamics is given in Birkhoff (forthcoming), which goes well beyond this account in coverage and technical detail. For further information about the numerical analysis of fluid dynamics see two draft manuscripts of Garrett Birkhoff, Stan Ulam, and von Neumann, "Digital Computations in Hydrodynamics" (June 1952) and "Calculations of Unsteady Flows in Two or More Dimensions" (January 1954), VNLC.

25. See Richtmyer and Morton (1967) for a discussion of Courant-Frierich-Lewy stability.

26. This condition was also known as "the CFL condition," "the condition on numerical stability," and, as von Neumann was apparently fond of calling it, "the Courant criterium" (Goldstine 1972, p. 288).

27. Von Neumann to Werner Leutert, 15 October 1950, VNLC.

One of von Neumann's earliest extensions of the CFL stability analysis is given in a 12-page letter to Goldstine, 21 February 1947, HGAP. Von Neumann describes how his interest in meteorology in particular had led him to seek integration methods for hyperbolic differential equations where the CFL condition $cdt < dx$ does not hold.

28. Von Neumann to Werner Leutert, 10 November 1950, VNLC. This correspondence is part of a three-sided argument, which ran from July 1950 to August 1951 (all in VNLC), concerning the correctness and applicability of von Neumann's method as given in the authorized version in O'Brien, Hyman, and Kaplan (1950). Leutert, a mathematics professor at the University of Maryland, sent von Neumann a copy of his manuscript, "Eine neue Methode zur numerischen Loesung linearer partieller Differentialgleichungen mit konstanten Koeffizienten," and published

a paper, Leutert (1951), which claims that von Neumann's method does not adequately decide numerical stability and uses the heat equation to illustrate his point. In the course of the correspondence Hyman and Kaplan communicate to von Neumann, and in a different way von Neumann communicates to Leutert, errors in Leutert's reasoning, but Leutert remained resolute. Von Neumann wrote in exasperation to Kaplan on 15 August 1951: "I would like to restate, that I think Leutert misses the point completely. As far as I can see, he treats the heat equation by a different numerical method from the one for which the particular stability condition in question was derived. I have been trying to make it clear at every occasion, including in my correspondence with Leutert, that a stability criterium, in the sense in which I use this word, always relates to a specific numerical method for solving a (partial) differential equation, and not to the differential equation itself."

29. Lectures von Neumann gave at Los Alamos Laboratories in February 1947 are referenced and summarized in von Neumann and Richtmyer (1947a). A lecture given in August 1947 to the Mechanics Division of the Naval Ordnance Laboratory at White Oak, Silver Spring, Maryland, is reported in Hyman (1947). Von Neumann authorized an account of his White Oak results to be incorporated in the paper by O'Brien, Hyman, and Kaplan (1950).

In the White Oak lecture von Neumann considers the wave-equation

$$\frac{\partial^2 u}{\partial x^2} = \frac{\partial^2 u}{\partial t^2}$$

He showed how the Courant, Friedrichs, Lewy difference representation is numerically stable whenever $\Delta x/\Delta t > 1$ and how under a different difference representation involving a parameter a stability is assured when $\Delta x/\Delta t \geq \sqrt{1-4a}$. Von Neumann claims that although he had restricted himself to the simple problem of the wave equation, his method applies equally well to more complicated equations.

30. Von Neumann (1948a).

31. The oil well and oil field have distinct but similar equations governing their flows. Von Neumann treats the two cases, which he calls circular symmetry (CS) and linear parallelity (PL), in the same report.

32. Apparently Standard Oil could rent time on the SSEC. Von Neumann had already indicated there is no known analytic solution to the problem. He had shown further that if one assumes that the flow is horizontal, the equations can be simplified greatly to a total differential equation, which can be solved by a straightforward step-wise numerical integration. However, he was dubious whether such an idealized result could be of any practical value.

For information about the SSEC see Bashe et al. (1986).

33. Von Neumann (1948a, Taub 689).

34. Von Neumann (1947a, Taub 683–684).

35. A similar account is given in Goldstine and von Neumann (1946, pp. 15-17) and Goldstine (1957).

36. The crux of von Neumann's stability analysis is the following: given a Fourier expansion of the error expression, trace the values assumed by the general term of the expansion to determine whether the error expression exceeds one. One might also include as part of his heuristic method his promotion of implicit difference representation to achieve numerical stability. O'Brien, Hyman, and Kaplan (1950) provide a systematic discussion of von Neumann's method. They also indicate that he had applied it to a wide range of problems during World War II, though this seems doubtful given how late in the war his interest in high-speed computing devices developed.

37. The method is discussed in von Neumann and Richtmyer (1947a).

38. Von Neumann (1948b).

39. For an example of von Neumann's work on flow of incompressible fluids, a case in which shocks do not present a problem, see Blair, Metropolis, von Neumann, Taub, and Tsingou (1959).

40. Von Neumann (1944b). This report was submitted by the Applied Mathematics Group at the Institute for Advanced Study to the Applied Mathematics Panel of the National Defense Research Committee on 20 March, 1944, under contract OSRD-3617.

41. Von Neumann points out that the Aberdeen experiments had convinced him that 14 bead molecules would be satisfactory for shocks in one dimension but that as many as 3000 beads may be required in two- and three-dimensional problems. This many beads would probably have placed the problem beyond the range of calculating equipment then available.

42. According to Carson Mark (private communication, 28 May 1987), the artificial viscosity method was a result of computations Richtmyer and von Neumann made between 1947 and 1950 for the Trinity atomic bomb test.

43. Von Neumann (1951a)·adopts a similar method to treat shocks.

44. The direct numerical approach is reported in Goldstine and von Neumann (1955). The work was support by Army Ordnance contract DA-36-034-ORD-1330 and Office of Naval Research contract N-7-onr-388.

45. At about the same time, H. L. Brode of the Rand Corporation made an independent, but similar, approach to the blast wave problem. See Brode (1954).

46. OH 124, 18 November 1986, interviewed by the author, OHCB.

47. Actually the Monte Carlo method was not entirely new; it was a type of model sampling statisticians had used for years before the introduction of the computer.

48. Ulam's most complete account of these origins is given in an unpublished manuscript, "The Origin of Monte Carlo," SUAP.

49. Ibid.

50. Von Neumann knew of the method by August 1946, since he refers to the possibility of using it on a bombing problem in his Moore School lecture on 13 August.

51. "Origin of Monte Carlo."

52. The Los Alamos report is published as Richtmyer and von Neumann (1947). In an unpublished manuscript, "Introduction to Papers on The Monte Carlo Method," 12 April 1983, Ulam states that this letter is probably the first written account of the method.

53. Von Neumann also suggested that several man-days using manual-graphical methods might work and planned to ask Princeton University statistician S. S. Wilks about his experience using such techniques on a bombing problem during the war.

When people consider the Monte Carlo method, they generally think of it as being carried out on a computer. In the early postwar years, when computers were scarce, all sorts of calculating devices were used. Cuthbert Hurd made this point in his discussion of the Monte Carlo symposium at the Institute for Numerical Analysis in 1949: "The computational devices were varied and interesting. In order of appearance, save one: Wilson utilized a spinning cylinder, which I believe was constructed from a Quaker Oats container; Spinrad, et al. used nomographs; Householder described the use of Rand random digit cards and IBM punched card equipment; DeMarcus and Nelson described a Gauss and Seidel solution which was later implemented on the IBM Selective Sequence Electronic Calculator; King describes the use of an IBM 405 Tabulator and a 513 Reproducing Punch; Mayer speaks of an Eniac calculation; Hammer gives a flow chart for the use of IBM machines which includes a 602 Multiplier; Brown refers to an electronic roulette wheel to be used in generating random numbers; Forsythe refers to a 604 Calculating Punch; Neyman refers to dice throwing and to an instrument constructed by Lehmer to carry out experiments concerning expected bomb damage; Wishart refers to the use of a hand computing machine by Karl Pearson. Shoor, et al., refer to a calculation made on the 'IBM Card Programmed Calculator' which they say had been facetiously dubbed as 'the poor man's Eniac' and then they proceed to describe the 'Betsy'" "A Note on Early Monte Carlo Computations and Scientific Meetings," SUAP.

54. A talk given by R. D. Richtmyer, "Monte Carlo Methods," at a meeting of the American Mathematical Society 24 April 1959, SUAP, describes these early Monte Carlo calculations and other points about the development of the method.

55. These meetings, held from June 29 through July 1, 1949, are described in a manuscript by Cuthbert C. Hurd, "A Note on Early Monte Carlo Computations and Scientific Meetings," SUAP. Ulam and von Neumann participated in both these conferences. Hurd (1950) also discusses another early meeting on Monte Carlo organized by IBM's Department of Education in November 1949.

56. A copy of the program for the Monte Carlo symposium is in SUAP.

57. Ulam's method is to consider a definite multiple integral as representing in the standard way the volume of an n-dimensional solid. Random numbers are then used to generate random points in a finite region of n-space that contains the solid and has known volume. By calculating the percentage of points falling inside the solid and multiplying this by the total volume, he obtains an estimate of the solid's volume and hence of the value of the multiple integral. This estimate can be made to any specified degree of accuracy.

58. This method is described in Forsythe and Leibler (1950).

59. This method is described in a 13-page letter von Neumann wrote to Abraham Taub, 5 July 1949, SUAP. The equation describes one-dimensional Lagrangean hydrodynamics with an equation of state where p depends on v alone:

$$\frac{\partial^2 X}{\partial t^2} = \frac{-v}{\frac{\partial X}{\partial x}} \diamond \frac{\partial p}{\partial x} \ , \quad v = \frac{\partial X}{\partial x} \ , \quad p = F(v)$$

60. Von Neumann (1951e).

61. Von Neumann discusses these methods in a letter of 3 February 1948 to Alston Householder, VNLC.

62. Von Neumann describes the two tests he used in a letter to Cuthbert Hurd, 3 December 1948, VNLC. First, form the matrix a_{ij} ($i, j = 1, \ldots, 10$), where a_{ij} is the frequency with which value $i+1$ occurs for the jth digit in the sequence of 3400 10-digit pseudo-random numbers he had generated. Submit this matrix to a X^2 test for both rows and columns. Second, calculate the correlation coefficients b_{jkl} ($j, k = 1, \ldots, 10; l = 0,1, \ldots, 5$) of the stochastic variables digit j on one punched card and digit k on the punched card formed l iterations later. Calculate the expected size b for the correlation coefficients, and check to see that the b_{jkl} have a normal distribution with dispersion b.

63. In his investigation of this matter von Neumann introduces the concept of an efficient pseudo-random generating function as one that will generate sequences of length $10^{n/2}$ before cycling, if n is the number of digits (fixed word length) used.

64. Von Neumann advocated arithmetic methods for generating these numbers when using the computer with Monte Carlo methods but the use of tables of "guaranteed" random numbers, such as those of Kendall and Smith (1939), when working with slower calculating devices.

65. Von Neumann (1951e, p. 768) remarks: "Any one who considers arithmetical methods of producing random digits is, of course, in a state of sin. For, as has been pointed out several times, there is no such thing as a random number—there are only methods to produce random numbers, and a strict arithmetic procedure of course is not such a method."

66. This technique is described without being named in von Neumann (1951e). Also see Hammersley and Handscomb (1964, pp. 36–37).

67. Goldstine (1972, p. 293) suggests a conversation with Ulam as the inspiration to von Neumann for this research program.

68. The results of these investigations are reported in Metropolis, Reitwiesner, and von Neumann (1950). The details of the calculation are reported in Reitwiesner (1950). e is calculated using the formula

$$e = \sum_{n=0}^{\infty} (n!)^{-1}$$

The calculation required 11 hours of machine time for computing and checking and an equal amount of time for punched card handling. π was calculated using the formulas:

$\pi/4 = 4 \arctan (1/5) - \arctan (1/239)$

$$\arctan (x) = \sum_{n=0}^{\bullet} (-1)^n (2n+1)^{-1} x^{2n+1}$$

Including card-handling time, the calculation took approximately 70 hours.

In a letter of 8 September 1949 (HGAP), von Neumann gives details to Reitwiesner of his analysis of the ENIAC calculations. He summarizes his findings by stating: "The first 2000 digits of e *do not look like a random sample* of decimal digits. Oddly enough, they seem to deviate from randomness by being *too uniformly distributed!* This is very remarkable, and it would seem to deserve further study."

69. This account is drawn largely from Dantzig (1963, 1984) and an unpublished manuscript kindly supplied by Dantzig, "Impact of Linear Programming on Computer Development." I also gratefully acknowledge access to Professor Dantzig's correspondence on linear programming as it relates to von Neumann. The account has also been improved by suggestions of Albert Tucker.

70. Duality results express a relationship between the original set of equations (or inequalities) and another (dual) set of equations (or inequalities) formed from the coefficients of the original set.

71. SCOOP stands for Scientific Computation of Optimal Programs. The air force provided the National Bureau of Standards with $400,000 in 1948 and with approximately $1 million by the early 1950s. The bureau used this money to support its development of SEAC as well as work on methods including linear programming. Project SCOOP and the general environment of computing in the air force at this time is described in an interview with Murray A. Geisler (interview II, 22 February 1971 (?)) interviewed by Richard R. Mertz, OHSM.

72. Dantzig (1963, p. 15). Many other economists and mathematicians who went on to have distinguished careers were involved in the early years of linear programming, including Albert Cahn, John Curtis, Robert Dorfman, Leonid Hurwicz, Tjalling Koopmans, William Orchard-Hays, Paul Samuelson, and Albert Tucker.

73. Von Neumann (1938), translated into English by D. Champernowne and republished as von Neumann (1945). Dantzig (1963, pp. 16–17) describes von Neumann's economic model in more detail and assesses it as an interesting mathematical, if not economic, result. It did receive attention from the originators of linear programming at the time of the subject's development. See, for example, the letter of 17 February 1948 from von Neumann to T. C. Koopmans in which von Neumann describes several results from this paper and his and Morgenstern's book on the theory of games.

74. Von Neumann and Morgenstern (1944); von Neumann (1928f,h). Of particular importance was their theorem of the alternative for matrices.

75. Dantzig (1984, p. 5).

76. Von Neumann never published the duality theorem, but see his privately circulated "Discussion of a Maximum Problem" written 15–16 November 1947, which appears in his *Collected Papers*. The duality theorem was written up by Dantzig in a report, "A Theorem on Linear Inequalities" (dated 5 January 1948), circulated privately to his colleagues at the Pentagon. The first rigorous proof to be published was by Tucker, Kuhn, and Gale (1950).

77. George Dantzig's private collection containing about a dozen letters between Dantzig and von Neumann, dating from November 1947 to September 1950, that discuss linear programming.

78. Dantzig to von Neumann, 28 April 1948. (Dantzig personal papers) The work was carried out at the New York Mathematical Tables Project under the supervision of Jack Laderman.

79. Dantzig describes the problem to von Neumann in a letter of 22 December 1948; von Neumann replies with his time estimates for ENIAC six days later (Dantzig personal papers). Von Neumann's estimate assumes ENIAC is operating two shifts (16 hours) a day and can be effectively used ten hours each day.

80. Von Neumann (1954).

81. Arthur Burks has pointed out (private correspondence, 1988) that this change can be traced back to the war because of the changes it caused in work in applied science and engineering and because of the willingness of high-caliber scientists to work on numerical problems because of the war.

82. One example not discussed was von Neumann's effort to find numerical methods appropriate to a computer for determining optimal strategies for two-person games with up to a few hundred strategies (von Neumann to Warren Weaver, 1 March 1948, VNLC).

83. Goldstine (1972, p. 292).

84. An interview with Forman Acton, conducted by Richard Mertz on 21 January 1971, gives a general description of numerical analysis and its personalities in America in this period. OHSM.

85. In an interview Stanley Frankel has remarked that the study of computational methods was at the time "an intensely unpopular field" and "the world of mathematics looked on it with scorn" (interview of 5 October 1972 conducted by Robina Mapstone, OHSM).

Chapter 6

1. The exception is the Colossus, which was built and operated by the British government during the war for cryptanalysis. Because of strict security classification, von Neumann and most other computer pioneers did not know of its existence.

2. I believe this somewhat simplified account of weather prediction in this period is fair, though it is based on the comments of two early partisans of the numerical approach (Smagorinsky 1983, p. 4; Thompson 1961, pp. 1–2). Some numerical and graphical methods were used in this period (e.g., to determine pressure), and there were also some scientific advances in dynamics that contributed to prediction techniques.

3. Douglas (1952, p. 16).

4. Thompson (1978, p. 137).

5. Many of these papers are reprinted in English translations in Abbe (1893). Nineteenth-century research on circulation of the atmosphere is described in Smagorinsky (1972) and Khrgian (1970).

6. Kutzbach (1979, pp. 159–160).

7. See Nebeker (1989).

8. Bjerknes (1904), as quoted in Platzman (1967, p. 538). The translation is by Mintz (1966).

9. Bjerknes (1914), as quoted in Platzman (1967, p. 537).

10. Ibid. (p. 538).

11. Bjerknes (1904) as quoted in Platzman (1967, p. 538). The graphical methods are described in detail in Bjerknes, Hesselberg, and Devik (1911).

12. Richardson (1922, p. vii).

13. Douglas (1952, p. 7).

14. Richardson (1922, p. viii).

15. That is, for variable w, one assumes that $\partial w/\partial t$ is constant over the time interval Δt, and therefore the value of w at time $t+\Delta t$ is approximated by $w + \Delta t\, \partial w/\partial t$.

16. Richardson described his method in his 1922 book. Platzman (1967) described Richardson's procedures and assumptions, analyzed his results, and discussed some of the reasons for the inaccuracy of the outcome. The errors were apparently the result of observational errors, lack of sufficient data, and simplifications in the method. The failure of the prediction does not vitiate the numerical method. Philip Thompson has indicated in a private conversation (October 1987) that Richardson's errors were probably not due to Courant instabilities in the finite difference method, contrary to the claim made by Herman Goldstine (1972, p. 300) and others.

17. See Nebeker (1989) and Platzman (1967).

18. Richardson (1922, p. 219) assumed the use of a 3-hour time step, a 200-kilometer square space grid, a calculating system in which complicated operations are broken into a series of simple tasks to improve speed and accuracy, and certain simplifications in calculation based upon the predictability of tropical weather.

19. Von Neumann gave an assessment of Richardson's contribution to numerical meteorology after he had had extensive experience with the theoretical and mathematical analysis and after making some initial meteorological calculations on the ENIAC but before he had had a chance to use the IAS computer for these purposes. The occasion for his comments was a response to Lewis Strauss, who had sent him a paper Richardson had published in *Nature* on the mathematical theory of war. Von Neumann wrote in this letter (21 November 1951, VNLC): "Richardson is, as far as I know, a man of independent means who has been working on various scientific subjects, and has, in particular, a very distinguished record in theoretical meteorology. He suggested thirty years ago, what some people, including ourselves, are now trying to do by computing machines: the prediction of the weather by calculation. His effort did not succeed—in fact, he misjudged the proportions of various elements of the problem quite substantially. The attempt was, nevertheless, remarkable and bold, and I think that Richardson will be remembered as a very imaginative precursor of what seems to be proving to be possible now, when both the mathematical and the instrumental techniques have been developed considerably further."

20. Joseph Smagorinsky (private communication, 18 November 1986) has described an argument put forth in the 1940s by the MIT meteorologist Bernhard Haurwitz: the divergence cannot be measured, so you cannot do the vertical integration in the tendency equation that calculates the surface pressure, and therefore you cannot complete the numerical computation.

21. Joseph Smagorinsky, Oral History, conducted by Richard R. Mertz, Princeton, NJ, 19 May 1971, OHSM.

22. Jule Charney (1960, p. 13). Khrgian (1970) provides detailed information about meteorology during World War I and World War II. An excellent account of the Numerical Meteorology Project is given by Nebeker (1989, ch. 5).

23. The Allies felt this need especially in the invasion of Normandy. In anticipation of the invasion, because of the concern about forecasting reliability, the U.S. government commissioned Princeton University statistician S. S. Wilks to compare systems of prediction. His results were not reassuring. He found that no system was more reliable than assuming that tomorrow's weather will be exactly the same as today's. (Albert W. Tucker, oral history conducted by the author 8 May 1986, OHCB OH 129).

24. It is reported that the first American officer killed in action was a meteorologist, in Norway in 1940 (Hughes 1970, p. 75).

25. Private communication from Philip Thompson, 6 October 1987.

26. Thompson (1961, p. 15) argued that this enhanced knowledge of upper air phenomena assured Carl-Gustav Rossby of the effectiveness of his two-dimensional barotropic model and stimulated the synoptic work of J. Bjerknes on the importance of upper air waves to atmospheric motions. This work shifted attention from the polar fronts that had dominated the work of the Bergen School and of meteorologists generally in the 1930s.

27. Khrgian (1970, p. 347).

28. Thompson (1983, p. 757). In an interview, Murray Geisler gives a picture of the state of meteorological calculation during World War II (interviewed by Richard R. Mertz, 22 February 1971, OHSM).

29. In a private conversation in November 1986 Herman Goldstine recalled a number of occasions, in particular at the time of the flight of the Enola Gay, when von Neumann remarked on the importance of the weather to military operations.

30. For a detailed discussion of this point, see the discussion in chapter 3 concerning nonlinear phenomena and heuristic uses of the computer. Charney (1972, p. 117) and Goldstine (1972, p. 300) make similar points.

31. This information was provided by Marshall Stone in a private conversation in March 1987. Stone was also a participant in the workshop. Rossby was at Chicago at the time, administering a meteorology training program for the military.

Von Neumann may have first learned about Rossby from F. W. Reichelderfer, chief of the U.S. Weather Bureau (private conversation in November 1986 with Joseph Smagorinsky). Rossby became Reichelderfer's assistant at the Weather Bureau in 1939 and continued to commute between Washington and Chicago during the war years. See Byers (1959) for details about Rossby's career and his important role in organizing the meteorological profession.

A lecture given by Reichelderfer in October 1980 at the twenty-fifth anniversary celebration of the Geophysical Fluid Dynamics Research Laboratory in Princeton seems to give a slightly different account. Reichelderfer made the presentation at an advanced age, and his remarks rambled considerably. Adding to the problem is the poor quality of the tape recording, which one of those in attendance happened to make and which is still privately held. Reichelderfer seems to say that he had first learned about numerical meteorology when he attended a lecture by Vilhelm Bjerknes at the Carnegie Institution in Washington in 1920 or 1922, that there was tremendous pressure from the government for better long-range weather forecasts to assist military operations, that he had contacted Vannevar Bush, the Coast Geodetic Survey, and others unsuccessfully seeking the computing power he would need for effective numerical meteorology, that von Neumann had already been searching for problems for the electronic computer when he first came in contact with him, and that he had suggested the weather problem to von Neumann.

32. The point about Richardson was made by Smagorinsky in a private discussion with me in November 1986. On the other point, see von Neumann to Rossby, 6, 19 February 1946, VNLC.

33. "Also Dr. Zworykin has the same interest in weather prediction and control as myself, in fact he gave me the decisive impulse to interest myself in this subject." von Neumann to Rossby, 6 February 1946, VNLC. In an oral history, Jule Charney indicated that von Neumann probably first settled on the meteorology problem as a result of conversations with his friend Zworykin. George W. Platzman, "Conversations with Jule Charney," release 2, December 1982; now available as a report from the National Center for Atmospheric Research, Boulder, Colorado.

34. Von Neumann to Rossby, 6 February 1946, VNLC. In a 16 April 1946 letter (VNLC), following his visit to Princeton, Rossby described to Reichelderfer RCA's interest in building radiosondes and communication facilities for transmitting meteorological data from remote stations to central computing centers. Rossby also gave his "very strong impression" that RCA was not adequately informed of other development work on meteorological instrumentation and suggested that Reichelderfer put RCA in contact with the Joint Meteorolgical Committee or some other knowledgable organization.

35. Charney to Stan Ulam, 6 December 1957, SUAP.

36. Reichelderfer to Zworykin, 25 November 1945, VNLC. In a letter of 25 January 1946 to Harold Pender, Dean of the Moore School (HSRC), Reichelderfer stated that he had learned of Zworykin's and von Neumann's interest in October or November as a result of a visit to the RCA Princeton Labs and "subsequently through a communication from the Director of the Bureau of Standards."

37. Reichelderfer to von Neumann, 29 December 1945, VNLC.

38. Shallet (1946).

39. For example, see Thompson (1983, p. 758; 1987, p. 12). Stern (1980) reported that this newspaper article caused indignation at the University of Pennsylvania and consternation among the army sponsors of ENIAC because publicity had not yet been released on the ENIAC, and it was felt that the article unfairly portrayed von Neumann and RCA as the main pioneers in the computer field. John Mauchly

was especially upset because of his interest in applying automatic computing to meteorology. Von Neumann was aware of, and unsympathetic with, Mauchly's interest in using computers to reduce statistical meteorological data and test the correlation between weather phenomena and sunspot cycles. Arthur W. Burks, Oral History 136, 20 June 1987, OHCB. It should also be noted, however, that von Neumann was also upset with the appearance of the *New York Times* article and tried to have it stopped or delayed. See his letter after the fact to Charles Merz, the editor of the paper, dated 23 January 1946, and a related piece of correspondence from F. W. Reichelderfer to Zworykin, 11 January 1946 (with a copy to von Neumann), VNLC.

40. Letter dated 16 April 1946, VNLC.

41. This in fact was not the reason that the ENIAC was unsuitable for elaborate numerical weather prediction. Rather, the reasons were its critical limitations in programming, primary memory size, and slow switching speed.

42. Letter, dated 23 April 1946 on the front page and one day earlier on the second page, VNLC.

43. Letter, 23 April 1946. The impact of artificial modifications of the atmosphere is mentioned several times in von Neumann's writings, but there is never a systematic discussion of his thoughts on the subject.

44. The proposal submitted by the institute included funds for an additional meteorologist and amounted to $61,000 per year. Frank Aydelotte to Commander Rex, 8 May 1946, JCMI.

45. Letter, 4 May 1946, HSRC.

46. Frank Aydelotte, director of the Institute for Advanced Study, to Rex, 8 May 1946. A complete retyped copy is available in JCMI. An incomplete copy is available in VNLC.

47. The proposal lists some sample problems of meteorological theory that might be investigated in the initial period: a model for studying the general circulation of the atmosphere based on the assumption of zonal symmetry (averaging over the irregular distribution of continents), the adequacy of a one-layer tropospheric model of the atmosphere, stability analysis of the polar front, and a quantitative study of the release of local instabilities.

48. The proposal lists as possible consultants meteorologists Rossby of the University of Chicago, H. U. Sverdup of the Scripps Oceanographic Institution, and J. Bjerknes of UCLA; physicists with interests in radiation, molecular physics, and astrophysics E. Teller of the University of Chicago and S. Chandrasekhar of Yerkes Observatory; one or more aerodynamicists, including Th. von Karman of California Institute of Technology; and experts in other fields, including W. Weaver of NDRC and the Rockefeller Foundation and V. K. Zworykin of RCA Princeton Laboratories. The outside board of meteorologists was never convened.

49. Navy contract N6ori-139. Subsequent funding for the Meteorology Project came from the Office of Naval Research and, starting in 1951, jointly from ONR and the Geophysics Research Division of the Air Force Cambridge Research Center.

50. IAS Meteorology Project, Report of Progress during the period from 1 April 1947 to 15 December 1947, JCMI. Queney had been trained at the Sorbonne and was a senior scientist at the Institut de Meteorologie et de Physique du Globe in Algiers. He had been a visitor at Rossby's institute at Chicago in the spring of 1946, and it was Rossby who wrote to Pierre Auger at the French Ministere de l'Education Nationale in Paris to request Queney's leave to join the IAS project for the 1946–1947 academic year. Rossby to Auger, 11 May 1946, VNLC. Rossby may also have been responsible for the offer to Montgomery, whom Rossby knew through his long-term research associate position at Woods Hole.

Von Neumann also tried unsuccessfully to hire Rossby to lead the Meteorology Project: "I learned from Captain G. Hunt, that he had seen you at Woods Hole, and that he was under the impression that you might consider visiting Princeton more frequently, and participating more directly and continuously in our work. I would therefore like to take this opportunity to tell you how welcome this idea is to me, and how welcome you will be at any time, for any length of time." Von Neumann to Rossby, 7 October 1946, VNLC. Nothing came of this invitation, but on 13 June 1949, von Neumann wrote offering Rossby a high-level membership in the institute for two years, at the same level of appointment as had been held by P. A. M. Dirac and N. Bohr and also by J. W. Alexander after he had resigned his Institute faculty position (VNLC). Rossby did not accept the offer, but he did come to the institute as a consultant for two months in early 1951, and there was talk of his returning every year for a few months. Von Neumann to Robert Oppenheimer, 27 February 1951, VNLC.

51. IAS Meteorology Project, report of progress for the period 1 July 1946 to 15 November 1946, JCMI. It was apparently impossible to expedite new construction in 1946. Julian Bigelow secured some primitive coal furnace buildings, surplus WPA miner's houses, which they had trucked in. George W. Platzman, "Conversations with Jule Charney," Release 2, December 1982; now available as a report of the National Center for Atmospheric Research.

52. The purpose of the Divergence Project was to calculate surface pressure tendencies by integrating the hydrostatic and continuity equations from direct observations of wind and pressure. Thompson heard about the institute project when Professor Jorgen Holmboe of UCLA brought to his attention the *New York Times* article. Thompson, who had already become interested in numerical meteorology while at Chicago, convinced his commanding officer to let him fly to Princeton to talk to von Neumann. Based on that conversation, Thompson was immediately transferred by the air force to the Princeton project. For further details, see Thompson (1983) or the oral history I conducted with Thompson, 5 December 1986, OHCB, OH 125.

53. The long arm of Rossby can be seen here as well. Pekeris had been a student of Rossby at MIT, where Rossby was on the faculty in the 1930s.

54. Not only did von Neumann not have the time to direct the project, he probably also believed he did not have the right training to direct it. Philip Thompson described von Neumann's knowledge of meteorology in 1946 as follows: "He had a good feeling for fluid dynamics. He had done some work, in fact, was working at that time on some problems in fluid dynamics, particularly with regard to blast effects. He was working with Bob Richtmyer at Los Alamos. . . . Von Neumann did

not have any very specific knowledge of meteorology. He'd read enough to get some sort of feel as to what the state of the science was, what it was all about, what was missing, what ought to be done; but was not very definite about how it should be done in detail. He was relying, I think, more on people who had a background in physics and mathematics, numerical analysis and computing, and had the physical insight to see what you must retain in a fairly simple model in order to make it simulate reality in some specific respects." OH125, OHCB, 5 December 1986, conducted by the author.

Joseph Smagorinsky also points to von Neumann's complementary experience in hydrodynamic calculations associated with nuclear calculations and how these prepared him for the work in numerical meteorology. Oral history, 19 May 1971, conducted by Richard R. Mertz, OHSM.

55. Thompson oral history, interviewed by the author, 5 December 1986, OHCB, OH 125. It must be remembered that while Thompson had some training at Chicago and experience at UCLA, it was only later at MIT that he completed his graduate studies in meteorology.

56. Oral history, Thompson, Interviewed by the author, 5 December 1986, OHCB. Also see Thompson (1983).

57. Rossby to von Neumann, 12 August 1946, VNLC. Charney attended the conference in Princeton according to the minutes of the meeting. Conference on Meteorology. 29–30 August 1946, Minutes, JCMI.

58. See Thompson (1983) for more details.

59. Charney to Thompson, 4 November 1947, private collection of Philip Thompson, National Center for Atmospheric Research, Boulder, Colorado.

60. Charney to von Neumann, January 2, 1948, VNLC.

61. The Jule Charney Papers in the MIT Archives contain a complete set of the Meteorology Project progress reports for the period 1 July 1946–30 June 1955. Over three-quarters of the reports list project personnel, and it is possible to construct a reasonably complete list of those who participated. From these reports it is difficult to distinguish consultants from regular staff. The reports establish the following information: institute Computer Project staff participating: Herman Goldstine, John von Neumann; meteorologists and consultants: R. Berggren, Bert Bolin, Albert Cahn, Jule Charney, Philip Clapp, Thomas V. Davies, E. Eady, Arnt Eliassen, Walter M. Elsasser, Ragnar Fjortoft, George Forsythe, John C. Freeman, K. Gambo, Bruce Gilchrist, Bernhard Haurwitz, Ernst Hovmoller, Gilbert Hunt, H. L. Kuo, Edward N. Lorenz, G. C. McVittie, W. Munk, Morris Neiberger, Hans Panofsky, Chaim L. Pekeris, Norman Phillips, George Platzman, Paul Queney, P. Raethjen, Carl-Gustaf Rossby, J. S. Sawyer, R. S. Scorer, P. A. Sheppard, Joseph Smagorinsky, Margaret Smagorinsky, Victor Starr, H. Stommel, R. C. Sutcliffe, Philip D. Thompson, J. van Miegham, George Veronis, Harry Wexler, and Tucheng Yeh; computers, coders, and plotters: James Cooley, Norma Gilbarg, Glenn Lewis, Mary Lewis, A. Nussbaum, J. O'Kane, I. Rabinowitz, and Chih Li Tu Yang. In the final years of the project there were official representatives of the sponsoring organizations on site: J. Blackburn (air force), George Cressman (air force), F. Shuman (Weather Bureau), and A. Stickles (navy).

62. The conference is reported in a four-page summary; copies are available in VNLC and JCMI.

63. According to Sydney Chapman in the introduction to Richardson (1965, p. ix), there was extensive discussion of Richardson's work at the conference.

64. Charney (1972, p. 117). In 1957 Charney gave a somewhat harsher assessment: "A conference held at the I.A.S. in August 1946 failed to grip the imagination of the leading dynamical meteorologists who were invited, and few worth-while suggestions were proffered." Charney to Stan Ulam, 6 December 1957, SUAP.

65. Von Neumann used the word *preparatory* in his first two progress reports (1 July 1946–15 November 1946; 15 November 1946–1 April 1947). The three reports that cover the period 1 April 1947–15 September 1948 indicate a continuation of these preliminary investigations. The Final Report of the Meteorology Project, 31 December 1956, lists the thirty-two papers published by the project staff (fifteen different authors) between 1948 and 1956. (All of these reports are in JCMI.)

66. Other investigations listed in the progress reports for the period July 1946–June 1948 (JCMI) were: Hans Panofsky's assessment of observational data on the vertical motion of the atmosphere as a starting point for the mathematical effort to derive the vorticity and the divergence fields from observations; von Neumann's study of the numerical instability in the methods for integrating the hydrodynamic equations of the atmosphere; Thompson's study of the atmosphere as an incompressible fluid; a semiempirical measurement by Panosky, Haurwitz, and Miller (under subcontract at New York University) of the large-scale, horizontal components of stress as a way to compare changes in momentum that accounted for pressure, gravitational, and Coriolis forces; numerical experiments overseen by Philip Clapp of the Extended Forecast Section of the U.S. Weather Bureau to test variants of the method of finite differences conducted by personnel of the National Bureau of Standards and the statistical section of the Weather Bureau; and a mathematical study of the hydrodynamical equations of the atmosphere by Hunt that improved on the theoretical results of Oseen and Leray.

67. New York University had a subcontract under the institute's Office of Naval Research grant to do research on the general circulation of the atmosphere, representation of meteorological elements by mathematical expressions, and the distribution and changes of such meteorological elements as cyclones, anticyclones, and hurricanes. See the 22 April 1947 letter of IAS director Frank Aydelotte to the Branch Office of the ONR in New York City, VNLC.

68. It had been believed for decades that there was no analytical means for solving the primitive equations. In late 1946 or early 1947 von Neumann confirmed their numerical instability "under those conditions of spatial and temporal resolution which are essentially characteristic of the problem of meteorological prediction." Progress Report for the Period of November 15, 1946 to April 1, 1947, JCMI. Thompson explained the theoretical and practical difficulties in greater detail, as follows (report of Progress during the Period from 1 April 1947 to 15 December 1947, JCMI): "The fundamental equations, even for an isentropic ideal atmosphere, are not well suited to numerical analysis as they stand. Aside from the unfortunate but hard fact that hydrostatic equilibrium is implicit in all standard measurements of pressure, the vertical component of acceleration is invariably the

small difference between the pressure and gravitational accelerations; consequently, the local variation of the vertical speed is an even smaller quantity. Moreover, the vertical component of velocity is neither observed nor susceptible to exact measurement. In view of these considerata, it would be highly desirable to know the vertical component of velocity at any moment in time as an explicit function of the distributions of other variables at that particular instant. The required expression, an integral-differential function of the pressure and horizontal velocity fields, has been found.

"Another difficulty, also stemming from innate sensitivity of the fundamental equations, must be reduced to less formidable proportions; the local derivative of pressure is an integral of the local variation of density, which is always a very small difference between large terms. This circumstance can be obviated by an alternative expression involving the local changes of potential temperature. The latter are of the same order of magnitude as the advective variations of potential temperature."

69. Meteorology Project, Report of Progress during the Period from 1 April 1947 to 15 December 1947, JCMI.

70. Thompson pointed out in this same progress report (ibid.) that "several such 'filters' are frequently, though perhaps unwittingly incorporated in theoretical models of the atmosphere to make them more tractable to mathematical analysis." He mentioned the exclusion of sound waves by assuming a homogeneous fluid and the exclusion of gravity waves by assuming no change in potential energy. He went further to note "in fact, every idealized model is, in a manner of speaking, a filtering device. By imposing certain restrictions suggested by empirically known compensating mechanisms, it appears quite feasible to 'extract the essence' of the mode of behavior in question."

71. The 1 April–15 December 1947 progress report for the Meteorology Project (JCMI) refers to reports outlining these models: Queney, "A Theoretical Study of Free Atmospheric Perturbations. Elastic, Gravity, and Long-Period Waves," and Thompson, "Permanent Waves in Homogeneous, Plane Fluids."

72. In a letter of 4 December 1967 Charney wrote to George Platzman: "We certainly were aware of Richardson's book when we began work at the Institute for Advanced Study. Indeed, von Neumann and others first proposed to use Richardson's method, but when it was realized that there were difficulties connected with initial data and computational stability, and when my own quasi-geostrophic approach appeared to circumvent these difficulties, this approach was followed instead." Quoted in Platzman (1967, p. 496).

73. The original letter of 12 February is in Thompson's possession. It is printed in entirety in appendix B of Thompson (1983). It began with an amusing anthropomorphic argument that draws in the Bible, *Reader's Digest*, Beethoven, and Chopin. Later in the letter Charney explicitly adopted the electrical engineering metaphor (shades of Shannon): "This leads us to the next problem, namely, how to filter out the noise. Pardon me, but let us again think metaphorically. The atmosphere is a transmitter. The computing machine is the receiver. The receiver is a very good one indeed, for it produces no appreciable noise, itself, i.e. all noise comes from the input. (I am supposing that you can compute to any desired order of accuracy.)

Now there are two ways to eliminate noise in the output. The first is to make sure that the input is free from objectional noises, or the second is to employ a filtering system in the receiver. Translating, the first method implies that the unwanted harmonics shall be eliminated from the raw data by some type of harmonic analysis; the second that you transform the equations of motion and make approximations in such a way that the bad harmonics are automatically eliminated."

74. Thompson (1983, p. 759).

75. See George W. Platzman, "Conversations with Jule Charney," Release 2, December 1982; available as a report of the National Center for Atmospheric Research, Boulder, Colorado.

76. Progress Report of the Meteorology Group at the Institute for Advanced Study, July 1, 1948 to June 30, 1949, JCMI.

77. Ibid.

78. Charney (1972, pp. 117–118).

79. This paper gives Rossby's famous dispersion result, which accounted for the propagation of these waves in terms of perturbations on the uniform flow. Garrett Birkhoff (1983, p. 29) has pointed out that the idea goes back to Helmholtz.

80. The model assumes that the atmosphere has uniform density, motion is purely horizontal, surfaces of constant density and constant pressure coincide (barotropy), the pressure gradients are approximately balanced by the Coriolis force (quasi-geostrophy), the vorticity of a fluid element around its vertical axis remains constant over time (vorticity conservation), wind is parallel at all levels, and the system is thermodynamically closed. See Smagorinsky (1953), von Neumann, Charney, and Fjortoft (1950), and Charney (1949).

Charney's 1949 paper contains many additional results. See Smagorinsky (1983, p. 7).

81. The form of the equation solved in the ENIAC computations of 1950 was:

$$\frac{\partial z}{\partial t} = \frac{1}{a^2 \cos^2 f} \frac{\partial(z,y)}{\partial(f,1)} ,$$

where $z \equiv \nabla^2 \psi + 2\Omega \sin\phi$ for the stream functions $\psi(\phi,\lambda,t)$ on a rotating sphere of radius a, latitude ϕ, longitude λ, and angular speed Ω (Charney 1972, 118).

82. The one-dimensional model, in its refined form of the spring of 1949, was described by Joseph Smagorinsky of the Weather Bureau: "Essentially, the new method is a much refined form of the vorticity theorem enunciated by Rossby in the late 1930's. Although this model is, as Rossby's, a barotropic fluid in one-dimensional motion which only considers small perturbations, it can take into account [equivalent-barotropic] divergence, the mean finite lateral width of a disturbance, friction, topography, an arbitrary initial pressure disturbance, and the boundary conditions which arise from considering circular latitude lines. To construct this model, it was necessary to introduce a number of arbitrary parameters in order to describe more fully actual atmospheric motions. The parameters involve (1) a measure of the finite lateral extent of the disturbances and (2) a second approximation on the assumption of a constant basic zonal current." Memorandum to the Chief of Bureau [F. W. Reichelderfer], 30 June 1949, quoted in Smagorinsky (1983, pp. 7–8).

83. Charney and Eliassen (1949, pp. 42–43). The discrepancy reported at the end of this quotation led them to investigate topographically induced perturbations in the atmosphere.

84. These calculations were done at the Weather Bureau in Washington under the general guidance of the Meteorology Group. Independent tests were conducted at the Swedish Meteorological Institute in Stockholm under Rossby's supervision. Progress Report of the Meteorology Group. 1 July 1948 to 30 June 1949, JCMI.

85. The evidence for this paragraph is a memorandum from Joseph Smagorinsky, an employee of the Weather Bureau, to the Chief of Bureau F. W. Reichelderfer, 30 June 1949, quoted in Smagorinsky (1983, pp. 7–8).

Apparently some efforts were made to do hand calculations for the two-dimensional model, but the group had so many difficulties they decided to wait until the calculations could be carried out on the ENIAC. Charney to Smagorinsky, 3 November 1949, quoted in Smagorinsky (1983, p. 9).

86. Progress Report of the Meteorology Group, July 1, 1948 to June 30, 1949, JCMI.

87. Charney explained von Neumann's contributions to this work as follows: "Johnny had become impatient while waiting for Julian Bigelow to finish the computer and suggested we do the integration on the Eniac. Several problems were involved: (1) We had to determine the computational stability criteria. This was done by Johnny, who had already shown how to apply the Courant-Lewi-Friedrichs [*sic*] procedure to a variety of partial-differential equations. (2) We had to devise a method that would not overtax the limited memory capacity of the Eniac. I had previously obtained trial solutions by using both Green's functions and hand relaxation methods to solve for $\partial \psi / \partial t$ in the vorticity equations of the type

$$- {}^2\frac{\partial y}{\partial t} = \frac{\partial(-\overset{2}{y}, y)}{\partial(x, y)}$$

"But both of these methods were unsuitable for the ENIAC. Johnny suggested using finite Fourier transforms to solve the equation for * over a rectangular area; the method proved quite successful. (3) A third problem was to determine the boundary condition for a closed region immersed in the fluid. Physical reasoning suggested that one should prescribe both the normal velocity and the vorticity at inflow points, but only the normal velocity at outflow points, along the boundary. Johnny showed that these conditions were both necessary and sufficient in a case which, though special, appeared to exhibit the essential mathematical properties of the general flow." Charney to Stan Ulam, 6 December 1957, SUAP.

88. Others, including von Neumann, Rossby, and Wexler, visited Aberdeen during the course of the computations. See Platzman (1979, p. 308) about Rossby's visit. Rossby was enthusiastic about Charney and Eliassen's method as a means "to get rid of the horrible subjectivity which still characterizes all, or almost all forecast efforts." Rossby to Platzman, 8 May 1949, quoted in Platzman (1979, p. 308).

89. These problems are given as stated in a memorandum from Joseph Smagorinsky to Chief, Weather Bureau (F. W. Reichelderfer), 7 February 1950, quoted in Smagorinsky (1983, pp. 9–10).

90. Smagorinsky writes of the ENIAC's being "overtaxed" by the calculations of the barotropic model, showing it to be impractical for the more demanding calculations for a baroclinic model, which would have to await the completion of the IAS computer. Joseph Smagorinsky to Chief, Weather Bureau [F. W. Reichelderfer], memorandum, 14 April 1950, quoted in Smagorinsky (1983, p. 10).

91. The Meteorology Group returned to Aberdeen in 1951 to conduct the tests for hypothetical situations. The results were regarded as anticlimactic after the 1950 calculation and were never published. Platzman (1979, p. 303).

92. Charney to Platzman, 10 April 1950, quoted in Platzman (1979, p. 311). Charney continued in that same letter: "Even the turning of the wind, which Ragnar [Fjortoft] thought to be a baroclinic phenomenon, was correctly forecast." More details of the forecasts are given in Smagorinsky (1983, p. 10), quoting reports written at the time.

93. The results are reported in Charney, Fjortoft, and von Neumann (1950). The progress reports of the Meteorology Group for the periods 1 July 1949–30 June 1950 and 1 July 1950–31 March 1951 (JCMI) report some of the research following the ENIAC calculations. Charney and Fjortoft developed a three-dimensional model to account for errors in the ENIAC forecasts, von Neumann did some programming and numerical analysis in anticipation of running further tests of the barotropic model on the IAS computer, Platzman and Margaret Smagorinsky investigated methods of objective smoothing and interpolation of grid values (a problem in the ENIAC calculations), Freeman wrote a paper on blocking as a shock phenomenon, and Charney and Fjortoft studied the statistical and mechanical properties of two-dimensional incompressible flows and carried out other theoretical studies on the physical nature of the atmosphere. Preparations were also made for a three-dimensional baroclinic model, which is discussed in the next section. It is clear that by this time the group was stalling until the IAS computer was completed.

94. Joseph Smagorinsky to Chief [F. W. Reichelderfer], Weather Bureau, memorandum, 14 April 1950, quoted in Smagorinsky (1983, p. 10).

95. See the discussion in Smagorinsky (1983, pp. 10–11).

96. The term *retooling* is one that Charney used in the Progress Report, Meteorology Group, July 1, 1950 to March 31, 1951, JCMI. This progress report and the one for the period 1 July 1949–30 June 1950 describe these preliminary activities.

97. In the third quarter of 1951, Charney made a trip to Europe to confer with others interested in the problems of numerical weather prediction. He learned that computations done by R. C. Sutcliffe of the British Meteorological Office, Air Ministry, with a quasi-geostrophic advective model had been unsatisfactory, confirming the experiences of the IAS Meteorology Group. Charney came to the conclusion during his trip that "nothing less than an integration of the complete three-dimensional quasi-geostrophic model can lead to a major improvement in forecasting." He solicited the assistance of Rossby and his International Meteorological Research Institute in Stockholm to carry out some of the preliminary testing and synoptic analysis on this three-dimensional model. Progress Report, Meteorological Group, July 1, 1951 to September 30, 1951, JCMI.

98. Meteorology Group, Progress Report, October 1, 1951 to December 21, 1951, JCMI. Charney recalled this work as follows: "We gradually extended the methods to more complicated models in the hierarchy to models involving two, three, four and five degrees of freedom in the vertical. One of the chief mathematical problems here was to find a method of solving three-dimensional elliptic equations with variable coefficients. Johnny suggested using the extrapolated Liebmann technique. He worked out the proof for convergence for the special case of the Laplace equation, although it was later found that Frankel had already done it, and David Young had extended it to more general equations." Charney to Stan Ulam, 6 December 1957, SUAP.

99. These early tests of the machines and the coding are described in the Meteorology Group, Progress Report, December 22, 1951 to March 31, 1952.

100. In the period 1951–1953 six simple baroclinic models were devised: Phillips (1951), Eady (1952), Eliassen (1952), Charney and Phillips (1953), Sawyer and Bushby (1953), and Thompson (1953). See Thompson (1983) for additional information on these models.

101. The best description of these calculations is given in the Meteorology Project, Summary of Work during the calendar year 1952, JCMI. Additional information can be found in the quarterly progress reports for that year, also located in JCMI.

102. An overview of the mathematics of the meteorological calculations, which will not be discussed in detail here, is given in two reports: Final Report on Contract No. DA-36-034-ORD-1023, April 1954, pp. II–94 through II–137, and Final Report on Contract No. DA-36-034-ORD-1330, December 1954, part III. Both can be found in AONA.

103. Meteorology Project, Quarterly Progress Report, January 1, 1953 to March 31, 1953, JCMI. Also see Charney (1954).

104. Meteorology Project, Quarterly Progress Report, April 1, 1953 to June 31, 1953, JCMI.

105. Meteorology Project, Progress Report, July 1, 1953 to March 31, 1954, JCMI.

106. Ibid.

107. The details of this offer are described in the two-page "Outline for Discussion on Operational Numerical Weather Prediction Service" attached to a letter of 29 July 1952 from Weather Bureau Chief F. W. Reichelderfer to Captain R. O. Minter, Head, Naval Aerology Section, JCMI.

108. The minutes of the meeting (VNLC) indicate the attendance: von Neumann, Charney, and Phillips from the institute; Wexler and Smagorinsky from the Weather Bureau; Petterssen and Lewis from the Air Weather Service; Bodurtha and Hughes from the Office of Naval Research; Rex from the Aerology Branch of the Navy Bureau of Aeronautics; Craig and Touart from the Geophysics Research Division; Platzman from the University of Chicago; and Dolezel from the Air Research and Development Command.

109. Charney had in mind the three-dimensional baroclinic model they were then testing at the institute. Thompson, who could not attend the meeting, sent a report (attached to the meeting minutes) suggesting a two-dimensional model, which he believed would be more economical. Charney believed that Thompson's model

would be too simple for adequate forecasts, but von Neumann suggested that they wait to decide until there was more experience with the two models. There is a record in JCMI and VNLC of a frank, and occasionally testy, correspondence in 1952 between Charney and Thompson over appropriate atmospheric models and the actions each had taken to secure funding for the model he favored.

110. For further information about the origins of the Joint Numerical Weather Prediction Unit, see Thompson (1983, sec. 5) and Smagorinsky (1983, sec. 4).

111. A discussion of the mission, functions, and organizational, personnel, and physical requirements for JNWPU is given, complete with organizational chart and budget, in *"Report by the Ad Hoc Committee on Numerical Weather Prediction to the Joint Meteorological Committee on Joint Numerical Weather Prediction Unit,"* 10 August 1953, JCMI. Bigelow, Charney, and von Neumann from the institute were among the thirteen scientific consultants to the committee.

112. In October 1954 Herman Goldstine and Joseph Smagorinsky were commissioned to compare the two most powerful computers commercially available at the time, the IBM 701 and the Engineering Research Associates ERA Model 1103. Each of the machines was required to produce three numerical forecasts based on the three-level model developed by Charney and Phillips at the institute. It took 10 weeks to write and 15 hours to debug the ERA code and 17 weeks to write and 50 hours to debug the IBM code. The speeds of the two machines were found to be similar but with a slight advantage in favor of the 701. However, the 701 card equipment was found to process data six times faster than that of the 1103. For this reason, Goldstine and Smagorinsky recommended the 701 for the JNWPU. The recommendation was accepted by a Technical Advisory Group chaired by von Neumann, and a 701 was delivered to JNWPU in early 1955. See Goldstine (1972, p. 329) and Smagorinsky (1983, p. 24) for a discussion of these tests. The detailed results of Goldstine and Smagorinsky's findings are reported in "Report to the Ad Hoc Group for Establishment of a Joint Numerical Weather Prediction Unit: The ERA 1103 and the IBM 701," 26 January 1954, and "Additions and Corrections" to the report, 27 January 1954, JCMI.

Philip Thompson has reported that the 701 was "just barely adequate for our purposes." It took three hours to calculate the 24-hour forecast after the data had been coded, transmitted, and collected. These forecasts required on the order of a billion calculations. Thompson observed that it was only after moving to the IBM 704 that more sophisticated models could be introduced. OH 125, 5 December 1986, conducted by the author, OHCB.

113. The JNWPU became the National Meteorological Center in 1961, first under ESSA and later under NOAA. Smagorinsky's unit evolved into what is today the Geophysical Fluid Dynamics Laboratory at Princeton University, under the auspices of NOAA.

114. The progress report for the period 22 December 1951–31 March 1952 (JCMI) indicates the group's interest in these questions and describes their study of the influence of large-scale heating on the mean seasonal flow pattern.

115. Meteorology Project Progress Report, 1 July 1953–31 March 1954, JCMI.

116. More complete descriptions and evaluations of this work are given in Smagorinsky (1983) and Thompson (1983). See also Phillips (1956) for the original publication of his findings.

117. Progress report, 1 April 1954–30 June 1955, JCMI.

118. Ibid.

119. See the proceedings of the conference in Pfeffer (1956), especially the editor's preface.

120. This summary is based on the account given in Smagorinsky (1983) and verified by Pfeffer (1956).

121. See Charney (1972, p. 119) for a discussion of this issue.

122. Supplied by Philip Thompson.

123. See the discussion of the general circulation problem in Thompson (1983).

124. Drafts dated 29 July and 1 August 1955 of the "Proposal for a Project on the Dynamics of the General Circulation" are in VNLC.

125. It was estimated that the calculations of the general atmosphere for the entire northern hemisphere would require 900 hours on the institute computer or 450 hours if the problem were checked in a less time-consuming way, and that this calculation would run five times more rapidly on an IBM 701 because its intrinsic speed was twice that of the IAS computer and because it had fewer memory limitations. Thus the problem would require 90 hours on the 701, 45 hours on the IBM 704, or 22 hours on the NORC. The only fast computer that was accessible to the meteorological community was the JNWPU IBM 701, which was why the proposal called for this new group to be established in Suitland.

126. The name was changed in 1959 to the General Circulation Research Laboratory and in 1963 to the Geophysical Fluid Dynamics Laboratory. It is now housed on the Forrestal campus of Princeton University. In 1956, after Charney and Phillips left the institute for MIT and von Neumann's energies were being consumed by his work with the Atomic Energy Commission and his battle with cancer, the air force and navy withdrew their support from the general circulation project. The Weather Bureau assumed full support at the urging of Reichelderfer and Wexler (Smagorinsky 1983, p. 34).

127. Smagorinsky (1983) describes some of the early work of this group. Charney and Phillips made substantial contributions in the early years, including an application of the von Neumann–Richtmyer artificial viscosity as proposed at the 1955 conference.

"Weather Bureau, General Circulation Research Project, Summary of Work, October 1955 to April 1956" (JCMI) describes some of the early problems and successes of the project.

128. Von Neumann did continue to try to promote research in numerical meteorology. For example, he chaired the National Science Foundation Conference on Theoretical Geophysics in Washington, D.C., in February 1956 at which there was a call for the formation of a new institute to conduct research in this area. Materials from this meeting are in VNLC.

129. "There was a strong body of opinion on the part of a number of people who were otherwise his [von Neumann's] friends at the Institute for Advanced Study that nothing experimental should be undertaken . . .and that . . . penetrated . . . rather deeply into my own consciousness and it was probably the main reason I left

the Institute for Advanced Study." George M. Platzman, "Conversations with Jule Charney," Release 2, December 1982; now available as a report from the National Center for Atmospheric Research, Boulder, Colorado.

Von Neumann tried to make arrangements in 1956 for Charney and Phillips to join him as permanent faculty members at UCLA. Von Neumann's terminal illness and perhaps other reasons intervened. See, for example, von Neumann to Paul Dodd, dean at UCLA, 26 March 1956, VNLC, about the plan to bring Charney and Phillips to UCLA.

130. Charney (1955, p. 798). Philip Thompson has made a similar point in "The Maturing of the Science," lecture to the American Meteorological Society annual meeting, 12 January 1987, New Orleans.

131. Thompson, "The Maturing of the Science."

132. Private communication to author, 5 December 1986.

133. Charney (1972, pp. 121ff.). Charney's remarks should be compared with those of Philip Thompson on the use of the computer for experimentation and discovery. Oral history 125, esp. pp. 32ff., OHCB, 5 December 1986, conducted by the author.

134. Goldstine and von Neumann (1946, esp. p. 3). This topic is discussed in greater detail in chapter 3.

135. Some of the scientific computations (not in meteorology) described in chapter 7 can be regarded as heuristic uses of the computer.

136. See, for example, the 1953 memorandum, "On the requirements for aerological data from the point of view of numerical weather forecasting," JCMI.

137. Smagorinsky (1953) discusses some of these issues.

138. The agenda from the conference can be found in JCMI and the report of the conference in VNLC.

139. These problems are discussed briefly in an oral history with Philip Thompson that I conducted: OH 125, OHCB, 5 December 1986, pp. 34 ff.

Chapter 7

1. Parts of the computer were given to the National Museum of American History in Washington, D.C., where it can usually be seen on display.

2. Letter, 3 February 1948, VNLC. Even before the institute computer project, von Neumann had enumerated to Lewis Strauss applications of the computer to aerodynamics, hydrodynamics, elasticity and plasticity, optics, electrodynamics, dynamic meteorology, and sorting problems. In this list von Neumann explicitly restricted himself to scientific problems of interest to the U.S. Navy—blast waves in air and water, antenna design, meteorological turbulence, and others.

3. In a report to the IAS Joint Faculty-Trustee Study Committee in May 1956 (FASC), Goldstine reported that the institute computer was used one-third time for the meteorology project, a small percentage time for internally generated mathematical problems, and the rest for physics, astrophysics, and mathematics originating at the institute, Princeton University, and elsewhere.

4. See, for example, the nine letters written between Herman Goldstine and Eleanor Trefftz of the Ohio State University physics department between June

1952 and March 1953 (HGAP) about a wave equation calculation done for her on the IAS computer.

5. Klara von Neumann, Hedi Selberg, and Sonya Bargmann were some of the faculty wives who did coding.

6. Because of classification restrictions, information is also curtailed about use of the institute computer for atomic weapons research, especially for Los Alamos.

7. These calculations are discussed in Final Report on Contract No. DA-36-034-ORD-1023, April 1954, AONA, and in a report sent to Arthur Grad, head of the Mathematics Branch of the Office of Naval Research, by Herman Goldstine as an attachment to a letter of 10 December 1954, HGAP.

8. A floating-point calculation was necessary here since the solution function varied over a wider range than that fixed in the computer.

9. This problem may have concerned the electronic structure of iron. Such a problem was suggested by Joseph Calloway of the Princeton University Palmer Physical Laboratory in a letter to Herman Goldstine, 29 July 1953, HGAP.

10. See the discussion of the studies on truncation and round-off errors in the application of the Runge-Kutta method to a Bessel equation in the July 1953 Progress Report on Contract DA-36-034-ORD-19, SANB.

11. See Goldstine, Murray, and von Neumann (1959). The numerical experiments are described in Final Report on Contract No. DA-36-034-ORD-1023, April 1954, AONA.

12. Both calculations are described in the February 1953 Monthly Progress Report on Contract No. DA-36-034-ORD-19, SANB.

13. This calculation is described in Final Report on Contract No. DA-36-ORD-1330, December 1954, AONA.

14. This computation is described in the February and March 1955 Monthly Progress Reports, Contract No. DA-36-034-ORD-19, SANB; Final Report on Contract No. DA-36-034-ORD-1646, May 1957, NMAH; and in Hans J. Maehly, "Problem Squires," 14 August 1955, HGAP.

15. These calculations are described in three letters: von Neumann to Chandrasekhar, 22 May 1953, and Chandrasekhar to Goldstine, 26 May, 14 July 1953, HGAP; also in the May 1953 Monthly Progress Report on Contract No. DA-36-034-ORD-19, SANB, and in Final Report on Contract No. DA-36-034-ORD-1023, April 1954, AONA.

The functions are:

$$J_n(\alpha_{nj} y) \equiv J_n(x)$$

$$C_{n\eta}(\alpha_{n\eta} y) \equiv C_{n\eta}(x) \equiv Y_n(\alpha_{n\eta}\eta)J_n(x) - J_n(\alpha_{n\eta}\eta)Y_n(x)$$

where $J_{n(x)}$ and $Y_{n(x)}$ are the Bessel functions of the first and second kinds of integral order $n > 0$, α_{nj} and $\alpha_{n\eta}$ are the jth zeroes of $j_n(\alpha)$ and $Y_n(\eta\alpha)J_n(\alpha) - J_n(\eta\alpha)Y_n(\alpha)$, η is a parameter $0 < \eta < 1$, and J_n, Y_n, and C_n are the cylinder functions of order n.

16. This computation is described in the November 1955 Monthly Progress Report on Contract DA-36-034-ORD-19, SANB, and in Final Report on Contract No. DA-36-034-ORD-1646, May 1957, NMAH.

17. March 1957, Monthly Progress Report, Contract No. DA-36-034-ORD-19, SANB. An approximation was deemed suitable if its use did not undermine solutions, that is, if the difference between the solution using the transcendental function and its rational approximate would result in a difference that had no practical significance. Rational approximations were useful because they could be calculated much more quickly and precisely by the computer.

18. This computation is discussed in February 1952 Monthly Progress Report, Contract No. DA-36-034-ORD-19, SANB; the enclosure to a letter of 27 June 1952 from Edith Norris of the National Bureau of Standards to von Neumann concerning the write-up of the IAS computer project for *Mathematical Tables and Other Aids to Computation*; and letters to D. H. Lehmer from von Neumann on 8 October 1952 and Goldstine on 10 October 1952 describing the results of the computation, HGAP. This text is excerpted in part from Aspray (1987, pp. 183–184).

19. This computation is described in the May 1952 Monthly Progress Report, Contract DA-36-034-ORD-19, SANB; and in M. Kochen, "Report on Problem IA by Selmer—Code 98," 19 December 1953, HGAP. Also see Selmer (1954).

20. Private communication, 10 September 1986. Selmer is probably incorrect in his supposition that he was the first anywhere to do number theory research on advanced computing machines. For some time D. H. Lehmer had been carrying out such a research program on calculating machines of his own design.

21. Chapter 5 describes these calculations in greater detail and indicates their importance to the research program in numerical analysis. These numerical experiments are described in the February 1953, March 1954, April 1954, and May 1954 Monthly Progress Reports, Contract No. DA-36-034-ORD-19, SANB; Final Report on Contract No. DA-36-ORD-1330, December 1954, AONA; and Final Report on Contract No. DA-36-034-ORD-1023, April 1954, AONA.

22. This method is discussed in chapter 5.

23. Useful information about the application of desk calculators and IBM equipment, as well as the IAS computer, to Schwarzschild's research is given in an interview with Schwarzschild conducted by David DeVorkin and Spencer Weart, 3 June 1977, CHOP.

24. Schwarzschild oral history with the author, 18 November 1988, OH 124, OHCB. Schwarzschild, like many others, calls the institute computer the MANIAC. That name is reserved elsewhere in this book for an IAS-class computer built at Los Alamos in the early 1950s.

25. Final Report on Contract No. DA-36-034-ORD-1646, May 1957, NMAH.

26. The best discussion of these astrophysical calculations is given in Final Report on Contract No. DA-36-034-ORD-1646, May 1957, NMAH. Also see: Final Report on Contract No. DA-36-034-ORD-1023, April 1954, AONA; Final Report on Contract No. DA-36-034-ORD-1330, December 1954, AONA; various of the Monthly Progress reports on Contract No. DA-36-034-ORD-19, SANB; and a letter from Hans J. Maehly (acting director on the Electronic Computer Project) to Arthur Grad (head, Mathematics Branch, ONR), 1 November 1956, HGAP.

27. In addition to the calculations described above, there was a study in 1957 of pulsational stability of stars with convective envelopes. The use of the institute

computer for this astrophysical research program continued for another year or two after the Electronic Computer Project terminated and the computer was operated by Princeton University.

28. The blast wave calculations are described in Final Report on Contract No. DA-36-034-ORD-1330, December 1954, and Final Report on Contract No. DA-36-034-ORD-1023, April 1957, AONA; Final Report on Contract No. DA-36-034-ORD-1646, May 1957, NMAH; and the report attached to a letter from Goldstine to Arthur Grad, head, Mathematics Branch, ONR, 10 December 1954, HGAP.

29. The mixing problem calculations are described in Final Report on Contract No. DA-36-034-ORD-1646, May 1957, NMAH; September 1954, November 1954, and other Monthly Progress Reports, Contract No. DA-36-034-ORD-19, SANB; a letter from Hans J. Maehly (acting director, ECP) to Arthur Grad (Head, Mathematics Branch, ONR), 1 November 1956, HGLC; and Goldstine and Gillis (1955).

   Similar computations were done on the MANIAC computer at Los Alamos. John R. Pasta worked on the computations at both places. See Pasta to Stan Ulam, 11 March 1954; their joint manuscript, "Heuristic Numerical Work in Some Problems of Hydrodynamics," SUAP; and Pasta to Goldstine, 10 May 1954, HGAP.

30. Other hydrodynamic studies were carried out, including an effort in 1957 to integrate numerically the Navier-Stokes equations for a compressible, viscous, and heat-conducting gas in two dimensions. There were also other classified problems calculated for the AEC.

31. The Squires problem fits into this category of problems.

32. Kinoshita was a postdoctoral visitor at IAS, who had completed his Ph.D. at Tokyo University in 1952. The computations are described in Final Report on Contract No. DA-36-034-ORD-1646, May 1957, NMAH.

33. The results of these computations are reported in Kinoshita (1957).

34. This calculation is described in Final Report on Contract No. DA-36-034-ORD-1646, May 1957, NMAH; November 1955 Monthly Progress Report, Contract No. DA-36-034-ORD-19, SANB; Hans Maehly (acting director, ECP) to Arthur Grad (head, Mathematics Branch, ONR), 1 November 1956, HGAP. The theory is described in Lane, Thomas, and Wigner (1955) and Wigner (1955).

35. These calculations are described in the November 1956 Monthly Progress Report, Contract No. DA-36-034-ORD-19, SANB; and in Final Report on Contract No. DA-36-034-ORD-1646, NMAH.

36. This calculation is described in Final Report on Contract No. DA-36-034-ORD-1646, May 1957, NMAH; and in Hans Maehly (acting director, ECP) to Arthur Grad (head, Mathematics Branch, ONR), 1 November 1956, HGAP.

37. These calculations are described in the February 1955 and March 1956 Monthly Progress Reports, Contract No. DA-36-034-ORD-19, SANB; and Hans J. Maehly (acting director, ECP) to Arthur Grad (head, Mathematics Branch, ONR), 1 November 1956, HGAP. The physical problem is described in Tobocman and Kalos (1955).

38. The systems programs are described in Hans J. Maehly (acting director, ECP) to Arthur Grad (head, Mathematics Branch, ONR), 1 November 1956 (HGAP), and in Final Report on Contract No. DA-36-034-ORD-1646, May 1957, NMAH.

39. The network analysis research is described in greatest detail in M. Kochen and S. Y. Wong, "Automatic Network Analysis with a Digital Computational System," IAS Electronic Computer Project, Technical Report No. 55-02, August 1955. Also see the April, June, and July 1955 Monthly Progress Reports, Contract No. DA-36-034-19 (all in SANB); and the Final Report on Contract No. DA-36-034-ORD-1646, May 1957, NBAH.

40. This work is described in the April 1955 Monthly Progress Report, Contract No. DA-36-034-ORD-19, SANB.

41. This calculation is described in Final Report on Contract No. DA-36-034-ORD-1023, April 1954, AONA, and in the April 1953 Monthly Progress Report, Contract No. DA-36-034-ORD-19, SANB.

42. This calculation is described in Final Report on Contract No. DA-36-034-ORD-1023, April 1954, AONA; and in the February 1953 Monthly Progress Report, Contract No. DA-36-034-ORD-19, SANB.

43. The calculation is described in Final Report on Contract No. DA-36-034-ORD-1023, April 1954, AONA.

44. The calculation is described in Final Report on Contract No. DA-36-034-ORD-1646, May 1957, NMAH; the July 1955 Monthly Progress, Contract No. DA-36-034-ORD-19, SANB; and Bryant Tuckerman, "Plan for an Historical Ephemeris, 600-1 BC," HGAP.

45. Final Report on Contract No. DA-36-034-ORD-1646, May 1957, NMAH.

46. See Tuckerman (1962).

47. This numerical experiment is described in Final Report on Contract No. DA-36-034-ORD-1646, May 1957, NMAH.

48. These numerical experiments are described in Final Report on Contract No. DA-36-034-ORD-1023, April 1954, AONA; and in the July 1956 Monthly Progress Report, Contract No. DA-36-034-ORD-19, SANB. Also see Barricelli (1962, 1963).

49. Document attached to letter from Herman Goldstine to Arthur Grad (head, Mathematics Branch, Office of Naval Research), 10 December 1954, HGAP.

50. These limitations are discussed by Goldstine in a draft of a paper entitled "Mathematical and Design Problems in Fast Scientific Computation," which was intended for presentation in Stockholm, Sweden, HGAP. Apparently Goldstine had presented an earlier version of this paper to the New York Scientific Computing Center symposium, 10 July 1956, under the title "The Need for both Engineering and Mathematical Advances in the Computing Machine Field."

Chapter 8

1. This point is discussed by Stern (1981, p. 78). Eckert gives his position in his testimony in the Honeywell v. Sperry Rand, U.S. District Court, Dist. Minn., 4th Div. (1973), pp. 17412–17741; Mauchly gives his position in Mauchly (1979). HSRC.

2. These comparisons are made in sections 2, 4, and 5 of the EDVAC report. Also see the comments of Arthur Burks in Aspray and Burks (1987, pp. 7–9).

3. Maxwell (1875, pp. 328–329).

4. Szilard (1929). See the discussions of Szilard's 1929 paper and the connection between entropy and information in Brillouin (1956), Cherry (1957), and Singh (1966).

5. Von Neumann (1932b, chap. 5).

6. Von Neumann (1932b, p. 369). Von Neumann made explicit in a letter of 8 April 1947 to Edward Teller (VNLC) the importance of these aspects of statistical mechanics to his work on automata: "I have some definite ideas concerning automata, memory, 'clearing' and irreversibility and entropy, somewhat connected with Szilard's treatment of 'Maxwell's Demon' (Zschr. f. Phys., 1929) and my old treatment of entropy and observability in quantum mechanics." In this letter von Neumann also described his thoughts on superconductivity and its value to counting-switching mechanisms.

7. The nature, and even the existence, of these conversations between Shannon and von Neumann is based on strong but circumstantial evidence. I have been unable to obtain Shannon's comments on this matter. As the ensuing discussion shows, at the least von Neumann was certainly familiar with Shannon's work.

8. In a meeting on 6 November 1987 Julian Bigelow indicated that von Neumann read voraciously and had probably read the Hartley and Nyquist papers. This is surprising since mathematicians did not commonly read the Bell journal, according to Bigelow. According to Shizuo Kakutani (Lecture, von Neumann Conference, Hofstra University, June 1988) in the 1948–1949 academic year von Neumann had a preprint of Shannon and Wiener's book (1949) on the mathematical theory of communication.

9. Shannon and Weaver (1949, pp. 8–9).

10. Ibid.

11. Ibid. (p. 3).

12. According to Jack Cowan (private communication, May 1988) von Neumann discussed the subject of statistical mechanics and its relation to information with Gabor. Von Neumann also had the opportunity to discuss these ideas with Shannon at Bell Laboratories and with Hamming at Los Alamos.

13. The contact between Turing and von Neumann is discussed in Davis (1987) and Hodges (1983). Much of this account is taken from Hodges and is corroborated with archival sources, where possible.

14. This problem had been stated by Hilbert at the 1928 international congress of mathematicians held in Bologna. A statement is considered here as formally statable if it can be expressed in the language of a logical theory being used to develop a foundation for mathematics. One commonly used system was that developed by Bertrand Russell and Alfred North Whitehead in *Principia Mathematica.*

15. This statement is one version of what is commonly known as Church's Thesis, which claims that the informal notion of an effectively computable function is coreferential with the mathematically formal notion of Turing machine computability.

16. Turing (1937, pp. 231–232).

17. This information is given in notes prepared by Ulam for his planned biography of von Neumann, SUAP.

18. Julian Bigelow described how von Neumann gave him Turing's computability paper to read as his first assignment when he came to work on the institute computer project in 1946. Private communication, 6 November 1987.

19. Von Neumann discussed questions of the computer and the brain with a number of Hungarian scientists. Eugene Wigner read drafts of his works on automata. There is later correpondence between von Neumann and fellow Hungarians Zoltan Bay and Albert Szent-Gyorgyi. See, for example, von Neumann to Szent-Gyorgyi, 22 June 1949, VNLC.

20. See, for example, von Neumann to Ortvay, 29 March 1939. There are approximately sixty letters in their correspondence, all written in Hungarian. Some are in VNLC; others are in OMIK. Eight of these letters, chosen for what they contribute to the understanding of the development of von Neumann's ideas on the computer and the brain, are translated into English in D. Nagy, F. Nagy, and Horvath (1987). All of the letters cited here are from these eight, with occasional slight restructuring of the English translation. Denes Nagy has informed me that there is little of substance in the part of the correspondence they did not translate and that many of the letters von Neumann wrote merely asked Ortvay for additional information about the brain (private communication, 9 March 1988). I cannot read Hungarian and am in no position to evaluate these claims.

21. Von Neumann to Ortvay, 13 May 1940, as translated in D. Nagy, F. Nagy, and Horvath (1987).

22. See, for example, his letter of 30 May 1940, as translated in D. Nagy, F. Nagy, and Horvath (1987).

23. In a private conversation, 6 November 1987, Julian Bigelow indicated that although the McCulloch-Pitts model is "immensely naive," von Neumann was "enormously impressed" with it.

24. Wiener and Bigelow's role in introducing von Neumann to this work was related to me in a private communication with Julian Bigelow on 6 November 1987. According to Bigelow, von Neumann read widely in Nicholas Rashevsky's *Bulletin of Mathematical Biophysics* but complained about the lack of scientific depth of the papers.

25. This work is described in McCulloch (1965, pp. 9–10) and presented in historical context in Aspray (1985). A psychon is described by McCulloch as a least psychic event and noted as being similar to a Leibnizian monad.

26. McCulloch (1965, p.10). McCulloch and Pitts cite Turing machines as a model for their work.

27. See, for example, McCulloch (1945, 1947, 1950, 1952).

28. See, for example, McCulloch (1950), which describes the application of cybernetic techniques to understanding the functioning of the central nervous system. McCulloch and Pitts applied cybernetic principles in a 1947 project on prosthetic devices to enable the blind to read by ear (Wiener 1948, pp. 31–32; de Latil 1957, pp. 12–13).

29. According to Julian Bigelow (private conversation 6 November 1987), von Neumann met Pitts a few times and got to know McCulloch quite well.

30. Seymour Papert described the paper's publication as a "valiant" effort to present these ideas to "a hostile or indifferent world" (McCulloch 1965, p. xvii). McCulloch admitted the initial lack of interest in their work (McCulloch 1965, p. 9). The discussion following von Neumann's 1948 Hixon Symposium also gives several implicit and explicit criticisms of the physiological adequacy of these idealized neurons (von Neumann 1951d, pp. AB 424–431).

31. Von Neumann (1945b, p. AB 24).

32. "Thanks to Rashevsky's defense of logical and mathematical ideas in biology, it [the 1943 article] was published in his journal [*Bulletin of Mathematical Biophysics*], where, so far as biology is concerned, it might have remained unknown; but John von Neumann picked it up and used it in teaching the theory of computing machines." McCulloch (1965, p. 9).

33. This point is discussed by Klara von Neumann in the preface to *The Computer and the Brain*.

There is an indication that some time prior to 1944 von Neumann had discussions on the literature of neurophysiology with Princeton University biologist Newton Harvey. See, for example, von Neumann to the Princeton mathematics librarian, Miss Blake, 29 November 1944, VNLC.

34. No other information about von Neumann's lecture or the meeting itself has been found. See letters from Spiegelman on 3, 14, and 31 December 1946 and replies by von Neumann on 10 and 16 (two letters) December, VNLC.

35. In the first 16 December letter Spiegelman is told that his encouragment has convinced von Neumann to try to write up his own ideas on self-reproduction.

36. See von Neumann to Mortimer Spiegelman (no known relation to Sol Spiegelman) of Metropolitan Life Insurance Company, 13 February 1950, SUAP.

37. See von Neumann to Warren McCulloch, 16 March 1949, WMAP. Von Neumann found von Foerster to be "really very brilliant" but had serious reservations about his theory of memory.

38. See letters from von Neumann dated 17 February and 1 April 1949 and from Bonhoeffer dated 21 January, 10 March, and 7 May 1949, VNLC.

39. See von Neumann to Warren McCulloch, 17 March 1949, WMAP. Von Neumann compared Bonhoeffer's model favorably with one developed by Nicholas Rashevsky. Von Neumann to Bonhoeffer, 17 March 1949, VNLC.

40. About the work of McCulloch and Pitts, von Neumann wrote: "I think that they contain very good and important ideas and results, but are unfortunately burdened with philosophical terminology that is not entirely clear and a hyperformalized way of designating things. The latter pains me especially, as an ex-logician. In my opinion, it is the cumbersome and inappropriate logical apparatus of R. Carnap. In spite of this the real ideas and significant results are clear and effective." Von Neumann to Bonhoeffer, 1 April 1949, VNLC.

41. Letter, 12 December 1949, VNLC. Lashley suggests work in four areas: direct study of neurological phenomena, like the work at Swarthmore College of Wolfgang Kohler, who was trying to establish neurological activity as fundamen-

tally analog in nature; research on the relationship between switching elements and simultaneous input impulses, as might be obtained from examination of the rat's visual cortex; a study of precision and the kinds of errors made by the human nervous system, mainly to show the limitations of the McCulloch-Pitts model; and studies like those of Nicholas Rashevsky on the brain as a complex network of circuits but modified to use statistical tools and assume the circuits to be randomly distributed.

42. Arrellane to von Neumann, 1950, VNLC. Wiener had apparently interceded on behalf of Arrellane, who also hoped to gain Albert Einstein's participation.

43. No to von Neumann, 31 October 1951, VNLC.

44. There are letters from Lederberg on 4 and 10 August 1955 and replies by von Neumann of 8 and 15 August, VNLC. Their dispute revolves around the role of information in the process of self-reproduction. It is clear that they are talking at cross-purposes, partly because of semantic difficulties. No resolution is reached in the correspondence.

45. See the letter from Williams of 7 September 1955 and von Neumann's reply of 3 October. Von Neumann encouraged them to publish their paper, "Error Control in a Biological Information System." I located no paper with this title, but see Weddell, Taylor, and Williams (1955) on a related topic.

46. Aiken, von Neumann, and Wiener to Herman Goldstine, 22 December 1944, HGAP. The original invitation went out from these three organizers 4 December 1944, but I have found no copies of it. Aiken was director of the Harvard Computation Laboratory.

47. Aiken, von Neumann, and Wiener to Goldstine, 22 December 1944, HGAP.

48. Aiken, von Neumann, and Wiener to Goldstein [*sic*], 28 December 1944, HGAP.

49. Memorandum to the participants from von Neumann, 12 January 1945, VNLC. Von Neumann suggested adding to the group J. Presper Eckert, S. Chandrasekhar, and George Stibitz. Von Neumann to Wiener, 1 February 1945, NWMI.

50. Wiener to Arturo Rosenblueth, 24 January 1945, NWMI.

51. Aiken, von Neumann, and Wiener to Goldstein [*sic*], 28 December 1944, HGAP.

52. One informative letter on the topic exists from Wiener to von Neumann, dated 24 January 1945. Wiener reported that he and Pitts were working on their report and that they had added to their task "the problem of transition from the computing machine to the control machine." Wiener also addressed the prospects for MIT's becoming the home for this new organization: "The attitude at Tech towards making it the home of such a project is as far as I can see friendly but not decisive as yet. One disadvantage of our community is Harvard Medical to which we could naturally look for backing on the physiological side has become completely clinical and offers little prospect as a home for the physiological side of the undertaking. I strongly expect that if we can get outside funds available it will not be too difficult to persuade the Institute to embark to a limited extent on a physiological program tied to our plans, but I have no definite commitment in this direction. I think that Tech should be put very high up in the list of our possibili-

ties as a home for the undertaking, but the time is not yet come to assume that it represents the only solution." Von Neumann replied on 1 February 1945 (NWMI) with his encouragement to pursue the matter at an opportune time.

53. Private communication, 6 November 1987. Wiener explained one reason for the delay in forming a society: "While we are going to meet again in the Spring, we have not organized in a formal permanent society. The reasons are that owing to the control of different and by no means unified government departments over parts of our program, it is best not to stir up a fuss until the military situation makes matters of classification less important. However, we definitely do have the intention of organizing a society and a journal after the war, and founding either at Tech or elsewhere in the country a center of research in our new field. In this matter Moe is giving his good will and expects to be able to help us with fellowships. We are also getting a good backing from Warren Weaver, and he has said to me that this is just the sort of thing that the Rockefeller should consider pushing. In addition, McCulloch and von Neumann are very slick organizers, and I have heard from von Neumann mysterious words concerning a some thirty megabucks which is likely to be available for scientific research. Von Neumann is quite confident that he can siphon some of it off." Letter to Arturo Rosenblueth, 24 January 1945, NWMI.

54. 29 November 1946, VNLC. Von Neumann was sufficiently concerned about this letter to ask Julian Bigelow for comments before mailing it to Wiener. Bigelow's comments are also found in VNLC.

55. Von Neumann also mentioned work was carrying out on the theoretical front. He claimed to have formulated the problem of self-reproduction rigorously, in the style of Turing, and promised to complete the details in the next two months. He anticipated that he would learn that it takes in the high 10,000s or 100,000s in number of basic components to produce an automaton capable of self-replication. He also mentioned that he had been musing over aspects of the gene-enzyme relationship and mutation as they relate to self-reproduction.

56. See Langmuir's letter of 11 November 1946 and von Neumann's letter dated the next day, VNLC.

57. Von Neumann to Mina Rees, Office of Naval Research, 20 January 1947, VNLC.

58. See, for example, von Neumann to D. Harker of General Electric Research Laboratory, 16 December 1946, and von Neumann to Mina Rees, 20 January 1947, VNLC.

59. In this scaled-up model intra-atomic distances are 1 centimeter, and atoms are modeled by metal balls. This scaling greatly simplifies the measurement.

60. See the interdepartmental correspondence, Edward G. Ramberg to V. K. Zworykin, 27 December 1946, VNLC, estimating the equipment and personnel needs to realize von Neumann's plans.

61. Haraway (1981–1982) discusses these conferences in the larger context of information in post–World War II biology. See Heims (1975, 1977) for background on the conference and its participants. Gardner (1985) discusses the Macy Lectures in the context of other early work in cognitive science.

62. McCulloch to Walter Pitts, 2 February 1946, WMAP.

63. Warren McCulloch, "Summary of the Points of Agreement Reached in the Previous Nine Conferences on Cybernetics," in von Foerster (1955, p. 70).

64. Proceedings of the last five meetings were published by the Macy Foundation and are still available. There is little information available about the first five meetings other than an occasional letter, program, or unpublished summary in WMAP. The Josiah Macy, Jr. Foundation destroyed its administrative records of the conference, but possibly some documentation can be found among the papers of other participants.

65. Donald Marquis summarized the discussion following von Neumann's presentation. A copy of this summary can be found in WMAP.

66. "To the Members of the Conference on Teleological Mechanisms, Oct. 23 & 24, 1947," summary of the previous meetings prepared by McCulloch, WMAP.

67. It is not easy to trace the progression of von Neumann's ideas in the theory of automata. His work in the logical design of hardware and numerical meteorology was team research conducted under government contract, which present the historian with the opportunity to interview collaborators and examine project reports. The theory of automata was an individual research program. Von Neumann did not receive government support for this research that required regular progress reports, and the memories of his colleagues, none of whom worked closely with him in this area, are haphazard. The historian's task is further complicated by the fact that von Neumann's heavy administrative duties in Washington and his early death prevented him from completing his research or placing it in a finished published form. His Vanuxem Lectures at Princeton University, his notes for the Silliman Lectures at Yale University, and his manuscript "The Theory of Automata: Construction, Reproduction, Homogeneity" all were incomplete and unpublished at the time of his death.

68. Von Neumann noted that the published lecture was an only slightly edited version of the lecture he delivered at the symposium and that what he had to say was necessarily sketchy at places because of the constraint of what can be delivered in the time of one lecture. Von Neumann 1951d, p. AB 391. He was reluctant to write up this lecture for publication at all. At the urging of the organizer, Lloyd A. Jeffress, he made several unsuccessful efforts in this direction, including an attempt to work from the stenographic notes of his talk. Von Neumann to Jeffress, 14 March 1949, VNLC. Jeffress had K. S. Lashley, one of the other Hixon Symposium participants, write to encourage von Neumann (2 June 1949, VNLC), and this had the desired effect. Von Neumann wrote to Lashley six days later (VNLC) saying that "my knowledge was much too lacunary and my ideas too far from maturity to make it possible for me to produce a satisfactory write-up," but with Lashley's encouragement he would try again. This time von Neumann succeeded, for Lashley wrote to von Neumann, 12 December 1949 (VNLC) praising the manuscript and suggesting physiological research that needed to be carried out to follow up on von Neumann's ideas.

69. See Jeffress to von Neumann, 16 December 1947, VNLC. The program lists the following speakers in addition to von Neumann: Warren McCulloch (University of Illinois, College of Medicine), "Why the Mind Is in the Head"; K. S. Lashley (Harvard University and Yerkes Laboratories of Primate Biology), "The Problem of Serial Order in Behavior"; Heinrich Kluver (University of Chicago), "Functional

Differences between the Occipital and Temporal Lobes"; Wolfgang Kohler (Swarthmore College), "Relational Determination in Perception"; and Ward C. Halstead (University of Chicago), "Brain and Intelligence." The discussion panel consisted of H. W. Brosin (University of Chicago), R. W. Gerard (University of Chicago), J. M. Nielsen (UCLA), H. S. Liddell (Cornell University), Donald B. Lindsley (Northwestern University), and Paul Weiss (University of Chicago).

Von Neumann was invited to suggest possible speakers. In letters of 11 November 1947 and 27 April 1948 to Jeffress (VNLC), he suggested Norbert Wiener (MIT), Walter Pitts (MIT), Gerhart von Bonin (University of Illinois), H. J. Muller (Indiana University), S. Spiegelman (St. Louis), S. E. Luria (Indiana University), Delbruck, and Beadle.

70. The formal invitation to participate came from the conference organizer, Lloyd A. Jeffress, in a letter of 6 November 1947. (VNLC).

71. Jeffress to von Neumann, 16 December 1947, VNLC.

72. Von Neumann (1951d, p. AB 391–392). Von Neumann returned to this point on page AB 405 when he discussed the limitations of artificial automata to carry out complex applications. He pointed to certain physical limitations of the elements used in artificial automata but also to the "intellectual" limitation created by the lack of "a properly mathematical-logical theory" of automata.

73. Von Neumann (1951d, p. AB 392). Von Neumann did point out (p. 393) that the validation of the axiom systems, to show that the axioms realistically express the external functioning of neurons in the central nervous system (or vacuum tubes in a computer), is the province of physiology (or electrical engineering).

74. This discussion was preceded by a lengthy discussion of the differences between analog and digital devices. The distinctions von Neumann drew are those commonly made today. What is most interesting about this discussion is the fact that he employed the concepts of communication theory in his discussion. He referred to fluctuations in analog devices and round-off error in digital devices as noise, and the main difference he drew between the two kinds of devices was the quantitative difference between their signal-to-noise ratios (at best 10^2 for electrical analog devices and 10^5 for mechanical analog devices, as opposed to 10^{10} in digital devices) and the ease of increasing signal-to-noise ratio in digital devices.

75. Von Neumann (1951d, p. AB 405).

76. Ibid.

77. In the case of the first prediction, it is possible that von Neumann was aware of the potentials of the transistor, which had been discovered the same year as his lecture at Bell Laboratories. On the second prediction, he wrote (AB 402): "It is quite possible that computing machines will not always be primarily aggregates of switching organs, but such a development is as yet quite far in the future." He did not elaborate further on this prediction in this lecture.

78. Von Neumann (1951d, p. AB 409).

79. Ibid. (p. AB 407).

80. Von Neumann's work on reliable automata built from unreliable parts (described later in this chapter) is an example of the second change. Arthur Burks (private communication, 1988) has stated that Stan Ulam had told him that it was

Wiener who directed von Neumann to the probabilistic approach to reliability and that Ulam did not think it would be fruitful. Later researchers, including Richard Hamming, solved the reliability problem using deterministic redundancy rather than a probability approach.

81. Von Neumann (1951d, p. AB 407). This is the same tradition in physics out of which came Szilard's solution to the Demon problem and von Neumann's own study of thermodynamical paradoxes in quantum mechanics. In his 1952 California Institute of Technology lectures on probabilistic automata, von Neumann made the point even more explicitly. Having given the definition for information

$$H = \sum_{i=1}^{n} p_i \log_2 p_i$$

which he attributed to Shannon and implicitly to Szilard, he wrote: "An important observation about this definition is that it bears close resemblance to the statistical definition of the entropy of a thermodynamical system. If the possible events are just the known possible states of the system with their corresponding probabilities, then the two definitions are identical. Pursuing this, one can construct a mathematical theory of the communication of information patterned after statistical mechanics.... That information should thus reveal itself as an essentially thermodynamical discipline, is not at all surprising: The closeness and the nature of the connection between information and entropy is inherent in L. Boltzmann's classical definition of entropy (apart from a constant, dimensional factor) as the logarithm of the 'configuration number.' The 'configuration number' is the number of a *priori* equally plausible states that are compatible with the macroscopic description of the state—i.e. it corresponds to the amount of (microscopic) information that is missing in the (macroscopic) description." Von Neumann (1956a, p. AB 566).

82. Von Neumann (1951d, p. AB 411).

83. Ibid. (p. AB 412–413).

84. One of the undated, unpublished studies, entitled "Von Neumann's Interest in Automata" (SUAP), which Ulam wrote when he was working on a von Neumann biography, mentioned that "some of our discussions already before the war concerned problems of replication."

85. Possibly inspired by von Neumann's ideas, the Irish author Lord Dunsany wrote a novel, *The Last Revolution* (1951), in which a solitary inventor builds a thinking machine that is able to work in a foundry and make copies of itself. The novel has strong Luddite overtones: "One day there will be another Pender [the inventor of the self-reproducing machine]. It will be easy to control him, but shall we have the wisdom to do so? Are we not proud of the power of our slave the machine? Are we not drunk with wonder at what it can do? Shall we not go on delighting to give that slave more and more power, until it becomes our master? And that will be the last revolution, of which the first outbreak was crushed, and by what a lucky accident. It will be the last because, once monstrous machines that already exist are established, we shall have no more chance of dethroning them than a mouse would have to defeat a tiger. It is only our cunning that has kept them under. If Marconi can make a machine that can hear ten thousand miles, and others, jealous of the speed of sound, can make machines that outpace it; then in a world that has

machines already which can pick up an elephant as we could pick up a pebble, and can crush a ton of rock with a single blow, it is clear that all they need to displace us is some calculating machine whose genius need not exceed the cunning of those that we have already nearly so far as television exceeds the telescopes of our fathers" (p. 184).

86. Briefly, von Neumann's construction is as follows. Define automaton A, which, given instructions I (the analog of Turing's tape) describing the functions another automaton can carry out, will construct that automaton. Define automaton B, which makes a copy of any instructions I given to it. Combine automata A and B into automaton C, which serves as a "control mechanism." C functions in such a way that if its A component is supplied with instructions I, C will cause A to construct the automaton A(I) described by the instructions I, and C will have its B component copy instructions I, insert I into the new automaton A(I), and release this automaton. Define automaton D as the combination of automata A, B, and C, and let J be the instructions that describe D. Place instructions J into component A of D and define the resulting automaton as E. Von Neumann shows that E is self-reproductive.

87. At the time of this work the genetic process was under increasing scrutiny, but the mechanism of the genetic code had not yet been uncovered.

88. Von Neumann (1951d, p. AB 420).

89. Ibid. (p. AB 420–421). It is quite clear that von Neumann understood the differences between his model and genetic functioning in the biological realm. His approach seemed to be to gain as much explanatory value as possible, which was developed from first principles other than providing close biological similitude. I believe he hoped, as his models improved, to make them model the genetic function more closely.

90. It is likely that von Neumann presented these lectures again in 1950 at Bell Telephone Laboratories in Murray Hill, New Jersey. Von Neumann to Louis N. Ridenour, 23 March 1950, VNLC.

91. Von Neumann (1966, p. AB 435). These lectures were never published by von Neumann and are available to us only in incomplete form through an edited version provided by Arthur Burks. Von Neumann used the word *complication* where we would more likely say *complexity*. Von Neumann's usage is followed here.

It is difficult to determine the progression of von Neumann's ideas by comparing the Hixon Symposium and the Illinois lectures. The Hixon Symposium was one short lecture to a group composed mainly of physiologists and psychiatrists. In the five Illinois lectures, von Neumann had the opportunity to elaborate on ideas that he may have already had the year before. Also, his Illinois audience was mathematically more sophisticated, including many mathematicians and one of the most advanced groups of scientists and engineers building electronic computers. These factors, rather than a progression of his thought in the fifteen intervening months, may explain the differences between the two presentations.

92. Von Neumann (1966, p. AB 439).

93. At this point von Neumann used Shannon's definition of information to argue that memory rather than processing is the problem most worthy of the attention of computer designers. He likened the memory in a computer to human comput-

ers who have only a single piece of paper to use in the course of fifty man-years of calculation with a desk calculator. He also discussed the trade-off between memory capacity and access time and suggested the use of a hierarchy of memories.

94. One comment in particular suggests this attitude: "The insight that a formal neuron network can do anything which you can describe in words is a very important insight and simplifies matters enormously at low complication levels. It is by no means certain that it is a simplification on high complication levels. It is perfectly possible that on high complication levels the value of the theorem is in the reverse direction, namely, that you can express logics in terms of these efforts and the converse may not be true." Von Neumann 1966, p.AB 450–451.

95. But von Neumann also pointed clearly to the limitations of the McCulloch-Pitts approach in understanding the human nervous system. He repeated his Hixon discussion of the regulation of blood pressure as an analog process. He also argued that the memory systems that can be constructed from McCulloch-Pitts neurons are unlikely to occur in nature because they are so wasteful in number of switching elements. In summary, he pointed to fatigue and memory "as very obvious lacunae in the McCulloch and Pitts approach to the nervous system." Ibid. (p. AB 452).

96. The Halting Problem asks whether there is a Turing machine which, given an arbitrary Turing machine M and input i, will determine whether M will complete its computation on i in a finite number of steps. The answer is no. It is an important result in mathematical logic, for it shows that there is no effective procedure for determining whether a function is effectively computable.

97. Von Neumann (1966, p. AB 453).

98. Ibid. (p. AB 454). Von Neumann pointed out the relationship of this result to the theory of types and to some work of Kurt Gödel. Arthur Burks, in editing this lecture, wrote to Gödel to ascertain what result of his von Neumann referred to. Gödel replied: "I think the theorem of mine which von Neumann refers to is . . . the fact that a complete epistemological description of a language A cannot be given in the same language A, because the concept of truth of sentences of A cannot be defined in A. It is this theorem which is the true reason for the existence of undecidable propositions in the formal systems containing arithmetic . . . [which I formulated] in my Princeton lectures of 1934." Von Neumann (1949, p. AB 458). Given that von Neumann participated in bringing Gödel to the IAS and had an abiding interest in mathematical logic, it is likely that von Neumann attended these lectures. Even if he did not, he had the opportunity to read the lecture notes, which were written up by Stephen Kleene and J. Barkley Rosser and distributed widely.

99. Von Neumann (1966, p. AB 468) noted that this analysis probably errs in favor of the computer.

100. Von Neumann pointed out, however, that the neuron does not approach the theoretical minimum energy dissipation per binary act as calculated by thermodynamical analysis. He suggested that this may be an example of nature sacrificing efficiency for reliability.

101. Von Neumann (1966, p. AB 472–473).

102. Ibid. (p. AB 481).

103. Also see the discussion of the kinematic model in Burks (1984), where it is

discussed in the context of related ideas from automata theory, computer science, semiotics, and philosophy of mind.

104. This description, which was incomplete in von Neumann's manuscript of the lecture, is supplemented by the editor Arthur Burks with material from a series of three lectures that von Neumann delivered to Bigelow, Goldstine, Peirce Ketchum, and Abraham Taub at the IAS in June 1948, in which he described the elementary parts in more detail: a stimulus organ that realizes logical disjunction, a coincidence organ that realizes logical conjunction, an inhibitory organ that realizes "p and not-q," a stimuli producer that provides a source of stimuli, a rigid member that serves as a frame for the construction of the automaton, a fusing organ that solders parts together, a cutting organ that disconnects soldered parts, a muscle that moves parts and brings them together, feelers that identify parts, and a battery that supplies energy. See von Neumann (1966, p. AB 484–485) for further details. Also see Burks's unpublished account, "Historical Analysis of von Neumann's Theories of Artificial Self-Reproduction," 23 November 1960 (ATBB).

105. Von Neumann (1966, p. AB 486).

106. Von Neumann points to Keynesian probability theory and quantum mechanics as two fields in which a logical theory is similarly extended to a probabilistic theory. See Keynes (1921), von Neumann "Quantum Logics (Strict and Probability Logics)" (1937) in Taub (1962, 4: 195–197), von Neumann and Birkhoff (1936), and von Neumann and Morgenstern (1944, sec. 3.3.3).

107. McCulloch claims that von Neumann was motivated to develop a probabilistic theory of automata by a lecture given by Walter Pitts on randomly connected nets at one of the 1946 meetings of the Macy Conference on Cybernetics (McCulloch 1965, p. 11; originally published as "What Is a Number, That a Man May Know It, and a Man, That He May Know a Number" in 1961). In the following few pages McCulloch gives a critique of the underlying assumptions of von Neumann's theory and claims that von Neumann was himself upset about them. These assumptions are that failures are absolute (not dependent on the strength of signals or the thresholds of neurons), that all neurons are assumed to have two inputs, and that each neuron computes the same function (the Sheffer stroke) so that there is not the same differentiation among idealized neurons as one finds in nature.

108. Von Neumann (1966, p. AB 462).

109. Von Neumann cited the work of Boltzmann, Hartley, and Szilard in the first case and Shannon and Richard Hamming in the second. It is interesting that von Neumann placed Hartley's work with the work on entropy. Aspray (1985) shows that Shannon's theory of communication followed directly on this same work of Hartley.

110. Von Neumann (1966, p. AB 465).

111. Dr. R. S. Pierce took notes on the lectures and wrote up an account, which von Neumann revised slightly. It is this revised account that is available to us today. Von Neumann's results were also popularized in Goldstine (1953).

Von Neumann thanked K. A. Brueckner and M. Gell-Mann "to whose discussion in 1951 he owes some important stimuli on this subject" (von Neumann 1952, p. AB 553). Professor Brueckner (private communication, 8 February 1988) explained the situation: "The contact between von Neumann and Gellmann and me occurred in the summer of 1951 at the University of Illinois. Gellmann and I were participants in a summer study organized, I believe, by Professor Sid Dancoff, funded by DoD. The general problem concerned radar systems working in a noisy environment. There were several other participants in the study, including physicists, engineers, biophysicists and M.D.s, mostly from the University of Illinois.

"Gellmann and I decided to look at the problem in the nervous system in the brain operating at high precision and very high reliability with components of nonzero failure rate. This seemed to us to require very elaborate 'voting' and self-checking procedures. Accordingly we were developing the mathematical procedures to quantify this idea. When von Neumann visited the study, we asked him for his ideas and suggestions. He responded immediately and within an hour had started to outline the ideas he later followed; remarkable evidence of his grasp and quick comprehension of the problem.

"Gellmann and I thought no more about the problem after the summer of 1951 and were of course impressed by von Neumann's further development."

112. Von Neumann (1952, p. AB 553).

113. Arthur Burks (private communication, 27 January 1988) has pointed out that neither the set of primitives consisting of "or," "and," and "a and not-b" nor the majority organ is complete because neither set of primitives can produce a one from a zero. Burks also noted that von Neumann assumed and used a pulse clock in his account as a source of ones.

114. He meant by feedback that pulses can be returned to a neuron through which they had previously passed by means of a closed circuit of lines between neurons. Curiously, von Neumann wrote equivalently of obeying intuitionistic logic and being Turing computable. The unlimited memory is supposed to be supplied by an analog of Turing's infinite tape: "an infinite tape, and scanners connected to afferent organs, along with suitable efferent organs to perform motor operations and/or print on the tape." (von Neumann 1952, p. AB 565).

115. Clearly, $\varepsilon < \delta$ unless some measure to check errors is taken.

116. In another section of this paper, von Neumann considered methods for controlling error in single line automata but at the expense of three times as many basic organs as for the same reliability in a multiplexed automaton. At the end of the paper he suggested a method for using bundles of lines, like multiplexing does, but not processing the bundles in the all-or-none, digital fashion of multiplexing. In this alternative scheme, a neuron would use the ratio of the number of stimulated lines to the total number of lines in the bundle as its input rather than interpreting the input as one (bundle stimulated) or zero (bundle not stimulated). Von Neumann showed how addition can be realized simply in this system and how the system can calculate any continuous function of the closed unit interval into itself but that the accuracy can not exceed $1/N$, where N is the number of lines in the bundle.

117. The functions of these two organs are likened, respectively, to those tubes in computers that carry out logical functions (rectification, gating, or coincidence) and those that amplify signals.

118. The conditions von Neumann assumed in his calculation for the computer are that it is composed of 2500 vacuum tubes actuated every 5 microseconds and has a desired overall reliability of 8 hours mean time between failures. The calculations for the nervous system are done in several ways under several sets of assumptions but in each case assume there are 10^{13} neurons each actuated 10 times per second.

119. Von Neumann (1952, p. AB 592).

120. See Burks (1970, p. 99, n. 17).

121. For a review of developments in the theory of reliable computation by machines built from unreliable components, see Pippenger (forthcoming). Some of the leading researchers are N. Pippenger, R. L. Dobrushin and S. I. Ortyukov, P. Gacs, B. S. Cirelson, T. Feder, M. G. Taylor, D. Uhlig, and S. Winograd.

122. This manuscript in its edited, completed form is the second half of *Theory of Self-Reproducing Automata* (pp. 91–377).

123. Burks (1966, p. 94). In VNLC, there are cover letters of 27 and 28 October 1952 to O. Morgenstern, A. Taub, and S. Ulam sent with the introductory chapter, which set out the program for the rest of the manuscript. An undated handwritten reply from Ulam states that he is returning the first chapter with comments. He makes some suggestions about how von Neumann might mathematically implement the ideas in the introductory chapter. The ideas Ulam presents are similar to those von Neumann gives in his later chapters, but it is impossible to tell the influence Ulam's letter had on von Neumann's thinking.

In the same file is a cover letter, dated 24 November 1952, to Ulam sending a second chapter, which presents the basic cellular model. In the letter von Neumann points out that he has yet to write up the material on the excitation-fatigue and self-reproducing models or provide any of the constructions or the proof of universality of his automata. A distribution list indicates that copies of chapter 2 were sent for review to Julian Bigelow, Herman Goldstine, Abraham Taub, Oskar Morgenstern, Stan Ulam, Eugene Wigner, and John Kemeny.

124. Part of the agreement concerning von Neumann's lectures on complicated automata at the University of Illinois in December 1949 was that he would prepare them for publication by the University of Illinois Press. He felt an obligation to deliver this manuscript but was pressed by his other duties. On 27 July 1951 he wrote to his friend Oskar Morgenstern, "I think my Illinois lectures will take a year or so to appear—primarily because I have to write them first." On 5 December 1951 von Neumann wrote apologetically to Miodrag Muntyan, the director of the University of Illinois Press, to inform him that his pressing government commitments were interfering with the completion of the manuscript and ask if there was any alternative way in which he could fulfill his obligation. With the assistance of Abraham Taub, a professor of mathematics at Illinois and close friend of von Neumann, a new arrangement was made for von Neumann to submit his manuscript on the theory of automata in lieu of the lectures on complicated automata. Von Neumann to Muntyan, 4 November 1952; von Neumann to Taub, 13 November 1952, VNLC. In the end, von Neumann never finished either manuscript, and they were published together posthumously.

125. Ulam (1950) describes the cellular idea and credits it to his discussions with von Neumann.

126. Julian Bigelow and Herman Goldstine convinced von Neumann to work with two- instead of three-dimensional cellular structures. Two-dimensional arrays are easier to work with, and any finite automaton in cellular three-space can be mapped to an equivalent structure within cellular two-space. Von Neumann 1966, pp. 110–111; also confirmed by the author in independent conversations with Goldstine and Bigelow in 1986 and 1987.

127. That is, there is a fixed number of units of time delay before the automaton processes the information about its own state and those of the contiguous cells.

128. Burks has pointed out that, in such a system, each cell must have facility for switching, output delay, internal memory, and feedback to control incoming signals. In the fourth Vanuxem Lecture, von Neumann gave an example of a neuron with threshold 2 and fatigue period 6 that had most of the desired properties. Von Neumann 1966, p. 96.

129. Burks points out the similarity between this model and work Alan Turing carried out in the 1950s on morphogenesis in which Turing presented differential equations that govern chemical processes associated with the operation and formation of biological organs. See Turing (1952).

130. Von Neumann (1966, p. 91).

131. A useful summary of von Neumann's answers to these questions is given by Arthur Burks in Von Neumann (1966, pp. 286–296).

132. This is a paraphrase of the questions von Neumann sets out at the beginning of his manuscript. Von Neumann 1966, p. 92.

133. Arthur Burks shows that the class of automata constructible by the universal constructing automata is a proper subclass of the class of automata that can be described by an initial cell assignment. See von Neumann (1966, p. 291) for details. There is also a problem of certain automata self-destructing if one attempts to build them from within by means of the methods von Neumann provides. An example is given in figure 13b (von Neumann 1966, p. 316).

Von Neumann never completed the design of his universal constructor, but Burks completed it along von Neumann's lines in chapter 5 of *Theory of Self-Reproducing Automata*. Burks's student, James Thatcher, produced an alternative design. See Thatcher (1966).

134. Von Neumann (1966, p. 131).

135. Others moved toward more efficient designs. For example, see Burks (1970), McNaughton (1961), Holland (1965), and Codd (1968).

136. Letter to Goldstine, 28 October 1952, VNLC.

137. Letter to Miodrag Muntyan, an editor at the University of Illinois Press, 4 November 1952, VNLC. Arthur Burks noted this same point in von Neumann (1966, p. 279).

138. Burks carefully describes the nature of these inaccuracies and suggests how they might be corrected, either by technical comments in the text or by pointing the reader to published literature where these issues are addressed.

139. Von Neumann (1958).

140. At least at one point, Warren McCulloch did not believe that the Atlantic City talk was the basis for the Silliman Lectures because of their difference in substance. McCulloch to Arthur Burks, 6 December 1960, WMAP. The evidence leads incontrovertibly to the conclusion that the Atlantic City talk was indeed the origin. Since von Neumann's ideas evolved over time and the Silliman lectures were never completed, the difference in content that McCulloch remarked upon can be explained easily.

141. Maurice H. Greenhill (program organizer) to Warren McCullough [*sic*], 12 February 1955; von Neumann to McCulloch, 17 February 1955, WMAP.

142. Von Neumann to Herbert S. Bailey, Jr. (director, Princeton University Press), 26 October 1955, VNLC.

143. This is taken from page 129 of an unidentified manuscript, dated 15 October 1957, in WMAP. The top of the document is labeled "XVI. Neurophysiology." Below are listed the names W. S. McCulloch, R. C. Gesteland, W. H. Pitts, E. M. Duchane, J. Y. Lettvin, and P. D. Wall. Below that is listed a section title, "A. Three of Von Neumann's Biological Questions," and the section is signed by McCulloch. A footnote indicates that this was research supported by Bell Telephone Laboratories, Inc., the Teagle Foundation, Inc., and the National Science Foundation.

144. Warren McCulloch to Arthur Burks, 6 December 1960, WMAP.

145. Von Neumann to Dennis Flanagan (editor, *Scientific American*), 24 June 1955, VNLC.

146. Von Neumann to Flanagan, 26 October 1955, VNLC.

147. Memorandum of telephone conversation with Flanagan, 2 November 1955, VNLC. According to von Neumann's letter to Bailey of 26 October 1955, Flanagan was continuing to pressure von Neumann for an article or a series of articles, but von Neumann was convinced that the more appropriate form of presentation was a book. He discussed publishing the book with Princeton University Press but decided that his time commitments were such that he must use the material for his obligated Silliman Lectures publication.

148. Von Neumann (1957 p. 1).

149. Ibid. (p. 2).

150. Here are some typical examples of the estimates von Neumann gave in comparison: neuron response time including recovery of 1.5×10^{-2} seconds versus vacuum tube response of 10^{-6} or 10^{-7} seconds (ratio of 10^4 or 10^5 in favor of the computer); cell membrane size of 10^{-5} centimeters versus vacuum tube grid-to-cathode distance of 10^{-1} or 10^{-2} centimeters, or transistor distance between whisker electrodes of 10^{-2} centimeters (so ratio of 10^3 in favor of the brain); and energy dissipation (which approximates closely energy consumption) of 10^{-9} watts in a neuron, 5–10 watts in a vacuum tube, and 10^{-1} watts in a transistor (so a ratio of 10^8 or 10^9 in favor of the brain).

Von Neumann argued that the computer has greater memory requirements (because of its serial organization) but also greater precision (because of the brain's use of analog, frequency modulation techniques to represent numerical values).

151. Von Neumann also suggested (p. 2) that study of the nervous system "may alter the way in which we look on mathematics and logic proper."

152. Some participants in the cybernetic movement were the electrical engineers Claude Shannon and Denis Gabor, the physiological psychologists Warren McCulloch and Arturo Rosenblueth, the mathematicians Stephen Kleene, John von Neumann, and Alan Turing, and others, including Ross Ashby.

153. Wiener (1961, 1948 introduction).

154. Julian Bigelow (private communication, 6 November 1987). See Aspray (1985) for a survey of the work of six of the main participants in the cybernetic program: McCulloch, Pitts, Shannon, Turing, von Neumann, and Wiener.

155. Von Neumann's sympathy with the cybernetic program is evident in his review of Wiener's book, which appeared in *Physics Today* in 1949. In a letter to Wiener dated 4 September 1949 (NWMI), von Neumann wrote: "I hope I need not tell you what I think of 'Cybernetics,' and, more specifically, of your work on the theory of communications: We have discussed this many times, I hope we shall discuss it many more times, and I have even published my 'appraisal' (as a book review in 'Physics Today'). Hardly any two people ever agree 100% on hardly anything, but I think that we agree more-than-average on this subject."

156. This conclusion is from Burks (1984). The term *postmodern* science has also been used for this change.

157. Allanson and Whitfield (1956). Another example in this same vein is the work of Williams and Weddell described earlier.

158. See, for example, Bremermann (1962) or Quastler (1953, 1957, 1959).

159. For a survey of this work, see Harmon (1962a, 1962b) and Rosenblatt (1962, historical introduction).

160. See, for example, Maitra (1960), McCulloch (1959), and McCulloch, Arbib, and Cowan (1962).

161. Penrose (1959). In Penrose (1960) the author interprets his mechanical model in chemical terms and applies what he has learned from the mechanical model to the question of RNA and DNA replication.

Moore (1964a) describes a kinematic model of self-reproduction inspired by von Neumann's work, built by Homer Jacobson of Brooklyn College. It consists of a train of scale-model railroad cars, which hold individual parts and accomplish control by electrical circuits mounted in each car. When a train of different kinds of cars is arranged in a particular sequence and placed on a particular track layout, the train will move around bumping unattached cars, rearranging them on sidings, and coupling them in its own image. Jacobson designed one train model for trains of arbitrary length and built a demonstration model two cars long.

162. See, for example, Muroga (1962) and Moore (1964b), respectively. One of the leading figures in the development of theoretical computer science, John Hopcroft, has indicated that he does not believe that von Neumann played an important role in the development of the central areas of theoretical computer science (e.g., automata and complexity theory). Private communication, 11 April 1988. That is probably a fair assessment. Certainly von Neumann did not have any fundamental results, like those of Turing on computability, that could become a foundation for these new theoretical subjects. However, a survey of the literature of this field for the 1960s uncovered a number of references to von Neumann's work. Thus, it is

also probably fair to state that his results were part of the context in which these theoretical disciplines originated. Von Neumann's influence on the development of other theoretical disciplines, including cellular automata and reliable machine design, is much more significant. This assessment has been corroborated by Michael Arbib (private communication, 1989), one of the early theoretical computer scientists.

163. See, for example, Allanson (1959), Blum (1960), Cowan (1960), McCulloch (1960b), Muroga (1960), and Verbeek (1960).

164. The first attempts to apply Hamming's error-correcting codes to von Neumann's ideas were made by Cowan (1960), Eden (1959), Elias (1958), and Peterson and Rabin (1959). More successful was the extension by Winograd and Cowan (1963) of Shannon's noisy channel coding theorem to the case of noisy computation. Winograd and Cowan provide an overview of these efforts.

165. The best example is Burks (1970), which includes papers by Burks, Holland, and Thatcher of the Michigan group and also by Moore, Myhill, and Ulam. The papers by Ulam and collaborators are interesting for their heuristic use of the computer to investigate growth patterns in cellular automata. Also see Langton (1986) for his reexamination of von Neumann's work in the light of later contributions to the study of "artificial life" (artificial systems that exhibit behavior characteristics of natural living systems).

Chapter 9

1. In Britain, Douglas Hartree came closest to meeting these two criteria.

2. I will not trace von Neumann's role as a consultant to Los Alamos. It might be possible to do so in part from a set of correspondence from 1947 and 1948 about this subject in VNLC. Of particular interest is a seven-page single-spaced letter dated 7 October 1947 in which von Neumann advised the laboratory director Norris Bradbury on the development of a computing program, choice of computer hardware, personnel needs, and some individuals who might be available to fill these positions. On von Neumann's role in hiring Nicholas Metropolis to run the computer operations at Los Alamos, see Bradbury's letter of 24 June 1948 and von Neumann's reply of 2 July.

3. Two interviews with Harry Polachek describe the computing work in army and navy laboratories during and in the decade following the war (interviews of 24 March 1970 and 23 April 1970, conducted by Richard R. Mertz, OHSM). Dr. Polachek was well positioned to describe this work. During the war he worked first for Army Ordnance at Aberdeen and then for Navy Ordnance. After the war he worked for the Naval Ordnance Laboratory and then the David Taylor Model Basin. At the first three of these he came into contact with von Neumann. Polachek described, for example, doing a complicated calculation for von Neumann in 1944 using IBM multipliers at the Navy Bureau of Ordnance and Bureau of Ships concerning the motion of a fluid in the area of a cylindrical explosion; other calculations he, von Neumann, and Raymond Seeger made during the war on shock waves, their interaction, and their reflection; and his verification on a desk calculator of von Neumann's paper-and-pencil calculation of the height at which to detonate an atomic bomb in order to take advantage of the Mach effect and thereby maximize the blast's impact.

4. G. A. E. Hindman (Navy Department, Bureau of Ordnance, Section Re 2) to von Neumann, 24 April 1945, memorandum, Subject: Computing Service," VNLC.

5. Memo: Von Neumann to Re 2, Re: Computing Service, 27 August 1945, HSRC.

6. Some of von Neumann's findings might surprise today's readers who believe that computers rapidly swept aside all previous computing technologies. Von Neumann found something positive about every type of machine except those used in fire control. Differential analyzers were recommended for use in problems involving continuously increasing independent variables and those with implicit functions. Standard IBM equipment was regarded as generally deficient in its degree of automation, flexibility, and plugboard setup procedure but useful for its wide availablity. Harvard Mark I, although considered to reflect "in many details the state of the relay- and tape-techniques of 5 and more years ago," was argued to be well designed and useful still. The larger Bell Labs relay machines were judged to be useful complements to the ENIAC for their effective automatic checking and straightforward control. Harvard Mark II, still two years from completion, was anticipated to be a first-rate device. ENIAC was praised for its electronic speed and EDVAC for its smaller size, greater speed, larger internal memory, and advanced logical control.

7. See von Neumann to Richard S. Burlingame, Navy Bureau of Ordnance, 1 February 1951, VNLC, in which he described the value of a high-speed computing machine for use by the navy in calculating air flows and shock waves, multidimensional flows in incompressible media such as water, elasticity and plasticity of solid structures attacked by blast waves, deflagration and detonation of high explosives, the aerodynamics of missile design, and the basic properties of atomic weapons and motors. Von Neumann also described the design objectives of the proposed NORC. The history of NORC and an assessment of NORC's value in moving the technology to a new plateau are given in Bashe et al. (1986).

In an oral history conducted 24 March 1970, Harry Polachek described von Neumann's role as a consultant to IBM and the navy in the design of the NORC. Polachek described von Neumann as playing an important role in conversations about the design of the computer's architecture, the speed requirements, and the selection of input-output equipment. Interview by Richard R. Mertz, OHSM.

8. Von Neumann also had an important impact on the ONR. Mina Rees, head of ONR's Mathematics Section after the war, has indicated that she relied heavily on von Neumann's advice on computers and that he had a practice of visiting her each time he came to Washington. Oral history, 20 October 1972, conducted by Henry Tropp, OHSM.

9. Franz Alt, in an interview of 12 September 1972 with Henry Tropp, OHSM, described the postwar computing environment at Aberdeen: the types of personnel and machines used and the self-education process the staff went through.

10. Von Neumann to Aydelotte, 11 October 1945, HGAP.

11. The memorandum is dated 30 January 1945, as is von Neumann's letter to Simon, both in VNLC.

12. See von Neumann to L. Dederick, 12 October 1945, and an undated memorandum by von Neumann and Goldstine, "Recommended Changes in BTL Machine," both VNLC. Also see Haskell Curry to Goldstine asking him and von Neumann to

write up the changes they had discussed for the BTL machine, 12 September 1945, HSRC. "Recommended Changes" is probably the response to Curry's request.

13. See the Summary Report of the Conference on the EDVAC Held 9 October [1944] at Aberdeen Proving Ground, Maryland; Report on Meeting, Ballistic Research Laboratory, 9 October 1946; "EDVAC 1.5"; Memo: EDVAC 1.5—Submission of Brief Description Proposal for, Irven Travis to Colonel G.F. Powell (Office of the Chief of Ordnance), 28 October 1946; and a letter from von Neumann to Powell, 5 November 1946, all in HSRC.

14. R. F. Clippinger makes the connection between these events explicit in "Adaptation of the ENIAC to Von Neumann's Coding Technique," summary of a paper delivered at the meeting of the Association for Computing Machinery, Aberdeen, Maryland, December 11–12, 1947; summary written 15 March 1948, SANB.

W. Barkley Fritz, "A Survey of ENIAC Operations and Problems 1946–1952" (Ballistic Research Laboratories, Memorandum Report No. 617, August 1952, HGAP), made a different claim for the origins of von Neumann's ideas: that in early 1948 Richard Clippinger and his colleagues at BRL were trying to use the ENIAC to solve a system of five simultaneous hyperbolic partial differential equations, that the size of the problem forced them to use the ENIAC in a novel way to make the problem fit involving coding for parallel operations using numerical information from the function tables for logical control, and that this was the origin of von Neumann's idea to make the ENIAC into a stored-program machine. Clippinger gave an account, consonant with that of Fritz, in an interview of 17 December 1970 conducted by Richard R. Mertz (archives, NMAH, OHSM). However, it appears that von Neumann already had the idea by the beginning of 1948, when this problem was to have been programmed.

Also see the description given by Goldstine in a letter to Douglas Hartree, 18 July 1947, and a different version given by Nicholas Metropolis (1980, p. 459).

15. Von Neumann to Ulam, 27 March 1947, HSRC.

16. See Goldstine (1971, p. 233). He refers to a report I was unable to locate: "Description and Use of the ENIAC Converter Code, Ballistic Research Laboratories, Technical Note No. 141, November 1949. Elizabeth Holberton, Nicholas Metropolis, and Homer Spence also seem to have contributed to the implementation. Private communication, Arthur Burks, 27 January 1988.

17. Clippinger, interview.

18. See "Actual Technique—The Use of the ENIAC," unpublished, n.d., anonymous report (1948?), VNLC.

19. See von Neumann to Ulam, 11 May 1948, HSRC.

20. Von Neumann to R. H. Kent, 13 June 1947, VNLC. Von Neumann spread the knowledge of this new programming method to more than 300 people in his keynote address in late 1947 at the first national meeting of the Association for Computing Machinery in Aberdeen. Franz Alt (1972, p. 694) describes von Neumann's talk: "He mentioned the 'new programming method' for ENIAC and explained that its seemingly small vocabulary was in fact ample: that future computers, then in the design stage, would get along on a dozen instruction types, and this was known to be adequate for expressing all of mathematics. . . . Von

Neumann went on to say that one need not be surprised at this small number, since about 1,000 words were known to be adequate for most situations of real life, and mathematics was only a small part of life, and a very simple part at that. This caused some hilarity in the audience, which provoked von Neumann to say: 'If people do not believe that mathematics is simple, it is only because they do not realize how complicated life is.'"

21. Von Neumann to Weaver, 15 January 1944, HSRC.

22. Some of these, involving Schilt at Columbia, have been discussed earlier. See, for example, von Neumann to Warren Weaver (AMP, NDRC), 6 February 1945, HSRC.

23. See, for example, the memo from S. Feltman (Office of the Chief of Ordnance) to the CO, Aberdeen Proving Ground, 17 April 1945; J. H. Frye (Office of the Chief of Ordnance) to Warren Weaver (AMP, NDRC), 8 May 1945; von Neumann to Haskell B. Curry (BRL Ordnance Department), 20 August 1945, all in HSRC.

24. See the account in Goldstine (1972, pp. 215–216).

25. There is an extensive paper trail of the committee in VNLC. The most significant of these records are the following: Minutes of the Meeting of the Committee, 23 April 1947; Memorandum to the N.R.C. Committee on High-Speed Computing by the Subcommittee Appointed to Consider Several High-Speed Computing Machine Proposals for the National Bureau of Standards, 12 March 1948; von Neumann to Marston Morse, 16 May 1951.

26. Interestingly, the committee decided unanimously at its 23 April 1947 meeting that it was not yet time to form an association of people interested in the new technology, as the one-of-a-kind conferences such as that held at MIT in 1945 and at Harvard in early 1947, were sufficient. Minutes of meeting, VNLC. See also Revens (1987), which quotes von Neumann's letter of 15 September 1947 regarding the newly formed Association for Computing Machinery: "As you may know, my personal opinion was, and still is, that such an association is a highly desirable one ultimately but that the general situation has not yet matured sufficiently to make the present moment the optimum one to found it. This does not mean, however, that I will not be very glad if you succeed in furnishing the proof of the opposite, and I want to use this occasion to wish you the best of luck in your efforts." Von Neumann never became a member of the ACM.

27. Some of von Neumann's work with the Standard Oil companies is described in chapter 5. He did work under this contract for Standard Oil of New York City, Esso Standard Oil of Linden, New Jersey, Humble Oil of Baytown, Texas, and Carter Oil of Tulsa, Oklahoma. The work included statistical, mathematical, and numerical analyses of flow calculation problems. An extensive correspondence relating to this work and some consultants' reports are in VNLC.

Another example of von Neumann's consulting on computers for industry was the advice he gave in 1950 to Northrop Aircraft about its Magnetic Digital Differential Analyzer (MADDIDA). See, in particular, von Neumann to John K. Northrop, 14 March 1950, on the soundness of the design and engineering embodiment, and his twenty-one-page letter to L. A. Ohlinger about further applications of the machine, both in VNLC.

28. Retainer Agreement: Von Neumann and IBM, 1 May 1945, VNLC.

29. See Lt. Colonel Chas. E. Herrstrom (Ordnance Department) to Chief, Research and Development, Patent Branch, Legal Division of 4 August 1945, memorandum, "Proposed Agreement between Consultant for U.S. Government and IBM"; also see Robert A. Lavender (OSRD) to Herrstrom, 31 July 1945, VNLC.

30. See von Neumann to W. J. Eckert, 6 March 1946, VNLC, who had initiated the consulting offer.

31. The information given here about von Neumann and IBM, except when noted otherwise, is taken from a private conversation with Cuthbert Hurd on 3 March 1989, in which he repeated and expanded on information he gave to Nancy Stern in an oral history of 20 January 1981, OH 76, OHCB.

32. See John McPherson (IBM vice-president) to von Neumann, 5 October 1951, and the attached consulting contract. The contract also called for additional days of consulting over thirty to be compensated at $400 per day.

33. See L. H. Thomas, "J. Von Neumann's views on the desirability of drums for the N.O.R.C. as expressed at a conference with H. Polachek and L.H. Thomas, 29/2/52," and von Neumann's letter to Thomas, 5 March 1952, about Thomas's report, VNLC.

34. Von Neumann pointed out that the only technical disadvantage of his proposal was that it led to an overall reduction of storage capacity, but he viewed this as insignificant because this machine would not be used to solve problems involving three-dimensional point-net approximations (which consume large quantities of memory).

Cuthbert Hurd remembers similar discussions with von Neumann about trade-offs between different kinds of memory configurations. At that time IBM was working on a new 4K reliable cathode ray tube memory based on the spot-ditch method. Von Neumann did calculations and suggested a 512-word internal memory and an 8K drum instead.

35. Private communication, 19 September 1989. Sheldon mentioned specifically a discussion he, von Neumann, John Greenstadt, and others had on a general method for triangularizing matrices and other discussions on iterative methods for solving boundary value partial differential equations. Sheldon also said that IBM had little call at the time for expert help in numerical analysis since L. H. Thomas was already on the IBM staff with this expertise.

36. Enclosure in von Neumann to Cuthbert Hurd, 11 November 1954, VNLC.

37. This topic is discussed in Bashe et al. (1986, pp. 420ff.). I also discussed it privately with John Palmer and Lyle Johnson of the IBM Technical History Project in November 1988, Stephen Dunwell in February 1989, and Cuthbert Hurd in March 1989.

38. The argument in the text summarizes a position taken by Stephen Dunwell (private communication, February 1989). Lyle Johnson and John Palmer (private communication, 20 November 1989) have indicated that this analysis perhaps oversimplifies the cause-and-effect analysis by ignoring customer preferences as well as an initial step in this direction in the marketing of the IBM 709 system.

39. For further information, see Bashe et al. (1986, pp. 421–422).

40. The speech is published in von Neumann's *Collected Works* (5: 238–247). An audiotape of the speech, one of the very few extant recordings of von Neumann, is in VNLC.

41. By this time von Neumann had received an appointment to the Atomic Energy Commission.

42. According to Hurd, this idea came to von Neumann after he had met a man in Los Angeles (probably from Hughes) who was able to produce 1000 megacycle wave signals—ones fast enough to serve as one of the sources for his discrete subharmonics. Von Neumann's subharmonic generator is described in Aspray and Burks (1987, pp. 313–315). Goto (1959) developed a similar idea a few years later.

43. Hurd remembers the following people as being present at these meetings: himself, von Neumann, Byron Havens, Robert Walker, John Lentz, and perhaps Wallace Eckert and L. H. Thomas.

44. There is a contract dated 14 October 1954 for the patent "Non-linear Capacitance or Inductance Switching, Amplifying and Memory Organs." Also see von Neumann to R. A. Anderson, 3 December 1954, VNLC, describing the patent he sold to IBM and his prior plans for developing it with some computer manufacturer.

   In early 1955, when von Neumann left the institute for the AEC, the institute trustees awarded him $25,000 and a scroll. Strauss was a trustee and was probably behind the award of this gift. Minutes, Special Meeting of the Executive Committee of the Board of Trustees, 30 July 1956, FASC.

45. The general story about the negotiations with the Japanese government over IBM-Japan is told in an interview with James Birkenstock conducted by Erwin Tomash and Roger Stuewer, 12 April 1980, OH 4, OHCB.

46. *New York Times* (24 October 1955).

47. It is not clear whether this problem was run on the computer over the opposition of then IAS director Robert Oppenheimer. Oppenheimer was against thermonuclear research, and we know that he had several long discussions with von Neumann about this matter. Whether he tried to influence the use of the institute computer for this research is unknown. The IAS calculation was the first extensive calculation of a thermonuclear bomb. In fact, the coding was ready a year and a half before the computer. However, the first such bomb built at Los Alamos was of a different design. Private communication, Carson Mark, 28 May 1987.

48. "Nomination of John von Neumann to be a Member of the United States Atomic Energy Commission," 8 March 1955, hand-corrected draft of testimony, VNLC.

49. Strauss stated that he had wanted von Neumann to serve on the commission for a long time and asked him at the first vacancy. He also claims that von Neumann consented at once when asked if he would be willing to be nominated. Ulam tells a different story: von Neumann knew of his scientific colleagues' worries over McCarthyism, the Oppenheimer security hearing, and the extreme attitudes of Strauss, and he was concerned that by joining the commission he would alienate these colleagues, many of them already unhappy with his heavy involvement with the AEC, Los Alamos, and bomb design. Ulam tells of a long conversation he had

with von Neumann in which von Neumann stated how flattered he was as a foreign born to be asked to serve, how he felt he could contribute, and how Strauss was pressuring for acceptance. See Strauss to Ulam, 12 November 1957, and Ulam's study of von Neumann, "Johnny Becomes an AEC Commissioner," SUAP.

50. See *Scientific American* (December 1954, pp. 52–53).

51. See Unna (1955). The term was to end 30 June 1959.

52. Ibid. (p. 7E).

53. "AEC Policy for Support of High-Speed Computers and Their Development," memorandum, 20 February 1956, AECA.

54. Ibid.

55. One positive step he did take, however, was to hire John Pasta in 1956 to the AEC Division of Research. Pasta shared von Neumann's view of the importance of computers in atomic energy research. For further information about Pasta, see Curtis et al. (1983).

56. See the cover letter of 16 March 1956 by Colonel Vincent Ford (who was attending to von Neumann's scientific work in the hospital) to a letter of 6 March 1956 on New York University Computing Facilities, DOEA.

57. For example, on 1 September 1955 von Neumann met with Cuthbert Hurd, Stephen Dunwell, and Lloyd Hunter to discuss new technologies for the Stretch: continuous transition layer transistors, the concurrent flux method for improving speed limitations in magnetic core memory, and the characteristics of a machine that could be built with these technologies. Von Neumann, Memorandum for the Record, Re: Conference, September 1, 1955, with Representatives of IBM Company on their High-Speed Machines Proposal, VNLC. Cuthbert Hurd (private communication, 3 March 1989) indicated that on several visits to von Neumann's Washington home they discussed these matters and von Neumann expressed his support of both the Stretch and LARC projects.

58. Von Neumann made a similar point as a consultant to the IBM 704 project when he stated that more than 1000 words of primary memory was "frivolous." Interview with Nathaniel Rochester, 24 July 1973, conducted by Henry S. Tropp, NMAH, OHSM.

59. See von Neumann to Sidney Fernbach, 5 October 1955, and Edward Teller to von Neumann, 28 October 1955, in support of Fernbach. Von Neumann had written, "Possibly a shortage of satisfactory planners and coders might justify facilitating those activities by providing such a large and expensive primary memory. Yet, I would think that in 2½ years (when LARC is to be delivered) we should have succeeded in raising the standard, or the availability of skill in those departments." Teller replied that he was doubtful that the programming problem would be solved in two and a half years, that in fact he saw it as getting worse. Teller also unsuccessfully lobbied Commissioner von Neumann to build both a LARC and a Stretch for each of Los Alamos and Livermore (letter, 22 April 1955). All in VNLC.

60. Ulam study, "Johnny Was Anti-Russian," SUAP.

61. The account given here is drawn largely from Vincent T. Ford to Ulam, 4 May 1970, SUAP; Gilpin (1962); Von Braun and Ordway (1969); and Von Karman (1967).

62. Other members of the committee were Hendrik Bode, Louis Dunn, Lawrence Hyland, George Kistiakowsky, Charles Laurintsen, Clark Millikan, Allen Puckett, Simon Ramo, Jerome Wiesner, and Dean Wooldridge.

63. President Eisenhower had a high regard for von Neumann. He awarded him the Medal of Freedom in 1956 and arranged for him to have a special room in Walter Reed Hospital in Bethesda, Maryland, for the last nine months of his life. The importance of von Neumann to this program can be seen from the fact that Air Force Colonel Vincent Ford and eight airmen were assigned to von Neumann while he was in Walter Reed Hospital.

64. See von Neumann to Deane Montgomery, 22 March 1956, VNLC. Apparently von Neumann had been giving thought to leaving the IAS for some time. In a letter to his wife, Klara, on Friday, August 28 [1953 probably, since August 28 was a Friday that year], he mentioned that he had been working for several years toward an appointment in California and that that was part of his reason for establishing consulting relations with the RAND Corporation and Livermore laboratory (all VNLC).

65. Ulam claims that Strauss arranged the contact with the University of California only to cheer von Neumann up; he did not believe von Neumann would recover from his cancer. Biographical study, "Coversations with Johnny Towards the End of His Life," SUAP. Von Neumann also received and gave "very serious" consideration to an offer from MIT for an "Institute professorship." See von Neumann to MIT president James Killian, 24 February 1956, VNLC.

66. See Sproul's offer to von Neumann of 5 February 1956 and von Neumann's acceptance letter, 19 March 1956, VNLC.

67. Von Neumann to University of California president Robert Sproul, 21 February 1956, VNLC. Von Neumann requested that he not be located at the UCLA computing center, emphasizing his interest in being a user rather than a developer or maintainer of computer hardware. Memorandum to President Sproul, Re: Professor John von Neumann, 21 November 1955, VNLC.

68. See UCLA chancellor Raymond Allen to von Neumann, 23 November 1955, and von Neumann to Paul Dodd (dean, College of Letters and Science, UCLA), 26 March 1956.

Herman Goldstine and James Pomerene left IAS for IBM, although Goldstine retained his IAS affiliation. Julian Bigelow remained at the institute.

General Bibliography

This bibliography contains only works cited in the text or used directly in its preparation. A more comprehensive bibliography relating to von Neumann and the context of his computing work can be found in William Aspray and Arthur Burks, eds., *Papers of John von Neumann on Computing and Computer Theory* (Cambridge: MIT Press and Los Angeles: Tomash Publishers, 1987).

Abbe, Cleveland. 1893. *The Mechanics of the Earth's Atmosphere.* Miscellaneous Collections, vol. 34. Washington, DC: Smithsonian.

Alexander, Franz. 1960. *The Western Mind in Transition: An Eyewitness Story.* New York: Random House.

Allanson, J. T. 1959. The Reliability of Neurons. *Proceedings of the First International Congress on Cybernetics,* pp. 687–694. Paris: Gauthier-Villars.

Allanson, J. T., and I. C. Whitfield. 1956. The Cochlear Nucleus and Its Relation to Theories of Hearing. In Colin Cherry, ed., *Information Theory,* pp. 269–286. Papers read at a Symposium on "Information Theory" held at the Royal Institution, London, 12–16 September, 1953. New York: Academic Press.

Alt, Franz. 1972. Archaeology of Computers—Reminiscences, 1945–1947. *Communications of the Association for Computing Machinery* 15 (July), pp. 693–694.

Anderson, Herbert L. 1986. Metropolis, Monte Carlo, and the MANIAC. *Los Alamos Science* 14 (Fall), pp. 96–107.

Anderson, Herbert L. 1986. Scientific Uses of the MANIAC. *Journal of Statistical Physics* 43, pp. 731–748.

Anon. 1955. Von Neumann, John. *Current Biography Yearbook,* pp. 624–624.

Arbib, Michael A. 1969. Automata Theory as an Abstract Boundary Condition for the Study of Information Processing in the Nervous System. In K. N. Leibovic, ed., *Information Processing in the Nervous System,* pp. 3–19. New York: Springer-Verlag.

Ashby, W. R. 1947. The Nervous System as a Physical Machine: With Special Reference to the Origins of Adaptive Behavior. *Mind* 56, pp. 113–127.

Ashby, W. R. 1952. *Design for a Brain.* New York, Wiley.

Ashby, W. R. 1956. *Introduction to Cybernetics.* New York, Wiley.

Ashford, Oliver M. 1985. *Prophet—or Professor? The Life and Work of Lewis Fry Richardson.* Bristol and Boston: Adam Hilger.

Aspray, William. 1985. The Scientific Conceptualization of Information: A Survey. *Annals of the History of Computing* 7, pp. 117–140.

Aspray, William, ed. 1985. *Proceedings of a Symposium on Large-Scale Digital Calculating Machinery.* Cambridge, MA: MIT Press and Los Angeles/San Francisco: Tomash Publishers.

Aspray, William. 1986. International Diffusion of Computer Technology, 1945–1955. *Annals of the History of Computing* 8 (October), pp. 351–360.

Aspray, William. 1987. The Mathematical Reception of the Modern Computer: John von Neumann and the Institute for Advanced Study Computer. In Esther R. Phillips, ed., *Studies in the History of Mathematics*, pp. 166–194. Washington, DC: Mathematical Association of America.

Aspray, William. 1988. The Emergence of Princeton as a World Center for Mathematical Research, 1896–1939. In William Aspray and Philip Kitcher, eds., *History and Philosophy of Modern Mathematics*, pp. 346–366. Minneapolis: University of Minnesota Press.

Aspray, William, ed. 1990. *Computing before Computers.* Ames: Iowa State University Press.

Aspray, William, and Arthur Burks, eds. 1987. *Papers of John von Neumann on Computing and Computing Theory.* Cambridge, MA: MIT Press.

Barricelli, Nils Aall. 1962. Numerical Testing of Evolution Theories: Part I, Theoretical Introduction and Basic Tests. *Acta Biotheoretica* 16, pp. 69–98.

Barricelli, Nils Aall. 1963. Numerical Testing of Evolution Theories: Part II, Preliminary Tests of Performance. Symbiogenesis and Terrestrial Life. *Acta Biotheoretica* 16, pp. 99–126.

Barto, Andrew G. 1975. Cellular Automata as Models of Neural Systems. Ph.D. dissertation, University of Michigan.

Bashe, Charles J., Lyle R. Johnson, John H. Palmer, and Emerson W. Pugh. 1986. *IBM's Early Computers.* Cambridge, MA: MIT Press.

Bates, Charles C., and John F. Fuller. 1986. *America's Weather Warriors, 1814–1985.* College Station: Texas A&M University Press.

Benes, J. 1980. Whither Cybernetics: Past Achievements and Future Prospects. *Kybernetes* 9, pp. 283–288.

Bernkopf, Michael. 1966. The Development of Function Spaces with Particular Reference to their Origins in Integral Equation Theory. *Archive for the History of Exact Sciences* 3, pp. 1–96.

Bigelow, Julian. 1980. Computer Development at the Institute for Advanced Study. In N. Metropolis, J. Howlett, and Gian-Carlo Rota, eds., *A History of Computing in the Twentieth Century*, pp. 291–310. New York: Academic Press.

Birkhoff, Garrett. 1958. Von Neumann and Lattice Theory. *Bulletin of the American Mathematical Society* 64, pp. 50–56.

Birkhoff, Garrett. 1981. Fifty Years of Numerical Linear Algebra. In Martin H. Schultz, ed., *Elliptic Problem Solvers.* Orlando, Florida: Academic Press.

Birkhoff, Garrett. 1983. Numerical Fluid Dynamics. *SIAM Review* 25, 1 (January), pp. 1–34.

Birkhoff, Garrett. 1990. Fluid Dynamics, Reactor Computations, and Surface Representations. In Stephen G. Nash, ed., *A History of Scientific Computation*, pp. 72–101. Reading, MA: Addison-Wesley.

Birkhoff, Garrett. Forthcoming. *History of Numerical Fluid Dynamics.*

Birkhoff, Garrett, and M. K. Bennett. 1987. Hilbert's "Grundlagen der Geometrie." *Rendiconti del Circolo Matematico di Palermo* ser. 2, 36, pp. 343–389.

Birkhoff, Garrett, Herman H. Goldstine, and E. H. Zarantello. 1953–1954. Calculation of Plane Cavity Flows Past Curved Obstacles. *Universita e Politecnico di Torino Rendiconti del Seminario Matematico* 13, pp. 205–224.

Birkhoff, Garrett, and Surender Gulati. 1979. Isotropic Distributions of Test Matrices. *Journal of Applied Mathematics and Physics* 30, pp. 148–158.

Birkhoff, Garrett, D. P. MacDougall, E. Pugh, and Sir Geoffrey Taylor. 1948. Explosives with Lined Cavities. *Journal of Applied Physics* 19, pp. 563–582.

Birkhoff, George D. 1931. Proof of the Ergodic Theorem. *Proceedings of the National Academy of Sciences* 17, pp. 656–660.

Birkhoff, George D., and B. O. Koopman. 1932. Recent Contributions to the Ergodic Theory. *Proceedings of the National Academy of Science* 18, pp. 279–282.

Bjerknes, J. 1964. Half a Century of Change in the "Meteorological Scene." *Bulletin of the American Meteorological Society* 45, 6 (June), 312–315.

Bjerknes, Vilhelm. 1904. Das problem der Wettervorhersage, betrachtet von Standpunkte der Mechanik und der Physik. *Meteorologische Zeitschrift* 21, 1–7.

Bjerknes, Vilhelm. 1914. Meteorology as an Exact Science. *Monthly Weather Review* 42, pp. 11–14.

Bjerknes, Vilhelm 1919. Wettervorhersage. *Meteorologische Zeitschrift, Braunschweig* 36, p. 68.

Bjerknes, Vilhelm, J. Bjerknes, H. Solberg, and T. Bergeron. 1934. *Hydrodynamique physique avec applications à la meteorologie dynamique.* Paris: Les Presses Universitaires.

Bjerknes, Vilhelm, T. Hesselberg, and O. Devik. 1911. *Kinematics.* pt. II of *Dynamic Meteorology and Hydrography.* Publication 88. Washington, DC: Carnegie Institution.

Blachman, Nelson M. 1953. *A Survey of Automatic Digital Computers.* Washington, DC: Office of Naval Research.

Blair, Clay, Jr. 1957. Passing of a Great Mind. *Life*, 25 February, pp. 89–104.

Blum, Manuel. 1960. Properties of a Neuron with Many Inputs. In *Bionics Symposium: Living Prototypes—the Key to New Technology*, pp. 55–82. Wright Air Development Division Technical Report 60–600 (December).

Blum, Manuel. 1962. Properties of a Neuron with Many Inputs. In H. von Foerster and G. Zopf, *Principles of Self-Organization*, pp. 95–119. New York: Pergamon.

Boardman, Robert C. 1952. New Computer Able to Do 100,000 Additions a Second. *New York Herald Tribune*, 11 June, p. 2.

Bonhoeffer, K. F. 1948. Activation of Passive Iron as a Model for the Excitation of Nerve. *Journal of General Physiology* 32(1), 20 September, pp. 69–91.

Born, Max, and Norbert Wiener. 1926. A New Formulation of the Laws of Quantization of Periodic and Aperiodic Phenomena. *Journal of Mathematics and Physics* 5, pp. 84–98.

Bremermann, H. J. 1962. Optimization through Evolution and Recombination. In Marshall C. Yovits, George T. Jacobi, and Gordon D. Goldstine, eds., *Self-Organizing Systems 1962*, pp. 93–106. Washington, DC: Spartan.

Brillouin, Leon. 1956. *Science and Information Theory.* New York: Academic Press.

Brode, H. L. 1954. Numerical Solutions of Spherical Blast Waves. Report P-571-AEC. Santa Monica: RAND.

Brode, H. L. 1955, Numerical Solutions of Spherical Blast Waves. *Journal of Applied Physics* 26, pp. 766–775.

Bronowski, Jacob. 1973. *The Ascent of Man.* Boston: Little, Brown.

Brunt, David. 1951. A Hundred Years of Meteorology (1851–1951). *Advancement of Science* 8, pp. 114–124.

Burks, Arthur W. 1950. The Logic of Programming Electronic Digital Computers. *Industrial Mathematics* 1, pp. 36–52.

Burks, Arthur W. 1960. Computation, Behavior, and Structure in Fixed and Growing Automata. In Marshall C. Yovits and Scott Cameron, eds., *Self-Organizing Systems*, pp. 282–311. Proceedings of an Interdisciplinary Conference, 5–6 May 1959. New York: Pergamon.

Burks, Arthur W. 1963. Towards a Theory of Automata Based on More Realistic Primitive Elements. In *Proceedings of the IFIP Congress 62*, pp. 379–385. Amsterdam: North-Holland.

Burks, Arthur W. 1966. *Theory of Self-reproducing Automata.* Urbana: University of Illinois Press.

Burks, Arthur W. 1970. *Essays on Cellular Automata.* Urbana: University of Illinois Press.

Burks, Arthur W. 1984. Computers, Control, and Intentionality. In Donald M. Kerr, ed., *Science, Computers, and the Information Onslaught*, pp. 29–55. New York: Academic Press.

Burks, Arthur W. 1986. A Radically Non–von Neumann Architecture for Learning and Discovery. In Wolfgang Handler, Dieter Haupt, Rolf Jeltsch, Wilfried Juling, and Otto Lange, eds., *CONPAR 86: Conference on Algorithms and Hardware for Parallel Processing*, pp. 1–17. Proceedings, Aachen, 17–19 September, 1986. Lecture Notes in Computer Science. Berlin: Springer-Verlag.

Burks, Arthur W., and Alice R. Burks. 1981. The ENIAC: First General-purpose Electronic Computer. *Annals of the History of Computing* 3, pp. 310–399.

Bush, Vannevar. 1970. *Pieces of the Action.* New York: William Morrow.

Byers, Horace R. 1959. Carl-Gustaf Rossby, the Organizer. In Bert Bolin, ed. *The Atmosphere and the Sea in Motion*, pp. 56–59. New York: Rockefeller Institute Press.

Campbell, Jeremy. 1982. *Grammatical Man.* New York: Simon and Schuster.

Ceruzzi, Paul. 1983. *Reckoners.* Westport, CT: Greenwood.

Charney, Jule. 1947. The Dynamics of Long Waves in a Baroclinic Westerly Current. *Journal of Meteorology* 4, 5 (October), pp. 135–162.

Charney, Jule. 1948. On the Scale of Atmospheric Motions. *Geofysiske Publikasjoner* 17, no. 2.

Charney, Jule. 1949. On a Physical Basis for Numerical Prediction of Large-Scale Motions in the Atmosphere. *Journal of Meteorology* 6, 6 (December), pp. 371–385.

Charney, Jule. 1954. Numerical Prediction of Cyclogenesis. In *Proceedings of the National Academy of Science* 40, 2, pp. 99–110.

Charney, Jule. 1955. Numerical Methods in Dynamical Meteorology. In *Proceedings of the National Academy of Science* 41, 11 (November), pp. 798–802.

Charney, Jule. 1960. Numerical Prediction and the General Circulation .In Richard L. Pfeffer, ed., *Dynamics of Change*, pp. 12–17. New York: Pergamon.

Charney, Jule. 1972. Impact of Computers on Meteorology. *Computer Physics Communications* 3, Supp., pp. 117–126.

Charney, Jule, and Arnt Eliassen. 1949. A Numerical Method for Predicting the Perturbations of the Middle Latitude Westerlies. *Tellus* 1, pp. 38–54.

Charney, Jule, and Norman A. Phillips. 1953. Numerical Integration of the Quasigeostrophic Equations for Barotropic and Simple Baroclinic Flows. *Journal of Meteorology* 10, pp. 71–99.

Cherry, E. C. 1952. The Communication of Information (an Historical Review). *American Scientist* 40, 4, pp. 640–664.

Cherry, E. C. 1957. *On Human Communication.* Cambridge, MA: MIT Press.

Chu, J. C. 1980. Computer Development at Argonne National Laboratory. In N. Metropolis, J. Howlett, and Gian-Carlo Rota, eds., *A History of Computing in the Twentieth Century*, pp. 345–346. New York: Academic Press.

Codd, E. F. 1964. Propagation, Computation, and Construction in Two-Dimensional Cellular Spaces. Technical Report 06921-1-T, ORA. Ann Arbor: University of Michigan.

Codd, E. F. 1968. *Cellular Automata.* New York: Academic Press.

Courant, Richard, Karl Friedrichs, and Hans Lewy. 1928. Uber die partiellen Differenzengleichungen der Mathematischen Physik. *Mathematische Annalen* 100, pp. 32–74.

Cowan, Jack D. 1960. Toward a Proper Logic for Parallel Computation in the Presence of Noise. *Bionics Symposium: Living Prototypes—the Key to New Technology*, pp. 93–152. Wright Air Development Division Technical Report 60-600. December.

Cowan, Jack D. 1962. Many Valued Logics and Reliable Automata. In H. von Foerster and G. Zopf, eds., *Principles of Self-Organization.* pp. 135–179. New York: Pergamon.

Curtis, Kent K., Nicholas C. Metropolis, William G. Rosen, Yoshia Shimamoto, and James N. Snyder. 1983. John R. Pasta, 1918–1981—An Unusual Path toward Computer Science. *Annals of the History of Computing* 5, pp. 224–238.

Dantzig, George B. 1963. *Linear Programming and Extensions.* Princeton, NJ: Princeton University Press.

Dantzig, George B. 1984. Reminiscences about the Origins of Linear Programming. *Memoirs of the American Mathematical Society* 48, pp. 1–11.

Dantzig, George B. Forthcoming. Origins of the Simplex Method. In Stephen G. Nash, ed., *A History of Scientific Computation*, pp. 164–176. Reading, MA: Addison-Wesley.

Davis, Martin. 1987. Mathematical Logic and the Origin of Modern Computers. In Esther R. Phillips, ed., *Studies in the History of Mathematics*, 26: 137–165. Mathematical Association of America Studies in Mathematics. Washington, DC: Mathematical Association of America.

Davis, Philip J. 1988. The State and Dreams of Numerical Analysis (with Some Recollections of Rods and Bones). *SIAM News* (May), pp. 6, 18–19.

de Latil, Pierre. 1957. *Thinking by Machine.* Boston: Houghton Mifflin.

Devik, Olaf, Tor Bergeron, and Carl Ludvig Godske. 1963. Vilhelm Bjerknes. *Geofysiske Publiksjoner* 24, 7–25.

Dieudonne, J. 1976. Von Neumann, Johann (or John). *Dictionary of Scientific Biography* 14: 88–92.

Dirac, P. A. M. 1930. *The Principles of Quantum Mechanics.* Oxford: Clarendon.

Douglas, C. K. M. 1952. The Evolution of 20th-Century Forecasting in the British Isles. *Quarterly Journal of the Royal Meteorological Society* 78, 335 (January), pp. 1–20.

Dunsany, Lord. 1951. *The Last Revolution.* London: Jarrolds.

Dyson, Freeman. 1979. *Disturbing the Universe.* New York: Harper & Row.

Eady, E. T. 1952. Note on Weather Computing and the So-called 2 1/2 Dimensional Model. *Tellus* 4, pp. 157–167.

Eckert, Wallace J. 1948. The IBM Pluggable Sequence Relay Calculator. *Mathematical Tables and Other Aids to Computation* 23 (July), pp. 149–161.

Eden, Murray. 1959. A Note on Error Detection in Noisy Logical Computers. *Information and Control* 2, pp. 310–313.

Elias, Peter. 1958. Computation in the Presence of Noise. *IBM Journal of Research and Development* 2, pp. 346–353.

Eliassen, Arnt. 1952. Simplified Dynamic Models of the Atmosphere, Designed for the Purpose of Numerical Prediction. *Tellus* 4, pp. 145–156.

Feynman, Richard. 1982. Los Alamos from Below. *Annals of the History of Computing* 4 (January), pp. 61–63.

Fleming, Donald, and Bernard Bailyn, eds. 1969. *The Intellectual Migration.* Cambridge, MA: Belknap Press of Harvard University Press.

Forsythe, George E., and P. Henrici. 1960. The Cyclic Jacobi Method for Computing the Principal Values of a Complex Matrix. *Transactions of the American Mathematical Society* 94, pp. 1–23.

Forsythe, George E., and Richard A. Leibler. 1950. Matrix Inversion by a Monte Carlo Method. *Mathematical Tables and Other Aids to Computation* 4, pp. 127–129.

Fox, L., H. D. Huskey, and J. H. Wilkinson. 1948. Notes on the Solution of Algebraic Linear Simultaneous Equations. *Quarterly Journal of Mechanics and Applied Mathematics* 1, pp. 149–173.

Fraenkel, Abraham A. 1967. The Notion of "Definite" and the Independence of the Axiom of Choice. In *From Frege to Gödel*, pp. 285–289. Edited by J. van Heijenoort. 1967. Cambridge, MA: Harvard University Press.

Frechet, Maurice. 1953. Commentary on the Three Notes of Emile Borel. *Econometrica* 21, pp. 118–127. (Includes communication on the Borel notes from John von Neumann).

Friedman, Robert Marc. 1978. "Vilhelm Bjerknes and the Bergen School of Meteorology, 1918–1923." Ph.D. dissertation, Johns Hopkins University.

Frisinger, H. Howard. 1974. Mathematicians in the History of Meteorology: The Pressure-Height Problem from Pascal to Laplace. *Historia Mathematica* 1, pp. 263–286.

Fustoss, Laszlo. 1984. *Ortvay Rudolf.* Budapest: Akademia Kiado (Hungarian Academy of Sciences).

Gardner, Howard. 1985. *The Mind's New Science: A History of the Cognitive Revolution.* New York: Basic Books.

Gilpin, Robert. 1962. *American Scientists and Nuclear Weapons Policy.* Princeton: Princeton University Press.

Gilstrap, L. O., and R. J. Lee. 1961. Learning Machines. In *1st Bionics Symposium: Living Prototypes—The Key to New Technology*, pp. 437–450. Wright Air Development Division Technical Report 60-600. 13–15 September.

Goldstine, Herman H. 1951. Numerical Inverting of Matrices of High Order. II. In *Proceedings of the American Mathematical Society* 2, pp. 188–202.

Goldstine, Herman. 1953a. Some Experience in Coding and Programing with the Institute Computer. In *Symposium on Large Scale Digital Computing Machinery, Proceedings*, pp. 273–278. U.S. Atomic Energy Commission ANL-5181.

Goldstine, Herman H. 1953b. Some Remarks on Logical Design and Programming Checks. In *1953 Eastern Joint Computer Conference Proceedings*, pp. 96–98.

Goldstine, Herman H. 1957. On the Relation between Machine Developments and Numerical Analysis. *Bonner Mathematische Schriften* 2–3, pp. 1–7.

Goldstine, Herman H. 1972. *The Computer from Pascal to von Neumann.* Princeton: Princeton University Press.

Goldstine, Herman H. 1990. Remembrance of Things Past. In Stephen G. Nash, ed., *A History of Scientific Computing*, pp. 5–19. Reading, MA: Addison-Wesley.

Goldstine, Herman H., and J. Gillis. 1955. On the Stability of Two Superposed Compressible Fluids. *Annali di Mathematica Pura ed Applicata* ser. 4, 40, pp. 261–267.

Goldstine, Herman H., and Adele Goldstine. 1946. The Electronic Numerical Integrator and Computer (ENIAC). *Mathematical Tables and Other Aids to Computation* 2, pp. 97–110.

Goldstine, Herman H., and Eugene P. Wigner. 1957. Scientific Work of John von Neumann. *Science*, 12 April, pp. 683–684.

Goto, E. 1959. The Parametron, a Digital Computing Element Which Utilizes Parametric Oscillation. In *Proceedings of the Institute of Radio Engineers* 47, pp. 1304–1316.

Grafton, Samuel. 1956. Married to a Man Who Believes the Mind Can Move the World. *Good Housekeeping* (September), pp. 80–81, 282–292.

Gregory, Robert T. 1953. Computing Eigenvalues and Eigenvectors of a Symmetric Matrix on the ILLIAC. *Mathematical Tables and Other Aids to Computation* 7, pp. 215–220.

Gruenberger, F. J. 1968. *The History of the JOHNNIAC.* Memorandum RM-5654-PR. Santa Monica, CA: RAND Corporation, October.

Haar, Alfred. 1933. Der Massbegriff in der Theorie der Kontinuierlichen Gruppen. *Annals of Mathematics* 34, pp. 147–169.

Halmos, Paul R. 1958. Von Neumann on Measure and Ergodic Theory. *Bulletin of the American Mathematical Society* 64, pp. 86–94.

Halmos, Paul R. 1973. The Legend of John von Neumann. *American Mathematical Monthly* 80, pp. 382–394.

Halmos, Paul R. 1985. *I Want to Be a Mathematician.* New York: Springer-Verlag.

Hammersley, John M., and D. C. Handscomb. 1964. *Monte Carlo Methods.* London: Methuen.

Harmon, Leon D. 1962a. Neural Analogs. In *Proceedings of the Spring Joint Computer Conference*, pp. 153–158.

Harmon, Leon. 1962b. Natural and Artificial Synapses. In Marshall C. Yovits, George T. Jacobi, and Gordon D. Gondstein, eds., *Self-Organizing Systems 1962*, pp. 177–202. Washington, DC: Spartan.

Harraway, Donna J. 1981–1982. The High Cost of Information in Post–World War II Evolutionary Biology: Ergonomics, Semiotics, and the Sociobiology of Communication Systems. *Philosophical Forum* 13 (Winter–Spring), pp. 244–278.

Hartley, R. V. 1928. Transmission of Information. *Bell System Technical Journal* 7, 535–553.

Hawkins, J. K. 1961. Self-Organizing Systems—A Review and Commentary. In *Proceedings of the Institute of Radio Engineers* 49, 1, 31–48.

Heims, Steve P. 1975. Encounter of Behavioral Sciences with New Machine-Organism Analogies in the 1940's. *Journal of the History of the Behavioral Sciences* 11, pp. 368–373.

Heims, Steve P. 1977. Gregory Bateson and the Mathematicians: From Interdisciplinary Interaction to Societal Functions. *Journal of the History of the Behavioral Sciences* 13, pp. 141–159.

Heims, Steve J. 1980. *John von Neumann and Norbert Wiener: From Mathematics to the Technologies of Life and Death.* Cambridge, MA: MIT Press.

Helmholtz, H. von. 1889. Uber atmospharische Bewegungen: II. Zur Theorie von Wind und Wellen. *Nachrichten von der Gesellschaft der Wissenschaften zu Gottingen* 3, 309–332.

Herald Tribune Bureau. 1957. John von Neumann Dies; Helped to Create H-Bomb. *New York Herald Tribune*, 9 February, p. 10.

Hewes, Laurence Ilsley, and Herbert Lee Seward. 1923. *Design of Diagrams for Engineering Formulas and the Theory of Nomography.* New York: McGraw-Hill.

Hilbert, David. 1904. On the Foundations of Logic. In *From Frege to Gödel*, pp 129–138. Edited by J. van Heijenoort. Cambridge, MA: Harvard University Press.

Hilbert, David. 1912. Begrundung der Kinetischen Gastheorie. *Mathemtische Annalen* 72, pp. 562–577.

Hilbert, David. 1935. Begrundung der elementaren Strahlungstheorie. *Gesammelte Abhandlungen* 3, pp. 217–289. Berlin: Verlag von Julius Sperlag.

Hodges, A. 1983. *Alan Turing: The Enigma.* New York: Simon & Schuster.

Holland, John. 1965. Universal Embedding Spaces for Automata. In Norbert Wiener and J. P. Schade, eds., *Cybernetics of the Nervous System*, pp. 223–243. Progress in Brain Research, vol. 17. New York: Elsevier.

Hopcroft, John E. 1987. Computer Science: The Emergence of a Discipline. *Communications of the ACM* 30, 3 (March), pp. 198–202.

Hopf, Eberhard. 1937. *Ergoden Theorie.* Berlin: J. Springer.

Hotelling, Harold. 1943. Some New Methods in Matrix Calculation. *Annals of Mathematical Statistics* 14, pp. 1–34.

Hughes, Patrick. 1970. *A Century of Weather Service: A History of the Birth and Growth of the National Weather Service, 1870–1970.* New York: Gordon and Breach.

Hurd, Cuthbert C., ed. 1950. *Seminar on Scientific Computation.* New York: International Business Machines Corporation.

Hurwicz, Leonid. 1945. The Theory of Economic Behavior. *American Economic Review* 35, pp. 909–925.

Hyman, M. A. 1947. *Stability of Finite Difference Representation.* Mechanics Division Technical Note SB/Tm-18.2-11. Silver Spring, MD: Naval Ordnance Laboratory, White Oak, 16 October.

Jackson, Willis. 1950. *Symposium on Information Theory: Report of Proceedings.* London: Ministry of Supply.

Jeffress, Lloyd A. 1951. *Cerebral Mechanisms in Behavior.* The Hixon Symposium. New York: John Wiley.

Jewell, Ralph. 1981. The Bergen School of Meteorology. *Bulletin of the American Meteorological Society* 62, 6 (June), pp. 824–830.

Kadison, Richard V. 1958. Theory of Operators, Part II. Operator Algebras. *Bulletin of the American Mathematical Society* 64, pp. 61–85.

Kaplansky, Irving. 1977. *Hilbert's Problems.* Preliminary ed. Chicago: University of Chicago Department of Mathematics, Lecture Notes in Mathematics.

Kemeny, John G. 1955. Man Viewed as a Machine. *Scientific American* (April), pp. 58–67.

Kendall, M. G., and B. Babbington Smith. 1939. *Tables of Random Sampling Numbers.* Tracts for Computers, 24. Cambridge: Cambridge University Press.

Keynes, J. M. 1921. *A Treatise on Probability.* London: Macmillan.

Khrgian, Aleksander Khristoforovich 1970. *Meteorology: A Historical Survey.* Vol. I. Jerusalem: Israel Program for Scientific Translations.

Kinoshita, Toichiro. 1957. Ground State of the Helium Atom. *Physical Review* 105, pp. 1490–1502.

Knuth, Donald E. 1970. Von Neumann's First Computer Program. *Computing Surveys* 2 (December), pp. 247–260.

Koestler, Arthur. 1952. *Arrow in the Blue: An Autobiography.* New York: Macmillan.

Koestler, Arthur. 1954. *The Invisible Writing.* New York: Macmillan.

Kuhn, H. W., and A. W. Tucker. 1958. John von Neumann's Work in the Theory of Games and Mathematical Economics. *Bulletin of the American Mathematical Society* 64, pp. 100–122.

Kutzbach, Gisela. 1979. *The Thermal Theory of Cyclones: A History of Meteorological Thought in the Nineteenth Century.* Boston: American Meteorological Society.

Lane, J. A., R. G. Thomas, and E. P. Wigner. 1955. Giant Resonance Interpretation of the Nucleon-Nucleus Interaction. *Physical Review* 98, pp. 693–701.

Langton, Christopher G. 1986. Studying Artificial Life with Cellular Automata. *Physica* 22D, pp. 120–149.

Langton, Christopher G. 1989. *Artificial Life.* Redwood City, CA: Addison-Wesley.

Legendi, Tamas, and Tibor Szentivanyi. 1983. *Leben und Werk von John von Neumann.* Mannheim, Wien, Zurich: Bibliographisches Institut.

Lettvin, J. Y., H. R. MaTorana, W. S. McCulloch, and W. H. Pitts. 1959. What the Frog's Eye Tells the Frog's Brain. In *Proceedings of the Institute of Radio Engineers* 47, 11, pp. 1940–1959.

Leutert, Werner. 1951. On the Convergence of Approximate Solutions of the Heat Equation to the Exact Solution. In *Proceedings of the American Mathematical Society* 2, pp. 433–439.

Lofgren, Lars. 1958. Automata of High Complexity and Methods of Increasing Their Reliability by Redundancy. *Information and Control* 1, 127–147.

Luce, Robert Duncan, and Howard Raiffa. 1957. *Games and Decisions.* New York: Wiley.

McCagg, William O., Jr. 1972. *Jewish Nobles and Geniuses in Modern Hungary.* New York: Columbia University Press.

McCulloch, Warren S. 1945. A Heterarchy of Values Determined by the Topology of Nervous Nets. *Bulletin of Mathematical Biophysics* 7, pp. 89–93.

McCulloch, Warren S. 1947. How We Know Universals: The Perception of Auditory and Visual Forms. *Bulletin of Mathematical Biophysics* 9, pp. 127–147.

McCulloch, Warren S. 1950. Brain and Behavior. In W. C. Halstead, ed., *Comparative Psychology*, pp. 39–50. Berkeley: University of California Press.

McCulloch, Warren S. 1952. *Finality and Form in Nervous Activity.* Publication No. 11. American Lecture Series. Springfield, IL: Thomas.

McCulloch, Warren S. 1957. Biological Computers. *Transactions of the Institute of Radio Engineers* (September), pp. 190–192.

McCulloch, Warren S. 1958. The Stability of Biological Systems. *Brookhaven Symposia in Biology No. 10, Homeostatic Mechanisms* (May), pp. 207–215.

McCulloch, Warren S. 1959. Agatha Tyche of Nervous Nets—the Lucky Reckoners. *National Physical Laboratory Symposium No. 10, Mechanization of Thought Processes* 2, pp. 613–633.

McCulloch, Warren S. 1960a. What Puzzles Me Most? In H. von Foerster and G. Zopf, Jr., eds., *Principles of Self-Organization*, pp. 91–94. New York: Pergamon.

McCulloch, Warren S. 1960b. The Reliability of Biological Systems. In Marshall C. Yovits and Scott Cameron, eds., *Self-Organising Systems*, pp. 264–281. Proceedings of an Interdisciplinary Conference, 5–6 May, 1959. New York: Pergamon.

McCulloch, Warren S. 1961. What Is a Number, That a Man May Know It, and a Man, That He May Know a Number? *General Semantics Bulletin* 26–27, pp. 7–18.

McCulloch, W. S. 1965. *Embodiments of Mind.* Cambridge, MA: MIT Press.

McCulloch, Warren S., Michael A. Arbib, and Jack D. Cowan. 1962. Neurological Models and Integrative Processes. In Marshall C. Yovits, George T. Jacobi, and Gordon D. Goldstein, eds., *Self-Organizing Systems 1962*, pp. 49–59. Washington, DC: Spartan.

McCulloch, W. S., and W. Pitts. 1943. A Logical Calculus of the Ideas Immanent in Nervous Activity. *Bulleltin of Mathematical Biophysics* 5, pp. 115–133.

McDonald, John. 1950. *Strategy in Poker, Business, and War.* New York: W. W. Norton.

Mackey, George W. 1957. Quantum Mechanics and Hilbert Space. *American Mathematical Monthly* 64 (October), pp. 45–57.

McNaughton, Robert. 1961. On Nets Made of Badly Timed Elements. Part I: Slow But Perfectly Timed Elements. Mimeographed. Philadelphia: Moore School of Electrical Engineering, University of Pennsylvania.

Maitra, K. K. 1960. Synthesis of Reliable Automata and Stable Neural Nets. In *Bionics Symposium: Living Prototypes—The Key to New Technology,* pp. 353–394, December. Wright Air Development Division Technical Report 60-600.

Makarov, V., and A. Rubinov. 1987. Von Neumann Technology. In John Eatwell, Murray Milgate, and Peter Newman, eds., *The New Palgrave: A Dictionary of Economics*, 4: 824–826 New York: Stockton.

Marschak, Jakob. 1946. Neumann's and Morgenstern's New Approach to Static Economics. *Journal of Political Economy* 54, pp. 97–115.

Mauchly, John. 1979. Amending the ENIAC Story. *Datamation* (October), pp. 217–220.

Maxwell, James Clerk. 1875. *Theory of Heat.* London: Longman, Green.

Metropolis, Nicholas 1980. The MANIAC. In N. Metropolis, J. Howlett, and Gian-Carlo Rota, eds., *A History of Computing in the Twentieth Century*, pp. 457–464. New York: Academic Press.

Metropolis, Nicholas, and E. C. Nelson. 1982. Early Computing at Los Alamos. *Annals of the History of Computing* 4 (October), pp. 348–357.

Mintz, Yale. 1966. A Collection of Papers Related to the 1966 NMC Primitive-Equation Model. Technical Memorandum 9. Washington, DC: Environmental Science Services Administration, Weather Bureau, Western Region.

Moore, Edward F. 1964a. Mathematics in the Biological Sciences. *Scientific American* 211, pp. 149–163.

Moore, Edward F. 1964b. *Sequential Machines.* Reading, MA: Addison-Wesley.

Moore, Edward F., and Claude E. Shannon. 1956. Reliable Circuits Using Less Reliable Relays. *Journal of the Franklin Institute* 262, pt. 1. (September), 191–208, pt. 2. (October), pp. 281–297.

Moore, Gregory H. 1986. Gödel and Cohen: The Origins of Forcing. In *Logic Colloquium 86*. Proceedings of the Colloquium held in Hull, U.K., 13–29 July. Edited by F. R. Drake and J. Kitruss. New York: Holland.

Morgenstern, Oskar. 1958. Obituary. John von Neumann, 1903–1957. *Economic Journal* 68, pp. 170–174.

Morgenstern, Oskar. 1968. Von Neumann, John. *International Encyclopedia of the Social Sciences* 16, pp. 385–387.

Morgenstern, Oskar. 1976. The Collaboration between Oskar Morgenstern and John von Neumann on the Theory of Games. *Journal of Economic Literature* 14, 2 (September), pp. 805–816.

Morishima, Michio. 1964. *Theory of Growth: The von Neumann Revolution*. Technical Report No. 130. Stanford, CA: Institute for Mathematical Studies in the Social Sciences, Stanford University.

Morse, Philip M. 1977. *In at the Beginnings: A Physicist's Life*. Cambridge, MA: MIT Press.

Mukhopadhyay, Amar. 1968. Representation of Events in the von Neumann Cellular Model. *ACM Journal* 15, pp. 693–705.

Mulholland, H. P. 1952. On the Distribution of a Convex Even Function of Several Independent Rounding-Off Errors. *Proceedings of the American Mathematical Society* 3, pp. 310–321.

Muroga, Saburo. 1960. Preliminary Study of the Probabilistic Behavior of a Digital Network with Majority Decision Elements. Technical Note 60–146. Rome, NY: Rome Air Development Center.

Muroga, Saburo. 1962. Majority Logic and Problems of Probabilistic Behavior. In Marshall C. Yovits, George T. Jacobi, and Gordon D. Goldstine, eds., *Self-Organizing Systems 1962*, pp. 243–261. Washington, DC: Spartan.

Murray, F. J. 1958. Theory of Operators. Part I. Single Operators. *Bulletin of the American Mathematical Society* 64, 3, pt. 2, pp. 57–60.

Nagy, Denes, Ferenc Nagy, and Peter Horvath. 1987. The Computer, the Brain, and the Missing Link (In Memoriam John von Neumann). Pamphlet. Budapest-Tempe: National Technical Information Centre and Library.

Namias, Jerome. 1968. Long Range Weather Forecasting—History, Current Status and Outlook. *Bulletin of the American Meteorological Society* 49, 5 (May), pp. 438–470.

Nash, Stephen G., ed. 1990. *A History of Scientific Computation*. Reading, MA: Addison-Wesley.

Nebeker, Frederik. 1989. The 20th-Century Tranformation of Meteorology. Ph.D. dissertation, Princeton University.

New York Times Staff. 1952. Machine to Figure Impact of Defense. *New York Times*, 15 June, p. 21.

New York Times Staff. 1954a. Oppenheimer Friend Named to the A.E.C. *New York Times*, 24 October , pp. 1, 5.

New York Times Staff. 1954b. New Atomic Aide Sees Lag in Power. *New York Times*, 25 October, p. 15.

New York Times Staff. 1957. Dr. Von Neumann of A.E.C., 53, Dies. *New York Times,* 9 February, p. 19.

Nyce, James M., and Paul Kahn. 1989. Innovation, Pragmatism, and Technological Continuity: Vannevar Bush's Memex. *Journal of the American Society for Information Science* 40, pp. 214–220.

Nyquist, H. 1924. Certain Factors Affecting Telegraph Speed. *Bell System Technical Journal* 3, pp. 324–346.

O'Brien, George C., Morton A. Hyman, and Sidney Kaplan. 1950. A Study of the Numerical Solution of Partial Differential Equations. *Journal of Mathematics and Physics* 29, pp. 223–239.

Oncken, Wilhelm. 1878–1892. ed. *Allgemeine Geschichte in Ginzeldarstellungen.* Berlin: G. Grote'sche Verlagsbuchhandlung.

Pasta, John R., and S. Ulam. 1959. Heuristic Numerical Work in Some Problems of Hydrodynamics. *Mathematical Tables and Other Aids to Computation* 13, 65 (January), pp. 1–12.

Peaceman, Donald W. 1990. A Personal Retrospection of Reservoir Simulation. In Stephen G. Nash, ed., *A History of Scientific Computation.* pp. 124–150. Reading, MA: Addison-Wesley.

Pekeris, C. L. 1972. Adventures in Applied Mathematics. *Quarterly Journal of Applied Mathematics* 30 (April), pp. 67–83.

Penrose, L. S. 1959. Automatic Mechanical Self-Reproduction. *New Biology* 28, pp. 92–117.

Penrose, L. S. 1960. Developments in the Theory of Self-Replication. *New Biology* 31, pp. 57–66.

Peterson, Victor L. 1984. Impact of Computers on Aerodynamics Research and Development. *Proceedings of the IEEE* 72, 1 (January), 68–79.

Peterson, W. W., and M. O. Rabin. 1959. On Codes for Checking Logical Operations. *IBM Journal of Research and Development* 3, 2 (April), pp. 163–168.

Pfeffer, Richard L. 1956. *Dynamics of Climate.* Proceedings of a Conference on the Application of Numerical Integration Techniques to the Problem of the General Circulation held 26–28 October, 1955. New York: Pergamon.

Phillips, Norman A. 1951. A Simple Three-Dimensional Model for the Study of Large-Scale Extratropical Flow Patterns. *Journal of Meteorology* 8, pp. 381–394.

Phillips, Norman A. 1956. The General Circulation of the Atmosphere: A Numerical Experiment. Royal Meterological Society, *Quarterly Journal* 82, 352 (April), 123–164

Pierce, J. R. 1973. The Early Days of Information Theory. *IEEE Transactions on Information Theory* IT-19, pp. 3–8.

Pippenger, Nicholas. 1990. Developments in "The Synthesis of Reliable Organisms from Unreliable Components." In John Impagliazzo and James Glimm, eds., *The Legacy of John von Neumann.* Providence, RI: American Mathematical Society.

Pitts, Walter, and Warren S. McCulloch. 1947. How We Know Universals: The Perception of Auditory and Visual Forms. *Bulletin of Mathematical Biophysics* 9, pp. 127–147.

Platzman, George W. 1967. A Retrospective View of Richardson's Book on Weather Prediction. *Bulletin of the American Meteorological Society* 48, 8 (August), 514–550.

Platzman, George W. 1968. Richardson's Weather Prediction. *Bulletin of the American Meteorological Society* 49, 5 (May), pt. 1, pp. 496–500.

Platzman, George W. 1979. ENIAC Computations of 1950: Gateway to Numerical Weather Prediction. *Bulletin of the American Meteorological Society* 60, 4, (April), pp. 302–312.

Pope, D., and C. Tompkins. 1957. Maximizing Functions of Rotations—Experiments Concerning Speed of Diagonalization of Symmetric Matrices Using Jacobi's Method. *Journal of the Association of Computing Machinery* 4, pp. 459–466.

Porter, Laura Smith. 1988. From Intellectual Sanctuary to Social Responsibility: The Founding of the Institute for Advanced Study, 1930–1933. Ph.D. dissertation, Princeton University.

Pugh, Emerson W. 1984. *Memories That Shaped an Industry.* Cambridge, MA: MIT Press.

Quastler, Henry, ed. 1953. *Essays on the Use of Information Theory in Biology.* Urbana: University of Illinois Press.

Quastler, Henry, ed. 1955. *Information Theory in Psychology.* Proceedings of a Conference on the Estimation of Information Flow, Monticello, Illinois, 5–9 July, 1954. Glencoe, IL: Free Press.

Quastler, Henry. 1957. The Complexity of Biological Computers. *Institute of Radio Engineers Transactions on Electronic Computers* (September), pp. 192–194.

Quastler, Henry. 1959. Storage and Actuation of Genetic Information. The Information Theory Approach. *Laboratory Investigation* 8, pp. 480–494.

Rajchman, Jan. 1980. Early Research on Computers at RCA. In N. Metropolis, J. Howlett, and Gian-Carlo Rota, eds., *A History of Computing in the Twentieth Century,* pp. 465–470. New York: Academic Press.

Reid, Constance. 1970. *Hilbert.* New York: Springer-Verlag.

Reid, Constance. 1976. *Courant in Gottingen and New York.* New York: Springer-Verlag.

Reitwiesner, George W. 1950. An ENIAC Determination of π and e to more Than 2000 Decimal Places. *Mathematical Tables and Other Aids to Computation* 4, pp. 11–15.

Revens, Lee. 1987. The First 25 Years: ACM 1947–1962. *Communications of the Association for Computing Machinery* (October), pp. 860–865.

Rhodes, Richard. 1986. *The Making of the Atomic Bomb.* New York: Simon and Schuster.

Richardson, Lewis Fry. 1922. *Weather Prediction by Numerical Process.* Cambridge: Cambridge University Press.

Richardson, Lewis Fry. 1965. *Weather Prediction by Numerical Process.* New York: Dover.

Richtmyer, Robert D., and K. W. Morton. 1967. *Difference Methods for Initial-Value Problems.* New York: Interscience.

Robertson, James E. 1980. The ORDVAC and the ILLIAC. In N. Metropolis, J. Howlett, and Gian-Carlo Rota, eds., *A History of Computing in the Twentieth Century*, pp. 347–364. New York: Academic Press.

Rosen, Robert. 1969. Hierarchical Organization in Automata Theoretic Models of the Central Nervous System. In K. N. Leibovic, ed., *Information Processing in the Nervous System*, pp. 21–35. New York: Springer-Verlag.

Rosenblatt, Frank. 1962. *Neurodynamics: Perceptrons and the Theory of Brain Mechanisms*. Washington, DC: Spartan.

Rosenblueth, A., N. Wiener, and J. Bigelow. 1943. Behavior, Purpose, Teleology. *Philosophy of Science* 10, pp. 18–24.

Rossby, Carl-Gustaf et al. 1939. Relation between Variations in the Intensity of the Zonal Circulation of the Atmosphere and the Displacements of the Semi-Permanent Centers of Action. *Journal of Marine Research* 2, 38–55.

Rubinov, A. 1987. von Neumann Ray. In John Eatwell, Murray Milgate, and Peter Newman, eds., *The New Palgrave: A Dictionary of Economics*, 4: 822–824. New York: Stockton.

Sandek, Lawrence. 1971. Von Neumann: Gentle Man with a Giant Mind. *Think* (March), pp. 40–42.

Sawyer, J. S., and F. H. Bushby. 1953. A Baroclinic Model Atmosphere Suitable for Numerical Integration. *Journal of Meteorology* 10, pp. 54–59.

Scientific American Editorial Staff. 1954. Science and the Citizen. *Scientific American* 191 (December), pp. 52–54.

Selmer, Ernst S. 1954. The Diophantine Equation $ax^3 + by^3 + cz^3 = 0$. Completion of the Tables. *Acta Mathematica* 92, pp. 191–197.

Shallet, Sidney. 1946. Electronics to Aid Weather Figuring. *New York Times*, 11 January, p. 12.

Shannon, Claude E. 1940. Symbolic Analysis of Relay and Switching Circuits. Master's thesis, MIT.

Shannon, Claude E. 1958. Von Neumann's Contributions to Automata Theory. *Bulletin of the American Mathematical Society* 64, pp. 123–129.

Shannon, Claude E. 1971. Information Theory. *Encyclopaedia Britannica*, 12: 246–249. 14th ed.

Shannon, Claude E., and W. Weaver. 1949. *The Mathematical Theory of Communication*. Urbana: University of Illinois Press.

Singh, Jagjit. 1966. *Great Ideas in Information Theory, Language, and Cybernetics*. New York: Dover.

Smagorinsky, Joseph. 1953. Data Processing Requirements for the Purposes of Numerical Weather Prediction. *Eastern Joint Computer Conference Proceedings*, pp. 22–30.

Smagorinsky, Joseph. 1972. The General Circulation of the Atmosphere. In D. P. McIntyre, ed., *Meteorological Challenges: A History*, pp. 3–42. Ottawa, Canada: Information Canada.

Smagorinsky, Joseph. 1974. Global Atmospheric Modeling and the Numerical Simulation of Climate. In Wilmot N. Hess, ed., *Weather and Climate Modification,* pp. 633–686. New York: Wiley.

Smagorinsky, Joseph. 1983. The Beginnings of Numerical Weather Prediction and General Circulation Modeling: Early Recollections. *Advances in Geophysics* 25, pp. 3–37.

Squires, G. L. 1956. Relation between the Vibration Frequencies of a Crystal and the Scattering of Slow Neutrons. *Physical Review* 103, pp. 304–312.

Stern, Nancy. 1980. John von Neumann's Influence on Electronic Digital Computing, 1944–1946. *Annals of the History of Computing* 2, 4 (October), pp. 349–362.

Stern, Nancy. 1981. *From ENIAC to UNIVAC: An Appraisal of the Eckert-Mauchly Computers.* Bedford, MA: Digital Press.

Strauss, Lewis L. 1962. *Men and Decisions.* Garden City, NY: Doubleday.

Sutton, O. G. 1954. The Development of Meteorology as an Exact Science. *Nature,* 12 June, 1112–1114.

Szilard, Leo. 1929. Uber die Entropieverminderung in einem Thermodynamischen System bei Eingriffen Intelligenter Wesen. *Zeitschrift fur Physik* 53, p. 840.

Taub, A. H., ed. 1961. Collected Works of John von Neumann. New York: Pergamon Press.

Teller, Edward, with Allen Brown. 1962. *The Legacy of Hiroshima.* Garden City, NY: Doubleday.

Thatcher, J. W. 1964. Universality in the von Neumann Cellular Model. Technical Report 03105-30-T, ORA. Ann Arbor: University of Michigan.

Thatcher, J. W. 1966. Universality in the von Neumann Cellular Model. In Arthur W. Burks, ed., *Essays on Cellular Automata,* pp. 132–186. Urbana: University of Illinois Press.

Thompson, Gerald L. 1987. von Neumann, John (1903–1957). In John Eatwell, Murray Milgate, and Peter Newman, eds., *The New Palgrave: A Dictionary of Economics,* 4: 818–822. New York: Stockton.

Thompson, Philip Duncan. 1953. On the Theory of Large-Scale Disturbances in a Two-dimensional Baroclinic Model of the Atmosphere. *Quarterly Journal: Royal Meteorological Society* 79, pp. 51–69.

Thompson, Philip D. 1961. *Numerical Weather Analysis and Prediction.* New York: Macmillan.

Thompson, Philip Duncan. 1978. The Mathematics of Meteorology. In Lynn Arthur Steen, ed., *Mathematics Today,* pp. 127–152. New York: Springer-Verlag.

Thompson, Philip Duncan. 1983. A History of Numerical Weather Prediction in the United States. *Bulletin of the American Meteorological Society* 64, 7, pp. 755–769.

Tobocman, W., and M. H. Kalos. 1955. Numerical Calculation of (dp) Angular Distributions. *Physical Review* 97, 1 (January), pp. 132–136.

Todd, John. 1974. John von Neumann and the National Accounting Machine. *SIAM Review* 16 (October), pp. 526–530.

Tribbia, Joseph J., and Richard A. Anthes. 1987. Scientific Basis of Modern Weather Prediction. *Science,* July 31, 493–499.

Tucker, Albert W., Harold W. Kuhn and David Gale. 1950. On Symmetric Games: Contributions to the Theory of Games. p. 81–87. *Annals of Mathematics Studies*, no. 24. Princeton, NJ: Princeton University Press.

Tuckerman, Bryant. 1962. *Planetary, Lunar, and Solar Positions 601 B.C. to A.D. 1 at Five Day and Ten-Day Intervals.* Memoirs of the American Philosophical Society, vol. 56. Philadelphia. American Philosophical Society.

Turing, Alan M. 1937. On Computable Numbers, with an Application to the Entscheidungsproblem . . . *Proceedings of the London Mathematical Society,* ser. 2, 42, pp. 230–265.

Turing, Alan M. 1948. Rounding-Off Errors in Matrix Processes. *Quarterly Journal of Mechanics and Applied Mathematics* 1, pp. 287–308.

Turing, Alan M. 1953. The Chemical Basis of Morphogenesis. *Philosophical Transactions of the Royal Society* B237, pp. 37–72.

Ubell, Earl. 1954. New Computer May Yield 60-Day Weather Forecasts. *New York Herald Tribune,* 3 December, p. 12.

Ulam, S. 1950. Random Processes and Transformations. *Proceedings of the International Congress of Mathematicians* 2, pp. 264–275.

Ulam, Stanislaw M. 1958a. John von Neumann 1903–1957. *Bulletin of the American Mathematical Society* 64, pp. 1–49.

Ulam, Stanislaw M. 1958b. The Late John von Neumann on Computers and the Brain. *Scientific American* (June), pp. 127–130.

Ulam, Stanislaw M. 1960. *A Collection of Mathematical Problems.* New York: Interscience.

Ulam, Stanislaw M. 1962. On Some Mathematical Problems Connected with Patterns of Growth of Figures. *Proceedings of Symposia in Applied Mathematics* 14, pp. 215–224.

Ulam, Stanislaw M. 1963. Electronic Computers and Scientific Research. *Computers and Automation* 12, pt. I (August), pp. 20–24, and pt. II (September), 35–40.

Ulam, Stanislaw M. 1986. *Science, Computers, and People.* Boston: Birkhauser.

U.S. Atomic Energy Commission. *In the Matter of J. Robert Oppenheimer.* Transcript of Hearing before the Personnel Security Board. 12 April–6 May 1954.

U.S. Congress. 1955. Hearings before the Senate Section of the Joint Committee on Atomic Energy, 84th Cong. 1st sess. on the Confirmation of AEC Commissioners, June 1953–March 1955. Held 27 June, 20 July, 1953, 18 November, 1954, and 8 March, 1955.

U.S. House of Representatives. 1954. *Organization and Administration of the Military Research and Development Programs.* Hearings before a Subcommittee of the Committee on Government Operations, 83d Cong., 2d sess. (von Neumann testimony, 15 June, 1954, pp. 371–386.)

Unna, Warren. 1955. AEC's von Neumann Knows His Factors. *Washington Post and Times Herald,* 5 June, p. 7E.

Van Heijenoort, Jean. 1967. *From Frege to Gödel.* Cambridge, MA: Harvard University Press.

Van Hove, Leon. 1958. Von Neumann's Contributions to Quantum Theory. *Bulletin of the American Mathematical Society* 64, pp. 95–99.

Verbeek, L. A. M. 1960. Reliable Computation with Unreliable Circuitry. In *Bionics Symposium: Living Prototypes—the Key to New Technology.* Technical Report 60–600. Wright Air Development Division, December.

Verbeek, L. A. M. 1962. On Error Minimizing Neuronal Nets. In H. von Foerster and G. Zopf, Jr., eds., *Principles of Self-Organization,* pp. 121–133. New York: Pergamon.

Von Braun, Wernher, and Frederick I. Ordway III. 1969. *History of Rocketry and Space Travel.* New York: Thomas Y. Crowell.

Von Foerster, Heinz. 1950. *Cybernetics: Circular Causal and Feedback Mechanisms in Biological and Social Systems.* Transactions of the Sixth Conference, 24–25 March 1949, New York. New York: Josiah Macy, Jr. Foundation.

Von Foerster, Heinz. 1952. *Cybernetics: Circular Causal and Feedback Mechanisms in Biological and Social Systems.* Transactions of the Eighth Conference, 15–16 March 1951, New York. New York: Josiah Macy, Jr. Foundation.

Von Foerster, Heinz. 1953. *Cybernetics: Circular Causal and Feedback Mechanisms in Biological and Social Systems.* Transactions of the Ninth Conference, 20–21 March 1952, New York. New York: Josiah Macy, Jr. Foundation.

Von Foerster, Heinz. 1955. *Cybernetics: Circular Causal and Feedback Mechanisms in Biological and Social Systems.* Transactions of the Tenth Conference, 22, 23, 24 April 1953, Princeton, N.J. New York: Josiah Macy, Jr. Foundation.

Von Karman, Theodore, with Lee Edson. 1967. *The Wind and Beyond.* Boston: Little, Brown.

Vonneuman, Nicholas A. 1987. *John von Neumann as Seen by His Brother.* Meadowbrook, PA: 1987. The author.

Walter, W. G. 1953. *The Living Brain.* New York: W. W. Norton.

Watson, J. B. 1919. *Psychology from the Standpoint of a Behaviorist.* Philadelphia: Lippincott.

Weddell, Graham, D. A. Taylor, and C. M. Williams. 1955. Studies on the Innervation of Skin. III. The Patterned Arrangement of the Spinal Sensory Nerves to the Rabbit Ear. *Journal of Anatomy* 89, pp. 317–342.

Weik, Martin H. 1955. *A Survey of Domestic Electronic Digital Computing Systems.* Ballistic Research Laboratories Report No. 971. Aberdeen Proving Ground, MD, December.

Weintraub, E. Roy. 1983. On the Existence of a Competitive Equilibrium: 1930–1954. *Journal of Economic Literature* 21, 1 (March), pp. 1–39.

Whittaker, Edmund, and G. Robinson. 1924. *The Calculus of Observations: A Treatise on Numerical Mathematics.* 1st ed. London and Glasgow: Blackie & Son.

Wiener, N. 1948. *Cybernetics: Or Control and Communication in the Animal and the Machine.* Cambridge, MA: Technology Press.

Wigner, E. P. 1955. Characteristic Vectors of Bordered Matrices with Infinite Dimensions. *Annals of Mathematics* 62, p. 548–564.

Wilkes, Maurice V., David J. Wheeler, and Stanley Gill. 1982. The Preparation of Programs for an Electronic Digital Computer, with Special Reference to the EDSAC and the Use of a Library of Subroutines. Los Angeles: Tomash.

Wilkinson, J. H. 1963. *Rounding Errors in Algebraic Processes.* Englewood Cliffs, NJ: Prentice-Hall.

Wilkinson, J. H. 1965. *The Algebraic Eigenvalue Problem.* Oxford: Clarendon Press.

Wilkinson, J. H. 1971. Modern Error Analysis. *SIAM Review* 13 (October), pp. 548–568.

Williams, F. C., and T. Kilburn. 1948. A Storage System for Use with Binary-Digital Computing Machines. *Institution of Electrical Engineers* 96, 3 (March 1949), pp. 81–100.

Williams, Michael R. 1985. *A History of Computing Technology.* Englewood Cliffs, NJ: Prentice-Hall.

Winograd, S., and J. D. Cowan. 1963. *Reliable Computation in the Presence of Noise.* Cambridge, MA: MIT Press.

Writings of John von Neumann

Listed here are the writings authored or coauthored by von Neumann. Almost all of these have been compiled in one of two collections of his work: A. H. Taub, ed., *John von Neumann: Collected Works* (New York: Macmillan, 1960–1963), 6 vols., and William Aspray and Arthur Bruks, eds., *Papers of John von Neumann on Computing and Computer Science* (Cambridge, MA: MIT Press and Los Angeles: Tomash Publishers, 1987). Square brackets at the end of each entry indicate where in these collections the article appears: T for the Taub volume, AB for the Aspray-Burks volume.

1922. Michael Fekete and v. N. Uber die Lage der Nulstellen gewisser Minimumpolynome. *Jahresbericht der deutschen Mathematiker-Vereinigung* 31, pp. 125–138. [T,I,10–23]

1923. Zur Einfuhrung der transfiniten Zahlen. *Acta literarum ac scientiarum Requiae Universitatis Hungaricae Francisco-Josephinae, Sectio scintiarum mathematicarum* 1, pp. 199–208. [T,I,24–33]

1925a. Egyenletesen suru szamsorozatok. *Mathematikai Phyzikai Lapok* 32, pp. 32–40. [T,I,58–66]

1925b. Eine Axiomatisierung der Mengenlehre. *Journal fur die reine und andgewandte Mathematik* 154, pp. 219–240. [T,I,34–56]

1926a. Zur Pruferschen Theorie der idealen Zahlen. *Acta Universitatis Szegediensis* 2, pp. 193–227. [T,I,68–103]

1926b. Az altalanos nalmazelmelet axiomatikus folepitses. Thesis, University of Budapest.

1927a. Mathematishche Begrundung der Quantenmechanik. In *Nachrichten von der Gesellschaft der Wissenschaften zu Gottingen*, pp. 1–57. [T,I,150–207]

1927b. Thermodynamik quantenmechanischer Gesamtheiten. *Nachrichten von der Gesellschaft der Wissenschaften zu Gottingen*, pp. 273–291. [T,I,236–254]

1927c. Wahrenscheinlichkeitstheoretischer Aufbau der Quantenmechanik. *Nachrichten der Gesellschaften der Wissenschaften zu Gottingen*, pp. 245–272. [T,I,208–235]

1927d. Zur Hilbertschen Beweistheorie. *Mathematische Zeitschrift* 26, pp. 1–46. [T,I,256–300]

1927e. Zur Theorie der Darstellungen kontinuierlicher Gruppen. *Sitzungsberichte der Preussischen Akademie*, pp. 76–90. [T,I,134–148]

1927. David Hilbert, v. N., and Lothar Nordheim. Uber die Grundlagen der Quantenmechanik. *Mathematische Annalen* 98, pp. 1–30. [T,I,104–133]

1928a. Die Axiomatisierung der Mengenlehre. *Mathematische Zeitschrift* 27, pp. 669–752. [T,I,339–422]

1928b. Die Zerlegung eines Intervalles in abzahlbar viele kongruente Teilmengen. *Fundamenta Mathematicae* 11, pp. 230–238. [T,I,302–311]

1928c. Eigenwerteproblem symmetrischer Functionaloperatoren. *Jahresberichte der deutschen Mathematiker-Vereinigung* 37, pp. 11–14.

1928d. Einige Bemerkungen zur Diracschen Theorie des Drehelektrons. *Zeitschrift fur Physik* 48, pp. 868–881. [T,I,423–436]

1928e Ein System algebraisch unabhangiger Zahlen. *Mathematische Annalen* 99, pp. 134–141. [T,I,312–319]

1928f. Sur la théorie des jeux. *Comptes Rendus des Séances. Académie des sciences. Paris* 186, pp. 1698–1791.

1928g. Uber die Definition durch transfinite Induktion, und verwandte Fragen der allgemeinen Mengenlehre. *Mathematische Annalen* 99, pp. 373–391. [T,I,320–338]

1928h. Zur Theorie der Gesellschaftsspiele. *Mathematischen Annalen* 100, pp. 295–320. Translated by S. Bargmann as On the Theory of Games of Strategy. *Annals of Mathematics Studies* 40, pp. 13–42. [T,VI,1–26]

1928a. v. N. and Eugene Wigner. Zur Erklarung einiger Eigenschaften der Spektren aus der Quantenmechanik des Drehelektrons I. *Zeitschrift fur Physik* 47, pp. 203–220. [T,I,438–456]

1928b. v. N. and Eugene Wigner. Zur Erklarung einiger Eigenschaften der Spektren aus der Quantenmechanik des Drehelectrons II. *Zeitschrift fur Physik* 49, pp. 73–94. [T,I,457–493]

1928c. v. N. and Eugene Wigner. Zur Erklarung einiger Eigenschaften der Spektren aus der Quantenmechanik des Drehelektrons III. *Zeitschrift fur Physik* 51, pp. 844–858.

1929a. Allgemeine Eigenwerttheorie Hermitescher Funktionaloperatoren. *Mathematische Annalen* 102, pp. 49–131. [T,II,3–85]

1929b. Beweis des Ergodensatzes und des *H*-Theorems in der neuen Mechanik. *Zeitschrift fur Physik* 57, pp. 30–70. [T,I,558–598]

1929c. Uber die analytischen Eigenschaften von Gruppen linearer Transformationen und ihrer Darstellungen. *Mathematische Zeitschrift* 30, pp. 3–42. [T,I,509–548]

1929d. Uber eine Widerspruchfreiheitsfrage der axiomatischen Mengenlehre. *Journal fur die reine und angewandte Mathematik* 160, pp. 227–241. [T,I,494–508]

1929e. Zur algebra der Funktionaloperatoren und Theorie der normalen Operatoren. *Mathematicsche Annalen* 102, pp. 370–427. [T,II,86–143]

1929f. Zur allgemeinen Theorie des Masses. *Fundamenta Mathematicae* 13, pp. 73–116. [T,I,599–642]

1929g. Zur Theorie der unbeschrankten Matrizen. *Journal fur reine und angewandte Mathematik* 161, pp. 208–236. [T,II,144–172]

1929h. Zusatz zur Arbeit "Zur allgemeinen Theorie des Masses." *Fundamenta Mathematicae* 13, pp. 333. [T,I,543]

1929a. v. N. and Eugene Wigner. Uber das Verhalten von Eigenwerten bei adiabatischen Prozessen. *Physikalissche Zeitschrift* 30, pp. 467–470. [T,I,553–556]

1929b. v. N. and Eugene Wigner. Uber merkwurdige diskrete Eigenwerte. *Physycalische Zeitschrift* 30, pp. 465–467. [T,I,550–552]

1930. Uber einen Hilfssatz der Variationsrechnung. *Abhandlungen aus dem mathematischen Seminar der Hamburgischen Universitat* 3, pp. 28–31. [T,II,173–176]

1931a. Algebraische Reprasentanten der Funktionen "bis auf eine Menge vom Masse Null." *Journal fur reine und angewandte Mathematik* 165, pp. 109–115. [T,II,213–219]

1931b. Bermerkungen zu den Ausfuhrungen von Herrn St. Lesniewski uber meine Arbeit "Zur Hilbertschen Beweistheorie." *Fundamenta Mathematicae* 17, pp. 331–334. [T,II,230–233]

1931c. Die Eindeutigkeit der Schrodingerschen Operatoren. *Mathematische Annalen* 104, pp. 570–578. [T,II,220–229]

1931d. Die formalistische Grundlegung der Mathematik. *Erkenntniss* 2, pp. 116–121. [T,II,234–239]

1931e. Uber Funktionen von Funktionaloperatoren. *Annals of Mathematics* 32, pp. 191–226. [T,II,177–212]

1932a. Einige Satze uber messbare Abbildungen. *Annals of Mathematics* 33, pp. 574–586. [T,II,294–306]

1932b. *Mathematische Grundlagen der Quantenmechanik.* Berlin: Springer; New York, Dover Publications, 1943; Presses Universitaires de France, 1947; Madrid, Instituto de Matematicas "Jorge Juan," 1949. Translated by Robert T. Beyer. Princeton University Press, 1955.

1932c. Physical Applications of the Ergodic Hypothesis. *Proceedings of the National Academy of Sciences* 18, pp. 263–266. [T,II,274–277]

1932d. Proof of the Quasi-Ergodic Hypothesis. *Proceedings of the National Academy of Sciences* 18, pp. 70–82. [T,II,260–273]

1932e. Uber adjungierte Funktionaloperatoren. *Annals of Mathematics* 33, pp. 294–310. [T,II,242–258]

1932f. Uber einen Satz von Herrn M. H. Stone. *Annals of Mathematics* 33, pp. 567–573. [T,II,287–293]

1932g. Zum Beweise des Minkowskischen Satze uber Linearformen. *Mathematische Zeitschrift* 30, pp. 1–2. [T,II,240–241]

1932h. Zur Operatorenmethode in der klassischen Mechanik. *Annals of Mathematics* 33, pp. 587–642. [T,II,307–362]

1932i. Zusatze zur Arbeit "Zur Operatorenmethode in der klassischen Mechanik." *Annals of Mathematics* 33, pp. 789–791. [T,II,363–365]

1932. Bernard O. Koopman and v. N. Dynamical Systems of Continuous Spectra. *Proceedings of the National Academy of Sciences* 18, pp. 255–263. [T,II,278–286]

1933a. A koordinata-meres pontossaganak hatarai az elektron Dirac-fele elmelete-ben (Uber die Grenzen der Koordinatenmessungs-Genauigkeit in der Diracschen Theorie des Elektrons). *Mathematikai es Termeszettudomanyi ertesito, a M. Tud. akademie III. esztalganak folyoirata. Mathematischer und naturwissenschaftlicher anzeiger der Ungarnischen akademie der wissenschaft* 50, pp. 366–385. [T,II,387–406]

1933b. Die Einfuhrung analytischer Parameter in topologischen Gruppen. *Annals of Mathematics* 34, pp. 170–190. [T,II,366–386]

1934a. Almost Periodic Functions in a Group I. *Transactions of the American Mathematical Society* 36, pp. 445–492. [T,II,454–502]

1934b. Zum Haarschen Mass in topologischen Gruppen. *Compositio Mathematica* 1, pp. 106–114. [T,II,445–453]

1934. Pacual Jordan, v. N., and Eugene Wigner. On an Algebraic Generalization of the Quantum Mechanical Formalism. *Annals of Mathematics* 35, pp. 29–64. [T,II,409–444]

1934. Abraham H. Taub, Oswald Veblen, and v. N. The Dirac Equation in Projective Relativity. *National Academy of Sciences: Proceedings* 20, pp. 383–388. [T,II,502–507]

1935a. Charakterisierung des Spektrums eines Integraloperators. *Actualites Scientifique et Industrielles* 229. Exposés Math., publiés a la memoire de J. Herbrand, no. 13 (Paris). [T,IV,38–55]

1935b. On Complete Topological Spaces. *Transactions of the American Mathematical Society* 37, pp. 1–20. [T,II,508–527]

1935c. On Normal Operators. *Proceedings of the National Academy of Sciences* 21, pp. 366–369. [T,IV,56–59]

1935a. Salomon Bochner and v. N. Almost Periodic Functions in Groups II. *Transactions of the American Mathematical Society* 37, pp. 21–50. [T,II,528–557]

1935b. Salomon Bochner and v. N. On Compact Solutions of Operational-Differential Equations I. *Annals of Mathematics* 36, pp. 255–291. [T,IV,1–37]

1935. Pascual Jordan and v. N. On Inner Products in Linear, Metric Spaces. *Annals of Mathematics* 36, pp. 719–723. [T,IV,60–64]

1935. With Marshall H. Stone. The Determination of Representative Elements in the Residual Classes of a Boolean Algebra. *Fundamenta Mathematicae* 25, pp. 353–378. [T,IV,65–90]

1936a. Continuous Geometry. *Proceedings of the National Academy of Sciences* 22, pp. 92–100. [T,IV,126–142]

1936b. Examples of Continuous Geometries. *Proceedings of the National Academy of Sciences* 22, pp. 101–108.

1936c. On a Certain Topology for Rings of Operators. *Annals of Mathematics* 37, pp. 111–115. [T,III,1–5]

1936d. On an Algebraic Generalization of the Quantum Mechanical Formalism (Part I). *Matematicheskie Sbornik* 1, pp. 415–484. [T,III,492–559]

1936e. On Regular Rings. *Proceedings of the National Academy of Sciences* 22, pp. 707–713. [T,IV,143–149]

1936f. The Uniqueness of Haar's Measure. *Matematicheskie Sbornic* 1, pp. 721–734. [T,IV,91–104]

1936. Garrett Birkhoff and v. N. The Logic of Quantum Mechanics. *Annals of Mathematics* 37, pp. 823–843. [T,IV,105–125]

1936. Francis J. Murray and v. N. On Rings of Operators. *Annals of Mathematics* 37, pp. 116–229. [T,III,6–119]

1937a. Algebraic Theory of Continuous Geometries. *Proceedings of the National Acadademy of Sciences* 23, pp. 16–22. [T,IV,150–156]

1937b. Continuous Rings and Their Arithmetics. *Proceedings of the National Academy of Sciences* 23, pp. 341–349. [T,IV,158–167]

1937c. Some Matrix-Inequalities and Metrization of Matrix-Space. *Tomskii University Review* 1, pp. 286–300. [T,IV,205–219]

1937d. Uber ein okonomisches Gleichungssystem und eine Verallgemeinerung des Brouwerschen Fixpunktsatzes. *Ergebnisse eines Mathematischen Kolloquiums* 3, pp. 73–83.

1937. K. Kuratowski and v. N. On Some Analytic Sets Defined by Transfinite Induction. *Annals of Mathematics* 38, pp. 521–525. [T,IV,200–204]

1937. Francis J. Murray and v. N. On Rings of Operators II. *Transactions of the American Mathematical Society* 41, pp. 208–248. [T,III,120–160]

1938. On Infinite Direct Products. *Compositio Mathematica* 6, pp. 1–77. [T,III,322–399]

1940. On Rings of Operators III. *Annals of Mathematics* 41, pp. 94–161. [T,III,161–228]

1940. v. N. and Isreal Halperin. On the Transivity of Perspective Mappings. *Annals of Mathematics* 41, pp. 87–93. [T,IV,168–174]

1940. With Robert H. Kent. The Estimation of the Probable Error from Successive Differences. Ballistic Research Laboratory Report 175, 14 February.

1940. Eugene Wigner and v. N. Minimally Almost Periodic Groups. *Annals of Mathematics* 41, pp. 746–750. [T,IV,220–224]

1941a. Distributions of the Ratio of the Mean Square Successive Difference to the Variance. *Annals of Mathematical Statistics* 12, pp. 367–395. [T,IV,452–480]

1941b. Optimum Aiming at an Imperfectly Located Target. Appendix to *Optimum Spacing of Bombs of Shots in the Presence of Systematic Errors*, by Louis S. Dederick and Robert H. Kent. Ballistic Research Laboratory Report 241, 3 July. [T,IV,492–506]

1941c. Shock Waves Started by an Infinitesimally Short Detonation of Given (Positive and Finite) Energy. National Defense Research Council, Div. 8, 30 June. U.S. Govt. Doc. AM-9.

1941. v. N. and Isaac J. Schoenberg. Fourier Integrals and Metric Geometry. *Transactions of American Mathematical Society* 50, pp. 226–251. [T,IV,225–250]

1941. v. N., Robert H. Kent, H. R. Bellinson, and Bertha I. Hart. The Mean Square Successive Difference. *Annals of Mathematical Statistics* 12, pp. 153–162. [T,IV,442–452]

1942a. A Further Remark Concerning the Distribution of the Ratio of the Mean Square Successive Difference to the Variance. *Annals of Mathematical Statistics* 13, pp. 86–88. [T,IV,481–483]

1942b. Approximate Properties of Matrices of High Finite Order. *Portugaliae Mathematica* 3, pp. 1–62. [T,IV,270–331]

1942c. Note to "Tabulation of the Probabilities for the Ratio of the Mean Square Successive Difference to the Variance." by Bertha I. Hart. *Annals of Mathematical Statistics* 13, pp. 207–214. [T,IV,484–491]

1942d. Theory of Detonation Waves. Progress report to 1 April 1942. U.S. Govt. Doc. PB 31090, 4 May. [T,VI,203–218]

1942. Subrahmanyan Chandrasekhar and v. N. The Statistics of the Gravitational Field Arising from a Random Distribution of Stars I. *Astrophysical Journal* 95, pp. 489–531. [T,VI,102–144]

1942. Paul R. Halmos and v. N. Operator Methods in Classical Mechanics II. *Annals of Mathematics* 43, pp. 332–350. [T,IV,251–269]

1943a. *Oblique Reflection of Shocks.* U.S. Govt. Doc. PB 37079, 12 October. [T,VI,238–299]

1943b. On Some Algebraical Properties of Operator Rings. *Annals of Mathematics* 44, pp. 709–715.

1943c. Theory of Shock Waves. Progress report to 31 August 1942. U.S. Govt. Doc. PB 32719, 29 January. [T,VI,178–202]

1943d (?) Progress Report on "Theory of Shock Waves." Report No. 1140 (final report under contract OEMsr-218). January.

1943e (?). Shadowgraph determination of shock-wave strength, Bureau of Ordnance Explosive Research Reports, No. 11. 25 October.

1943. Subrahmanyan Chandrasekhar and v. N. The Statistics of the Gravitational Field Arising from a Random Distribution of Stars II. The Speed of Fluctuations; Dynamical Friction; Spatial Correlations. *Astrophysical Journal* 97, pp. 1–27. [T,VI,145–171]

1943. Francis J. Murray and v. N. On Rings of Operators IV. *Annals of Mathematics* 44, pp. 716–808. [T,III,229–321]

1943. With Raymond J. Seeger. On Oblique Reflection and Collision of Shock Waves. U.S. Govt. Doc. PB 31918. 20 September.

1944a. Introductory Remarks (Sec. I), Theory of the Spinning Detonation (Sec. XII), Theory of the Intermediate Product (Sec. XIII). In *Report of Informal Technical Conference on the Mechanism of Detonation.* U.S. Govt. Doc. AM-570. 10 April.

1944b. Proposal and Analysis of a Numerical Method for the Treatment of Hydrodynamical Shock Problems. Report 108.1R AMG-IAS No. 1, submitted by the Applied Mathematics Group, Institute for Advanced Study to the Applied Mathematics Panel National Defense Research Committee, 20 March. U.S. Govt. Doc. OSRD-3617. [T,VI,361–379]

1944c. Riemann Method; Shock Waves and Discontinuities (One-Dimensional), Two-Dimensional Hydrodynamics. Lectures in *Shock Hydrodynamics and Blast Waves*, by H. A. Bethe, K. Fuchs, J. von Neumann, R. Peierls, and W. G. Penney. Notes by J. O. Hirschfelder. U.S. Govt. Doc. AECD-2860. 28 October.

1944d (?). Surface Water Waves Excited by an Underwater Explosion. Memo to J. Robert Oppenheimer. LASL, LAMS-128. 28 August. Secret, restricted data.

1944e (?). Remarks on Report of R. R. Halverson, "The Effect of Air Burst on the Blast from Bombs and Small Charges, Part II." Memo to J. Robert Oppenheimer. (AM-863) C. 23 October.

1944. v. N. and Oskar Morgenstern. *Theory of Games and Economic Behavior.* Princeton: Princeton University Press.

1944. Digest of *J. von Neumann's lecture at meeting on optimum heights on Sept. 22, 1944.* Memo to N. F. Ramsey from B. Waldman. Los Alamos Scientific Laboratory (LAMD-46), 7 December. Secret, restricted data.

1944. (By Harry Polachek and Raymond J. Seeger.) Regular Reflection of Shocks in an Ideal Gas. Bureau of Ordnance Explosive Research Reports, No. 13. 12 February.

1944. (By Harry Polachek and Raymond J. Seeger.) Interaction of Shock-Waves in Water-like Substances. Bureau of Ordnance Explosive Research Reports, No. 14. 16 August.

1944. (By P. C. Keenan and Raymond J. Seeger.) Analysis of Data on Shock Intersections. Progress Rpt I. Bureau of Ordnance, Explosives Research Report No. 15. "This analysis was made with J. von Neumann." (AM-496). C. 3 February.

1945a. A Model of General Economic Equilibrium. *Review of Economic Studies* 13, pp. 1–9. [T,VI,29–37]

1945b. First Draft of a Report on the EDVAC. Report prepared for U.S. Army Ordnance Department under Contract W-670-ORD-4926. Reprinted in Nancy Stern, *From ENIAC to UNIVAC*, pp. 177–246. Bedford, MA: Digital Press, 1981. [AB,17–82]

1945c. Refraction, Intersection and Reflection of Shock Waves. In *Conference on Supersonic Flow and Shock Waves.* U.S. Govt. Doc. AM-1663, 16 July, pp. 4–12. [T,VI,300–308]

1945d. *Some Considerations on Shaped Charge Assembly.* Outcome of discussions at Ballistics Research Laboratory, Bruceton, with MacDougall, Paul and Messerly. Los Alamos Scientific Laboratory, LAMS-196. 23 January. Secret, restricted data.

1945. John W. Calkin, v. N., and R. Peierls. *The Similarity Solution for a Collapsing Spherical Cavity Near Zero Radius.* LASL, LA-210. S. 31 January.

1945. (By Hans A. Bethe.) Radiation Hydrodynamics, Part I. Work done by J. von Neumann and others. Los Alamos Scientific Laboratory, LA-322. 3 July. Secret, restricted data.

1945. With Abraham H. Taub. Flying Wind Tunnel Experiments. U.S. Govt. Doc. PB 33263, 5 November.

1946a. Report on Instrumentation Program of Technical Staff, vol. 2. Operation Crossroads. Enclosure Q. Comments Concerning Dr. W. G. Penney's Report, Depth for Test C. Bureau of Ships Instrumentation Group, Joint Task Force One. XRD-210 (XR-156, v. 2) 1 December. Secret, restricted data.

1946b. Statement, 31 January. Hearings before the Special Committee on Atomic Energy, U.S. Senate. 77th Cong., 2d. sess., on S. 1717, A Bill for the Development and Control of Atomic Energy.

1946. Egon Bretscher, D. F. Frankel, Darol K. Froman, Nicholas Metropolis, Philip Morrison, Lothar W. Nordheim, Edward Teller, A. Turkevich, and v. N. *Report on the Conference on the Super.* Los Alamos Scientific Laboratory, LA-575. 12 June. Secret, restricted data.

1946. Herman H. Goldstine and v. N. On the Principles of Large Scale Computing Machines. Unpublished. [T,V,1–32;AB,315–348]

1946. Robert Schatten and v. N. The Cross-Space of Linear Transformations II. *Annals of Mathematics* 47, pp. 608–630. [T,IV,386–408]

1946. v. N. and Maurice M. Shapiro. *Underwater Explosion of a Nuclear Bomb.* LASL, LA-545. Also issued as Chap. 14 in vol. 7, pt. III, of the Los Alamos Technical Series (LA-1022). 8 April. Secret, restricted data.

1946. Valentine Bargmann, Deane Montgomery, and v. N. Solution of Linear Systems of High Order. Report prepared for Navy Bureau of Ordnance under contract Nord-9596. [T,V,421–477]

1946. Arthur W. Burks, Herman H. Goldstine and v. N. Preliminary Discussion of the Logical Design of an Electronic Computing Instrument. Part I, Vol. I. Report prepared for U.S. Army Ordnance Department under contract W-36-034-ORD-7481. [T,V,34–79;AB,97–142]

1947a. The Mathematician. In *The Works of the Mind*, pp. 180–196. Edited by Robert B. Heywood. Chicago: University of Chicago Press. [T,I,1–9]

1947b. The Point Source Solution. In *Blast Wave.* U.S. Govt. Doc. LA-2000, 13 August, pp. 27–55. [T,VI,219–237]

1947c. The Future Role of Rapid Computing in Meteorology. *Aeronautical Engineering Review* 6, 4 (April), p. 30.

1947d. Discussion of a Maximum Problem. Unpublished manuscript dated 15–16 November 1947. Edited by A. W. Tucker and H. W. Kuhn. [T,VI,89–95]

1947a. v. N. and Herman H. Goldstine. Numerical Inverting of Matrices of High Order. *Bulletin of the American Mathematicaal Society* 53, pp. 1021–1099. [T,V,478–557]

1947b. Herman H. Goldstine and v. N. Planning and Coding of Problems for an Electronic Computing Instrument. Part II, Vol. I. Report prepared for U.S. Army Ordnance Department under contract W-36-034-ORD-7481. [T,V,80–151; AB,151–222]

1947. Frederick Reines and v. N. The Mach Effect and the Height of Burst. In *Blast Wave.* U.S. Govt. Doc. LA-2000, 13 August, X-11-X-84. [T,VI,309–347]

1947a. v. N. and Robert D. Richtmyer. On the Numerical Solution of Partial Differential Equations of Parabolic Type. U.S. Govt. Doc. LA-657, 25 December. [T,V,652–663]

1947b. Robert D. Richtmyer and v. N. Statistical Methods in Neutron Diffusion. U.S. Govt. Doc. LAMS-551, 9 April. [T,V,751–764]

1948a. First Report on the Numerical Calculation of Flow Problems. 22 June–6 July. Unpublished. [T,V,664–712]

1948b. On the Theory of Stationary Detonation Waves. File No. X122, BRL, Aberdeen Proving Ground, MD, 20 September.

1948c. Second Report on the Numerical Calculation of Flow Problems. 25 July–22 August. Unpublished. [T,V,713–750]

1948a. Herman H. Goldstine and v. N. Planning and Coding of Problems for an Electronic Computing Instrument. Part II, Vol. II. Report prepared for U.S. Army Ordnance Department under contract W-36-034-ORD-7481. [T,V,152-214; AB,223-285]

1948b. Herman H. Goldstine and v. N. Planning and Coding of Problems for an Electronic Computing Instrument. Part II, Vol. III. Report prepared for U.S. Army Ordnance Department under contract W-36-034-ORD-7481. [T,V,215-235;AB,286-306]

1948. Robert Schatten and v. N. The Cross-Space of Linear Transformations III. *Annals of Mathematics* 49, pp. 557-582. [T,IV,409-434]

1949a. On Rings of Operators: Reduction Theory. *Annals of Mathematics* 50, pp. 401-485. [T,III,400-491]

1949b. Recent Theories of Turbulence. Report made to Office of Naval Research. Unpublished. [T,VI,437-472]

1949c. Review of Norbert Wiener's *Cybernetics. Physics Today* 2, pp. 33-34.

1949. G. Foster Evans, v. N., and Stanislaw M. Ulam. *Outline of a Method for the Calculation of the Progress of Thermonuclear Reactions.* LASL, LAMS-831. 7 January. Secret, restricted data.

1950. *Functional Operators.* 2 vols. Annals of Mathematics Studies no. 21, 22. Princeton: Princeton University Press.

1950. George W. Brown and v. N. Solutions of Games by Differential Equations. *Annals of Mathematics Studies* (Princeton University Press), 24, pp. 73-79. [T,VI,38-43]

1950. v. N. and Robert D. Richtmyer. A Method for the Numerical Calculation of Hydrodynamic Shocks. *Journal of Applied Physics* 21, pp. 232-237. [T,VI,380-385]

1950. Irving E. Segal and v. N. A Theorem on Unitary Representations of Semisimple Lie Groups. *Annals of Mathematics* 52, pp. 509-517. [T,IV,332-340]

1950. Jule G. Charney, Ragnar Fjortoft, and v. N. Numerical Integration of the Barotropic Vorticity Equation. *Tellus* 2, pp. 237-254. [T,VI,413]

1950. Nicholas C. Metropolis, George Reitwiesner, and v. N. Statistical Treatment of Values of First 2000 Decimal Digits of e and of pi Calculated on the ENIAC. *Mathematical Tables and Other Aids to Computation* 4, pp. 109-111. [T,V,765-767]

1951a. Discussion on the Existence and Uniqueness or Multiplicity of Solutions of the Aerodynamical Equations. In *Problems of Cosmical Aerodynamics*, pp. 75-84. Central Air Documents Office.

1951b. Eine Spektraltheorie fur allgemeine Operatoren eines unitaren Raumes. *Mathematische Nachrichten* 4, pp. 258-281. [T,IV,341-364]

1951c. The Future of High-Speed Computing. In *Proceedings. Computation Seminar*, 5-9 December 1949, p. 13. New York: IBM Corporation. [T,V,236;AB,349]

1951d. The General and Logical Theory of Automata. In *Cerebral Mechanisms in Behavior—The Hixon Symposium*, pp. 1-31. Edited by L. A. Jeffrees. New York: Wiley. [T,V,288-328;AB,391-431]

1951e. Various Techniques Used in Connection with Random Digits. *Journal of Ressearch of the National Bureau of Standards*, Applied Mathematics Series, 12, pp. 36-38. [T,V,768-770]

1951f. Description of the Conformal Mapping Method for the Integration of Partial Differential Equation Systems with 1 plus 2 Independent Variables. Unpublished paper, written in the period 16 December 1950–8 January 1951. Reviewed by A. H. Taub. [T,VI,473–476]

1951. John W. Calkin, Cerda Evans, Foster Evans, v. N., and Klari von Neumann. *The Burning of D-T Mixtures in a Spherical Geometry.* Los Alamos Scientific Laboratory, LA-1233. 23 April. Secret, restricted data.

1951. John W. Calkin, Cerda Evans, Foster Evans, v. N., and Klari von Neumann. Supplement to *The Burning of D-T Mixtures in a Spherical Geometry.* Los Alamos Scientific Laboratory, LA-1237. 23 April. Secret, restricted data.

1951. Herman H. Goldstine and v. N. Numerical Inverting of Matrices of High Order II. *Proceedings of the American Mathematical Society* 2, pp. 188–202. [T,V,558–572]

1951. (By Robert D. Richtmyer.) Project Hippo. (Mechanized Calculation of Efficiencies and of Other Features of a Fission Bomb Explosion). Final report on the original Hippo project and results for problems I and II. (Work done by J. von Neumann and others.) Los Alamos Scientific Laboratory, LA-1282. 10 August. Secret, restricted data.

1951. (By Arturo W. Rosenbluth.) Aberdeen Calculation on the Cylinder. (Work done by J. von Neumann and others.) Los Alamos Scientific Laboratory, LA-1288. 31 January. Secret, restricted data.

1951. Discussion Remark Concerning Paper of C. S. Smith, "Grain Shapes and Other Metallurgical Applicaitons of Topology." In *Metal Interfaces*, pp. 108–110. Cleveland: American Society for Metals.

1953a. A Certain Zero-Sum Two-Person Game Equivalent to the Optimal Assignment Problem. *Annals of Mathematics Studies* (Princeton University Press), 28, pp. 5–12. [T,VI,44–49]

1953b. Communication on the Borel Notes. *Econometrica* 21, pp. 124–125. [T,VI,27–28]

1953. Enrico Fermi and v. N. *Taylor Instability at the Boundary of Two Incompressible Liquids.* U.S. Govt. Doc. AECU-2979, pt. 2, pp. 7–13. [T,VI,431–434]

1953. v. N. and Herman H. Goldstine. A Numerical Study of a Conjecture of Kummer. *Mathematical Tables and Other Aids to Computation* 7(42), pp. 133–134. [T,V,771–772]

1953. With Donald B. Gillies and J. P. Mayberry. Two Variants of Poker. *Annals of Mathematics Studies* (Princeton University Press), 28, pp. 13–50. [T,VI,50–81]

1954a. A Numerical Method to Determine Optimum Strategy. *Naval Research Logistics Quarterly* 1, pp. 109–115. [T,VI,82–88]

1954b. Entwicklung und Ausnutzung neuerer mathematischer Maschinen. *Arbeitsgemeinschaft fur Forschung des Landes Nordrhein-Westfalen*, vol. 45. [T,V,148–187]

1954c. Non-linear Capacitance or Inductance Switching, Amplifying and Memory Devices. Basic paper for patent 2,815,488, filed 28 April 1954. Unpublished. [T,V,379–419]

1954d. The NORC and Problems in High Speed Computing. Speech at first public showing of the IBM Naval Ordnance Research Calculator, 2 December 1954. [T,V,238–247;AB,350–359]

1954e. The role of Mathematics in the Sciences and in Society. Address at Fourth Conference of Association of Princeton Graduate Alumni, June 1954. [T,VI, 477–490]

1954. v. N. and Edward Teller. *Applications of the Hot Sphere Generated by an A-Bomb.* University of California Radiation Laboratory, Livermore. UCRL-4412. November. Secret, restricted data.

1954. Eugene P. Wigner and v. N. Significance of Loewner's Theorem in the Quantum Theory of Collisions. *Annals of Mathematics* 59, pp. 418–433. [T,IV,365–380]

1955a. Can We Survive Technology? *Fortune* (June), pp. 106–108, 151–152. [T,VI,504–519]

1955b. Defense in Atomic War. *The Scientific Bases of Weapons*, pp. 21–23. [T,VI,523–525]

1955c. Impact of Atomic Energy on the Physical and Chemical Sciences. *Technical Review* (November), pp. 15–17. [T,VI,520–522]

1955d. Method in the Physical Sciences. In *The Unity of Knowledge*, pp. 157–164. Edited by L. Leary. New York: Doubleday. [T,VI,491–498]

1955e. *Mathematical Foundations of Quantum Mechanics.* Translated from the German by Robert T. Beyer. Princeton: Princeton University Press.

1955. Herman H. Goldstine and v. N. Blast Wave Calculation. *Communications on Pure and Applied Mathematics* 8, pp. 327–353. [T,VI,386–412]

1955. v. N. and Bryant Tuckerman. Continued Fraction Expansion of $2^{1/3}$. *Mathematical Tables and Other Aids to Computation* 9, pp. 23–24. [T,V,773]

1955. Allen Devinatz, Adolf E. Nussbaum, and v. N. On the Permutability of Self-Adjoint Operators. *Annals Mathmatics* 62, pp. 199–203. [T,IV,381–385]

1956a. Probabilistic Logics and the Synthesis of Reliable Organisms from Unreliable Components. In *Automata Studies*, pp. 43–98. Edited by Claude E. Shannon and John McCarthy. Princeton: Princeton University Press. [T,V,329–378;AB,553–602]

1956b. The Impact of Recent Developments in Science on the Economy and on Economics. *Looking Ahead* 4, pp. 11. [T,VI,100–101]

1958a. *The Computer and the Brain.* New Haven: Yale University Press.

1958b. Non-isomorphism of Certain Continuous Rings. *Annals of Mathematics* 67, pp. 485–496. [T,IV,176–188]

1959. Herman H. Goldstine, Francis J. Murray, and v. N. The Jacobi Method for Real Symmetric Matrices. *Association for Computing Machinery. Journal* 6, pp. 59–96. [T,V,573–610]

1959. A. Blair, Nicholas Metropolis, v. N., Abraham H. Taub, and M. Tsingou. A Study of a Numerical Solution to a Two-Dimensional Hydrodynamical Problem. *Mathematical Tables and Other Aids to Computation* 13, pp. 145–184. [T,V,611–651]

1960. *Continuous Geometry.* Princeton: Princeton University Press.

1966. *Theory of Self-Reproducing Automata.* Edited and completed by Arthur W. Burks. Urbana: University of Illinois Press. [AB 432–552]

Index

The MIT Press, with Peter Denning as general consulting editor, publishes computer science books in the following series:

ACM Doctoral Dissertation and Distinguished Dissertation Awards

Artificial Intelligence
Patrick Winston, founding editor
Michael Brady, Daniel Bobrow, and Randall Davis, editors

Charles Babbage Institute Reprint Series for the History of Computing
Martin Campbell-Kelly, editor

Computer Systems
Herb Schwetman, editor

The MIT Electrical Engineering and Computer Science Series

Exploring with Logo
E. Paul Goldenberg, editor

Foundations of Computing
Michael Garey and Albert Meyer, editors

History of Computing
I. Bernard Cohen and William Aspray, editors

Information Systems
Michael Lesk, editor

Logic Programming
Ehud Shapiro, editor; Koichi Furukawa, Jean-Louis Lassez, Fernando Pereira, and David H. D. Warren, associate editors

Research Monographs in Parallel and Distributed Processing
Christopher Jesshope and David Klappholz, editors

Scientific and Engineering Computation
Janusz Kowalik, editor

Technical Communications
Ed Barrett, editor

Printed in the United States
by Baker & Taylor Publisher Services

Printed in the United States
by Baker & Taylor Publisher Services